2011
CONDOMINIUM
BLUEBOOK®

FOR
CALIFORNIA

By BRANDEN E. BICKEL

23rd Edition

PIEDMONT PRESS

Special Acknowledgment to:

Cover design by Archer Design, Inc., Half Moon Bay, California
Editorial assistance by Joan Anspach

The Condominium Bluebook is published by:

Piedmont Press
6114 La Salle Avenue, Suite 510
Oakland, California 94611
Tel: (510) 595-8400 Fax: (510) 595-8600
piedmontpress@condolawfirm.com
www.condobook.com

Library of Congress No. ISSN 1066-9310

PRINTED IN THE UNITED STATES OF AMERICA
The Parliamentary Procedure segment of this book has been adapted, with permission, from a booklet entitled "The A-B-C's of Parliamentary Procedure" published by the Community Associations Institute.

Please Note: This publication is a compilation of statutes currently in force in California. The information contained in this book may not be sufficient to address a particular problem and the user is encouraged to consult a licensed attorney for legal advice.

PREFACE

STATUTORY CHANGES FOR 2011

Statutory changes for 2011 are highlighted in ***bold italic type.*** Reliance on past editions of The Condominium Bluebook® may be misleading because of subsequent changes in the law. New statutory law becomes effective January 1st of the year following enactment, unless enacted as emergency legislation, in which case it becomes effective upon enactment. All regular and emergency legislation enacted during the calendar year 2010 is reflected in this edition of The Condominium Bluebook®.

Table of Contents

Table of Statutes

FEDERAL

CALIFORNIA

CODE OF CIVIL PROCEDURE

GOVERNMENT CODE

HEALTH & SAFETY CODE

REVENUE & TAXATION CODE

UNITED STATES INTERNAL REVENUE CODE

VEHICLE CODE

WELFARE & INSTITUTIONS CODE

Code sections amended by legislation enacted during the 2010 Legislative Session are in bold print.

CHAPTER 1

AN OVERVIEW OF
CALIFORNIA CONDOMINIUM LAW

I.   COMMON INTEREST DEVELOPMENTS

The term "common interest development" (or "CID") describes a form of real estate where each owner holds exclusive rights to a portion of the property typically called a unit or lot, and shared rights to portions of the property typically called the common area.

Members of a homeowners' association are the owners of individual units or lots, and the terms "members" and "owners" are used interchangeably in this chapter.

A. TYPES OF COMMON INTEREST DEVELOPMENT

The most numerous forms of CIDs, and the focus of The Condominium Bluebook, are the condominium and the planned development. The two other types of CIDs, the stock cooperative and the community apartment, are less common, although they are governed by many of the same laws. For additional information, see Civil Code § 1351, in Chapter 2. A timeshare and a tenancy-in-common are not CIDs.

Other types of common interest developments that are becoming increasingly common, particularly in large urban areas, are the mixed-use condominium development and live-work lofts. Live-work lofts typically are conventional condominiums zoned for both residential and commercial use. The mixed-use development combines a commercial (or more rarely, an industrial) component with a residential component. The commercial component is governed by a commercial association, and the residential component is governed by a residential association. The mixed-use project as a whole is governed by a master association of which both the commercial and residential association are members. In a mixed-use common interest development, the commercial (or industrial) association will generally be exempt from certain requirements of the Davis-Stirling Act, Civil Code §§ 1350 *et seq*, in Chapter 2. However, the residential and master associations will not be exempt from these requirements. For more information, see "HOA Record Keeping and Reporting Requirements" at page 48 of this chapter; see also Civil Code § 1373, in Chapter 2.

B. DIFFERENCES BETWEEN CONDOMINIUM PROJECTS, PLANNED DEVELOPMENTS AND STOCK CO-OPS

The determination of whether a property is developed as a condominium project or a planned development is usually based on the physical characteristics of the buildings. Projects with only vertically-stacked units are always condominiums. Projects with only detached homes are almost always planned developments. Projects involving horizontally attached homes, or a combination of different home types, can be formed as either condominiums or planned developments.

The most significant difference between condominium projects and planned developments is the distinct nature of the individually owned and group owned portions of the property. The individually owned portion of a condominium is called the **unit**, and typically consists of interior space within a defined set of walls, floors and ceilings. Condominium owners also frequently have exclusive use of decks, patios, and parking areas. The individually owned portion of a planned development is called the **lot** and typically consists of a piece of land and everything on it. The common area in a condominium is usually all of the structural elements of the building(s) housing the units, and all land and exterior areas. The common area in a planned development is usually streets, open space, and recreational facilities.

Condominium projects and planned developments also differ with respect to the form of joint ownership of common area. Title to at least some portion of the common area in a condominium must be held by the owners in percentage shares, and, in most condominiums, title to all of the common area is held this way. By contrast, title to the common area in a planned development is almost always held by the homeowner association. For additional information, see Civil Code § 1351, in Chapter 2.

There are marked distinctions between a stock cooperative and a condominium. A stock cooperative is a corporation formed to hold title to real property, usually an apartment building. The shareholders are given a proprietary interest in occupying a portion of the property, that is - an apartment, under a proprietary lease. The right of occupancy is generally made by transfer of stock in the corporation and the leasehold rights to a purchase of a shareholder's interest. The shareholder in a stock cooperative is merely a lessee, who has a landlord-tenant relationship with the stock cooperative as the owner of the land. A community apartment is similar in structure. While the Davis-Stirling Common Interest Development Act, Civil Code §§ 1350 *et seq.*, in Chapter 2, applies to stock cooperatives and community apartments, some provisions must be interpreted in light of the structural differences among the several types of organizations.

II. HOMEOWNERS' ASSOCIATION STRUCTURE

A. LEGAL STRUCTURE OF HOMEOWNERS' ASSOCIATIONS

The law allows a homeowners' association (or "HOA" for short) to be either **incorporated** or **unincorporated**. An incorporated association has a legal identity that is separate from that of its members, just as Microsoft has a legal identity that is separate from its shareholders. Unlike Microsoft, which is a for-profit corporation, an incorporated homeowners' association is a non-profit mutual benefit corporation which means that its powers are limited to those normally exercised for the mutual benefit of the homeowners, and it is exempt from certain governmental fees and taxes.

Traditionally, homeowners' associations have been incorporated to protect owners from responsibility for association debts, losses and liabilities. But recent laws have extended most of these protections to owners of unincorporated associations provided the associations have proper insurance. (For additional information on these protections, see Civil Code §§ 1365.7 and 1365.9, in Chapter 2, and Corporations Code § 18610.) Under current law, the advantages of incorporation are some additional protection from owner liability, ease of opening association accounts with certain banks and vendors, and qualification of the units or lots for mortgage loans from lenders that require an incorporated association. Balanced against these advantages are the costs of forming the corporation, the burden of annually filing forms with the California Secretary of State, and additional procedural formalities such as having officers and directors, and conducting formal meetings.

An unincorporated association can be incorporated by its members at any time. The process of incorporation involves amending the governing documents, preparing articles of incorporation, and filing with the California Secretary of State.

B. GOVERNING DOCUMENTS AND PLANS

The term "**governing documents**" is used as a general reference to the entire group of legally recognized paperwork that creates and controls a condominium project or planned development. The governing documents typically include a subdivision map and/or condominium plan, a declaration of covenants, conditions and restrictions (often referred to as "CC&Rs"), articles of incorporation, bylaws, and rules.

1. Subdivision Map or Condominium Plan

The terms "subdivision map" and "condominium plan", as well as the less common terms "final map" and "parcel map", describe types of drawings that illustrate how a property is divided into units or lots. These drawings show the exact location and boundaries of each unit or lot, and of the common area. They are prepared by licensed land surveyors, reviewed by government agencies, and recorded with the county at the time a condominium project or planned development is formed. Once recorded, the drawings become connected to every deed and mortgage on every unit or lot within the property, and this connection makes changing the map or plan very difficult without the consent of everyone with an interest in the property. There can be several maps or plans recorded at different times as new portions of a project are added. In some condominium projects, a condominium plan is attached to the CC&Rs rather than recorded separately.

2. Declaration of Covenants, Conditions and Restrictions (often simply called the "declaration" or the "CC&Rs")

CC&Rs describe the rights and obligations of the homeowners' association and of each owner. CC&Rs vary widely in content and length, but usually cover the following topics: (1) the boundaries of the common area and of each unit or lot; (2) the owner usage restrictions, typically including common area use restrictions, pet regulations, and alteration controls; (3) the maintenance responsibilities of the association and the individual owners; (4) the allocation of association operating costs among the owners, and the mechanism for collecting owner payments; (5) the dispute resolution procedure; (6) the enforcement powers; and (7) the rights and protections of mortgage lenders.

CC&Rs are required for all condominiums and planned developments. They are prepared by the developer's attorney, reviewed by a government agency, the California Department of Real Estate (unless the project has fewer than five units or lots), and recorded with the county at the time a condominium project or planned development is formed. For additional information, see Civil Code § 1353, in Chapter 2.

3. Articles of Incorporation

The articles of incorporation (or simply the "articles") are usually short and often contain only the name of the homeowners' association, the name of the association's initial agent for the service of process (the person authorized to receive legal notices), and a statement that the association is a non-profit mutual benefit corporation. Sometimes the articles also include language about voting, directors, amendments, and dissolution of the association. Articles are required only when an association is incorporated. (Unincorporated associations sometimes have articles of association, but these are not required.) Articles are prepared by the developer's attorney, reviewed by a government agency (unless the project has fewer than five units or lots), and filed with the Secretary of State. For additional information, see Corporations Code §§ 7130-7132, in Chapter 3.

4. Bylaws

The bylaws describe the mechanics of association decision-making and management. Bylaws vary widely in content and length, but usually include the following: (1) number of and selection methods for officers and directors; (2) notice, meeting and voting procedures for owner and board decisions; and (3) association record keeping and reporting requirements.

Although bylaws are common for both incorporated and unincorporated associations, they are required only for certain incorporated associations. Bylaws are prepared by the developer's attorney and reviewed by a government agency (unless the project has fewer than five units or lots) at the time a condominium project or planned development is formed. But unlike articles and CC&Rs, bylaws are not recorded or filed with any government agency, and this makes them easier to change. For additional information, see Corporations Code § 7151, in Chapter 3.

5. Rules

The CC&Rs usually empower the homeowners' association to adopt rules and give the rules the same binding power as the other governing documents. The rules often provide usage restrictions relating to alterations, signage, waste disposal, parking, pets, and recreational facilities. Where the same topics are discussed in the CC&Rs, the rules may add to or explain the CC&Rs but cannot conflict with them. Association rules are usually enacted after some of the units or lots have been sold and the owners have taken control of the association. They are not subject to any governmental review and do not need to be filed or recorded with any governmental agency.

The procedures for adopting and amending association rules are discussed in detail in "Procedures for Adopting and Changing Homeowners' Association Rules" in Section IV of this chapter.

C. LAW GOVERNING THE GOVERNING DOCUMENTS

1. Statutory Law

The California State Legislature has passed numerous statutory laws governing the formation and operation of condominium and planned development homeowners' associations. The most important of these laws is the Davis-Stirling Common Interest Development Act (Civil Code §§ 1350-1378), which is included in its entirety in Chapter 2 of this book. The Davis-Stirling Act sets out detailed requirements regarding the governing documents, including the enforcement and amendment of governing documents, operating rules, ownership rights and interests, homeowners' association governance and operations, fiscal requirements, assessment collection, transfer of ownership rights, improvements, and construction defect litigation.

The California Legislature has enacted various other statutes, many contained in the Civil Code and other California Codes, which are relevant to the creation and operation of common interest developments. Chapters 3 through 11 of this book contain statutory provisions concerning powers and procedures of the homeowners' association board of directors, HOA membership meetings and voting, HOA records and record keeping, taxation, litigation and construction defects, civil rights and restrictions, vehicle issues, and requirements for professional managers.

2. Case Law

A second important source of law governing common interest developments are the legal decisions rendered by California courts. A summary of the significant judicial decisions affecting common interest developments is contained in Chapter 12 of this book.

3. California Department of Real Estate Regulations

The California Department of Real Estate ("DRE") has also enacted various regulations which concern the development of common interest developments. However, the DRE regulations apply to common interest developments only until the developer relinquishes control over the CID to the homeowners' association. Once the HOA is in control, only the governing documents and statutory and case law regulate the common interest development. Projects with fewer than five units or lots are exempt form DRE regulation.

D. OTHER ISSUES REGARDING THE GOVERNING DOCUMENTS AND THE LAW

1. Binding Effect of Governing Documents

The law provides that the use of real estate can be restricted when a document describing the restrictions is recorded with the county where the property is located. The restrictions "run with the land", meaning they apply to each owner who acquires the property after the restrictions are recorded. The map or plan, and the CC&Rs, are different types of recorded restrictions which "run with the land", and that is why they bind each and every owner of a unit or lot. The articles, bylaws, and rules are not recorded, but derive their binding power from the recorded CC&Rs. With the articles and bylaws, this binding power arises because the CC&Rs make each owner a member of the homeowners' association, and the law makes each member of the association subject to the association's articles and bylaws. With the rules, the binding power arises because the CC&Rs specifically empower the association to enact additional binding restrictions in the form of rules.

2. Liberal Construction of Governing Documents

The law provides that the governing documents for a common interest development shall be liberally construed to facilitate the operation of the common interest development. This means that a court or other adjudicative decision maker asked to determine the meaning of the governing documents will read the provisions broadly so that they may accomplish the purpose for which they were written. The law also provides that if any provisions of the governing documents are judged unenforceable or impermissible, other provisions of the governing documents that are otherwise enforceable will remain enforceable. See Civil Code § 1370, in Chapter 2.

3. Conflicts Between the Governing Documents and Statutory Law

The resolution of a conflict between the governing documents and statutory law depends upon the intent of the governmental body that enacted the statutory law. Where the apparently conflicting statutory law contains a phrase like "notwithstanding the provisions of the declaration" or "notwithstanding anything to the contrary in the governing documents" in its text, the intent to override the governing documents is clear and the statutory law controls. Where the apparently conflicting law contains a phrase like "unless otherwise provided in the declaration" or "subject to the provisions of the governing documents" in its text, the intent not to override is clear and the governing document provision controls. Where the apparently conflicting statutory law contains no clear indication of whether it is intended to supersede conflicting provisions in governing documents, intent must be determined from the language and context of the statutory law, and also from historical records of its enactment. Consult an attorney in these cases.

4. Ambiguous or Unclear Governing Document Provisions

The meaning of ambiguous or unclear language depends on the intent of its author(s). The intent can sometimes be determined by examining other parts of the document relating to similar issues or analogous situations. Where this approach fails, ambiguous or unclear language should be given its most reasonable interpretation in light of laws relating to similar issues or analogous situations, and local custom and practice (i.e. how governing documents in similar projects are written and how other similar associations operate.) Consult an attorney if a significant legal issue is at stake.

5. Unreasonable or Unfair Governing Document Provisions

Provisions of the CC&Rs, bylaws and rules are upheld unless they are arbitrary, impose burdens on some residents that substantially outweigh their benefits to other residents, or violate fundamental public policy. Consult an attorney if a provision does not seem to meet these standards. For additional information, see *Nahrstedt v. Lakeside Village Condominium Assn. (1994) 8 Cal.4th 361, 33 Cal.Rptr.2d 63,* in Chapter 12.

6. Owner's Right to Inspect and Copy Governing Documents and HOA's Books, Records, Minutes and Rules

Unit or lot owners, or their designated representatives, have the right to inspect and copy "association records" and "enhanced association records". "Association records" are defined as: (1) all financial documents required by statute to be provided to an owner; (2) interim unaudited financial statements (balance sheet, income and expense statement, budget comparison, general ledger); (3) executed contracts (except privileged contracts); (4) written board approvals of vendor contracts; (5) federal and state income tax returns; (6) reserve account statements and records; (7) agendas and minutes of board, member and committee meetings (except executive session meetings); (8) membership lists, including name, property address and mailing address; and (9) check registers. "Enhanced association records" are defined as: (1) invoices, receipts and canceled checks; (2) approved purchase orders; (3) credit card statements for accounts held in the association's name; (4) statements for services rendered; and (5) reimbursement requests submitted to the association.

Association records for the current fiscal year and two previous fiscal years must be made available. Minutes of owner and board meetings must be made permanently available. Minutes of committees with decision-making authority must be made permanently available commencing January 1, 2007. Association records for the current fiscal year must be made available within 10 days of a request. Association records for the previous two fiscal years must be made available within 30 days of a request. Minutes of committees with decision-making authority must be made available within 15 days after approval, but only for committee meetings held after January 1, 2007.

The association may, but is not required to, copy documents at an owner's request. The association may charge the owner for the actual cost of copying records, provided the owner agrees to pay the costs in advance. The association must make the records available at the association's on-site business office or, if there is no office, at a place where the owner and association agree. If the association and owner can't agree or an owner submits a request for specifically identified records, the association can satisfy the request by mailing copies of the records to the owner by first-class mail. The association may bill the owner the cost of copying and mailing the records, as well as an amount not to exceed $10 per hour or $200, whichever is less, for redacting "enhanced association records," provided the owner has agreed to pay the costs in advance.

The association may withhold or redact information that is likely to lead to identify theft or fraud, is likely to compromise the privacy of another owner, or is privileged under law or otherwise protected by statute. Examples of protected information are personal identification information (i.e., social security numbers, driver's license numbers, credit card account numbers, bank account numbers, etc.), personal disciplinary records, personal delinquent assessment records, executive session records, personnel records (other than compensation) and interior architectural and security system plans. But the association may not withhold information pertaining to compensation paid to employees, contractors or vendors. The association must provide an written explanation for withholding information if requested by an owner and the association bears the burden of demonstrating in court that withholding was justified. An owner is prohibited from making commercial or any other use of association records that does not pertain to the owner's interest as an owner.

A violation of an owner's inspection rights can result in severe penalties. An owner may bring a civil action to enforce his/her inspection rights, and if a court finds that the association unreasonably withheld access to association records, the court must award the owner reasonable cost and expenses, including reasonable attorney's fees, and impose a civil penalty of up to $500 for each separate violation. Notably the statute does not allow an association to recover its cost of defending an owner's civil action unless the court finds the request was frivolous, unreasonable, or without foundation. For additional information, see Civil Code § 1365.2, in Chapter 2.

7. Amending Governing Documents: Procedural Requirements

Every common interest development will need to revise or restate its governing documents at some point. Revision usually involves modification of existing documents by amendment. Restatement means completely replacing the existing documents with an entirely new set of governing documents. Revision and restatement will be referred to in this chapter as simply "amendment" for the sake of brevity.

Governing documents of a condominium project and a planned development typically include the CC&Rs, bylaws, articles of incorporation, articles of association, condominium plans, and operating rules which govern the association. Governing documents of a stock cooperative and community apartment project typically involve bylaws, articles of incorporation, a proprietary lease, and operating rules. For information on amending operating rules, see "Procedures for Adopting and Changing Homeowners' Association Rules" at page 45 of this chapter.

When amendment of governing documents is under consideration, the documents themselves should first be consulted for amendment procedures. If those procedures are inadequate, the statutory law regulating the method of amendment for that type of document should be examined.

Most governing documents can be amended by a simple majority vote of the owners. Sometimes a higher percentage vote is required when certain provisions are given special protection against amendment, such as changing the method of allocation assessments or voting rights among owners, altering the boundaries of exclusive use common area, or terminating the development.

a. CC&Rs

CC&Rs may be amended by the owners as provided in the CC&Rs or as provided by statute. CC&Rs that fail to include provisions permitting amendment may be amended at any time by a simple majority vote. CC&Rs that specify they are not amendable may not be amended without an order of court overriding the restriction.

When the CC&Rs provide a method of amendment, the effective date of the amendment is after the amendment has been approved by the required percentage of owners on a secret ballot vote, the approval has been certified in writing by an authorized officer of the association and the amendment has been properly recorded in each county where the development is located. A copy of the amendment must be distributed by first-class mail or personal delivery to all owners as soon as possible after recording. For further information, see Civil Code § 1355(a), in Chapter 2.

In rare cases when CC&Rs do not contain amendment procedures, statutory law specifies the method of amendment. The proposed amendment must be distributed to all owners by first-class mail or personal delivery not less than 15 days nor more than 60 days prior to a secret ballot vote. Then amendment must be approved by a majority of the owners, certified in writing by an authorized officer of the association, and recorded in each county where the development is located. Again, the effective date is the recording date and not the distribution date. For further information, see Civil Code § 1355(b), in Chapter 2.

(i) Eliminating Developer-Related CC&R Provisions

The law allows an abbreviated method of eliminating developer-related CC&R provisions after the developer has terminated its onsite activities. The board of directors, with a reduced percentage approval of the owners, may adopt an amendment deleting from the CC&Rs any provision which is unequivocally designed and intended to facilitate the developer's access over or across the common are for completing the construction or marketing of the development or a particular phase of the development.

In order to adopt such an amendment, the board of directors must mail to all owners by first-class mail: a copy of the proposed amendment, and a notice of the time, date and place the board will consider adopting the amendment at a meeting open to all owners. Owners attending the meeting must have an opportunity to comment on the proposed amendment. All board deliberations must be conducted in open session. Once approved by the board of directors, the proposed amendment must be submitted for approval of the owners on a secret ballot vote. Owner approval requires only a majority of votes cast once a quorum is established. For further information, see Civil Code § 1355.5, in Chapter 2.

(ii) Court Ordered Amendment of CC&Rs

Often CC&Rs require approval of more that a majority of owners to amend a particularly sensitive CC&R provision. Some older CC&Rs require approval of more than a majority to amend any provision of the CC&Rs. The law establishes a method for overriding a super-majority approval requirement by court order.

When faced with a super-majority approval requirement, the association or an owner may petition the court for an order reducing the percentage approval requirement necessary for the amendment. The association must first put the proposed amendment to a vote of the owners. If the amendment receives approval by at least a bare majority of the owners but not the required super-majority, the association or an owner may petition the court for judicial approval of the amendment without a further vote.

The petition must describe the efforts made by the association to solicit the percentage owner approval specified in the CC&Rs, the number of affirmative and negative votes actually received, the percentage of affirmative votes required by the CC&Rs and any other relevant facts. The petition must include a copy of the CC&Rs, the text of the amendment, the notice and solicitation material sent to the owners, and an explanation of the reason for the amendment. The court will set a hearing and require the petitioner to give at least 15 days notice of the time and place of the hearing to all members, mortgagee/ lenders entitled to notice under the CC&Rs, and to any governmental agency entitled to notice under the CC&Rs. If the court finds that all procedural steps in the statute have been satisfied and the proposed amendment is reasonable, it may confirm the amendment as being validly approved on the basis of the vote actually received instead of the super-majority required by the CC&Rs. The amendment becomes effective upon recording in each county where the development is located. A copy of the amendment must be sent to each owner together with a statement that the amendment has been recorded. For further information, see Civil Code § 1356, in Chapter 2.

This procedure is not available when the proposed amendment would: (1) result in approval by less than a majority of each class of voters in a multi-class voting system; (2) eliminate any special rights, preferences or privileges of the developer without the developer's approval; (3) impair the security of lender holding a mortgage or deed of trust on the property without the lenders' approval as specified in the CC&Rs.

(iii) Extending Life of the CC&Rs
Most CC&Rs contain an automatic renewal provision extending the term during which they are valid in increments of 5, 10 or 20 years. A typical provision states an initial term and then provides that upon

expiration of the initial term, the term shall be automatically extended for successive periods of 10 years, unless the association is terminated and it records a notice of termination with the county recorder. An automatic renewal provision does not require any action on the part of the association to trigger renewal.

Occasionally CC&Rs provide a termination date but make no provision for extension of that termination date. Without further action, the CC&Rs would expire on the termination date and the CC&Rs would then cease to have any legal effect. The state legislature determined that as a matter of public policy CC&Rs are an appropriate method of protecting common interest developments and providing financial support for the upkeep of common areas, systems and facilities, which if allowed to lapse would adversely impact the housing supply. Accordingly, the legislature enacted a statute that allows an association to extend the term or life of the development beyond the initial term even where there is no automatic renewal provision by adopting a CC&R amendment approved by a majority of the owner before the expiration of the initial term. If the renewal amendment requires super-majority approval, then the association may seek approval of the amendment by court order using the procedures is Civil Code § 1356. An amendment to extend the term of CC&Rs may be used on more than one occasion, but it is simpler to adopt an automatic renewal provision as part of the first extension amendment.

(iv) Special Approvals

CC&Rs may require special approvals from lenders, governmental agencies or master associations. The purpose of granting special approval rights to lenders is to allow them to participate in an amendment that might impair their security interests. These right are usually granted only lenders in first position or to "eligible" lenders who have given notice of a desire to participate in an amendment affecting its security interest. Governmental agencies may require participation in an amendment affecting a condition imposed by the agencies as part of the initial governmental approval of the development. Sometimes a city or county redevelopment agency will require special approval rights to achieve a planning objective. Sometimes federal agencies, such as the Department of Housing and Urban Affairs (HUD) or the Veterans Administration require special approval rights as a condition of providing the developer with federal financing. A master association may require approval of amendments affecting architectural restrictions under the jurisdiction of the master association.

Special approval rights are enforceable. Failure to obtain special approvals may void the amendment. When an association officer certifies that all of the requisite approvals have been obtained, the officer is certifying that all special approvals as well as owner approvals have been obtained.

(v) Ballot Solicitation

Approval of a proposed amendment must be done by secret ballot in accordance with the procedure se forth in Civil Code § 1363.03. The procedures for a secret ballot are discussed in the section entitled "Director Nomination and Election" at page 36 in this chapter. Approval may be by a mail-in ballot alone. The secret ballot must be sent out at least 30 days prior to the voting deadline, but there is no outside limit within which the secret ballot must be returned other than a general restriction that it must be returned within a reasonable time. There is no precise definition of a reasonable time but customary practice is to allow between 60 and 120 days for the return of the secret ballots. The voting deadline must be stated on the ballot or in the voting instructions. For further information, see Civil Code § 1363.03, in Chapter 2 and Corporations Code §§ 7513, 7514, in Chapter 4.

There is no clear authority whether the voting deadline can be extended by the board of directors to allow the association to obtain additional approvals. The safest course is to resubmit the amendment on a new secret ballot with a new voting deadline if the necessary approvals are not received by the end of the initial voting deadline.

b. Bylaws

Bylaws may be amended by the board of directors or the owners depending upon which is given the power to amend. Bylaws specifically authorizing amendment by board action alone are rare. Most bylaws require owner approval of an amendment. The only statutory requirement for owner approval is when the amendment: materially and adversely affects the voting rights, dissolution, transfer or status of memberships; changes the number or terms of directors;

increases quorum requirements; affects proxy rights; or affects cumulative voting provisions or termination of the association. See Corporations Code §§7150, 7151, 7220, 7224, in Chapter 3 and §§ 7512-7515, in Chapter 4.

Bylaws amended by the members must be approved by the percentage of owners specified in the bylaw; and if a percentage is not specified in the bylaws, then by a majority of those voting once a quorum has been established. See Corporations Code § 7150(b).

Bylaws do not have to be filed with the California Secretary of State or recorded with the county recorder. Some bylaws have been recorded because they contain provisions usually found in CC&Rs or may be combined with the CC&Rs in a single document. If bylaws have been improperly recorded, they should be separated from the CC&Rs when the documents are next revised.

c. Articles of Incorporation

Articles of incorporation are a document that is filed with the California Secretary of State at the time a corporate association is formed. They are required only to set forth: the name of the corporation; a statement that it is a non-profit mutual benefit corporation organized to engage in any lawful activity; and the name and address of the agent for service of process. They may contain optional provisions as specified in Corporations Code § 7132. Because of their brevity articles of incorporation rarely need revision, unless the association wants to change its name, agent for service of process or an optional provision is inconsistent with amended CC&Rs or amended bylaws. They should always be checked for consistency when the other governing documents are revised.

Articles of incorporation, unless restricted to a vote by the owners, are amendable by a majority of the directors present at a duly constituted board meeting. If the articles require a owner vote, those requirements must be fulfilled. An amendment to the articles becomes effective when the association files with the California Secretary of State a certificate of amendment consisting of an officer's certificate containing the text of the amendment and attesting to its approval by the board or members. See Corporations Code §§ 7810-7820, in

Chapter 5.

d. Condominium Plans and Subdivision Maps

Condominium plans and subdivision maps are drawings that depict the common area, exclusive use common area and individual ownership interests in three dimensional space. These documents will only need to be amended if there are errors in the original plan or map, or if there is an intent to change the boundaries of the several interests. For example, if an association decided to add a subterranean garage below an existing building or acquire an adjacent parcel for additional common area, an amended plan or map would have to be recorded. As stated earlier in this chapter, where the owners of the separate interests own the common area as tenants-in common, it may be difficult to amend the original map or plan because every owner and every lender of record must approve the amended plan or map before it can be recorded. These approval can be difficult to obtain in large projects with numerous owners and lenders. If the association owns the common area, amendment is much simpler because only the association's approval is necessary.

The first step in the amendment process is to have the reconfigured space drawn on a new plan or map by a registered civil engineer or a licensed surveyor. The next step is to obtain the requisite approvals of the owners and lenders. The final step is to record the amended plan or map in every county in which the project is located. The recording is usually handled by a title company.

For more information on amending condominium plans and subdivision maps, see the section entitled "Sale or Exchange of Portions of the Unit or Lot" at page 24 of this chapter, and Government Code §§ 66469-66472.1, in Chapter 5.

8. Identity of "Declarant"

For most common interest developments, the governing documents refer to a "declarant" who formulates the CC&Rs and other documents. The declarant is the original developer of the project, and it has special privileges and rights because it had virtually complete control over the content of the documents when they were prepared. It is advisable for homeowners' associations to amend their governing documents to remove the developer-specific provisions as soon as the project is completely built out and sold. For additional information, see Checklist 1 in Chapter 15, and Civil Code §§ 1351(g) and 1355.5, in Chapter 2.

III.   OWNERSHIP, ACCESS AND USAGE

A. INDIVIDUALLY OWNED PORTIONS OF THE CONDOMINIUM PROJECT

In a condominium project, the individually owned area is called a **unit**. The exact physical location of each condominium unit within a particular project is shown on the recorded map or condominium plan. The map or plan, and/or the CC&Rs, will also contain a definition of the term "unit" as it is used for that particular project, listing the elements of the building that are part of the unit. These definitions vary significantly from project to project, and it is unwise to apply generalizations or assumptions. Instead, read the definition in the CC&Rs with the following questions in mind:

(1) Does the unit include any exterior surfaces such as roofing, siding or foundation?

(2) What portions of the interior walls does the unit include: the whole wall (i.e. both sides and everything in between), half the wall (i.e. everything from one side to a point halfway to the other side), one finished surface (i.e. only the wallboard or plaster on one side), or just the finish (i.e. the paint or paper)? Note that some unit definitions distinguish perimeter walls (i.e. walls between units, or between a unit and the common area) from partition walls (i.e. walls between rooms in the same unit); or structural walls (i.e. walls that help hold up the building) from non-structural walls (i.e. those that simply divide rooms). Where these wall-type distinctions are made, the portions of the wall that are part of the unit will vary depending on wall type.

(3) What portions of the floors and ceilings does the unit include: the entire floor or ceiling, all portions up to a midpoint, the finished portion (i.e. ceiling plaster or sheet rock, finished wood flooring), or just the finish (i.e. paint or carpet)? Here again, some definitions distinguish floors and ceilings between units, or between a unit and the common area, from floors and ceilings between levels of the same unit.

(4) What portions of the windows and doors does the unit include:

the entire window or door, or only glass and screens? Note that some definitions distinguish interior doors from exterior doors. Does the definition include window and door frames? Does it include window and door hardware?

(5) Does the unit include all of the fixtures and appliances located within it? Note that the term "fixtures," when used in this context, encompasses cabinets, lights, electrical outlets, sinks, showers, and tubs.

(6) What portions of the plumbing, electrical, heating and air conditioning systems are part of the unit: all elements that serve only the unit, or only elements visible from within the unit?

(7) Does the unit include any decks, balconies, or patios, and if so, how does the definition describe the boundaries of these areas?

Note that even if the unit does not include these areas, they may be assigned as exclusive use common areas, as discussed in the section entitled "Exclusive Use or Restricted Common Areas," at page 22 of this chapter.

B. INDIVIDUALLY OWNED PORTIONS OF PLANNED DEVELOPMENT

In a planned development, the individually owned area is called the **lot** and typically consists of a piece of land and everything on it. The exact physical location of each lot within a particular project is shown on the recorded map for that project. Where there are walls or fences that sit on the border of two lots, ownership is considered to be shared unless the CC&Rs provide otherwise. Note that the map and/or CC&Rs for planned developments sometimes give neighbors and even the general public the right to cross a private lot (a type of "easement"). For additional information, see Civil Code § 1351, in Chapter 2.

C. OWNERSHIP OF COMMON AREAS

Title to common area can be held by the homeowners' association or by the owners in percentage shares as "tenants in common." The decision is made by the developer at the time the governing documents are prepared, and is very difficult to change later. To determine who owns the common area, refer to the CC&Rs. The method of common area ownership has no significant consequences in a properly insured association. Note that in condominium projects, title to at least some common area must be held as tenants in common. The percentage held by each owner does not determine that owner's usage rights or cost responsibility. For additional information, see Civil Code §§ 1351 and 1362, in Chapter 2.

D. USE OF COMMON AREAS

1. By the Unit or Lot Owner

Each owner in a condominium project or planned development is equally entitled to use all common area (other than exclusive use or restricted common area) regardless of ownership or assessment percentage.

2. By a Non-Resident Unit or Lot Owner

If there is no provision in any of the governing documents prohibiting a non-resident owner from using the recreational facilities while his/her unit or lot is rented, he/she may continue to use them. If there is such a provision, the law is not entirely clear as to whether the prohibition can be enforced. However, if the prohibition against non-resident owners is contained in the original CC&Rs, or was created shortly after the homeowners' association took control of the common interest development and before the owner against whom the prohibition is sought to be enforced purchased his/her unit or lot, the prohibition is probably enforceable. For additional information, see *Liebler v. Point Loma Tennis Club (1995) 40 Cal.App.4th 1600, 47 Cal.Rptr.2d 783* (enforcing a restriction), and *MaJor v. Miraverde Homeowners Assn. (1992) 7 Cal.App.4th 618, 9 Cal.Rptr.2d 237* (invalidating a restriction), in Chapter 12.

3. By Guests and Tenants

An owner's guests and tenants have the same common area usage rights as the owner unless the governing documents specifically provide otherwise.

4. Restrictions on or Fees for Use of Common Areas

A homeowners' association may charge fees for the use of recreational facilities and refuse access without payment, provided the charge applies equally to all owners and is not specifically prohibited by the governing documents. Such fees can be initiated and adjusted by the HOA board of directors unless the governing documents specifically require an owner vote. However, a fee may not exceed the amount necessary to defray the costs for which it is levied. See Civil Code § 1366.1, in Chapter 2.

The HOA may also temporarily remove an owner's recreational facilities usage privileges as discipline for a violation of the governing documents. This type of discipline is permitted only if (i) the governing documents do not specifically prohibit it, (ii) the board of directors has adopted the discipline policy in advance, (iii) notice of the policy has been provided to all of the owners in advance, and (iv) the violating owner is given notice of the violation and a board hearing before the recreational facilities usage privileges are removed.

E. EXCLUSIVE USE OR RESTRICTED COMMON AREAS

The terms "exclusive use common area" and "restricted common area" are used interchangeably. They refer to portions of a condominium project or planned development that are not within the defined boundaries of a unit or lot, but are intended to be used exclusively by one owner. Technically, exclusive use or restricted common area is part of the common area owned either by the homeowners' association or by all of the owners, but one particular owner holds a type of easement which gives him/her exclusive usage rights. The easement is permanent and cannot be taken away by the association or by the other owners. Decks, patios, parking spaces, and storage spaces are often assigned as exclusive use or restricted common area on the recorded plan or map, in the CC&Rs, or in the deed conveying the lot or unit to its first owner. The law automatically assigns all elements designed to serve only one particular unit or lot as exclusive use common area, but the automatic assignments operate only if they do not conflict with the governing documents. Unless the CC&Rs otherwise provide, the board of directors may not grant an owner exclusive use of any portion of the general common area without the approval of 67% of all owners in the development. For additional information, see Civil Code §§ 1351 and 1363.07, in Chapter 2.

F. "PERCENTAGE INTEREST" OR "COMMON INTEREST"

The terms "percentage interest" and "common interest" are used only when the common area is jointly owned by the individual owners (rather than by the association). In these cases, the terms "percentage interest" and "common interest" refer to the percentage share of common area owned by a particular owner. An owner's "percentage interest" or "common interest" does not determine that owner's usage rights, voting rights or cost responsibilities.

G. PARTY WALLS

The term "party wall" in a planned development usually means a wall, fence, or other building element that sits on the border of two or more lots. Sometimes the CC&Rs will define "party wall" more broadly so that it includes any building element that is within a prescribed distance of the lot border. Where party walls exist, the CC&Rs will usually allocate responsibility for maintenance, impose restrictions on alterations, and provide access rights for maintenance. When the CC&Rs are silent on any of these issues, general rules of law apply. These laws are complex and beyond the scope of *The Condominium Bluebook*. For additional information, consult an attorney.

H. PARTITION

When used in a legal context in connection with jointly owned real estate, the term "partition" refers to a court-supervised process where jointly owned real estate is sold and the proceeds divided among the owners. Contrary to common usage, partition never involves a physical division of one parcel of real estate into multiple parcels. Partition is the law's remedy when changed circumstances or disagreements prevent co-owners from jointly managing their shared property; and, in most joint ownership arrangements, any owner can force a partition at any time. However, although the common areas of condominiums and planned developments are often jointly owned, the law prohibits partition unless the project has become substantially damaged or obsolete. For additional information, see Civil Code § 1359, in Chapter 2.

I. INDIVIDUAL UNIT OR LOT SPLIT OFF

By the time a condominium or planned development home is sold, documents have been recorded with the county government which firmly bind it to the rest of the project. A condominium unit in a multi-unit, vertically-stacked building can never be split off; but, if the building is substantially damaged, the law and the governing documents sometimes allow the entire project to be sold and the proceeds divided. A condominium or planned development home located in a structure containing no other homes, or attached to other homes on a horizontal plane, can be split off, but only with the approval of the county government as well as the percentage of owners and lenders required by the governing documents.

J. SALE OR EXCHANGE OF PORTIONS OF UNIT OR LOT

The boundaries of units and lots within a condominium project or planned development appear on the recorded map or plan, and they cannot be changed without amending that map or plan. The amendment must be prepared by a registered civil engineer or a licensed surveyor. If the map or plan to be amended is recorded separately from the CC&Rs, the amendment must be reviewed by a governmental agency, signed by all owners and all lenders with an interest in the project, and recorded. The signature requirement is especially difficult to fulfill because it requires the cooperation of every lender that has a mortgage on any of the units or lots in the complex (including those not directly affected by the amendment), and sometimes lenders are not anxious to cooperate in this process. If the map or plan to be amended is recorded only as an exhibit to the CC&Rs, the amendment will need to be approved only by the percentage of owners required by the CC&Rs, and the lenders with mortgages on the directly affected units or lots. The approval of other lenders, and of a governmental agency, is required only if the CC&Rs so state. For additional information, see Government Code §§ 66469 *et seq.,* in Chapter 5.

K. SALE OR EXCHANGE OF EXCLUSIVE USE OR
RESTRICTED COMMON AREAS

If the exclusive use or restricted common area is assigned to a particular unit or lot on a map or plan recorded separately from the CC&Rs, the sale or exchange of such area would require an amendment of the map or plan as described in the previous subsection. If the exclusive use or restricted common area is assigned to a particular unit or lot only in the CC&Rs and/or the initial deed conveying the unit or lot, and is not assigned on the map or plan, the sale or exchange will require an amendment to the CC&Rs and/or a new deed. In these cases, the owners directly involved with the sale or exchange will need the approval and cooperation of their mortgage lenders. The CC&Rs may also require approval and cooperation of some or all of the other owners and their mortgage lenders. For additional information, see Civil Code § 1363.07, in Chapter 2.

L. COMBINATION OF TWO OR MORE UNITS OR LOTS

The ability of an owner to physically combine units or lots (i.e. join them together with doorways, stairs etc.) will be determined by the alteration provisions of the CC&Rs and the local building and planning codes. In most cases, the owner will need to get association approval for these types of physical alterations as well as a building permit from a governmental agency. The ability of an owner to legally combine units or lots (i.e. make them into a single unit or lot) will be determined by specific CC&R provisions relating to unit or lot combination or changing boundaries. Even if the CC&R requirements can be satisfied, if the combination involves the use of a portion of the general common area, then it will require the approval of 67% of all owners in the development and may require an amendment to the map or plan, as described in the previous section.

M. ACCESS

1. Homeowners' Association Access to Individually Owned Units or Lots

Most CC&Rs state that the homeowners' association has the right to enter any unit or lot whenever necessary to fulfill the association's duties. Among the duties that would justify entry is common area maintenance and verification of an owner's compliance with owner maintenance requirements and alteration restrictions. Often, the CC&Rs will require that the association provide advance notice of the entry except in an emergency. When the CC&Rs are silent on these issues, both the right of entry and the requirement for advance notice will be implied.

2. Unit or Lot Owner Access to Neighboring Unit or Lot

Most CC&Rs state that each owner has the right to enter a neighbor's unit or lot, and all common area, whenever such entry is necessary to maintain the owner's unit or lot, provided advance notice is given or there is an emergency. When the CC&Rs are silent on the issue, the entry right will be implied. The right does not exist when the purpose is to facilitate owner alterations or improvements rather than necessary maintenance.

N. RENTAL RESTRICTIONS

Rental restrictions in governing documents are probably permissible if they are uniformly applied to all owners, do not discriminate against a particular group of potential renters, and can be shown to serve some legitimate purpose. Note that rental restrictions may affect the owners' ability to obtain mortgage loans from some lenders. Rental restrictions are discussed in detail in the section entitled "Other Common Usage Restrictions," at page 88 of this chapter. See also *Laguna Royale Owners Assn. v. Darger (1981) 119 Cal.App.3d 670, 174 Cal.Rptr. 136;* and *City of Oceanside v. McKenna (1989) 215 Cal.App.3d 1420, 264 Cal.Rptr. 275*, in Chapter 12.

O. TRANSFER OF OWNERSHIP

A homeowners' association may not adopt any rule or regulation which unreasonably or arbitrarily restricts an owner's ability to market his/her unit or lot. An association may not impose any assessment or fee in connection with the marketing of an owner's interest except fees and charges no greater than the actual costs to the association to change its records and to provide copies of various documents to the selling owner which the selling owner must provide to the prospective purchaser. An association may not require that the sale or marketing of the owner's separate interest be conducted through a particular real estate broker, and the association may not prevent an owner from displaying a sign on his/her own unit or lot advertising the sale or lease of the unit or lot. See Civil Code §§ 712 and 713, in Chapter 9, and Civil Code §§ 1368 and 1368.1, in Chapter 2.

The law requires a selling unit or lot owner to make extensive disclosures to prospective purchasers. These disclosures include the common interest development's governing documents; a statement regarding any occupancy, residency or age restrictions in the governing documents; association financial documents for the most recent fiscal year; statements regarding current and approved, but not yet effective, regular and special assessments and fees; a notice regarding any unresolved owner discipline issues; and information regarding construction defects at the common interest development. For more information, see "Disclosures to Prospective Purchasers" at page 78 of this chapter and Civil Code § 1368, in Chapter 2.

IV. HOMEOWNERS' ASSOCIATION POWERS AND CONTROL

A. DISTRIBUTION OF POWERS BETWEEN OWNERS, BOARD OF DIRECTORS, HOA COMMITTEES, OFFICERS, AND PROPERTY MANAGER

In general, the distribution of power and authority within the homeowners' association is determined by the governing documents, but the law contains some restrictions on how the governing documents can distribute this power. The law presumes that most association power and authority will be exercised by a board of directors without the direct involvement of the owners. Where the governing documents simply give the association power to do or approve something without specifically requiring owner approval, the power can be exercised by the board without owner approval.

The law imposes very few restrictions on how much power the documents can give the board. The following is a list of the few acts which always require owner approval:

(1) Amending the CC&Rs (see Civil Code §§ 1355 and 1356, in Chapter 2, and note there is a limited exception allowing the board to amend the CC&Rs to remove developer preferences with a reduced membership vote or to remove discriminatory provisions);

(2) Amending the bylaws to (i) increase the number of owners necessary to hold owner meetings (the "quorum") (see Corporations Code § 7512(a), in Chapter 4), (ii) change the number of directors on

the board (see Corporations Code § 7151(b), in Chapter 3), or (iii)
change a provision allowing director election by cumulative voting
(see Corporations Code § 7615(a), in Chapter 4);

(3) Increasing regular assessments more than 20% (see Civil Code
§ 1366(b), in Chapter 2, and note that this limitation does not apply in
the emergency circumstances listed there);

(4) Imposing special assessments during one year that total more
than 5% of the budgeted expenses for that fiscal year (see Civil Code
§ 1366(b), in Chapter 2, and note that this limitation does not apply
in the emergency circumstances listed there); and

(5) Removing a director without cause (see Corporations Code §
7222, and note that "cause" is defined in Corporations Code § 7221,
in Chapter 3).

In practice, most governing documents also require owner approval
for a variety of major decisions including changing the items which the
association is responsible to maintain, changing the owners' assessment
percentages, changing the unit or lot boundaries, and imposing leasing
or resale restrictions.

The board has complete control over all committees, officers
and managers. This means that the board decides who will serve in
these capacities, and what authority they will have, subject only to
restrictions in the governing documents. The board retains the power
to override the decision of any committee, officer and manager. For
additional information, see Corporations Code §§ 7210-7214, in
Chapter 3.

B. ABILITY OF AN INDIVIDUAL OWNER OR A GROUP OF OWNERS TO OVERRIDE OR CHALLENGE DECISIONS OF THE BOARD OF DIRECTORS

Except for reversing a rule change, owners cannot override a board,
committee, officer or manager decision. If the owners are unhappy
with a board decision, they can convene a meeting, vote to remove one
or more directors, and hope the replacement directors make a more
satisfactory decision. If the owners are unhappy with a committee,
officer, or manager decision, they can attempt to convince the board
to overrule it; or, if that does not work, they can vote to change the

board. Alternatively, one or more owners could challenge any board, committee, officer or manager decision through litigation or arbitration on the basis that the decision was not reasonable, made in good faith, and/or in compliance with the governing documents or the formally established policies or procedures.

If an individual owner wishes to challenge or change a decision made by the homeowners' association, the owner should begin by attempting to discuss the matter with the HOA president, a director, committee chair or property manager. If this attempt does not yield satisfactory results, the owner should attend a board meeting or call an owner meeting to discuss the problem with the other owners. If the owner wishes to pursue the matter further, he/she should consult an attorney.

An exception to the limitation on owners' right to override a board decision exists when the board adopts, amends or repeals an operating rule that affects use of the common areas or exclusive use common areas, architectural or aesthetic standards for alteration of a unit or lot, member discipline, and standards and procedures for assessment collection. In such cases individuals owning 5 percent or more of the units or lots may call a special meeting of the owners to reverse a rule change. Written notice of the meeting must be given within 30 days of the rule change. The rule change will be reversed if a majority (or greater percentage if required by the CC&Rs or bylaws) of those present at a duly held meeting at which a quorum is present, vote for reversal. If a rule change is reversed, it may not be readopted by the board for one year. For more information, see Civil Code §§ 1357.100-1357.150, in Chapter 2.

C. HOA DECISION-MAKING PROCESS AND STANDARDS/LIMITS ON HOA POWER

The first step in board of directors decision-making is determining whether the course of action under consideration would be reasonable and in the best interests of all owners as a group. If this question can be answered affirmatively, the next step is to review the governing documents and *The Condominium Bluebook* with the following questions in mind:

(1) Is a particular action or decision required under the governing documents and/or the law?

(2) Is a particular procedure for making the decision required under the governing documents and/or the law?

(3) Does the decision under consideration require an owner vote?

Questionable action should be reviewed by an attorney. If the action could have a significant impact on one or more owners, it is wise to get a written opinion of counsel (upon which the board can rely in the event of a legal challenge) before the board takes action. A legal opinion may protect the board from liability for an erroneous decision by allowing it to assert reasonable reliance on the advice of counsel as a defense. But remember that the failure of an association to follow the advice of counsel or its own internal decision-making procedures will make inappropriate action vulnerable to a legal challenge.

Further, each board member's decision must adhere to the following standards:

(1) it must be within the scope of the association's authority under the governing documents and the law;

(2) it must be based upon a reasonable investigation;

(3) it must be intended to serve the best interests of the association and the owners as a group;

(4) it must be made in good faith; and,

(5) it must be reasonable in light of the information available at the time the decision is made.

Where the association has formally established policies or procedures, they must be uniformly applied and followed. However, the fact that the association has permitted or approved a certain activity or alteration by a particular owner at one time does not necessarily mean that the association must permit or approve that same activity by the same or a different owner at a later time. Further, there is no governmental agency with authority to oversee homeowners' associations. Association duties and standards must be enforced by owners and lenders through the court system or through some alternative dispute resolution process such as mediation or arbitration. In evaluating an association decision for compliance with the standards described above, the courts or an arbitrator will defer to the board's authority and presumed expertise. For additional information, see *Lamden v. La Jolla Shores Clubdominium Homeowners Assn. (1999) 21 Cal.4th 249, 87 Cal.Rptr.2d 237; Dolan-King v. Rancho Santa Fe Assn. (2000) 81 Cal.App.4th 965, 97 Cal.Rptr.2d 280*; *Clark v. Rancho Santa Fe Association (1989) 216 Cal.App.3d 606, 265 Cal.Rptr. 41; Cohen v. Kite Hill Community Assn. (1983) 142 Cal.App.3d 642, 191 Cal.Rptr. 209;* and *Laguna Royale Owners Assn. v. Darger (1981) 119 Cal.App.3d 670, 134 Cal.Rptr.136*, in Chapter 12.

D. AUTHORITY TO WRITE CHECKS OR SIGN CONTRACTS

The law states that the signatures of at least two directors, or of one officer and one director, are required for withdrawals from the association reserve account(s). See Civil Code § 1365.5(b), in Chapter 2. Withdrawal requirements for other association accounts are usually set in the governing documents, but if they are not, the requirements can be established by the board.

A decision whether the association should enter into a particular contract is made by the board unless the governing documents require owner approval or unless the board has delegated the decision to an officer, committee, or manager. The law is currently unclear regarding how many officers, and which officers, must sign the contract in order for it to be valid. Until this issue is settled by the courts, it is prudent to have the contract signed by two officers: (i) the president or vice president, and (ii) the secretary or chief financial officer.

The law provides that a contract signed by an officer can be binding even if there was never a proper association decision to enter into it. To avoid liability for non-approved contracts, the board should exercise care in selecting responsible officers, and provide written notice to all of its vendors that no contract should be considered valid unless it is signed by a designated person or the vendor receives a board resolution authorizing the agreement. A sample board resolution is provided in Chapter 15. For additional information, see Civil Code § 1365.5(b), in Chapter 2, and Corporations Code § 7214, in Chapter 3.

E. OFFICER AND DIRECTOR COMPENSATION FOR SERVICES

While it is legal to pay directors and officers for their service unless prohibited by the governing documents, it is not a good idea. Under the law, volunteer directors and officers of properly insured homeowners' associations face no personal liability for their decisions absent intentional fraud or self-dealing. Paid directors and officers can face personal liability for bad judgement and unintentional mistakes. For additional information, see Code of Civil Procedure § 425.15, in Chapter 7, Corporations Code § 7231.5, in Chapter 3, and Civil Code § 1365.7, in Chapter 2.

F. OWNERS MEETINGS AND DECISIONS

1. Regular and Special Owners Meetings

A regular owner meeting is one held on a regular schedule prescribed in the governing documents. Most governing documents require one regular meeting (the "annual meeting") each year. A special owner meeting is one that is not required by the governing documents, but rather has been convened for a special purpose. A special owner meeting can be convened by the board, the chairman of the board (if any), the president, or any group consisting of at least 5% of the owners.

2. Notice Requirements for Owners Meetings

Both regular and special owner meetings require a written notice to all owners. The notice must include the place, time and date of the meeting, an agenda of the matters to be discussed, and, in cases where directors are to be elected, the names of those who have been nominated (if any) prior to the notice date. The notice may be mailed or hand delivered. Posting the notice in the common area is not sufficient for owner meetings. If the notice is mailed by first class registered or certified mail, or if it is hand delivered, it must be given between 10 and 90 days before the meeting; if it is mailed by any other method, it must be given between 20 and 90 days before the meeting. Notice is not required when the meeting is actually the continuation of another meeting that was adjourned within the previous 45 days as long as the time and place of the continuation meeting had been announced at the original meeting.

When a group of owners, acting independently from the board, wishes to convene a special meeting, they must send a written request to the board chairman (if any), president, vice president, or secretary, and that person is required to notify all of the owners of the meeting between 35 and 90 days of the request. The date of the special meeting is set by the board.

Sample owner meeting notices are provided in Chapter 15. For additional information on owner meeting notices, see Corporations Code § 7511, in Chapter 4, and Civil Code § 1363(e), in Chapter 2.

Decisions made at an owner meeting held without proper notice are valid only if all of the following occur: (i) enough owners (a "quorum") were present to allow decisions to be made at a properly noticed meeting, (ii) none of the owners at the meeting objected to the improper notice at the beginning of the meeting, and (iii) every owner who did not attend the meeting signs a waiver of notice or an approval of the meeting minutes. For additional information, see Corporations Code § 7511(e), in Chapter 4.

Generally, at a regular owner meeting, the owners can vote on matters not mentioned in the meeting notice, except when less than 1/3 of the voting power is present. At a special owner meeting, the owners cannot vote on matters not mentioned in the meeting notice. For additional information, see Civil Code § 1363(e), in Chapter 2, and Corporations Code §§ 7511-7512, in Chapter 4.

3. Quorum Requirement

The governing documents generally specify the minimum amount of owner voting power (the "quorum") that must be present for decisions to be made at an owner meeting. The law does not specify a minimum or maximum quorum requirement, but does provide that if the governing documents permit decisions by a quorum of less than 1/3 of the total voting power and a quorum of less than 1/3 of the voting power is present at an owner's meeting, the only matters that can be voted on are those mentioned in the meeting notice. The law also provides that if the governing documents fail to specify a quorum requirement, it will automatically be set at 1/3 of the voting power. For additional information, see Corporations Code § 7512, in Chapter 4.

4. Procedural Rules for Owners Meetings

The law requires that owner meetings be conducted "in accordance with a recognized system of parliamentary procedure or any parliamentary procedures the association may adopt." For additional information, see Civil Code § 1363(d), in Chapter 2. Suggested owner meeting procedures are provided in Chapter 14.

5. Proxy Voting

An owner who cannot attend an owner meeting but who wishes to vote on a matter has two choices. The owner may use a mail-in ballot or give another owner a proxy authorizing the other owner to vote on his/her behalf at the meeting. The use of proxies is of diminished importance with the advent of mail-in ballots commencing in July 2006. For more information on proxies, see the section entitled "Proxies" at page 39 of this chapter.

6. Decision-Making Without an Owners Meeting

Any matter that could be decided at an owner meeting can also be decided without a meeting. To make owner decisions without an owner meeting, written ballots must be distributed to all owners. The ballots must contain the following information for each proposed action:

(1) a description of the action;

(2) a place to indicate approval or disapproval;

(3) the response deadline;

(4) the number of ballots that must be received by the deadline to satisfy the association's quorum requirements; and

(5) the percentage of approvals required for passage.

Owners must be given a reasonable time to return their ballots. Once returned, a ballot cannot be changed or revoked. A sample ballot form is provided in Chapter 15. For additional information, see Corporations Code §§ 7513, 7514, and 7516, in Chapter 4.

7. Owner Voting Power

A particular owner's voting power is determined by the governing documents. In most homeowners' associations, the owners of each unit have one vote of equal weight regardless of their ownership or assessment percentage, or the value or size of their units or lots. If voting power is not specified in the governing documents, the law presumes that the owners of each unit have one vote of equal weight. For additional information, see Corporations Code § 7610, in Chapter 4.

8. Super-Majority Voting Requirements

The level of owner voting power required for approval of a particular matter is determined by the governing documents and tends to vary depending on the type of decision. Most governing documents list a group of decisions requiring greater than majority approval, specify the level of approval required for each, and state that all other owner decisions are made by a majority. In instances where the governing documents do not specifically state that a particular type of decision requires a super-majority vote for approval, a majority approval requirement is presumed.

When interpreting voting requirements in governing documents or in the law, it is important to pay close attention to wording. When a matter requires the approval of a specified percentage, or the majority "of all owners" or "of the total voting power of the association" it means that the voting power cast for approval must be measured against the total voting power of all owners including those who did not cast votes. When a matter requires the approval of a specified percentage, or a majority, "of the owners" (i.e. without using the word "all"), or "of the votes cast," it means that the voting power cast for approval is only measured against the total voting power cast. For more information, see Corporations Code § 5033 and § 5034, in Chapter 4.

9. Meeting Minutes Requirement

The law requires that the association prepare and maintain minutes of all owner meetings, and that these minutes be made available to owners for inspection on written demand at any reasonable time for any reasonable purpose. The governing documents usually provide that the secretary is to prepare the minutes within a prescribed number of days following the meeting. For additional information, see Corporations Code § 8320, in Chapter 5 and Civil Code § 1363, in Chapter 2.

G. ELECTION AND TERMS OF HOMEOWNERS' ASSOCIATION DIRECTORS

1. Director Requirements and Qualifications

Incorporated associations are legally required to have directors. Unincorporated associations need not have directors. The governing documents can require that directors have certain qualifications so long as the qualifications are reasonable. In most associations, directors must be owners. Some governing documents require directors be residents as well as owners.

2. Director Nomination and Election

The governing documents usually specify nomination procedures for director candidates. For associations with fewer than 500 owners, the only requirement imposed by law is that the procedures be reasonable. (See Corporations Code §§ 7521-7524 for requirements applicable to associations with 500 or more members, in Chapter 4.) In fact, it is not necessary to have any formal nomination procedures if the association allows any owner to nominate a director. However, if any nominations have been made prior to the date the meeting notice is sent to the owners, the nominees should be identified in the notice.

Civil Code § 1363.03 requires an association to adopt rules that (1) ensure candidates equal access to association media, newsletters, and internet web-sites for campaign purposes, whether the candidate is supported by the board or not; (2) ensure equal access to common area meeting space for campaign purposes; (3) specify the qualifications for candidates and procedures for the nomination of candidates; (4) specify the qualifications for voting, the voting power of the association members, requirements for proxies, and voting schedules; and (5) specify the method of selecting one or three independent third parties as inspectors. The duties of inspectors of elections are enumerated in the statute.

Regardless of what the governing documents provide, elections involving the selection or removal of directors, amendments to the governing documents, assessments requiring owner approval, and the grant of exclusive use common area to a member must be by secret ballot. All other elections will be governed by the provisions of the governing documents.

Secret ballot elections must be held as follows: ballots and two pre-addressed envelopes with instructions on how to return ballots must be mailed by first-class mail or delivered to every member not less than 30 days before the voting deadline. Voters may not be identified by name, address, or lot, parcel, or unit number on the ballot. The ballot itself is not signed by the voter, but is inserted into an envelope that is sealed. This envelope is inserted into a second envelope that is sealed. In the upper left hand corner of the second envelope, the voter prints and signs his/her name, address, and lot, or parcel, or unit number that entitles him/her to vote. The second envelope is addressed to the inspector(s) of elections who tallies the votes. The envelope may be mailed or delivered by hand to a location specified by the inspector(s). The member may request a receipt upon delivery.

A quorum for a secret ballot election is required if stated in the governing documents. If a quorum is required, each ballot received by the inspector(s) is treated as a voter present at a meeting for the purposes of establishing a quorum.

All votes must be counted by the inspector(s) in an open meeting of the board or owners. Any owner may witness the counting of ballots. No one may open a secret ballot before all of the ballots are counted. The results must be promptly reported to the board, recorded in the minutes of the next board meeting and available for review by the members. Within 15 days of the election, the board must notify all owners of the election results. The ballots must remain in the custody of the inspector(s) until they are counted and then delivered to the association for safe storage for no less than one year.

In the event of a challenge, the association must make the ballots available for inspection by the owners or their authorized representatives. For additional information, see Civil Code § 1363.03, in Chapter 2.

The law prohibits the use of association funds for campaign purposes in the election of directors. For additional information, see Civil Code § 1363.04, in Chapter 2.

A violation of secret voting requirements invokes several penalties. Any owner may bring a civil action to challenge the election within one year after the date of the election, and if a court finds that the secret election rules were not adopted or the required procedures were not followed, the court may void the results of the election, award the challenging owner reasonable attorney's fees and court costs, and impose a civil penalty of up to $500 for each violation, except that a single violation affecting all owners equally is subject to only one civil penalty. Notably the statute does not allow an association its cost of defending an election challenge unless the court specifically finds that the challenger's civil action is frivolous, unreasonable, or without foundation. For additional information, see Civil Code § 1363.09, in Chapter 2.

A claim for many violations of secret voting requirements may be brought in Small Claims Court if the amount of the claim does not exceed the jurisdictional limit of Small Claims Court (now $7,500 for an action brought by a natural person and $5,000 for an action brought by a corporation or other business entity). For further information, see Civil Code § 1363.09, in Chapter 2 and Code of Civil Procedure § § 116.220, 116.221.

3. Cumulative Voting

In an election of directors using cumulative voting, each owner is allowed to cast a total number of votes equal to the number of directors to be elected, and may combine or "cumulate" those votes in any way he/she wishes. Thus if there are five seats on the board to be filled at the election, each owner will be entitled to five votes, but will not be required to vote for five candidates. As an alternative to casting one of his/her votes for each of five candidates, an owner can cast five votes for one candidate, or three votes for one candidate and two votes for another, and so on. The purpose of cumulative voting is to give each owner a stronger likelihood of electing at least one or two directors who share his/her views.

The law allows cumulative voting only if it is specifically authorized in the governing documents. If it is authorized, the association must allow cumulative voting using secret ballot procedures including mail-in ballots. The former requirement that cumulative voting will be triggered only if prior to the voting, at least one owner states his/her intention to cumulative his/her vote, has been eliminated. For additional information, see Civil Code § 1363.03, in Chapter 2.

4. Proxies

"Proxy" means a written authorization signed by an owner that gives another owner the power to vote on his/her behalf. A photocopy, facsimile or electronic transmission bearing an owner's signature is valid. Proxies may not be used in lieu of a ballot or combined with a ballot. They must be a separate, distinct document. In addition, if there are any voting instructions accompanying a proxy, the instructions must be on a separate sheet of paper that can be detached from the proxy when it is delivered to the inspector(s) of elections and retained by the proxy holder. For additional information, see Civil Code § 1363.03(d), in Chapter 2.

A proxy is valid only for 11 months from the date it is signed, unless the proxy specifically states that it is valid for a longer period. No proxy is valid for more than 3 years from the date it is signed under any circumstances. A proxy may be revoked at any time before a ballot is received by the inspector(s) of elections. For additional information, see Corp. Code § 7613, in Chapter 5 and Civil Code § 1363.03(d), in Chapter 2.

The use of proxies for election of directors is of diminished importance with the advent of mail-in ballots commencing July 2006.

5. Length of Director Terms/Staggered or Concurrent Terms

The length of the directors' terms is usually specified in the governing documents. By law, however, directors' terms may not exceed four years. If the governing documents do not specify term length, the law provides that it will be one year. It is not necessary for all directors to have terms of the same length, or for all directors' terms to expire in the same year. Frequently, the governing documents provide for staggered terms, so that fewer than all of the board seats are open to election at one time providing continuity in transition. For further information, see Corporations Code § 7220, in Chapter 3.

6. Removal of Directors Prior to Expiration of Term

A director may be removed by owner vote at any time using secret ballot procedures. The owners do not need a reason for the removal. The number of owner votes needed to remove a director is determined as follows:

(1) If the governing documents allow cumulative voting, a director can be removed only if the total number of votes of the owners opposing removal, if cumulated and all cast in favor of the director, would be insufficient to elect him/her (see Corporations Code § 7222(b)(1), in Chapter 3, for additional details);

(2) If the governing documents provide for voting in classes or subgroups, a director elected by a particular class or subgroup can be removed only by a majority vote of that class or subgroup (see Corporations Code § 7222(b)(2) and (3), in Chapter 3, for additional details);

(3) If neither of the first two paragraphs apply, and the association has fewer than 50 owners, director removal requires a majority of the total voting power of the association (rather than just a majority of the votes cast in the removal election); and

(4) If neither of the first two paragraphs apply, and the association has 50 or more owners, director removal requires a majority of the voting power cast in the removal election.

A director may also be removed by the other directors, but only if there is cause for removal. Appropriate cause for removal by the other directors includes mental incapacity and felony conviction. In addition, the governing documents may allow the board to remove directors for missing a specified number of meetings. For additional information, see Corporations Code § 7221(a), in Chapter 3.

7. Director Vacancies

The method of selecting a director to fill a vacancy following a resignation or removal is usually prescribed in the governing documents. If the governing documents are silent on the issue, a vacancy created by resignation is filled by board vote, and a vacancy created by removal is filled by owner vote (regardless of whether the removal was executed by the owners or by the board). For additional information, see Corporations Code § 7224, in Chapter 3.

H. DIRECTOR MEETINGS

1. Authority to Convene and Frequency of Board Meetings

In general, the governing documents will prescribe the frequency of regular board meetings, but will allow the board to establish the exact time and place of each meeting. The governing documents usually also provide that the time and place of a regular meeting can be changed, or a special meeting can be scheduled, by the chairman of the board (if any), the president, or a specified number of directors. If the documents are silent on the issue of who may call a special board meeting, the law provides that the chairman of the board (if any), the president, the vice president, the secretary, or any two directors may do so. Owners who are not directors or officers cannot call board meetings. For additional information, see Corporations Code § 7211(a), in Chapter 3.

2. Notice Requirements for Board Meetings

For a regular board meeting occurring at a time and place specified in the governing documents, no notice need be given to directors or owners unless notice is required by the governing documents. In other non-emergency situations, owner notice is always required, and director notice is usually required (see Corporation Code § 7211(a), in Chapter 3, for a list of the rare occasions when director notice is not required). In emergency situations as defined in Civil Code § 1363.05(g), in Chapter 2, owner notice is never required.

Where owner notice is required, it must be given at least four days in advance, and the governing documents may require a longer notice period. The notice must be posted in a prominent place within the common area, or delivered personally or by mail to each unit or lot. If the notice is posted, a written copy must be sent to every owner who requests written notice. The notice may be included in a newsletter or other general mailing. The notice must contain the agenda for the meeting. Sample notices are provided in Chapter 15. For additional information on owner notice requirements, see Civil Code § 1363.05(f), in Chapter 2.

Where director notice is required, it may be given four days in advance by first-class mail, or 48 hours in advance by telephone, voice mail, fax, electronic mail or personal delivery. Each director can waive his/her notice rights. For additional information on director notice requirements, see Corporation Code § 7211, in Chapter 3.

3. Quorum Requirement

The governing documents generally specify the minimum number of directors (the "quorum") that must be present for decisions to be made at a board meeting. The law will not permit this number to be less than the greater of 1/5 of the total number of directors or two directors. When the governing documents do not specify a director quorum, a majority of directors shall be required for a quorum. A majority vote of the directors, attending a meeting where a quorum is established, can make decisions unless the governing documents impose a higher voting requirement. Directors may attend meetings by conference telephone and still be considered present for quorum and voting purposes. For additional information, see Corporations Code § 7511, in Chapter 4.

4. Owner Attendance and Participation at Board Meetings

Owners are entitled to attend all board meetings except meetings held in executive session. The board is permitted to hold an executive session only to discuss litigation, contracts with non-owners, owner discipline (in which case the subject owner may attend), and personnel matters. If only part of the meeting will be an executive session, owners may attend the remainder. If the entire meeting will be an executive session, owners may not attend but are still entitled to advance notice. Any gathering (including a conference telephone call) where a majority of directors discuss any item of association business scheduled to be heard by the board is considered a director meeting, and triggers owner notice and attendance rights. For additional information, see Civil Code § 1363.05, in Chapter 2.

Owners must be permitted to speak at all board meetings except executive sessions, but the board may establish a reasonable time limit for owner speeches. Owners are not entitled to participate in board deliberations. For additional information, see Civil Code § 1363.05, in Chapter 2.

5. Procedures for Board Meetings

The law does not require formal procedures during board meetings.

Nevertheless, board meetings are likely to be more productive and less frustrating for participants, if formal procedures are adopted and followed. Suggested owner meeting procedures are provided in Chapter 14. A suggested agenda for board meetings is provided as Checklist 2 of Chapter 15.

Effective January 1, 2008, the board of directors may not discuss or take action on any item of business at a non-emergency meeting unless the item was placed on the agenda and the agenda was included with the meeting notice, unless the board makes one of three special findings: (1) an emergency situation exists that could not have been reasonably foreseen at the time the meeting notice was given; or (2) upon a vote of two-thirds of the board members (or upon a unanimous vote if less than two-thirds of the directors are present) that immediate action is necessary and the situation came to the attention of the board after the meeting notice was given and could not be included in the agenda; or (3) the item appeared on an agenda of a prior meeting more than 30 days before and the item was continued to the specific date on which action is to be taken. Before taking action under any one of these exceptions, the board must openly identify the item and the exception that justifies a special finding. For further information, see Civil Code § 1363.05(f) and (i), in Chapter 2.

These restrictions do not limit a director, a property manager or other association representative from discussing the following without regard to the content of the agenda: (1) briefly responding to statements made or questions posed by an owner; (2) asking questions for clarification; (3) making a brief announcement; (4) making a brief report on his or her own activities; (5) providing references, resources or factual information to the property manager and staff; (6) requesting the property manager or staff to report back at a subsequent board meeting on a matter; (7) directing the property manager or staff to place an item of business on a future agenda; and (8) directing the property manager or staff to perform administrative tasks necessary to fulfill these meeting procedures. For further information, see Civil Code § 1363.05(i), in Chapter 2.

However, these restrictions do not prohibit an owner who is not a board member from speaking on any issue not on the agenda.

6. Board Decisions Without Meeting

Board decisions cannot be made without a meeting except in two situations. The board may approve action without the necessity of a formal meeting by written unanimous consent of all the board members. The unanimity requirement eliminates the necessity of a board meeting because, if all of the directors agree to the action, there is no need for a meeting to discuss the merits of the action. The law is unclear on what right of notice and involvement an owner has in a board decision by unanimous written consent.

The board may also act without a meeting in emergency situations when all of the following occur:

(1) immediate attention is required;

(2) the circumstances of the emergency situation could not have been reasonably foreseen;

(3) it is impracticable to provide owner notice; and

(4) all directors have signed a written approval of the decision

A director approval form is provided in Chapter 15. For additional information, see Corporations Code § 7211, in Chapter 3, and Civil Code § 1363.05, in Chapter 2.

Board action is not required for all corporate activities. The activities and affairs of the corporation must be conducted and all corporate powers shall be exercised by **or** under the direction of the board. However, the board may delegate the management of day-to-day activities to any person, including an officer, director, committee, or property manager, so long as all corporate powers are exercised at the ultimate direction of the board. The board is not intended to be the executive body in the corporate structure, but rather the policy-making body pursuant to whose overall supervision and control those who actually carry on the daily operations of the association act. For additional information, see Corporations Code § 7211, in Chapter 3.

7. Standard for Board Decisions: Business Judgment Rule

The standard to which the board is held regarding discretionary management decisions or whether to bring suit for a violation of the governing documents is called the "business judgment rule." Under this standard, each director and the board as a whole must act in good faith and in a manner the director believes to be in the best interests of the homeowners' association. Further, each director must act with the care, including reasonable inquiry, that an ordinary prudent person in a similar position would exercise under similar circumstances. Under this standard the board of directors cannot be held liable for an erroneous decision or a poor choice in the absence of a showing of fraud, bad faith or negligence. The business judgment rule also permits the board of directors to rely on the opinions, reports, statements and financial data provided by (1) officers and employees of the homeowners' association whom the board reasonably believes to be competent; (2) legal counsel, independent accountants and other persons as to matters which the board believes to be within such person's professional competence; and (3) a committee of the board as to matters within its designated authority, provided that the board reasonably believes the committee to merit confidence. See *Lamden v. La Jolla Shores Clubdominium Assn. (1999) 21 Cal.4th 249, 87 Cal.Rptr.2d 237; Beehan v. Lido Isle Community Assn. (1977) 70 Cal. App.3d 858, 137 Cal.Rptr. 528,* in Chapter 12.

8. Meeting Minutes Requirements

The law requires that the association maintain minutes of all director meetings except executive sessions, that the minutes be prepared (at least in draft form) within 30 days of the meeting, and that the association provide copies of the minutes to any owner upon request. We recommend that the board also maintain separate minutes for executive sessions, which should be maintained separately from minutes for open meetings and **not** distributed to members. The governing documents usually state that the secretary is responsible for preparing the minutes, but this is frequently delegated to a property manager. For additional information, see Corporations Code § 8320, in Chapter 5, and Civil Code § 1363.05(d), in Chapter 2. A sample board resolution is provided in Chapter 15.

9. Procedures for Adopting and Changing Homeowners' Association Rules

The board of directors is responsible for adopting, amending or repealing homeowners' association operating rules. Any rules adopted by the board must be (i) in writing, (ii) within the authority of the board to make pursuant to the law, the CC&Rs, the articles of incorporation and the bylaws, (iii) not inconsistent with the law, the CC&Rs, the articles or the bylaws, (iv) made in good faith, and (v) reasonable. See Civil Code § 1357.110, in Chapter 2.

For rule adoption or amendment regarding use of common areas or exclusive use common areas, architectural or aesthetic standards for alterations of a unit or lot, member discipline, delinquent assessment payment plans or assessment dispute resolution, and election procedures, the board must provide all members with thirty (30) days advance written notice which contains the text of the proposed new or amended rule, unless the rule is necessary to address an imminent threat to public health or safety, or an imminent risk of substantial economic loss to the association. The board must adopt a proposed rule change at a board meeting after consideration of any comments by association members. Once a rule change has been approved, the board must deliver notice of the change to all owners within 15 days. 5% of the owners may convene a special owners' meeting to consider reversing the rule change by delivering a written request to the president or secretary within 30 days after notification of adoption of a rule change. If a majority of owners, at an owner meeting at which a quorum is present, vote to reverse the rule change, the rule change is reversed and may not be readopted by the board for one year, although the board may adopt a different rule on the same subject without a time restriction. In lieu of calling a meeting requested by 5% of the owners, the board may distribute a ballot to every member of the association for a vote by written ballot.

The procedural rules set forth in the preceding paragraph do not apply to board decisions regarding maintenance of common areas, specific matters not intended to apply to unit or lot owners generally, the amounts of regular or special assessments, rule changes required by law if the board has no discretion as to the substantive effect of the rule change, or the issuance of a document that merely restates existing law or the governing documents. For more information regarding these procedural rules, see Civil Code §§ 1357.120 through 1357.150, in Chapter 2.

I. HOMEOWNERS' ASSOCIATION OFFICERS AND COMMITTEES

1. Officer Requirements

Incorporated associations are legally required to have at least (i) a chairman of the board or president, (ii) a secretary, and (iii) a chief financial office or treasurer, but, unless prohibited by the governing documents, one person may hold all of these offices. Unincorporated associations need not have officers but most do. For additional information, see Corporations Code § 7213(a), in Chapter 3.

2. Differences between Directors and Officers

The main difference between officers and directors in both incorporated and unincorporated associations is the nature of their responsibilities. Directors are generally responsible for decisions on major issues affecting the association, such as whether to conduct an inspection of the development for latent construction defects, whether to initiate a law suit against the developer for construction defects, adopting a budget and determining yearly regular assessments, and determining the amount that should be maintained in the reserve funds. Officers are generally responsible for day-to-day decision-making and operation of the association. For example, in an association which has officers, the officers are generally responsible for day-to-day maintenance of the common interest development and the collection of owner assessments. Where a homeowners' association contracts with a professional manager to run the day-to-day operations of the association, the manager will usually perform some or all of the duties that officers would perform in a common interest development without a professional manager.

3. Election and Removal of Officers

Officers are chosen by the board unless the governing documents specifically provide for election by the owners. Officers chosen by the board may be replaced by the board at any time and for any reason. For additional information, see Corporations Code § 7213(b), in Chapter 3.

4. Officer Decision-Making Authority

The power and authority of each officer is determined by the governing documents, or, if the documents are silent, by the board.

Regardless of how power and authority is delegated among the officers, the board can override the decision of any officer on any matter. For additional information, see Corporations Code § 7210, in Chapter 3.

5. Committees

Most governing documents authorize the formation of one or more specific committees, but the board has the authority to create committees even if that power is not specifically mentioned in the governing documents. Unless the governing documents specify the size of the committee, the qualifications required of the members, and the method of selecting and removing the members, these matters can be determined by the board. Committee recommendations are not binding on the board, and committee decisions may be overridden by the board. The law prohibits certain matters from being delegated to a committee, and these matters are listed in Corporations Code § 7212(a), in Chapter 3. For additional information, see Corporations Code §§ 7151(c)(4) and 7210, also in Chapter 3.

J. HOA RECORD KEEPING AND REPORTING REQUIREMENTS

The law imposes strict record keeping and reporting requirements on homeowners' associations, and the governing documents often impose even more stringent requirements. Some of the records and reports must be distributed to the owners automatically on a prescribed schedule, and the remainder must be available to owners upon request. The following is a summary of the minimum requirements imposed by law, organized by general category:

1. Financial Information

Budget: The association must prepare a *pro forma* operating budget each year which projects the income and expenses for the upcoming year, and the amount needed in reserve for future upkeep and eventual replacement of the major parts of the project which the association maintains. The exact content requirements for the *pro forma* operating budget are listed in Civil Code § 1365(a). Either the entire *pro forma* operating budget, or a summary of it, must be distributed to all owners each year. If only a summary is distributed, it must include a statement that the full budget is available upon request.

As part of the budget or summary, the association must include the following additional material:

(1) A statement that board meeting minutes are available upon request (see Civil Code § 1363.05 for required content (all of the citations to the Civil Code contained in this section can be found in Chapter 2));

(2) A statement of whether the association anticipates any special assessments for reserves (see Civil Code § 1365(a)(3) for required content);

(3) A statement describing how the reserve needs were calculated (see Civil Code §§ 1365(a)(4) and 1365.2.5 for required content);

(4) A statement of the association's policy for collecting delinquent assessments (see Civil Code §§ 1365(e) and 1365.1);

(5) A summary of association insurance coverage (see Civil Code § 1365(f) for required content); and

(6) A summary of the association's dispute resolution procedures (see Civil Code § 1369.590 for required content).

Annual Report: The association must prepare a financial report **each year** which includes an income and expense statement, a balance sheet, a statement of changes in financial position, and notification of the location of the owner name and address list. If the association has collected less than $75,000 during the year, it must notify all owners that the annual report is available upon request; if the association has collected more than $75,000 during the year, it must retain an accountant to review the report and then automatically provide it to all owners. For more information, see Corporations Code § 8321, in Chapter 5, and Civil Code § 1365(c), in Chapter 2.

Reserve Study: The association must prepare a reserve study every three years which includes a list of the major association-maintained components with a remaining life of less than 30 years, and estimates of (i) the remaining life of each component; (ii) the costs of maintaining and replacing these components; (iii) the annual contribution required to fund these costs; and (iv) the percentage to which the estimated costs are funded compared to the total amount of reserve funds on deposit. The reserve study must be based upon a physical inspection of all accessible areas of the property. For more information, see Civil Code § 1365.5(e), in Chapter 2. For a detailed discussion of reserve studies, see the section entitled "Reserve Studies" at page 62 of this chapter.

2. Decisions

Meeting Minutes: The association must prepare minutes of each owner and board meeting, and provide copies of the minutes to any owner upon request. The minutes or a summary of the minutes must be made available to the owners within 30 days of a board meeting. A notice that the board meeting minutes are available for review must be included with the *pro forma* operating budget each year. For additional information, see Corporations Code § 8320, in Chapter 5, and Civil Code § 1363.05, in Chapter 2.

Monetary Penalties: If the association imposes monetary penalties or fees for violation of the governing documents, it must provide a schedule to all owners each time a penalty or fee is established or adjusted. For additional information, see Civil Code § 1363, in Chapter 2.

Litigation: If the association is contemplating litigation against the developer, it has various reporting requirements. For further information, see Civil Code §§ 1365.5(d), 1375, and 1375.1, in Chapter 2.

3. Membership

Address List: The association must maintain a list of owner names and addresses. The list need not include members' telephone numbers, fax numbers or e-mail addresses. Owners must be notified of the location of the list as part of the annual report, and a copy of the list must be provided to owners upon request. For additional information, see Civil Code § 1365.2, in Chapter 2.

4. Information Statement Submitted to Secretary of State

The law requires all homeowners' associations, whether incorporated or unincorporated, to file a biennial information statement with the California Secretary of State. The information statement must contain various information as required by statute, including the name of the association, the type of common interest development at issue, the common interest development's location, and the name, address and telephone number of the association's office or managing agent. The association must promptly notify the Secretary of State of any changes that occur to the information previously provided. For more information, see Civil Code § 1363.5, in Chapter 2.

The penalty for an incorporated association's noncompliance with the filing requirements is a suspension of the association's rights, privileges, and powers as a corporation, and monetary penalties. For more information on this requirement, see Civil Code § 1363.6, in Chapter 2.

5. Insurance

Homeowners' associations are required to provide a summary of the terms of all of their insurance policies to each owner each year, and to provide complete copies of the policies upon request. For additional information, see Civil Code § 1365(f)(1), in Chapter 2.

6. Disclosures to Prospective Unit or Lot Purchasers

Homeowners associations are not required to provide or disclose any information to prospective purchasers of units or lots but are required to provide a variety of documents to selling owners so that these owners can meet seller disclosure requirements. The documents may be made available in hard copy or electronic form and the association may charge a reasonable fee based on the association's actual cost. For additional information, see Civil Code § 1368, in Chapter 2, and *Kovich v. Paseo Del Mar Homeowners' Assn. (1996) 41 Cal.App.4th 863, 48 Cal. Rptr.2d 758,* in Chapter 12.

7. Reporting Requirements for Mixed-Use Developments

The law provides that common interest developments which are limited to industrial or commercial uses are exempt from some requirements of the Davis-Stirling Act, Civil Code § 1350 *et seq.,* in Chapter 2, including the annual report requirement described in "Financial Information" at page 48 of this chapter. In mixed use developments which contain a residential component, the commercial and/or industrial associations are exempt from the annual reporting requirement. However, the residential association and the master association, of which the residential association is a member, remain subject to all of the requirements of the Davis-Stirling Act, even if the commercial and/or industrial associations comprise a majority of voting power in the master association. See Civil Code § 1373, in Chapter 2.

V. MANAGING AGENTS/PROFESSIONAL MANAGERS

A. DEFINITION

A managing agent is a person or entity, such as a property management company, who for compensation or the expectation of compensation exercises control over the assets of a common interest development. However, the term "managing agent" does not include any full-time employee of the homeowners' association or any regulated financial institution operating within the normal course of its regulated business practice. See Civil Code § 1363.1(b), in Chapter 2, and Bus. & Prof. Code § 11500 *et seq.*, in Chapter 11.

B. REQUIREMENTS FOR PROFESSIONAL MANAGER

Some governing documents require professional management, or state that an owner vote (or even the approval of mortgage lenders) is required to discontinue professional management. Absent these provisions, professional management is not required, but it is generally advisable, particularly for larger associations. The law allows any association to retain a professional manager. For additional information, see Corporations Code § 7210, in Chapter 3.

C. SERVICES TYPICALLY PROVIDED BY
PROFESSIONAL MANAGERS

Professional managers offer a wide variety of services to homeowners' associations including accounting, budgeting, record keeping, assessment collection, bill payment, meeting coordination, and common area maintenance. Associations choose from among the services available, and enter into a contract with the manager describing the scope of work. The management contract should also include the fee, the duration of arrangement, and the circumstances under which the arrangement can be terminated before the contract expires. Some governing documents limit the duration of management agreements or require specific early termination provisions. A sample management agreement recommended by California Association of Community Managers is provided in Chapter 13.

While the law allows almost any association function to be delegated to a professional manager, most governing documents list certain association functions that cannot be delegated. Non-delegable functions typically include borrowing money, levying assessments, making capital expenditures in excess of budgeted amounts, and imposing discipline for violation of the governing documents. Regardless of what functions are delegated, and regardless of the content of the management agreement, the board retains the duty to supervise the manager and the authority to override any decision made by the manager. For additional information, see Corporations Code § 7210, in Chapter 3.

D. SELECTION OF PROFESSIONAL MANAGER AND MANAGEMENT CONTRACT

The board has the authority to select the manager and determine the content of the management contract, but it may appoint a committee to make recommendations. A sample management contract recommended by California Association of Community Managers is provided in Chapter 13.

E. DISCLOSURE REQUIREMENTS

Managers of homeowners' associations are not required to be licensed, but they must provide extensive written disclosures to the board of directors within ninety days prior to entering into a management agreement with the homeowners' association. The disclosures must include the names and business addresses of the professional manager's owners or general partners (or its officers and directors if it is a corporation) and any relevant licenses or professional certificates, including expiration dates, held by the professional manager or any of its employees. For additional information, see Civil Code § 1363.1, in Chapter 2.

F. RESTRICTIONS ON MANAGER'S HANDLING OF FUNDS

The law imposes stringent requirements on managers that handle homeowners' association funds to prevent commingling and fraud. For example, association monies held by the professional manager must be deposited into a trust account maintained by an in-state bank, savings and loan or credit union. However, the board of directors may instruct the professional manager to deposit funds in an interest-bearing account, subject to certain requirements. Further, the professional manager must maintain separate records for receipt and disposition of all association money it handles and may not commingle the funds of one homeowners' association with the funds of any other homeowners' association, unless strict contractual or bonding requirements are met. For additional information, see Civil Code § 1363.2, in Chapter 2.

VI. FINANCIAL MANAGEMENT

A. BUDGETING AND REGULAR ASSESSMENTS

1. Definition of Operating Funds and Reserve Funds

The term "operating funds" describes money collected for annually recurring expenses such as insurance, management, common area utilities, and janitorial service. The term "reserve funds" describes money collected for the repair and replacement of major components of the property which the homeowners' association maintains.

2. Homeowners' Association Budget: Definition, Creation and Review

The *pro forma* operating budget is a document listing the expected income, operating fund needs, and reserve fund needs, along with the basis for the calculation of the reserve fund needs. The exact content requirements for the budget are listed in Civil Code § 1365(a), in Chapter 2. A new budget must be prepared and circulated to all owners each year, but it can be based upon the budget from the previous year. The board is responsible for preparing the budget, but it can delegate this responsibility to an officer, committee, or professional manager provided the board retains final authority to review and approve the budget. For more information on budgets, see the section entitled

"Financial Information" at page 48 of this chapter.

3. Reserve Funds: Limitations on Use and Review Study Requirement

Reserve funds may only be spent to repair, restore, replace, maintain or pursue litigation involving the repair, restoration, replacement or maintenance of major components of the common interest development which the homeowners' association is required to maintain. However, the board may temporarily transfer funds in the association's reserve account to the general operating fund to meet short term cash-flow requirements, provided that the board first notifies the owners of an intent to consider the transfer, the reasons for the transfer and the repayment options and notice a board meeting at which the transfer will be considered. The board must then make a written finding recorded in the minutes explaining why the reserve funds are needed and how and when the monies will be repaid to the reserve fund. Any monies temporarily transferred from the reserved fund generally must be repaid to the reserve fund within one year, although the board may delay the repayment due date, after giving the same notice as required for the initial transfer, upon a finding that a temporary delay would be in the best interest of the association. See Civil Code § 1365.5(c), in Chapter 2.

At least once every three years, the board must conduct a reasonably competent and diligent visual inspection of the accessible areas of the major components the association is required to maintain as part of a study to determine reserve fund requirements. See also Civil Code § 1365.5(e), in Chapter 2.

4. Determination and Adjustment of Regular Assessment Amounts

Regular assessments must be based upon the funding needs projected in the budget. In general, the board is responsible for determining the amount of the regular assessments, but it can delegate this responsibility to an officer, committee, or professional manager provided the board retains final authority. Some governing documents require owner approval for changes in regular assessments. Regardless of any restrictions in the governing documents, the board may increase regular assessments up to 20% greater than the previous fiscal year without the approval of the owners. However, the board may not increase regular assessments by any amount without the approval of the owners if the association failed to provide a *pro forma* budget as required by Civil Code § 1365(a) on a timely basis. Even where the governing documents do not require owner approval, increases of more than 20% must be approved by the owners except in emergency situations. Owner approval for the purpose of an increase in regular assessments means approval by a majority of votes cast in an election where at least a majority of all owners vote. If approved, all owners must be notified of an increase in regular assessments by first-class mail between 30 and 60 days before the increase takes effect. For additional information, see Civil Code §§ 1366 and 1366.1; in Chapter 2.

5. Determination of Each Owner's Share of Assessments

The governing documents always specify how assessments are allocated among the owners, and usually require a high percentage of the owners and the mortgage lenders to approve any change in the allocation. The allocation is established by the developer at the time the governing documents are prepared, and is reviewed by a governmental agency (California Department of Real Estate) for projects consisting of five or more units or lots. Allocations may be based on the square footage of each unit as a percentage of the total square footage of all units in the development, an equal allocation whereby each unit owner pays the same assessment regardless of individual unit size, or a mixed method of allocation which combines elements of both the square footage and equal approaches. There are no legal grounds for an owner to challenge the assessment allocation based upon fairness or equity, provided that the allocation actually imposed upon each owner is consistent with the governing documents.

B. OTHER ASSESSMENTS

1. Definition and Creation of Special Assessments

A special assessment is an assessment for an association expense that was under-budgeted or not budgeted. It can be made payable in a single installment or in multiple installments. In general, the board has the power to impose small special assessments and to determine the payment schedule on these special assessments, but some governing documents require owner approval for all special assessments.

Regardless of the restrictions in the governing documents, the board may levy a special assessment of not more than 5% of the gross expenses for the current fiscal year without the approval of the owners. However, the board may not levy a special assessment of any amount without the approval of the owners if the association failed to provide a *pro forma* budget as required by Civil Code § 1365(a). Even where the governing documents do not require owner approval, special assessments during one year that total more than 5% of the budgeted expenses for that year require owner approval except in emergency circumstances. Owner approval for the purpose of levying a special assessment means approval by a majority of the votes cast in an election where at least a majority of all owners vote. The allocation of a special assessment among the owners is determined by the governing documents. If approved, all owners must be notified of a new or increased special assessment by first-class mail between 30 and 60 days before it is due. See Civil Code § 1366, in Chapter 2.

2. Definition and Creation of Emergency Assessments

Emergency assessments, either by an increase in regular assessments or the levy of a special assessment, may be imposed without prior owner approval in the following three circumstances:

(1) An extraordinary expense which is the result of a court order;

(2) An extraordinary expense necessary to repair or maintain any part of the common interest development for which the association is responsible where a threat of personal safety on the property is discovered; or

(3) An extraordinary expense necessary to repair or maintain any part of the common interest development for which the association is responsible that could not have been reasonably foreseen by the board when it prepared and distributed the annual *pro forma* operating budget, provided that the board passes a written resolution which contains findings as to the necessity of the expense and why it could not be reasonably foreseen. See Civil Code § 1366(b), in Chapter 2.

3. Definition and Creation of Personal Reimbursement Assessments

A personal reimbursement assessment is an assessment against only one owner. The most common type of personal reimbursement assessment is one imposed to reimburse the association for a cost which is a specific owner's individual responsibility under the governing documents. For example, if an owner or the owner's guest or tenant damages the common area, the association could levy a personal reimbursement assessment for the repair cost. Another type of personal reimbursement assessment is one imposed as a fine or penalty. Fines and penalties can only be imposed if a schedule of violations and corresponding fines has been distributed to all owners in advance. Often, the governing documents require that an owner be given a board hearing before a personal reimbursement assessment is imposed. For additional information, see Civil Code §§ 1363(g) and (h), in Chapter 2.

C. LIMITATIONS ON USAGE OR SERVICE FEES

The board may impose usage and service fees, separate from regular or other types of assessments, as long as they do not conflict with the governing documents. The amount of these additional charges must be reasonable and may not exceed the amount necessary to defray the costs for which the charges are levied. See Civil Code § 1366.1, in Chapter 2.

D. ASSESSMENT DISPUTES AND COLLECTION

1. Owner Challenges to Assessments

If an owner disagrees with the amount of an assessment, he/she can challenge the assessment through a court action or internal dispute resolution. An owner may, at his/her option, pay under protest any disputed charge or sum levied by the association, including an assessment, fine, penalty, late fee, collection cost, or monetary penalty, and by so doing, reserve the right to contest the disputed charge in court or otherwise.

Internal dispute resolution is initiated by an owner submitting a written request for dispute resolution. The exact requirements for challenging an assessment through this method are described in Civil Code § 1363.840, in Chapter 2. In addition, an association may not initiate a foreclosure without participating in alternative dispute resolution with a neutral third party if requested by the owner.

Alternatively, an owner who disputes a monetary assessment or other levy within the jurisdictional limit of Small Claims Court may, in addition to pursuing internal dispute resolution, pay under protest the disputed amount and commence an action in Small Claims Court for a judicial resolution of the dispute.

An owner may not withhold assessments owed to the association on the grounds that the owner is entitled to recover money or damages from the association for some other obligation. For additional information, see *Park Place Estates Homeowners Assn. v. Naber (1994) 29 Cal. App.4th 427, 35 Cal.Rptr.2d 51,* in Chapter 12. Further, an owner is not entitled to withdraw any funds held by the association when the owner sells his/her individual unit or lot. Allocation of assessments between the seller and buyer are handled through escrow.

2. Delinquent Assessments: Consequences for Unit or Lot Owners and Requirements for Homeowners' Association to Collect Delinquent Assessments

If an owner does not pay a regular or special assessment, he/she is subject to a variety of fees and penalties including non-judicial foreclosure, a lengthy procedure culminating in an auction-like sale of the delinquent owner's unit or lot to pay the assessment and the collection costs. In a non-judicial foreclosure, there is no trial or hearing. The procedure can be handled by an attorney or by a specialized assessment collection service.

If an owner does not pay a personal reimbursement assessment levied to reimburse the association for common area damage, non-judicial foreclosure is also possible so long as the governing documents authorize it. If an owner does not pay a personal reimbursement assessment levied for any other purpose, the association must collect its funds through a judicial process.

The association must have a written statement of policy for collecting delinquent assessments and must distribute that statement to all owners annually. The policy should require immediate and aggressive action by the association every time an assessment is delinquent. This approach avoids the awkwardness of responding to owners who request additional time to pay, which, if granted, creates a perception of leniency or inconsistent treatment. Moreover, in cases where the delinquent owner has also defaulted on his/her mortgage, quick action decreases the likelihood that a mortgage foreclosure will prevent the association from collecting unpaid assessments.

3. Lien and Foreclosure Procedures to Collect Delinquent Assessments

If an owner is delinquent in paying assessments, the association should record a lien upon the owner's unit or lot. Before an association can record a lien upon an owner's unit or lot, however, the association must first provide the owner with a written notice sent by certified mail thirty days prior to recording the lien. The notice must include various information as required by statute, including (1) a general description of the association's collection and lien enforcement procedures and method of calculation of the amount due, (2) an itemized statement of the charges owed by the owner, which includes the amount of the delinquent assessments, the fees and reasonable costs of collection, reasonable attorneys' fees, and any late charges or interest, (3) a statement that the owner shall not be liable to pay the charges, interest or costs of collection if it is determined the assessment was, in fact, paid on time, (4) a statement that the owner may request as meeting with the board regarding the delinquency if the owner so requests, and (5) a statement that the owner has the right to participate in non-binding internal dispute resolution ("meet and confer") or mediation with a neutral third party. Sample association notices relating to delinquent assessments are provided in Chapter 15. For additional information, see Civil Code §§ 1367.1, 1367.4 and 1367.5, in Chapter 2.

Thirty days after a lien is properly recorded on an owner's lot or unit, the association may pursue either a judicial or non-judicial foreclosure if the assessment, not including late charges or fees, exceeds $1,800 or is more than 12 months delinquent. A decision to record a lien must be made at an open meeting of the board; a decision to initiate foreclosure must be made in executive session. If an owner's lot or unit is sold by non-judicial foreclosure for delinquent assessments, there is a 90-day period for the owner to redeem the property after the sale by paying all arrears and costs. Judicial and non-judicial foreclosure each have their own advantages and disadvantages. Consult an attorney before pursuing either type of foreclosure proceeding. For additional information, see Civil Code §§ 1367.4 and 1367.5, in Chapter 2.

The lien and foreclosure remedies only apply to delinquent assessments and to late fees, costs of collection (including attorneys' fees), and interest on the delinquent assessments. The lien and foreclosure remedies can not be used to collect monetary penalties imposed by the association on an owner as a disciplinary measure for violation of the governing documents. See Civil Code § 1367.1(e), in Chapter 2.

Another benefit for an association which diligently enforces its lien procedures against delinquent owners is that if the association has appropriately recorded a lien against an owner's lot or unit and the owner later files for bankruptcy, the association will be considered a secured creditor of the owner. Thus, if a lien is already in place, the association will have a much better chance of recovering delinquent assessments than it otherwise would.

E. HOA ACCOUNTING PROCEDURES AND FINANCIAL REPORTING REQUIREMENTS

The law requires that a homeowners' association segregate its reserve funds from its operating funds and perform a quarterly financial review that includes:

(1) a reconciliation of both the operating and reserve accounts;

(2) a comparison of the actual reserve revenue and expenses to the budgeted reserve revenues and expenses;

(3) an analysis of the bank statements for both operating and reserve accounts; and

(4) an analysis of the income and expense statements for operating and reserve accounts.

Some governing documents increase the scope or frequency of this review. The law also requires preparation and distribution of a budget and financial report each year as described in the section entitled "Homeowners' Association Budgets" at page 54 of this chapter, and a reserve study every three years as described in the following section.

Reserve funds can be used only for repair, restoration, replacement or maintenance of the portions of the property that the association is obligated to maintain, or litigation involving these items. In some circumstances, the association can borrow reserve funds to cover operating expenses, but the board must first notify the owners, make required findings, and then repay the reserve funds within one year, unless the repayment due date is extended after further notification to the owners and appropriate finding as required by statute. The board is responsible for fulfilling the association's accounting responsibilities, but it can delegate this responsibility to an officer, committee, or professional manager provided the board retains final authority. For additional information, see Checklists 4 and 5 in Chapter 15, Civil Code §§ 1365 and 1365.5, in Chapter 2, and Corporations Code §§ 8320-8322, in Chapter 5.

F. RESERVE STUDIES

An association is required to prepare a reserve study at least once every three years based on a diligent visual inspection of the accessible areas of the "major components". A "major component" is a component of the development that the association is required to maintain or replace with a service live of 30 years or less. Components with an estimated service life of more than 30 years may be included in the study as a capital asset or disregarded from the reserve calculations, so long as the decision is revealed in the reserve study and reported in the reserve disclosure form discussed below.

There are two exceptions to the requirement of a reserve study. When the current replacement value of all major components is less that one-half of the gross budget of the association a reserve study is not required. This rare exception applies only to associations with extremely limited common area improvements, such as a median strip, a single common area playground, a walking trail, or a common entry gate. Also, a reserve study is not required for a development that is limited exclusively to industrial or commercial uses. For additional information, see Civil Code §§ 1365.5(c) and 1373(a), in Chapter 2.

The board is required to review the reserve study annually and determine whether intervening events over the past year warrant adjustment of the reserve funding. If adjustment is warranted, then regular assessments should be adjusted to reflect the increase or decrease necessary to meet the funding goals. Professional reserve study preparers will provide interim annual updates when the board feels adjustments are appropriate. For additional information, see Civil Code § 1365.5(c), in Chapter 2.

A reserve study at a minimum must include: (1) an identification of the major components with a remaining service life of less than 30 years; (2) a determination of the remaining service life of those major components; (3) the cost of maintaining or replacing those major components over the next 30 years; and (4) an estimate of the annual contribution necessary to meet the cost of maintaining or replacing those major components over the next 30 years; and (5) a reserve funding plan that indicates how the association plans to fund the reserves. The funding plan may exclude those major components the board has determined not to repair or replace. The plan must include a schedule of the date and amount of any change in regular or special assessments that will be needed to sufficiently fund the reserve funding plan. The plan must be adopted by the board at a meeting open to the members. If the board determines that an assessment increase is necessary to fund the plan, any increase shall be approved in a separate action of the board consistent with the procedures described in Civil Code § 1366, in Chapter 2.

Reserves studies typically take into account the interest earned on reserve funds on deposit. By statute a reserve study may not assume an interest rate of return on cash reserves in excess of 2% above the discount rate published by the Federal Reserve Bank of San Francisco at the time the calculation is made. For additional information, see Civil Code § 1365(a)(4), in Chapter 2. The discount rate can be obtained at www.frbsf.org/banking under "Banking Data & Resources - FRBSF Discount Rate."

An association must set up a reserve account separate from its operating account in which to deposit reserve funds collected through assessments. The association may deposit in the reserve account funds received from a compensatory damage award or settlement for construction defects, but it must maintain a separate accounting for those funds even though they may be co-mingled with the other reserve funds. The purpose of reserve funds is to have available at a specific point in time the necessary funds to maintain and replace major components throughout their service life. For additional information, see Civil Code § 1365.5(b) and (c), in Chapter 2.

Reserve funds cannot be spent for any purpose other than the maintenance and replacement of major components for which the funds are set aside except in limited situations. Reserve funds set aside for a particular line item in a reserve study need not be restricted to expenditures on that line item alone, but rather the aggregate of all reserve funds may be used for aggregate of all reserve expenses at a particular time. Reserve funds should not be used for expenses on components not included in the reserve study. If major components not in the reserve study are in need or repair or replacement, the reserve study should be updated to include those components with an adjustment to the funding plan. For additional information, see Civil Code § 1365.5(c), in Chapter 2.

The board may authorize the temporary transfer of reserve funds to the operating account to meet short-term cash-flow requirement or other expenses - a liberal exception. However, before the board may transfer reserve funds, it must fulfill certain procedural requirements. It must notify the owners of the intent to consider a transfer at a meeting of the board open to the owners with not less than 4 days prior written notice. The notice must include the reasons for the transfer, the options for repayment, and whether a special assessment may be considered. If the board authorizes the transfer at an open meeting, it must prepare written findings, included in the minutes, explaining the reasons for the transfer, and describing when and how the funds will be repaid to the reserve account. For additional information, see Civil Code § 1365.5(c), in Chapter 2.

Funds transferred from the reserve account must be restored to reserve account within one year of the date of the initial transfer with one more liberal exception. The board may delay repayment upon making a written finding, supported by documentation, that temporary delay would be in the best interest of the association. Neither "temporary delay" nor "best interest" is defined by law and the rule of reason should apply. A decision to delay repayment can only be made by the board at an open meeting after giving notice to the owners in the same manner as required for the initial transfer. The board is required to exercise "prudent fiscal management" in maintaining the integrity of the reserve account at all times. Again, no definition is given for "prudent fiscal management" but it is generally understood that the standards are the same as those for any fiduciary entrusted with the custody and preservation of someone else's money. If the repayment plan proves inadequate, the association must levy a special assessment to replenish the reserve account. If the special assessment exceeds 5% of the budgeted gross expenses for the current fiscal year, the special must be put to a secret vote of the owners. The association is authorized to extend payment plans to the owners to meet a special assessment. For additional information, see Civil Code § 1365.5(c), in Chapter 2.

When reserve funds are transferred for litigation purposes, the association must notify the owners of that decision and the availability of an accounting in the next mailing to the owners. The association is then required to make a quarterly accounting of expenses related to litigation available to the owners on at least a quarterly basis. The accounting need not be sent to all owners, but must be available upon request by owners at the association's office. For additional information, see Civil Code § 1365.5(c), in Chapter 2.

Each year not less than 30 days nor more than 90 days prior to the beginning of the association's fiscal year, it must distribute with its *pro forma* operating budget a summary of the association's reserves based upon the most recent annual review or 3-year study and the cash and cash equivalents on deposit. For additional information, see Civil Code § 1365(a). The summary must be based upon information available at the end of the fiscal year upon which the summary is based, must include all of the following:

(1) The current estimated replacement costs, estimate remaining life, and estimated useful life of each major component;

(2) The current estimate of the amount of cash reserves necessary to meet its reserve funding goals;

(3) The current estimate of accumulated cash reserves actually available to meet its reserve funding goals, expressed both on a project-

wide basis and on a per unit basis;

(4) The amount of funds received for a compensatory damage award or settlement related to construction defects;

(5) The percentage the amount of accumulated cash reserves on deposit bears to the amount of currently estimated to be required to meet its reserve funding goals;

(6) A statement whether the association anticipates the levy of one or more special assessments to meet its reserve funding goals and the method of all anticipated assessments; and

(7) A statement of the anticipated mechanism for funding reserves over the life of the reserve study.

The *pro forma* operating budget must also contain a statement as to all of the following:

(1) Whether the board has decided to defer the repair or replacement of any major components included in the reserve study together with a justification for the deferral;

(2) Whether the board anticipates one or more special assessments to meet the reserve funding goals and, if so, the estimated amount, due dates and duration of the assessments;

(3) The mechanisms by which the reserves will be funded, including assessments, borrowing, use of other assets, deferral of selected repairs, and any other funding mechanisms; and

(4) Whether the association has any outstanding loans with an original term of more than one year, including the payee, interest rate, amount outstanding, annual payment, and when the loan matures.

Commencing January 1, 2009, a summary of the reserve funding plan adopted by the board must be provided to the owners with the *pro forma* operating budget and must include a notice that the full reserve funding study plan is available upon request of an owner.

Reserve disclosures are now prescribed by statute. Civil Code § 1365.2.5 provides at statutory form for reserve assessments and funding which includes: (1) current assessments per unit; (2) additional assessments that have been scheduled to be imposed; (3) whether current reserve balances will be sufficient to meet the requirements of the current funding goals; (4) if not, what is the plan to meet the requirements of the current funding goals; (5) identification of the major components included in the existing reserve study but not included in the reserve funding program; and (6) the current balance of reserve funds in cash or cash equivalent on deposit. The statutory reserve funding disclosure must accompany each *pro forma* operating budget sent out before the end of the fiscal year. The statutory form may be supplemented or modified to clarify the information so long as the minimum information required by statute is provided. For further information, see Civil Code § 1365.2.5, in Chapter 2.

For the purposes of calculating the amount of reserves needed to be accumulated for maintenance or replacement of a major component at a given time required by Civil Code § 1365.2.5, the amount needed is computed as the current cost of repair or replacement multiplied by the number of years the component has been in service divided by the remaining service life of the component. This is frequently referred to as "straight line" depreciation. This method of calculation is not a required method of funding the reserves. It is merely an analytical tool to evaluate how the reserves are funded against a "straight line" model of funding. There is no requirement for funding reserves at any particular level under California law.

G. INCOME TAX REQUIREMENTS

Residential homeowner associations may elect to be taxed either under Internal Revenue Code § 277 or under Internal Revenue Code § 528. Associations that elect Section 277 file Form 1120. Those that elect Section 528 file Form 1120-H. Many associations choose which tax form to file by selecting the form that yields the lowest tax. However, the decision whether to file Form 1120 or 1120-H is a complicated one that requires a full understanding of the tax consequences of the election.

Form 1120-H is a relatively simple form to prepare but has certain qualifying requirements and a higher tax rate for most associations than the alternative Form 1120. On the other hand, Form 1120 is complex. While it will normally result in a lower tax rate than Form 1120-H (for example, 15% for the first $50,000 of taxable income versus a flat rate of 30%), its complexity and the lack of specific rulings in several areas create a higher possibility for error. The ultimate decision is the association's but it should be made with the guidance of a professional tax advisor.

If an association elects to file under Section 277 (Form 1120), all net membership income is taxed at regular corporate rates but the association may be able to defer excess income by making an annual election under Revenue Ruling 70-604. With this option, taxable income is taxed at regular graduated corporate rates between 15% and 39%. Net membership losses may be carried forward to future years to offset future net membership income. Net non-membership income is taxed at regular corporate tax rates. Net non-membership losses are treated as net operating losses. Net membership income is the excess membership income over membership expenses for that year.

Revenue Ruling 70-604 allows associations filing under Section 277 to remove any excess membership income from taxable income by re-characterizing it as a return of capital. Under the ruling, associations may make an annual election to exempt or defer net membership income from taxation by, in effect, returning the excess to its members. As stated in the ruling, associations have the option of: (1) applying the excess of membership income over membership expenses to the following year's expenses; or (2) refunding the excess of membership income to the association's reserves. Applying excess income to the reserve fund is specifically authorized. While some tax practitioners believe that the ruling permits an indefinite carry over of excess membership income, the IRS has stated that the ruling allows only a one-year carry over. A conservative approach would be to create a loss equivalent to any carry over from the previous year thereby offsetting the carry over with an equivalent loss. The election could then be made anew in subsequent years. The election under Revenue Ruling 70-604 must be made by the members at an annual meeting; it may not be made by the board. (See Form No. 2 in Ch. 15.)

If an association elects to file under Section 528 (Form 1120-H), all membership income is not taxed, but no loss carry-forward is allowed and no election under Revenue Ruling 70-604 is allowed. With this option, taxable income is taxed at a flat rate of 30%. Net non-member income is taxed at the same flat rate. No net operating losses may be deducted.

The definition of gross income is all income from whatever source derived except as specifically excluded by the Internal Revenue Code. The receipts of an association typically are: (1) member operating assessments, (2) member reserve assessments, (3) member fees for services, (4) non-member fees for services, (5) litigation settlements and (6) passive income (i.e., interest). While most of these receipts are treated as gross income for tax purposes, the code excludes from income: (1) member reserve assessments, (2) special assessments for repair/reserve purposes; and (3) litigation proceeds. These are treated as a return on capital. For additional information, see Internal Revenue Code § 528, IRS Revenue Ruling 70-604, and California Rev. & Tax Code § 23701t, in Chapter 6.

VII. MAINTENANCE OBLIGATIONS

A. INDIVIDUAL OWNER'S MAINTENANCE OBLIGATIONS

1. Determining Responsibility for Maintenance

In condominium projects and planned developments, maintenance obligations are not necessarily determined by ownership. In other words, the fact that a particular element or area is individually owned does not necessarily mean that it is individually maintained. To determine whether an element or area is individually maintained, begin by reading the sections of the governing documents that specifically discuss maintenance obligations. The maintenance sections may or may not refer back to the ownership sections (such as the definition of the condominium unit). If responsibility for the element or area is not clear, attempt to determine the author's intent by analogy to similar elements or areas that are mentioned in the documents. If the documents provide no clues as to the author's intended allocation of responsibility, determine ownership of the element or area and allocate responsibility based on ownership.

Some governing documents contain "identification of components" schedules that list which parts of the common interest development, including the individual components of such parts, will be maintained by the association or by the individual owners.

2. Property Owner Must Maintain

In most **condominium projects**, individual owners are obligated to maintain the following elements of the property:

(1) everything included within the definition of the unit as explained in the section entitled "Individually Owned Portions of the Condominium Project" at page 19 in this chapter.

(2) the glass, screens, moving frame, and hardware of windows (even if they do not fall within the definition of the unit);

(3) all doors, door frames, and door hardware (even if they do not fall within the definition of the unit); and

(4) the finished wall surfaces of storage spaces assigned as exclusive use or restricted common area.

Where exterior areas such as decks, patios or yards are included as part of a condominium unit or assigned as exclusive use or restricted common area, individual maintenance obligations vary widely, and no generalizations are possible.

In most **planned developments**, individual owners are obligated to maintain the following elements of the property:

(1) all interior elements and areas of the homes;

(2) all portions of the plumbing, electrical, heating and air conditioning systems serving the homes;

(3) all foundations and structural elements of the homes (but not roofing and siding);

(4) all glass, screens, moving frame, and hardware of windows;

(5) all doors, door frames, and door hardware; and

(6) all patios and decks (except exterior paint on decks).

As discussed in later, owner maintenance obligations change when an element or area is damaged by negligence, or as a consequence of the malfunction of an element the owner is not responsible to maintain. See the section entitled "Maintenance Obligation for Damage Caused by Negligent or Intentional Action or Inaction" at page 72 of this chapter.

3. Standards for Owner Required Maintenance

The governing documents usually include a minimum standard for owner maintenance such as the statement "each owner shall maintain the elements of the property for which he/she is responsible in a condition which does not impair the value or desirability of other units or lots." Most governing documents also provide that if an owner fails to satisfy his/her maintenance requirements, the association may do so and assess any related expense against the responsible owner as a personal reimbursement assessment. It is advisable (and required by some governing documents) that the association provide a written warning, an opportunity to correct the problem, and a board hearing, before undertaking a repair for an owner.

4. Maintaining Items that Border Two or More Lots in a Planned Development

Maintenance responsibility for elements on the border of lots within a planned development (often called "party walls") is determined by the governing documents or, where the documents are silent on the issue, by general rules of law. In most cases, each of the bordering lot owners is responsible for a percentage of the cost which reflects the extent to which the element serves his/her lot. Any of the bordering lot owners can undertake necessary maintenance, and recover the appropriate share of the costs from the other bordering lot owners.

B. ASSOCIATION MAINTENANCE OBLIGATIONS

1. Property that Homeowners' Association Must Maintain

The allocation of maintenance responsibilities between the individual owners and the association is usually determined by the governing documents, and varies widely from project to project. A step-by-step procedure for determining responsibility is discussed in the previous section.

In most **condominium projects**, the association is obligated to maintain the following elements of the property:

(1) all exterior elements including siding and roofing (but not windows and doors);

(2) all foundations and other structural elements;

(3) all landscaping, exterior lighting, drives, and walks;

(4) all interior common areas including lobbies, hallways and stairs (except stairs connecting levels within units);

(5) all portions of the plumbing, electrical, heating and air conditioning systems serving more than one unit; and

(6) all fire protection alarms and equipment.

Where exterior areas such as decks, patios or yards are included as part of a condominium unit or assigned as exclusive use or restricted common area, association maintenance obligations vary widely, and no generalizations are possible.

In most **planned developments**, the association is obligated to maintain the following elements of the property:

(1) all common area;

(2) all exterior surfaces of homes, including roofing, siding, trim, decks, balconies, exterior stairs, railings, window frames, and door frames;

(3) all fences and exterior, non-structural walls;

(4) all landscaping on each lot; and

(5) all fire protection alarms and equipment except smoke detectors within homes.

As discussed in the next section, association maintenance obligations change when an element or area is damaged by negligence, or as a consequence of the misuse or malfunction of an element that an owner is responsible to maintain. For additional information relating to damage caused by wood-destroying pests, see Civil Code § 1364(b), in Chapter 2.

2. Homeowners' Association Inspection Requirement

A homeowners' association is required to regularly inspect the portions of the property it maintains as part of the reserve study process. Reserve study requirements are discussed in detail in the section entitled "Reserve Studies" at page 62 of this chapter. For additional information, see Civil Code § 1365.5(e), in Chapter 2.

C. MAINTENANCE OBLIGATION FOR DAMAGE CAUSED BY NEGLIGENT OR INTENTIONAL ACTION OR INACTION

Each owner is responsible for maintenance necessitated by the negligent or intentional action or inaction of him/herself, his/her guests, employees and contractors, the occupants of his/her unit (including tenants), and the guests, employees and contractors of these occupants. The association is responsible for maintenance necessitated by the negligent or intentional action or inaction of its employees and contractors.

D. "POINT OF ORIGIN" AND ITS EFFECT ON MAINTENANCE OBLIGATIONS

The term "point of origin" refers to the first event that sets in motion the series of other events leading to a maintenance need. The point of origin of the maintenance need determines responsibility for its cost. For example, if the bathtub of a condominium unit overflows, the owner is responsible for all resulting damage to other units and to the common area. This is true because the point of origin of the damage was either a malfunction of the faucet or drain (elements for which the owner is responsible), or an occupant's negligence in allowing the tub to overflow (an act for which the owner is responsible).

VIII. IMPROVEMENTS AND ALTERATIONS

A. HOA APPROVAL REQUIRED FOR CERTAIN IMPROVEMENTS/ALTERATIONS

Condominium governing documents usually require association approval for improvements and alterations of a unit which do any of the following:

(1) change the appearance of any exterior area;

(2) change any interior common area (except entirely separated exclusive use common areas such as storage closets);

(3) impair structural integrity; or

(4) interfere with plumbing, electrical, heating, or air conditioning service to other units or the common area.

Planned development governing documents usually require association approval for improvements and alterations of a lot which do any of the following:

(1) change any common area;

(2) involve the construction of new structures or additions, including fences, walls, pools, spas, balconies, patios, patio enclosures, screens, tents, awnings, window air conditioners, exterior shutters, exterior antennas, or exterior wiring;

(3) change the appearance of the exterior elements of existing structures including paint, siding and roofing;

(4) change the appearance of existing landscaping visible from the common area or other lots;

(5) obstruct the view from another lot or from the common area; or

(6) interfere with the water supply, sewage or drainage systems.

The law imposes some limitations on restrictions on noncommercial signs, posters, flags or banners (see Civil Code § 1353.6, in Chapter 2), real estate signs (see Civil Code § 712, in Chapter 9), U.S. flags (see Govt. Code § 434.5, in Chapter 9 and Civil Code § 1353.5, in Chapter 2), satellite dishes (see Civil Code § 1376, in Chapter 2), solar panels (see Civil Code §§ 714 and 714.1, in Chapter 9), and handicapped access (see Civil Code § 1360(a)(2), in Chapter 2). See also the section entitled "Signs and the United States Flag" at page 84 of this chapter.

B. PROCEDURE WHEN HOMEOWNERS' ASSOCIATION APPROVAL REQUIRED

Most governing documents contain detailed procedures for the submission, consideration, and approval of proposed alterations and improvements. Where the governing documents do not contain these procedures, or where the procedures are incomplete or ambiguous, the board should develop new or supplemental procedures and express them in a written resolution or rule (See Civil Code § 1378). If formal approval procedures are not established, or if they are not followed, the association may be prohibited from enforcing its architectural guidelines. See *Deane Gardenhome Assn. v. Denktas (1993) 13 Cal. App.4th 1394, 16 Cal.Rptr.2d 816,* in Chapter 12.

The architectural approval procedures should contain the following elements:

(1) A list of the items required before the association will consider the application, which would typically include:

(a) A description of the proposed alteration, including, as appropriate, its shape, height, width, elevation, materials, color, location and such further information as may be necessary to allow the association to evaluate it fully;

(b) A set of construction drawings prepared by a licensed architect and/or engineer; and

(c) A certificate by a licensed architect or engineer stating that the alteration (i) will not impair the structural integrity of any part of the property, and (ii) will not interfere with any utility or mechanical system;

(2) A provision allowing the association to make any reasonable request for additional information or details;

(3) A time limit for approval or disapproval along with a system for acknowledging receipt of information for the purpose of establishing compliance with the deadline;

(4) A statement of the standards that the association will apply in making its decision, such as the following: "The association has sole and complete discretion to approve or disapprove an alteration requiring approval. The association shall approve an alteration only if it makes an affirmative finding that the alteration (i) will not impair the structural integrity of any part of the property, (ii) will not interfere with any mechanical system, (iii) is consistent with the governing documents, (iv) will not detract from the appearance, harmony, attractiveness and enjoyability of the property, and (v) will not impose an unreasonable maintenance burden on the association";

(5) A description of any mechanism under which an applicant can appeal a disapproval, and/or another owner can appeal an approval, including the mechanics of the appeal procedure;

(6) Guidelines regarding the time limit for completion of the work, obtaining an extension, and consequences for failing to complete the work on time; and

(7) Guidelines regarding licensing, bonding, and insurance of a contractor hired to complete approved alterations.

Alteration approval is a responsibility of the board, but it may delegate this responsibility to an officer, committee, or professional manager provided the board retains final authority.

C. ASSOCIATION STANDARDS FOR CONSIDERING IMPROVEMENT/ALTERATION REQUESTS

Homeowners' associations are granted the same wide latitude ordinarily given government agencies in their decision making. Associations whose governing documents require architectural review and approval before an owner can make a physical change to his/her separate interest must have a written procedure for making its decision which provides for prompt deadlines. The decision must be: (i) reasonable, fair and made in good faith; (ii) consistent with local ordinances; (iii) in writing; and (iv) provide an explanation for the disapproval of a proposed change and procedure for reconsideration. For more information see Civil Code § 1378, in Chapter 2.

An association must annually provide the owners with notice of any requirements for association approval of physical changes to the property. The notice must describe the types of changes that require association approval and must include a copy of the procedure used to review and approve or disapprove a proposed change.

The fact that an association has permitted or approved a certain activity or alteration by a particular owner at one time does not mean that the association must permit or approve that same activity by the same or a different owner at a later time, provided that the association's later decision otherwise conforms to the standards listed in the preceding paragraph. For additional information, see *Lamden v. La Jolla Shores Clubdominium Homeowners Assn. (1999) 21 Cal.4th 249, 87 Cal.Rptr.2d 237; Dolan-King v. Rancho Santa Fe Assn. (2000) 81 Cal.App.4th 965, 97 Cal.Rptr.2d 280; Clark v. Rancho Santa Fe Association (1989) 216 Cal.App.3d 606, 265 Cal.Rptr. 41; Cohen v. Kite Hill Community Assn. (1983) 142 Cal.App.3d 642, 191 Cal.Rptr. 209; Deane Gardenhome Assn. v. Denktas (1993) 13 Cal.App.4th 1394, 16 Cal.Rptr.2d 816;* and *Laguna Royale Owners Assn. v. Darger (1981) 119 Cal.App.3d 670, 134 Cal.Rptr.136,* in Chapter 12.

D. PENALTIES WHEN OWNER MAKES IMPROVEMENT WITHOUT HOA APPROVAL

When an owner begins alterations or improvements without

required association approval, he/she is subject to a variety of penalties under the governing documents and the law. At a minimum, the association can order the owner to immediately cease all work and restore any altered areas or components to their original state. If the owner does not comply, the association can perform the restoration and assess the costs against the owner *via* a personal reimbursement assessment. The board has the power to undertake these actions, but may delegate responsibility to an officer, committee, or professional manager provided the board retains final authority. If the association does not act, it may find it more difficult to enforce similar restrictions in the future.

Each association should have provisions in its governing documents for discovering and responding to violations of alteration restrictions. These should include:

(1) The right to enter any unit or lot, following reasonable notice, to inspect all construction, whether or not approval was required or granted;

(2) A requirement that the association notify the owner of the violation in writing, and order the owner to cease work and restore the altered area within a prescribed time period;

(3) A procedure for the owner to obtain a hearing before the board if the owner wishes to argue that approval was not required, or that the work complies with an approval that the owner obtained; and

(4) A requirement that if the owner fails to remedy the situation by the deadline, the association may undertake the work and assess the costs against the owner.

IX. DEFECTS AND DISCLOSURES

A. CONSTRUCTION DEFECTS

When an owner discovers construction defects in a portion of the property which the association is obligated to maintain, he/she should report the problem to the manager or, if there is no manager, to an association officer or director. The association is obligated to repair the damage under the governing documents, regardless of whether the developer is ultimately responsible. The board is required to exercise prudent business judgement in deciding whether to attempt to recover repair costs from the developer.

When an owner discovers construction defects in a portion of the property which the owner is obligated to maintain, he/she must repair the defects under the governing documents. The repair obligation exists regardless of whether the developer is ultimately responsible, or whether a previous owner or real estate agent has violated disclosure laws. If the owner fails to repair, the association may do so and assess the costs against the owner. The owner may be entitled to recover his/her repair costs from the developer, a previous owner, or a real estate agent, and should consult an attorney.

B.   HOA RESPONSIBILITIES WHEN CONSTRUCTION DEFECTS ARE DISCOVERED

A homeowners' association should consult an attorney as soon as it discovers construction defects. Failing to act quickly could result in the loss of recovery rights. The law contains extensive requirements and procedures for construction defect dispute resolution. Further, the law expressly provides that the duties of association officers and directors include considering (i) whether to conduct an investigation of the common interest development for latent (hidden) construction defects before the relevant statute of limitations expires and (ii) whether to commence a lawsuit against the developer or builder of the common interest development for design or construction defects. For additional information, see Civil Code §§ 1365.7(f), 1368(a)(5) and (6), 1368.4, 1375, and 1375.1, all in Chapter 2, and Code of Civil Procedure §§ 337.1 and 337.15, in Chapter 7.

C.   DISCLOSURES TO PROSPECTIVE PURCHASERS

The seller of a unit or lot is required by law to disclose all material defects in the property, including defects located in the common area, and defects located in other units or lots if they affect the value or desirability of the unit or lot being sold. The disclosure requirements extend to all defects of which the seller is aware or should be aware, including construction defects. Additional disclosure requirements apply when construction defect litigation has been commenced or is under consideration. For additional information, see Civil Code §§

1102 et. seq., 1134, in Chapter 8, and Civil Code § 1368, in Chapter 2.

Any real estate agent involved in the sale is also required to disclose any defects of which he/she is aware or should be aware, and is further required to conduct a reasonably competent and diligent visual inspection. For additional information, see Civil Code §§ 2079 *et. seq.*

Homeowners' associations are not required to provide or disclose construction defect information to prospective purchasers of units or lots, but are required to provide such information to selling owners so that they can meet their disclosure requirements. See *Kovich v. Paseo Del Mar Homeowners' Assn. (1996) 41 Cal.App.4th 863, 48 Cal. Rptr.2d 758,* in Chapter 12.

X. INSURANCE ISSUES

A. ASSOCIATION PROPERTY/CASUALTY INSURANCE

1. Property/Casualty Insurance

The governing documents contain detailed property insurance requirements. In condominium projects, these typically require that the association obtain property damage insurance (sometimes called casualty insurance) for everything located on the property except the contents of the units. These policies usually cover damage to interior walls, floors and ceilings within units, but may not cover damage to cabinets, plumbing and electrical fixtures, appliances, wall and floor coverings, and built-in furniture. The individual owners are responsible for insuring the contents of their units against damage, and the governing documents for some common interest developments require owners to carry this insurance.

In planned developments, the governing documents usually require the association to insure all portions of the property which it is obligated to maintain. In some cases, however, the individual owners are required to insure everything on their lots even though the exterior surfaces of the homes are maintained by the association. The law does not require a particular amount or type of property insurance. Most governing documents include a minimum insurance requirement by stating that the limits of coverage shall not be less than the full current replacement cost of the structures. In other cases, the documents allow the board to determine the appropriate amount of insurance. Regardless of what the documents say, the board is empowered to exceed any minimum insurance requirement, and must use prudent business judgement in determining the amount and type of insurance to purchase.

2. Earthquake Insurance

Earthquake insurance is not typically part of the property/casualty policy. It is obtained by an additional policy or endorsement at additional expense. Most governing documents do not require earthquake insurance, and it is not required by law. Since earthquake insurance is usually expensive and typically involves a large deductible, its benefits are debatable, and a board probably will not face liability for choosing not to obtain it, unless it is required by the governing documents. Nevertheless, it is worth noting that property insurance generally does not provide coverage for damage caused by earthquakes (but will provide coverage for damage caused by fires started by earthquakes) and that homeowners' associations in areas likely to experience major earthquakes during the anticipated life of the common interest development may wish to purchase earthquake insurance.

3. When Repairs Exceed Insurance Coverage

In general, when insurance proceeds are insufficient to pay repair costs, the association must levy a special assessment or borrow to cover the shortfall. If a special assessment is voted down, or a loan is unavailable, most governing documents describe a procedure for dissolving the association and selling the property following a large uninsured or under-insured loss. These procedures are intended to provide an alternative to a special assessment so large that most owners could not pay it.

B. ASSOCIATION LIABILITY INSURANCE

1. General Liability Coverage

General liability insurance covers the association and sometimes its members for personal injuries, bodily injury and property damage to third parties. The policy may also cover liability for defamation, advertising injury, non-owned automobile accidents, employment practices, and similar additional coverages. All general liability policies contain a number of important exclusions that must be considered in assessing the validity of a claim. In the event of a disputed claim, consult an attorney as a coverage analysis is usually beyond the expertise of a lay person.

The law does not require a minimum amount of liability insurance, but most governing documents specify minimum policy limits. The law states that if certain minimum statutory policy limits are met, the individual owners cannot be held responsible if damages exceed the coverage. The statutory minimum is $2,000,000 if the project consists of 100 or fewer units or lots, and $3,000,000 if the project consists of more than 100 units or lots. For additional information, see Civil Code §§ 1365.7 and 1365.9, in Chapter 2.

2. Directors' and Officers' Liability Insurance

The law provides that a volunteer director or officer cannot be held liable for damages resulting from his/her service to the association if he/she performs his/her duties (i) in good faith, (ii) in a manner which he/she believes to be in the best interests of the association, and (iii) with such care, including reasonable inquiry, as an ordinarily prudent person in a like position would use in similar circumstances. At the risk of oversimplifying this standard, the idea is to protect honest directors and officers from liability for mistakes unless their actions are self-interested, unreasonable or negligent. Directors are entitled to rely on information and opinions provided by the association's officers, committees, and hired experts. For more information, see the section entitled "Standard for Board Decisions: Business Judgment Rule" at page 44 of this chapter.

To provide additional liability protection to directors and officers, most governing documents state that the association will indemnify them absent gross negligence, intentional misconduct, or fraud. Indemnity means that the association will pay for an attorney to defend the director or officer and will pay the damages if the defense fails. Most governing documents require the association to carry director and officer ("D&O") liability insurance for these costs, and such insurance is always a good idea. The law states that if the D&O insurance meets statutory minimums, the director or officer cannot be held personally liable even if the damages exceed the insurance coverage. The statutory minimum is $500,000 if the project consists of 100 or fewer units or lots, and $1,000,000 if the project consists of more than 100 units or lots. For additional information, see Corporations Code §§ 7231.5 and 7237, in Chapter 3, and Civil Code § 1365.7, in Chapter 2.

3. Managing Agent and Fidelity Bonds

Managing agent bonds and fidelity bonds are a form of insurance for the theft or misappropriation of funds. This type of insurance is not required by law, but is required by some governing documents. It is advisable for large associations to obtain this type of insurance unless their funds are handled by a professional manager who already has adequate bonding or insurance coverage.

C. DISCLOSURE OF INSURANCE COVERAGE TO OWNERS

Homeowners' associations are required to provide a summary of the terms of all of their insurance policies to each owner each year. The summary must include the name of the insurer, the type of insurance, the limits of the policy or policies, the amount of deductibles, and a notice to owners the language of which is specified in Civil Code § 1365(f)(4). Associations are also required to notify each owner as soon as reasonably practical by first-class mail whenever a policy has lapsed, been canceled, not renewed or replaced, or when the limits have been decreased or the deductibles increased. Associations must provide complete copies of the policies to an owner upon request. For additional information, see Civil Code § 1365(f), in Chapter 2.

D. OWNER LIABILITY FOR PERSONAL INJURIES/ PROPERTY DAMAGE IN THE COMMON AREA AND HOA DEBTS

If the association is incorporated, an individual owner can never be held responsible for personal injuries or property damage that occur in another owner's home or in the common area simply by reason of being an owner in the project. If the association is unincorporated, an individual owner can be held responsible only if the association is responsible and unable to satisfy the claim, and then only if the association does not carry liability insurance meeting the statutory minimums, which at the present time are at least $2,000,000 in projects of 100 or fewer homes and $3,000,000 in projects of more than 100 homes. Keep in mind that an owner can always be held responsible for personal injury or property damage caused by his/her own conduct and should carry personal liability insurance separate from the association's policies to cover that risk. For additional information, see Civil Code § 1365.9, in Chapter 2.

If the association is incorporated, an individual owner can never be held responsible for the association's debts. If the association is unincorporated, an individual owner can be held responsible only if the member (1) expressly assumes responsibility for the obligation in writing, (2) expressly authorizes the obligation, (3) receives the benefit of the obligation, or (4) executes a contract authorizing the obligation without authority to do so. For additional information, see Corporations Code § 18610.

E. OWNER REQUIRED INSURANCE AND MINIMUM COVERAGE

The law is unclear whether an association can require owners to carry personal insurance. Some governing documents have such requirements but they have not been tested in any appellate court decision to date. These typically mandate an owner to carry specified levels of personal liability insurance which could be invoked in the event of a claim for personal injury or property damage for which the owner and association may have some joint responsibility or in the event of a claim by the association against the owner for causing injury or damage.

XI. USAGE RESTRICTIONS

A. IMPERMISSIBLE USAGE RESTRICTIONS

Statutory law explicitly prohibits housing discrimination based upon race, color, religion, sex, sexual orientation, marital status, national origin, ancestry, familial status, source of income, and disability. See Govt. Code § 12955 *et seq.*, in Chapter 9. Further, the California Supreme Court, finding that this list of protected classes is "illustrative rather than restrictive," has held that discrimination against children, and against families because they have children, is also prohibited. The law against discrimination is so broad that any occupancy restriction could be interpreted as discriminatory, including limits on the maximum number of occupants in a home. The only limitations that are clearly valid and enforceable are those that track the language of local and state health codes, and those that establish a project as senior citizen housing. For additional information, see Civil Code §§ 51-53, in Chapter 9.

Homeowners' associations generally may not prevent unit or lot owners from installing solar panels. See Civil Code §§ 714 and 714.1, in Chapter 9.

B. SIGNS AND THE UNITED STATES FLAG

Since a condominium project or planned development is private property, there is no constitutional protection for freedom of expression. This means that sign restrictions and prohibitions in governing document provisions are generally valid and enforceable, provided that they are enforced consistently and without discrimination against some owners. There are several types of signs that cannot be prohibited. The association may not prohibit signs advertising a unit or lot for sale or rental, including related signs providing directions to the property, and the owner's or agent's name, address and telephone number. The association also may not prohibit non-commercial signs, posters or flags within the boundaries of a unit or lot (except for the protection of public health or safety) that are 9 square feet or less in size or non-commercial banners that are 15 square feet or less in size. No restriction can be imposed on the display of the U.S. flag in an owner's unit, lot or exclusive common area. The association may impose restrictions on the location, size, dimensions, and design of any signs in the common area. For additional information, see Civil Code §§ 712, 713 and Government Code § 434.5, in Chapter 9 and Civil Code §§ 1353.5 and 1353.6, in Chapter 2.

C. PETS

Governing documents adopted or amended after January 1, 2001, may not prohibit an owner from keeping at least one domesticated bird, cat, dog or aquatic animal in an aquarium, subject to reasonable rules and regulations, such as leashing and clean-up requirements. Civil Code § 1360.5, in Chapter 2. For additional information, see *Nahrstedt v. Lakeside Village Condominium Assn. (1994) 8 Cal.4th 361, 33 Cal.Rptr.2d 63*, in Chapter 12.

D. PARKING

Common interest developments often provide individual parking spaces for unit or lot owners. These parking spaces may be designated as either exclusive use common areas or a part of the unit or lot in the governing documents. In either case, governing documents may forbid the parking of certain vehicles such as boats, trailers, recreational vehicles, or broken-down automobiles in driveways or in parking spaces visible to other lot or unit owners.

The homeowners' association may designate private roads and other places within the common interest development as no parking areas where improperly parked vehicles are subject to towing or removal at the vehicle owner's expense, so long as the homeowners' association provides "no parking" signs which meet certain statutory requirements. See Vehicle Code §§ 22658 *et seq*. and 22853, in Chapter 10.

E. TELEVISION ANTENNAS AND SATELLITE DISHES

The law provides that a homeowners' association may **not** prevent the installation of video or television antennas or satellite dishes, provided that the antenna or dish is no more than one meter (roughly 39 inches) in diameter and is located in an area within the exclusive use or control of the owner, unless installation of the antenna or satellite dish creates a legitimate safety concern, or the building or common interest development has been designated an historical site. See 47 Code of Federal Regulations ("CFR") § 1.4000. This means that individual unit or lot owners probably are entitled to install antennas or satellite dishes in exclusive use common areas, such as decks and balconies, so long as the antenna or satellite dish does not encroach on general use common areas.

Even when installation of an antenna or satellite dish meets the size and exclusive use/control requirements, a homeowners' association may promulgate rules and restrictions which (i) require the owner to file an application or give notice to the association prior to installation; (ii) require an owner of a lot or unit to obtain permission from the association to install an antenna or satellite dish on any other owner's unit or lot; (iii) provide for the maintenance, repair or replacement of roofs or other building components affected by the installation; or (iv) require installers of antennas or satellite dishes to indemnify or reimburse the association or its members for loss or damage caused by the installation, maintenance or use of an antenna or satellite dish. However, such rules or restrictions are invalid if they (i) significantly delay or prevent installation, maintenance or use of the antenna or satellite dish system; (ii) significantly increase the cost of the antenna or satellite dish system; or (iii) significantly decrease the efficiency or performance of the system. See 47 CFR § 1.4000; see also Civil Code § 1376, in Chapter 2.

Any approval process required for installation of antennas or satellite dishes should be the same as the approval process the association uses for other proposed architectural modifications to the common interest development, provided it does not significantly delay or prevent installation. The standards which the association uses to consider whether or not to approve a request to install an antenna or satellite dish must conform to the legal requirements described in the previous paragraph of this subsection.

If a dispute arises regarding installation of an antenna or satellite dish at a common interest development, consult an attorney, because the law in this area is complicated by somewhat incongruous state and federal law requirements.

F. RENTAL RESTRICTIONS

The law prohibits "unreasonable" restrictions on the "alienation" or "transferability" of property. "Alienation" or "transferability" means the right to transfer title or possession of property to another person, whether by sale or by lease. The law also provides that any homeowners' association rule or regulation which "arbitrarily or unreasonably" restricts an owner's ability to market his/her separate interest is void. See Civil Code § 1368.1(a), in Chapter 2. Because the law disfavors restrictions on transferability, the person seeking to enforce the restriction (usually the homeowners' association) has the burden of demonstrating a strong justification.

Few decided cases address what restrictions on transferability in common interest developments will be enforced. One Court of Appeal decision provides a general test for the reasonableness of such restrictions: (1) whether the reason given by a homeowners' association for withholding approval of a proposed transfer is related to the "protection, preservation or proper operation" of the common interest development and also the "purposes of the association as set forth in the governing documents"; and (2) whether the association's power to decide was "exercised in a fair and non-discriminatory manner." See *Laguna Royale Owners Assn. v. Darger (1981) 119 Cal.App.3d 670, 174 Cal.Rptr. 136,* in Chapter 12.

Another factor a court might consider is "the nature and severity of the consequences of application of the restriction." *Id.* In the *Darger* case, the court found the association's refusal to allow a unit leaseholder to assign three one-quarter undivided interests in the unit to three other couples unenforceable.

Restrictions requiring that all purchasers or lessees (tenants) be at least a certain minimum age in common interest developments designed for senior citizens are permissible. See Civil Code §§ 51.3 and 51.4, in Chapter 9. Also, restrictions which prohibit non-resident owners from using common areas are probably enforceable so long as the restriction is contained in the original CC&Rs, or the restriction is added shortly after the homeowners' association assumes responsibility for the common interest development and **before** the non-resident owner against whom the restriction is to be enforced purchases his/her unit. See *Liebler v. Point Loma Tennis Club (1995) 40 Cal.App.4th 1600, 47 Cal.Rptr.2d 783*, but see *MaJor v. Miraverde Homeowners Assn. (1992) 7 Cal.App.4th 618, 9 Cal.Rptr.2d 237,* in Chapter 12.

As a general rule, rental restrictions contained in the original CC&Rs are more likely to be enforceable than rental restrictions added later by amendment to the CC&Rs or by rules adopted by the homeowners' association, because all unit purchasers are presumed to know about restrictions contained in the original CC&Rs prior to their decision to purchase. Because this area of the law is ill-defined, consult an attorney if a significant issue regarding rental restrictions arises.

G. ARCHITECTURAL CONTROLS AND RESTRICTIONS

CC&Rs generally contain architectural controls restricting the structural and aesthetic changes that can be made to the common interest development. Architectural controls are generally enforceable provided that the governing documents authorize the homeowners' association to enforce them, the association applies reasonable standards when it makes architectural decisions, and the association has adopted and consistently followed reasonable enforcement procedures. So long as these criteria are followed, the association may generally deny a proposed modification based solely on subjective aesthetic considerations. See *Clark v. Rancho Sante Fe Assn. (1989) 216 Cal. App.3d 606, 265 Cal.Rptr. 41,* in Chapter 12.

For more information on the procedures and standards a homeowners' association should apply when considering a proposed architectural modification, see the section entitled "Improvements and Alterations" at page 73 of this chapter.

H. OTHER COMMON USAGE RESTRICTIONS

Some other permissible usage restrictions commonly contained in CC&Rs include requiring that the unit or lot be used primarily for residential purposes, restricting the color of window coverings visible from the street or common areas, restrictions on changing floor coverings, restrictions on parking boats, trailers or recreational vehicles within the common interest development, prohibiting conversion of garages into living or recreational areas, prohibiting nuisances (activities that are noxious, illegal, annoying or offensive to a person of reasonable and normal sensitivity), restrictions on garbage disposal and use of storage spaces, and prohibition of outside clothes lines and garage sales.

I. OWNER RESPONSIBILITY FOR TENANT'S COMPLIANCE WITH USAGE RESTRICTIONS

An owner is responsible for his/her tenant's compliance with the governing documents, and can be fined or penalized for the tenant's violations. Any owner who rents his/her unit should have a written rental agreement incorporating all of the governing document usage restrictions, and making the tenancy subject to any additional restrictions that are enacted by the association during the rental term. The governing documents can require an owner to incorporate all of their restrictions in a lease and provide the association with tenant information before the commencement of the rental term.

XII. MORTGAGES AND LIENS

A. OWNER DEFAULT

When an owner defaults on his/her mortgage, the lender is entitled to undertake a foreclosure procedure that ultimately results in an auction-like sale of the defaulting owner's unit. The lender has no recourse against the association or any other owner. The purchaser at the foreclosure sale must comply with all of the provisions of the governing documents, including the obligation to pay assessments. But a foreclosure sale purchaser is not responsible for any unpaid, pre-foreclosure assessments.

B. "MORTGAGE PROTECTION" PROVISIONS IN GOVERNING DOCUMENTS

Most lenders will refuse to make mortgage loans on homes within condominium projects and planned developments unless there are special provisions in the governing documents to protect them. These provisions are designed to insure that the basic rights and responsibilities associated with the home at the time the loan is made cannot be easily changed. The lender is particularly concerned about changes that might devalue the home such as an increase in the home's assessment allocation, the removal of a parking or storage space, or an uninsured or under-insured loss. Most lenders review the mortgage protection provisions of the governing documents before they approve a mortgage within a condominium project or planned development.

C. MECHANICS' LIENS

The term "mechanics' lien" describes a document that can be recorded with county government by a contractor or construction materials supplier who has not been paid. The recording of a mechanics' lien relating to a particular property effectively prevents the owner from selling or refinancing the property without either paying the bill or establishing in court that the lien is invalid. When construction is performed for an individual owner on his/her condominium unit or planned development lot, the owner's contractors and construction materials suppliers can record mechanics' liens against that owner's unit or lot, but cannot record mechanics' liens against the common area or against any other owner's unit or lot. When construction is performed for the association on the common area, the association's contractors and construction materials suppliers can record mechanics' liens against the common area and every unit or lot. An owner who learns that a mechanics' lien has been recorded against his/her unit or lot should consult an attorney. For additional information, see Civil Code § 1369, in Chapter 2.

XIII. DISPUTES BETWEEN AN OWNER AND THE HOMEOWNERS' ASSOCIATION AND DISCIPLINARY ACTION AGAINST AN OWNER

A. OWNER VIOLATION OF GOVERNING DOCUMENTS

Checklist 6 in Chapter 15 provides step-by-step instructions for an association to enforce governing documents when an owner violates the governing documents.

B. OWNER'S NOTICE AND HEARING RIGHTS WHEN HOA CONSIDERS DISCIPLINARY ACTION

It is important for each homeowners' association to adopt a

written notice and hearing procedure to be used in handling alleged violations of the governing documents. The procedure should require:

(1) That the board provide a written notice to the owner specifying the nature of the problem and whether the matter might result in the levy of a personal reimbursement assessment or the imposition of some other sanction or penalty;

(2) That the notice state a time, date and place at which the owner will have an opportunity to be heard by the board, and that the notice be given to the owner at least 10 days before the hearing date;

(3) That at the time of the hearing, the owner who committed the alleged violation, and any other interested party, shall have an opportunity to speak for a reasonable period of time (the length of which can also be specified);

(4) That at the conclusion of the hearing, the board shall determine whether the violation has occurred, and whether to take action as permitted by the governing documents, and that the board's decision shall be final; and

(5) That the member will receive written notification of the board's decision within 15 days.

For additional information, see Civil Code § 1363(h), in Chapter 2.

C. TYPES OF DISCIPLINE THAT MAY BE IMPOSED

A homeowners' association has a wide range of possible discipline it can impose upon an owner in violation of the governing documents, including monetary fines, suspension of voting rights, and suspension of privileges (such as use of portions of the common area). However, an association may not deny an owner access to his/her home. When the association decides to discipline an owner, it must send the owner a written notice within 15 days following its decision. See Civil Code § 1363(h), in Chapter 2.

In order for discipline to be permissible, it must be reasonable in terms of its relationship to the owner's violation and proportionate to the seriousness of the violation. In order to assess monetary penalties, the association must provide in advance to each member a schedule of violations and the corresponding monetary penalty for each such violation. See Civil Code § 1363(g), in Chapter 2. Late fees on delinquent assessments may not exceed the greater of $10 or 10% of the delinquent assessment, and interest charges may not exceed 12% per annum commencing 30 days after the assessment becomes delinquent. See Civil Code § 1366(e), in Chapter 2.

The association may not discipline an owner for a violation unless the governing documents provide that the conduct at issue is impermissible and subject to specified disciplinary action by the association and the owner has reasonable notice of the existence of such provisions. In addition, no member may be expelled or suspended, and no membership may be terminated or suspended, unless the association has a preexisting procedure that complies with the requirements described in the preceding subsection. Any disciplinary action taken by the association must be fair and reasonable, made in good faith and applied in a non-discriminatory manner. See also Corporations Code § 7341, in Chapter 4.

An association may not treat a monetary penalty imposed on an owner for failure to comply with the governing documents as an assessment that my become a lien enforceable by non-judicial foreclosure. See Civil Code § 1367.1(e) in Chapter 2. The statute does not prohibit the association from recording a lien enforceable by judicial foreclosure. Prior to recording a lien, the association must follow a series of procedural steps, including providing a detailed notice to the owner and an opportunity for the owner to address the association's board regarding the matter. For more information, see the section entitled "Lien and Foreclosure Procedures to Collect Delinquent Assessments" at page 60 in this chapter; see also Civil Code §§ 1367.1, 1367.4 and 1367.5, in Chapter 2. In order to collect unpaid monetary fines levied for violation of the governing documents, the association may initiate a small claims court action against the owner.

D. CONFIDENTIALITY REQUIREMENTS

A lot or unit owner, who has received a notice informing him/her that the association board is considering disciplinary action against the owner or that the owner has unpaid delinquent assessments, may request that the board meet in executive session to consider the matter. The owner who elects to have such a matter heard in executive session is entitled to attend the executive session. See Civil Code §§ 1363(h) and 1363.05(b), in Chapter 2. If the owner has requested that the matter be heard in executive session, the board should keep confidential its discussion on the matter and its ultimate decision. However, the board should keep separate minutes for executive sessions in order to record the board's decision-making process.

A homeowners' association may publish a list of the units or lots upon which the association has recorded liens, so long as the association's lien procedures clearly provide for publication, the lien has been properly recorded and the owner at issue does, in fact, have outstanding delinquent assessments. On one hand, publishing lists of liened properties creates an additional incentive for owners to pay their assessments in a timely manner. On the other hand, such a policy may promote additional disputes and litigation.

E. ALTERNATIVE DISPUTE RESOLUTION

Mediation and arbitration are methods of alternative dispute resolution ("ADR"). Their purpose is to save time and money by resolving disputes without going to court. Mediation involves a neutral person who attempts to help the parties resolve their dispute through discussion and compromise. A mediator does not make rulings or decisions. Consequently, mediation is always informal and non-binding. Arbitration involves a neutral person who acts as a surrogate judge. An arbitrator considers the position of each side, and the applicable law, then makes a ruling. The parties decide in advance whether the ruling will be binding or non-binding.

Most governing documents require some form of ADR, but there is wide variation regarding the type of ADR required and the situations where the requirement applies. Regardless of what the governing documents say about ADR, the law requires that when a party is seeking declaratory relief (i.e. a judicial pronouncement on some issue), injunctive relief (i.e. a judicial order prohibiting some action), or either of those types of relief in connection with a damage claim of less than $5,000, the party must send a "Request For Resolution" to the opposing party offering to participate in some form of alternative dispute resolution. Failing to send a Request For Resolution prevents the filing of a lawsuit. A party receiving a Request For Resolution can decline to participate in ADR unless ADR is mandatory under the governing documents.

Sample requests and responses for alternative dispute resolution are provided in Chapter 15. For additional information, see Civil Code §§ 1363.810-1363.850 and 1369.510-1369.590, in Chapter 2.

F. AWARD OF ATTORNEYS' FEES TO PREVAILING LITIGANT

The law provides that in any legal action brought by an owner, or by a homeowners' association, to enforce the provisions of the governing documents, the prevailing party shall be entitled to recover his/her reasonable attorney's fees and costs. Some governing documents broaden the right to recover attorney's fees and costs so that it applies in all disputes relating to the property, including those that do not involve enforcement of the governing documents or even a legal action. Absent such provisions, a homeowners' association is not entitled to recover its attorneys fees from an owner unless it prevails in a court proceeding or arbitration, and the association cannot bill an individual owner for attorneys' fees if the association seeks legal advice to respond to an owner's concerns but no lawsuit or arbitration hearing is completed. In all instances where a right to recover attorney's fees exists, it will apply in arbitration as well as in court. For additional information, see Civil Code §§ 1363.810-1363.850 and 1369.510-1369.590, in Chapter 2.

G. HOA APPEARANCE IN COURT

The association may appear in small claims court by an officer, director, employee, designated agent, property manager, or a bookkeeper. For additional information, see Code of Civil Procedure § 116.540.

H. SETTLEMENT

The board must authorize any settlement of a legal proceeding by board resolution before the settlement is binding. Neither an officer, director, property manager or attorney is authorized to approve a settlement without a board resolution. A tentative settlement agreement can be reached provided it is conditioned on a subsequent board resolution approving the settlement. For an in-court settlement to be enforceable, an officer or director of the association must be present in court and represent that the board has authorized the settlement. Representations of board authorization by the property manager, an insurance representative or an attorney without an officer or director being present are insufficient to create a binding settlement agreement. See Code of Civil Procedure § 664.6, and *Elnekave v. Via Dolce Homeowners Association (2006) 142 Cal.App.4th 1193; 48 Cal.Rptr.3d 663,* in Chapter 12.

XIV. DISPUTES BETWEEN INDIVIDUAL OWNERS

A. HOA'S OBLIGATION TO ENFORCE GOVERNING DOCUMENTS

In general, homeowners' associations have discretion whether or not to enforce the governing documents. This discretion is removed, and enforcement mandatory, in instances where the governing documents explicitly require association action. Regardless of whether enforcement is mandatory, however, it is usually advisable for the association to act in order to avoid future enforcement problems. See *Beehan v. Lido Isle Community Assn. (1977) 70 Cal.App.3d 858, 137 Cal.Rptr. 528; Deane Gardenhome Assn. v. Denktas (1993) 13 Cal. App.4th 1394, 16 Cal.Rptr.2d 816,* in Chapter 12.

B. OWNER AUTHORITY TO ENFORCE GOVERNING DOCUMENTS AGAINST ANOTHER OWNER

Each owner in a condominium project or planned development has the right to independently enforce the CC&Rs against any other owner. A governing document other than the CC&Rs may be enforced by the association against a violating owner or by an owner against the association, but not by an owner against another owner. The mechanism for enforcement is either the court system or alternative dispute resolution depending on the nature of the violation and the dispute resolution provisions of the governing documents. In any action to enforce the governing documents, the prevailing party is entitled to recover reasonable attorney's fees and costs. For additional information, see Civil Code § 1354(a), in Chapter 2, and *Posey v. Leavitt (1991) 229 Cal.App.3d 1236, 280 Cal.Rptr. 568,* in Chapter 12.

C. ALTERNATIVE DISPUTE RESOLUTION

Alternative dispute resolution requirements imposed by law, and those imposed by the governing documents, are applicable to owner disputes. For a general discussion of alternative dispute resolution requirements, refer to the section entitled "Alternative Dispute Resolution" at page 93 in this chapter. Sample requests and response forms for alternative dispute resolution are provided in Chapter 15. For additional information, see Civil Code §§ 1363.810-1363.850 and 1369.510-1369.590, in Chapter 2.

XV. REMOVAL OF VEHICLES FROM COMMON INTEREST DEVELOPMENTS

An association may remove a parked vehicle to a storage facility under any one of the following circumstances:

(1) There is displayed, in plain view at all entrances to the property, a sign not less than 17 by 22 inches in size, with lettering not less than one inch in height, prohibiting public parking and indicating that vehicles will be removed at the owner's expense, and containing the telephone number of the local traffic law enforcement agency and the name and telephone number of each towing company with which the association has a written towing authorization agreement. The sign may also indicate that a citation will be issued for the violation.

(2) The vehicle has been issued a notice of parking violation and 96 hours have elapsed since the issuance of that notice.

(3) The vehicle on association property lacks an engine, transmission, wheels, tires, doors, windshield, or any other major part or equipment necessary to operate safely on the highways, the

association has notified the local traffic law enforcement agency, and 24 hours have elapsed since that notification.

The association must make available to the tow truck operator, if available, the name and address of the owner of the vehicle and indicate the grounds for removal. The tow truck operator has certain reporting requirements, but the association also must notify by telephone or, if impractical, by the most expeditious means available, the local traffic law enforcement agency within one hour of the tow.

If the vehicle owner arrives before the vehicle is removed from association property, the tow truck operator must immediately and unconditionally release the vehicle to the owner. Refusal to do so is a criminal offense. But the person to whom the vehicle is release must immediately remove the vehicle to a proper parking location. The towing company is entitled to charge one-half of the regular towing charge for releasing the vehicle before it has left the property but after it has been coupled to the tow truck. The regular tow charge may only be imposed after the vehicle has been removed from the property.

A towing company may not remove a vehicle until it has made a good faith effort to locate the vehicle owner and received written authorization to remove from the association or its property manager, who must be physically present at the time of removal and verify the violation. The written authorization must include: (i) the make, model, vehicle identification number and license plate number of the removed vehicle; (ii) the name, signature, job title, residential or business address and working telephone number of the person authorizing the removal; (iii) the grounds for removal; (iv) the time when the vehicle was first observed parked on the property; and (v) the time that authorization to tow was given. When the owner redeems the vehicle the towing company must provide him/her with a copy of the written authorization, but it is required to delete the information about the individual authorizing the tow.

Certain remedies are specified by statute for damage to a vehicle during removal from property and for an unauthorized tow. If a vehicle is damaged during a tow, the owner of the vehicle may recover compensation for damage resulting from any intentional or negligent act from the person causing the damage. Any person who is responsible for an unauthorized tow is liable for double the parking and storage charges.

CHAPTER 2

DAVIS-STIRLING COMMON INTEREST DEVELOPMENT ACT
(Civil Code §§ 1350-1378)

GENERAL PROVISIONS
Preliminary Provisions

Civ. Code § 1350. Short Title.

This title shall be known and may be cited as the Davis-Stirling Common Interest Development Act.

Civ. Code § 1350.5. Headings.

Division, part, title, chapter, and section headings do not in any manner affect the scope, meaning, or intent of this title.

Civ. Code § 1350.7. Delivery.

(a) This section applies to delivery of a document listed in Section 1363.005 or to the extent the section is made applicable by another provision of this title.

(b) A document shall be delivered by one or more of the following methods:

(1) Personal delivery.

(2) First-class mail, postage prepaid, addressed to a member at the address last shown on the books of the association or otherwise provided by the member. Delivery is deemed to be complete on deposit into the United States mail.

(3) E-mail, facsimile, or other electronic means, if the recipient has agreed to that method of delivery. The agreement obtained by the association shall be consistent with the conditions for obtaining consumer consent described in Section 20 of the Corporations Code. If a document is delivered by electronic means, delivery is complete at the time of transmission.

(4) By publication in a periodical that is circulated primarily to members of the association.

(5) If the association broadcasts television programming for the purpose of distributing information on association business to its members, by inclusion in the programming.

(6) A method of delivery provided in a recorded provision of the governing documents.

(7) Any other method of delivery, provided that the recipient has agreed to that method of delivery.

(c) A document may be included in or delivered with a billing statement, newsletter, or other document that is delivered by one of the methods provided in subdivision (b).

(d) For the purposes of this section, an unrecorded provision of the governing documents providing for a particular method of delivery does not constitute agreement by a member of the association to that method of delivery.

Definitions

Civ. Code § 1351. Definitions.

As used in this title, the following terms have the following meanings:

(a) "Association" means a nonprofit corporation or unincorporated association created for the purpose of managing a common interest development.

(b) "Common area" means the entire common interest development except the separate interests therein. The estate in the common area may be a fee, a life estate, an estate for years, or any combination of the foregoing. However, the common area for a planned development specified in paragraph (2) of subdivision (k) may consist of mutual or reciprocal easement rights appurtenant to the separate interests.

(c) "Common interest development" means any of the following:

(1) A community apartment project.

(2) A condominium project.

(3) A planned development.

(4) A stock cooperative.

(d) "Community apartment project" means a development in which an undivided interest in land is coupled with the right of exclusive occupancy of any apartment located thereon.

(e) "Condominium plan" means a plan consisting of (1) a description or survey map of a condominium project, which shall refer to or show monumentation on the ground, (2) a three-dimensional description of a condominium project, one or more dimensions of which may extend for an indefinite distance upwards or downwards, in sufficient detail to identify the common areas and each separate interest, and (3) a certificate consenting to the recordation of the condominium plan pursuant to this title signed and acknowledged by the following:

(A) The record owner of fee title to that property included in the condominium project.

(B) In the case of a condominium project which will terminate upon the termination of an estate for years, the certificate shall be signed and acknowledged by all lessors and lessees of the estate for years.

(C) In the case of a condominium project subject to a life estate, the certificate shall be signed and acknowledged by all life tenants and remainder interests.

(D) The certificate shall also be signed and acknowledged by either the trustee or the beneficiary of each recorded deed of trust, and the mortgagee of each recorded mortgage encumbering the property. Owners of mineral rights, easements, rights-of-way, and other nonpossessory interests do not need to sign the condominium plan. Further, in the event a conversion to condominiums of a community apartment project or stock cooperative has been approved by the required number of owners, trustees, beneficiaries, and mortgagees pursuant to Section 66452.10 of the Government Code, the certificate need only be signed by those owners, trustees, beneficiaries, and mortgagees approving the conversion.

A condominium plan may be amended or revoked by a subsequently acknowledged recorded instrument executed by all the persons whose signatures would be required pursuant to this subdivision.

(f) A "condominium project" means a development consisting of condominiums. A condominium consists of an undivided interest in common in a portion of real property coupled with a separate interest in space called a unit, the boundaries of which are described on a recorded final map, parcel map, or condominium plan in sufficient detail to locate all boundaries thereof. The area within these boundaries may be filled with air, earth, or water, or any combination thereof, and need not be physically attached to land except by easements for access and, if necessary, support. The description of the unit may refer to (1) boundaries described in the recorded final map, parcel map, or condominium plan, (2) physical boundaries, either in existence, or to be constructed, such as walls, floors, and ceilings of a structure or any portion thereof, (3) an entire structure containing one or more units, or (4) any combination thereof. The portion or portions of the real property held in undivided interest may be all of the real property, except for the separate interests, or may include a particular three-dimensional portion thereof, the boundaries of which are described on a recorded final map, parcel map, or condominium plan. The area within these boundaries may be filled with air, earth, or water, or any combination thereof, and need not be physically attached to land except by easements for access and, if necessary, support. An individual condominium within a condominium project may include, in addition, a separate interest in other portions of the real property.

(g) "Declarant" means the person or group of persons designated in the declaration as declarant, or if no declarant is designated, the person or group of persons who sign the original declaration or who succeed to special rights, preferences, or privileges designated in the declaration as belonging to the signator of the original declaration.

(h) "Declaration" means the document, however denominated, which contains the information required by Section 1353.

(i) "Exclusive use common area" means a portion of the common areas designated by the declaration for the exclusive use of one or more, but fewer than all, of the owners of the separate interests and which is or will be appurtenant to the separate interest or interests.

(1) Unless the declaration otherwise provides, any shutters, awnings, window boxes, doorsteps, stoops, porches, balconies, patios, exterior doors, door frames, and hardware incident thereto, screens and windows or other fixtures designed to serve a single separate interest, but located outside the boundaries of the separate interest, are exclusive use common areas allocated exclusively to that separate interest.

(2) Notwithstanding the provisions of the declaration, internal and external telephone wiring designed to serve a single separate interest, but located outside the boundaries of the separate interest, are exclusive use common areas allocated exclusively to that separate interest.

(j) "Governing documents" means the declaration and any other documents, such as bylaws, operating rules of the association, articles of incorporation, or articles of association, which govern the operation of the common interest development or association.

(k) "Planned development" means a development (other than a community apartment project, a condominium project, or a stock cooperative) having either or both of the following features:

(1) The common area is owned either by an association or in common by the owners of the separate interests who possess appurtenant rights to the beneficial use and enjoyment of the common area.

(2) A power exists in the association to enforce an obligation of an owner of a separate interest with respect to the beneficial use and enjoyment of the common area by means of an assessment which may become a lien upon the separate interests in accordance with Section 1367 or 1367.1.

(l) "Separate interest" has the following meanings:

(1) In a community apartment project, "separate interest" means the exclusive right to occupy an apartment, as specified in subdivision (d).

(2) In a condominium project, "separate interest" means an individual unit, as specified in subdivision (f).

(3) In a planned development, "separate interest" means a separately owned lot, parcel, area, or space.

(4) In a stock cooperative, "separate interest" means the exclusive right to occupy a portion of the real property, as specified in subdivision (m).

Unless the declaration or condominium plan, if any exists, otherwise provides, if walls, floors, or ceilings are designated as boundaries of a separate interest, the interior surfaces of the perimeter walls, floors, ceilings, windows, doors, and outlets located within the separate interest are part of the separate interest and any other portions of the walls, floors, or ceilings are part of the common areas.

The estate in a separate interest may be a fee, a life estate, an estate for years, or any combination of the foregoing.

(m) "Stock cooperative" means a development in which a corporation is formed or availed of primarily for the purpose of holding title to, either in fee simple or for a term of years, improved real property, and all or substantially all of the shareholders of the corporation receive a right of exclusive occupancy in a portion of the real property, title to which is held by the corporation. The owners' interest in the corporation, whether evidenced by a share of stock, a certificate of membership, or otherwise, shall be deemed to be an interest in a common interest development and a real estate development for purposes of subdivision (f) of Section 25100 of the Corporations Code.

A "stock cooperative" includes a limited equity housing cooperative which is a stock cooperative that meets the criteria of Section 817.

GOVERNING DOCUMENTS
Creation

Civ. Code § 1352. Requirements For Creation Of Common Interest Development.

This title applies and a common interest development is created whenever a separate interest coupled with an interest in the common area or membership in the association is, or has been, conveyed, provided, all of the following are recorded:

(a) A declaration.

(b) A condominium plan, if any exists.

(c) A final map or parcel map, if Division 2 (commencing with Section 66410) of Title 7 of the Government Code requires the recording of either a final map or parcel map for the common interest development.

Civ. Code § 1352.5. Covenants In Violation Of Gov't Code § 12955; Action For Injunctive Relief.

(a) No declaration or other governing document shall include a restrictive covenant in violation of Section 12955 of the Government Code.

(b) Notwithstanding any other provision of law or provision of the governing documents, the board of directors of an association, without approval of the owners, shall amend any declaration or other governing document that includes a restrictive covenant prohibited by this section to delete the restrictive covenant, and shall restate the declaration or other governing document without the restrictive covenant but with no other change to the declaration or governing document.

(c) If after providing written notice to an association requesting that the association delete a restrictive covenant that violates subdivision (a), and the association fails to delete the restrictive covenant within 30 days of receiving the notice, the Department of Fair Employment and Housing, a city or county in which a common interest development is located, or any person may bring an action against the association for injunctive relief to enforce subdivision (a). The court may award attorney's fees to the prevailing party.

Civ. Code § 1353. Contents Of Declaration.

(a)(1) A declaration, recorded on or after January 1, 1986, shall contain a legal description of the common interest development, and a statement that the common interest development is a community apartment project, condominium project, planned development, stock cooperative, or combination thereof. The declaration shall additionally set forth the name of the association and the restrictions on the use or enjoyment of any portion of the common interest development that are intended to be enforceable equitable servitudes. If the property is located within an airport influence area, a declaration, recorded after January 1, 2004, shall contain the following statement:

NOTICE OF AIRPORT IN VICINITY

This property is presently located in the vicinity of an airport, within what is known as an airport influence area. For that reason, the property may be subject to some of the annoyances or inconveniences associated with proximity to airport operations (for example: noise, vibration, or odors). Individual sensitivities to those annoyances can vary from person to person. You may wish to consider what airport annoyances, if any, are associated with the property before you complete your purchase and determine whether they are acceptable to you.

(2) For purposes of this section, an "airport influence area," also known as an "airport referral area," is the area in which current or future airport-related noise, overflight, safety, or airspace protection factors may significantly affect land uses or necessitate restrictions on those uses as determined by an airport land use commission.

(3) If the property is within the San Francisco Bay Conservation and Development Commission Jurisdiction, as described in Section 66610 of the Government Code, a declaration recorded on or after January 1, 2006, shall contain the following notice:

NOTICE OF SAN FRANCISCO BAY CONSERVATION DEVELOPMENT COMMISSION JURISDICTION

This property is located within the jurisdiction of the San Francisco Bay Conservation and Development Commission. Use and development of property within the commission's jurisdiction may be subject to special regulations, restrictions, and permit requirements. You may wish to investigate and determine whether they are acceptable to you and your intended use of the property before you complete your transaction.

(4) The statement in a declaration acknowledging that a property is located in an airport influence area or within the jurisdiction of the San

Francisco Bay Conservation and Development Commission does not constitute a title defect, lien, or encumbrance.

(b) The declaration may contain any other matters the original signator of the declaration or the owners consider appropriate.

Civ. Code § 1353.5. Right To Display The American Flag.

(a) Except as required for the protection of the public health or safety, no declaration or other governing document shall limit or prohibit, or be construed to limit or prohibit, the display of the flag of the United States by an owner on or in the owner's separate interest or within the owner's exclusive use common area, as defined in Section 1351.

(b) For purposes of this section, "display of the flag of the United States" means a flag of the United States made of fabric, cloth, or paper displayed from a staff or pole or in a window, and does not mean a depiction or emblem of the flag of the United States made of lights, paint, roofing, siding, paving materials, flora, or balloons, or any other similar building, landscaping, or decorative component.

(c) In any action to enforce this section, the prevailing party shall be awarded reasonable attorneys' fees and costs.

Civ. Code § 1353.6. Displaying Of Noncommercial Signs Or Flags.

(a) The governing documents, including the operating rules, may not prohibit posting or displaying of noncommercial signs, posters, flags, or banners on or in an owner's separate interest, except as required for the protection of public health or safety or if the posting or display would violate a local, state, or federal law.

(b) For purposes of this section, a noncommercial sign, poster, flag, or banner may be made of paper, cardboard, cloth, plastic, or fabric, and may be posted or displayed from the yard, window, door, balcony, or outside wall of the separate interest, but may not be made of lights, roofing, siding, paving materials, flora, or balloons, or any other similar building, landscaping, or decorative component, or include the painting of architectural surfaces.

(c) An association may prohibit noncommercial signs and posters that are more than 9 square feet in size and noncommercial flags or banners that are more than 15 square feet in size.

Civ. Code § 1353.7. Fire Retardant Roof Covering Materials.

(a) No common interest development may require a homeowner to install or repair a roof in a manner that is in violation of Section 13132.7

of the Health and Safety Code.

(b) Governing documents of a common interest development located within a very high fire severity zone, as designated by the Director of Forestry and Fire Protection pursuant to Article 9 (commencing with Section 4201) of Chapter 1 of Part 2 of Division 4 of the Public Resources Code or by a local agency pursuant to Chapter 6.8 (commencing with Section 51175) of Part 1 of Division 1 of Title 5 of the Government Code, shall allow for at least one type of fire retardant roof covering material that meets the requirements of Section 13132.7 of the Health and Safety Code.

Civ. Code § 1353.8. Architectural Guidelines - Use Of Low Water-Using Plants.

(a) Notwithstanding any other law, a provision of any of the governing documents of a common interest development shall be void and unenforceable if it does any of the following:

(1) Prohibits, or includes conditions that have the effect of prohibiting, the use of low water-using plants as a group.

(2) Has the effect of prohibiting or restricting compliance with either of the following:

(A) A water-efficient landscape ordinance adopted or in effect pursuant to subdivision (c) of Section 65595 of the Government Code.

(B) Any regulation or restriction on the use of water adopted pursuant to Section 353 or 375 of the Water Code.

(b) This section shall not prohibit an association from applying landscaping rules and regulations established in the governing documents, to the extent the rules and regulations fully conform with the requirements of subdivision (a).

Enforcement

Civ. Code § 1354. Covenants And Restrictions In Declaration; Enforcement.

(a) The covenants and restrictions in the declaration shall be enforceable equitable servitudes, unless unreasonable, and shall inure to the benefit of and bind all owners of separate interests in the development. Unless the declaration states otherwise, these servitudes may be enforced by any owner of a separate interest or by the association, or by both.

(b) A governing document other than the declaration may be enforced by the association against an owner of a separate interest or by an owner of a separate interest against the association.

(c)   In an action to enforce the governing documents, the prevailing party shall be awarded reasonable attorney's fees and costs.

Amendment

Civ. Code § 1355. Amendment Of Declaration.

(a) The declaration may be amended pursuant to the governing documents or this title. Except as provided in Section 1356, an amendment is effective after (1) the approval of the percentage of owners required by the governing documents has been given, (2) that fact has been certified in a writing executed and acknowledged by the officer designated in the declaration or by the association for that purpose, or if no one is designated, by the president of the association, and (3) that writing has been recorded in each county in which a portion of the common interest development is located.

(b) Except to the extent that a declaration provides by its express terms that it is not amendable, in whole or in part, a declaration which fails to include provisions permitting its amendment at all times during its existence may be amended at any time. For purposes of this subdivision, an amendment is only effective after: (1) the proposed amendment has been distributed to all of the owners of separate interests in the common interest development by first-class mail postage prepaid or personal delivery not less than 15 days and not more than 60 days prior to any approval being solicited; (2) the approval of owners representing more than 50 percent, or any higher percentage required by the declaration for the approval of an amendment to the declaration, of the separate interests in the common interest development has been given, and that fact has been certified in a writing, executed and acknowledged by an officer of the association; and (3) the amendment has been recorded in each county in which a portion of the common interest development is located. A copy of any amendment adopted pursuant to this subdivision shall be distributed by first-class mail postage prepaid or personal delivery to all of the owners of separate interest immediately upon its recordation.

Civ. Code § 1355.5. Amendment To Delete Developer Provisions.

(a) Notwithstanding any provision of the governing documents of a common interest development to the contrary, the board of directors of the association may, after the developer of the common interest development has completed construction of the development, has terminated construction activities, and has terminated his or her marketing activities for the sale, lease, or other disposition of separate interests within the development, adopt an amendment deleting from any of the governing documents any provision which is unequivocally designed and intended, or which by its nature can only have been designed or intended, to facilitate the developer in completing the construction or marketing of the development. However, provisions of the governing documents relative to a particular construction or marketing phase of the development may not be deleted under the authorization of this subdivision until that construction or marketing phase has been completed.

(b) The provisions which may be deleted by action of the board shall be limited to those which provide for access by the developer over or across the common area for the purposes of (a) completion of construction of the development, and (b) the erection, construction, or maintenance of structures or other facilities designed to facilitate the completion of construction or marketing of separate interests.

(c) At least 30 days prior to taking action pursuant to subdivision (a), the board of directors of the association shall mail to all owners of the separate interests, by first-class mail, (1) a copy of all amendments to the governing documents proposed to be adopted under subdivision (a) and (2) a notice of the time, date, and place the board of directors will consider adoption of the amendments. The board of directors of an association may consider adoption of amendments to the governing documents pursuant to subdivision (a) only at a meeting which is open to all owners of the separate interests in the common interest development, who shall be given opportunity to make comments thereon. All deliberations of the board of directors on any action proposed under subdivision (a) shall only be conducted in such an open meeting.

(d) The board of directors of the association may not amend the governing documents pursuant to this section without the approval of the owners, casting a majority of the votes at a meeting or election of the association constituting a quorum and conducted in accordance with Chapter 5 (commencing with Section 7510) of Part 3 of Division 2 of Title 1 of, and Section 7613 of, the Corporations Code. For the purposes of this section, "quorum" means more than 50 percent of the owners who own no more than two separate interests in the development.

Civ. Code § 1356. Petition To Court To Reduce Percentage Of Affirmative Votes To Amend Declaration; Recording Amendment; Mailing.

(a) If in order to amend a declaration, the declaration requires owners having more than 50 percent of the votes in the association, in a single class voting structure, or owners having more than 50 percent of the votes in more than one class in a voting structure with more than one class, to vote in favor of the amendment, the association, or any owner of a separate interest, may petition the superior court of the county in which the common interest development is located for an order reducing the percentage of the affirmative votes necessary for such an amendment. The petition shall describe the effort that has been made to solicit approval of the association members in the manner provided in the declaration, the number of affirmative and negative votes actually received, the number or percentage of affirmative votes required to effect the amendment in accordance with the existing declaration, and other matters the petitioner considers relevant to the court's determination. The petition shall also contain, as exhibits thereto, copies of all of the following:

(1) The governing documents.

(2) A complete text of the amendment.

(3) Copies of any notice and solicitation materials utilized in the solicitation of owner approvals.

(4) A short explanation of the reason for the amendment.

(5) Any other documentation relevant to the court's determination.

(b) Upon filing the petition, the court shall set the matter for hearing and issue an ex parte order setting forth the manner in which notice shall be given.

(c) The court may, but shall not be required to, grant the petition if it finds all of the following:

(1) The petitioner has given not less than 15 days written notice of the court hearing to all members of the association, to any mortgagee of a mortgage or beneficiary of a deed of trust who is entitled to notice under the terms of the declaration, and to the city, county, or city and county in which the common interest development is located that is entitled to notice under the terms of the declaration.

(2) Balloting on the proposed amendment was conducted in accordance with all applicable provisions of the governing documents.

(3) A reasonably diligent effort was made to permit all eligible members to vote on the proposed amendment.

(4) Owners having more than 50 percent of the votes, in a single class voting structure, voted in favor of the amendment. In a voting structure with more than one class, where the declaration requires

a majority of more than one class to vote in favor of the amendment, owners having more than 50 percent of the votes of each class required by the declaration to vote in favor of the amendment voted in favor of the amendment.

(5) The amendment is reasonable.

(6) Granting the petition is not improper for any reason stated in subdivision (e).

(d) If the court makes the findings required by subdivision (c), any order issued pursuant to this section may confirm the amendment as being validly approved on the basis of the affirmative votes actually received during the balloting period or the order may dispense with any requirement relating to quorums or to the number or percentage of votes needed for approval of the amendment that would otherwise exist under the governing documents.

(e) Subdivisions (a) to (d), inclusive, notwithstanding, the court shall not be empowered by this section to approve any amendment to the declaration that:

(1) Would change provisions in the declaration requiring the approval of owners having more than 50 percent of the votes in more than one class to vote in favor of an amendment, unless owners having more than 50 percent of the votes in each affected class approved the amendment.

(2) Would eliminate any special rights, preferences, or privileges designated in the declaration as belonging to the declarant, without the consent of the declarant.

(3) Would impair the security interest of a mortgagee of a mortgage or the beneficiary of a deed of trust without the approval of the percentage of the mortgagees and beneficiaries specified in the declaration, if the declaration requires the approval of a specified percentage of the mortgagees and beneficiaries.

(f) An amendment is not effective pursuant to this section until the court order and amendment have been recorded in every county in which a portion of the common interest development is located. The amendment may be acknowledged by, and the court order and amendment may be recorded by, any person designated in the declaration or by the association for that purpose, or if no one is designated for that purpose, by the president of the association. Upon recordation of the amendment and court order, the declaration, as amended in accordance with this section, shall have the same force and effect as if the amendment were adopted in compliance with every requirement imposed by the governing documents.

(g) Within a reasonable time after the amendment is recorded the association shall mail a copy of the amendment to each member of the association, together with a statement that the amendment has been recorded.

Civ. Code § 1357. Extending Term Of Declaration.

(a) The Legislature finds that there are common interest developments that have been created with deed restrictions which do not provide a means for the property owners to extend the term of the declaration. The Legislature further finds that covenants and restrictions, contained in the declaration, are an appropriate method for protecting the common plan of developments and to provide for a mechanism for financial support for the upkeep of common areas including, but not limited to, roofs, roads, heating systems, and recreational facilities. If declarations terminate prematurely, common interest developments may deteriorate and the housing supply of affordable units could be impacted adversely.

The Legislature further finds and declares that it is in the public interest to provide a vehicle for extending the term of the declaration if owners having more than 50 percent of the votes in the association choose to do so.

(b) A declaration which specifies a termination date, but which contains no provision for extension of the termination date, may be extended by the approval of owners having more than 50 percent of the votes in the association or any greater percentage specified in the declaration for an amendment thereto. If the approval of owners having more than 50 percent of the votes in the association is required to amend the declaration, the term of the declaration may be extended in accordance with Section 1356.

(c) Any amendment to a declaration made in accordance with subdivision (b) shall become effective upon recordation in accordance with Section 1355.

(d) No single extension of the terms of the declaration made pursuant to this section shall exceed the initial term of the declaration or 20 years, whichever is less. However, more than one extension may occur pursuant to this section.

Operating Rules

Civ. Code § 1357.100. "Operating Rule" And "Rule Change" Defined.
As used in this article:

Civil

(a) "Operating rule" means a regulation adopted by the board of directors of the association that applies generally to the management and operation of the common interest development or the conduct of the business and affairs of the association.

(b) "Rule change" means the adoption, amendment, or repeal of an operating rule by the board of directors of the association.

Civil Code § 1357.110. Validity.

An operating rule is valid and enforceable only if all of the following requirements are satisfied:

(a) The rule is in writing.

(b) The rule is within the authority of the board of directors of the association conferred by law or by the declaration, articles of incorporation or association, or bylaws of the association.

(c) The rule is not inconsistent with governing law and the declaration, articles of incorporation or association, and bylaws of the association.

(d) The rule is adopted, amended, or repealed in good faith and in substantial compliance with the requirements of this article.

(e) The rule is reasonable.

Civil Code § 1357.120. Application.

(a) Sections 1357.130 and 1357.140 only apply to an operating rule that relates to one or more of the following subjects:

(1) Use of the common area or of an exclusive use common area.

(2) Use of a separate interest, including any aesthetic or architectural standards that govern alteration of a separate interest.

(3) Member discipline, including any schedule of monetary penalties for violation of the governing documents and any procedure for the imposition of penalties.

(4) Any standards for delinquent assessment payment plans.

(5) Any procedures adopted by the association for resolution of disputes.

(6) Any procedures for reviewing and approving or disapproving a proposed physical change to a member's separate interest or to the common area.

(7) Procedures for elections.

(b) Sections 1357.130 and 1357.140 do not apply to the following actions by the board of directors of an association:

(1) A decision regarding maintenance of the common area.

(2) A decision on a specific matter that is not intended to apply generally.

(3) A decision setting the amount of a regular or special assessment.

(4) A rule change that is required by law, if the board of directors has no discretion as to the substantive effect of the rule change.

(5) Issuance of a document that merely repeats existing law or the governing documents.

Civ. Code § 1357.130. Notice Of Rule Change.

(a) The board of directors shall provide written notice of a proposed rule change to the members at least 30 days before making the rule change. The notice shall include the text of the proposed rule change and a description of the purpose and effect of the proposed rule change. Notice is not required under this subdivision if the board of directors determines that an immediate rule change is necessary to address an imminent threat to public health or safety or imminent risk of substantial economic loss to the association.

(b) A decision on a proposed rule change shall be made at a meeting of the board of directors, after consideration of any comments made by association members.

(c) As soon as possible after making a rule change, but not more than 15 days after making the rule change, the board of directors shall deliver notice of the rule change to every association member. If the rule change was an emergency rule change made under subdivision (d), the notice shall include the text of the rule change, a description of the purpose and effect of the rule change, and the date that the rule change expires.

(d) If the board of directors determines that an immediate rule change is required to address an imminent threat to public health or safety, or an imminent risk of substantial economic loss to the association, it may make an emergency rule change; and no notice is required, as specified in subdivision (a). An emergency rule change is effective for 120 days, unless the rule change provides for a shorter effective period. A rule change made under this subdivision may not be readopted under this subdivision.

(e) A notice required by this section is subject to Section 1350.7.

Civ. Code § 1357.140. Special Meeting Of Members To Reverse A Rule Change.

(a) Members of an association owning 5 percent or more of the separate interests may call a special meeting of the members to reverse a rule change.

(b) A special meeting of the members may be called by delivering a written request to the president or secretary of the board of directors, after which the board shall deliver notice of the meeting to the association's members and hold the meeting in conformity with Section 7511 of the Corporations Code. The written request may not be delivered more than 30 days after the members of the association are notified of the rule change. Members are deemed to have been notified of a rule change on delivery of notice of the rule change, or on enforcement of the resulting rule, whichever is sooner. For the purposes of Section 8330 of the Corporations Code, collection of signatures to call a special meeting under this section is a purpose reasonably related to the interests of the members of the association. A member request to copy or inspect the membership list solely for that purpose may not be denied on the grounds that the purpose is not reasonably related to the member's interests as a member.

(c) The rule change may be reversed by the affirmative vote of a majority of the votes represented and voting at a duly held meeting at which a quorum is present (which affirmative votes also constitute a majority of the required quorum), or if the declaration or bylaws require a greater proportion, by the affirmative vote or written ballot of the proportion required. In lieu of calling the meeting described in this section, the board may distribute a written ballot to every member of the association in conformity with the requirements of Section 7513 of the Corporations Code.

(d) Unless otherwise provided in the declaration or bylaws, for the purposes of this section, a member may cast one vote per separate interest owned.

(e) A meeting called under this section is governed by Chapter 5 (commencing with Section 7510) of Part 3 of Division 2 of Title 1 of, and Sections 7612 and 7613 of, the Corporations Code.

(f) A rule change reversed under this section may not be readopted for one year after the date of the meeting reversing the rule change. Nothing in this section precludes the board of directors from adopting a different rule on the same subject as the rule change that has been reversed.

(g) As soon as possible after the close of voting, but not more than 15 days after the close of voting, the board of directors shall provide notice of the results of a member vote held pursuant to this section to every association member. Delivery of notice under this subdivision is subject to Section 1350.7.

(h) This section does not apply to an emergency rule change made under subdivision (d) of Section 1357.130.

Civ. Code § 1357.150. Effective Date.

(a) This article applies to a rule change commenced on or after January 1, 2004.

(b) Nothing in this article affects the validity of a rule change commenced before January 1, 2004.

(c) For the purposes of this section, a rule change is commenced when the board of directors of the association takes its first official action leading to adoption of the rule change.

OWNERSHIP RIGHTS AND INTERESTS

Civ. Code § 1358. Interests Included In Conveyance, Judicial Sale Or Transfer Of Separate Interests; Transfers Of Exclusive Use Areas; Restrictions Upon Severability Of Component Interests.

(a) In a community apartment project, any conveyance, judicial sale, or other voluntary or involuntary transfer of the separate interest includes the undivided interest in the community apartment project. Any conveyance, judicial sale, or other voluntary or involuntary transfer of the owner's entire estate also includes the owner's membership interest in the association.

(b) In a condominium project the common areas are not subject to partition, except as provided in Section 1359. Any conveyance, judicial sale, or other voluntary or involuntary transfer of the separate interest includes the undivided interest in the common areas. Any conveyance, judicial sale, or other voluntary or involuntary transfer of the owner's entire estate also includes the owner's membership interest in the association.

(c) In a planned development, any conveyance, judicial sale, or other voluntary or involuntary transfer of the separate interest includes the undivided interest in the common areas, if any exist. Any conveyance, judicial sale, or other voluntary or involuntary transfer of the owner's entire estate also includes the owner's membership interest in the association.

(d) In a stock cooperative, any conveyance, judicial sale, or other voluntary or involuntary transfer of the separate interest includes the ownership interest in the corporation, however evidenced. Any conveyance, judicial sale, or other voluntary or involuntary transfer of the owner's entire estate also includes the owner's membership interest in the association.

Nothing in this section prohibits the transfer of exclusive use areas, independent of any other interest in a common interest subdivision, if authorization to separately transfer exclusive use areas is expressly stated in the declaration and the transfer occurs in accordance with the terms of the declaration.

Any restrictions upon the severability of the component interests in real property which are contained in the declaration shall not be deemed conditions repugnant to the interest created within the meaning of Section 711 of the Civil Code. However, these restrictions shall not extend beyond the period in which the right to partition a project is suspended under Section 1359.

Civ. Code § 1359. Restrictions On Partition Of Common Areas.

(a) Except as provided in this section, the common areas in a condominium project shall remain undivided, and there shall be no judicial partition thereof. Nothing in this section shall be deemed to prohibit partition of a cotenancy in a condominium.

(b) The owner of a separate interest in a condominium project may maintain a partition action as to the entire project as if the owners of all of the separate interests in the project were tenants in common in the entire project in the same proportion as their interests in the common areas. The court shall order partition under this subdivision only by sale of the entire condominium project and only upon a showing of one of the following:

(1) More than three years before the filing of the action, the condominium project was damaged or destroyed, so that a material part was rendered unfit for its prior use, and the condominium project has not been rebuilt or repaired substantially to its state prior to the damage or destruction.

(2) Three-fourths or more of the project is destroyed or substantially damaged and owners of separate interests holding in the aggregate more than a 50-percent interest in the common areas oppose repair or restoration of the project.

(3) The project has been in existence more than 50 years, is obsolete and uneconomic, and owners of separate interests holding in the aggregate more than a 50-percent interest in the common area oppose repair or restoration of the project.

(4) The conditions for such a sale, set forth in the declaration, have been met.

Civ. Code § 1360. Modification Of Unit By Owner; Facilitation Of Access For Handicapped; Association Approval.

(a) Subject to the provisions of the governing documents and other applicable provisions of law, if the boundaries of the separate interest are contained within a building, the owner of the separate interest may do the following:

(1) Make any improvements or alterations within the boundaries of his or her separate interest that do not impair the structural integrity or mechanical systems or lessen the support of any portions of the common interest development.

(2) Modify a unit in a condominium project, at the owner's expense, to facilitate access for persons who are blind, visually handicapped, deaf, or physically disabled, or to alter conditions which could be hazardous to these persons. These modifications may also include modifications of the route from the public way to the door of the unit for the purposes of this paragraph if the unit is on the ground floor or already accessible by an existing ramp or elevator. The right granted by this paragraph is subject to the following conditions:

(A) The modifications shall be consistent with applicable building code requirements.

(B) The modifications shall be consistent with the intent of otherwise applicable provisions of the governing documents pertaining to safety or aesthetics.

(C) Modifications external to the dwelling shall not prevent reasonable passage by other residents, and shall be removed by the owner when the unit is no longer occupied by persons requiring those modifications who are blind, visually handicapped, deaf, or physically disabled.

(D) Any owner who intends to modify a unit pursuant to this paragraph shall submit his or her plans and specifications to the association of the condominium project for review to determine whether the modifications will comply with the provisions of this paragraph. The association shall not deny approval of the proposed modifications under this paragraph without good cause.

(b) Any change in the exterior appearances of a separate interest shall be in accordance with the governing documents and applicable provisions of law.

Civ. Code § 1360.5. Pet Provision.

(a) No governing documents shall prohibit the owner of a separate interest within a common interest development from keeping at least one pet within the common interest development, subject to reasonable rules and regulations of the association. This section may not be contrued to affect any other rights provided by law to an owner of a separate interest to keep a pet within the development.

(b) For purposes of this section, "pet" means any domesticated bird, cat, dog, aquatic animal kept within an aquarium, or other animal as agreed to between the association and the homeowner.

(c) If the association implements a rule or regulation restricting the number of pets an owner may keep, the new rule or regulation shall not apply to prohibit an owner from continuing to keep any pet that the owner currently keeps in his or her separate interest if the pet otherwise conforms with the previous rules or regulations relating to pets.

(d) For the purpose of this section, "governing documents" shall include, but are not limited to, the conditions, covenants, and restrictions of the common interest development, and the bylaws, rules, and regulations of the association.

(e) This section shall become operative on January 1, 2001, and shall only apply to governing documents entered into, amended, or otherwise modified on or after that date.

Civ. Code § 1361. Rights Or Easements In Common Area.

Unless the declaration otherwise provides:

(a) In a community apartment project and condominium project, and in those planned developments with common areas owned in common by the owners of the separate interests, there are appurtenant to each separate interest nonexclusive rights of ingress, egress, and support, if necessary, through the common areas. The common areas are subject to these rights.

(b) In a stock cooperative, and in a planned development with common areas owned by the association, there is an easement for ingress, egress, and support, if necessary, appurtenant to each separate interest. The common areas are subject to these easements.

Civ. Code § 1361.5. Denial Of Access To Owner's Separate Interest.

Except as otherwise provided in law, an order of the court, or an order pursuant to a final and binding arbitration decision, an association may not deny an owner or occupant physical access to his or her separate interest, either by restricting access through the common areas to the owner's separate interest, or by restricting access solely to the owner's separate interest.

Civ. Code § 1362. Ownership Of Common Areas.

Unless the declaration otherwise provides, in a condominium project, or in a planned development in which the common areas are owned by the owners of the separate interests, the common areas are owned as tenants in common, in equal shares, one for each unit or lot.

GOVERNANCE
Association

Civ. Code § 1363. General Powers And Duties Of Association; Meetings; Access To Records; Disciplinary Action.

(a) A common interest development shall be managed by an association that may be incorporated or unincorporated. The association may be referred to as a community association.

(b) An association, whether incorporated or unincorporated, shall prepare a budget pursuant to Section 1365 and disclose information, if requested, in accordance with Section 1368.

(c) Unless the governing documents provide otherwise, and regardless of whether the association is incorporated or unincorporated, the association may exercise the powers granted to a nonprofit mutual benefit corporation, as enumerated in Section 7140 of the Corporations Code, except that an unincorporated association may not adopt or use a corporate seal or issue membership certificates in accordance with Section 7313 of the Corporations Code.

The association, whether incorporated or unincorporated, may exercise the powers granted to an association in this title.

(d) Meetings of the membership of the association shall be conducted in accordance with a recognized system of parliamentary procedure or any parliamentary procedures the association may adopt.

(e) Notwithstanding any other provision of law, notice of meetings of the members shall specify those matters the board intends to present for action by the members, but, except as otherwise provided by law, any proper matter may be presented at the meeting for action.

(f) Members of the association shall have access to association records, including accounting books and records and membership lists, in accordance with Article 3 (commencing with Section 8330) of Chapter 13 of Part 3 of Division 2 of Title 1 of the Corporations Code. The members of the association shall have the same access to the operating rules of the association as they have to the accounting books and records of the association.

(g) If an association adopts or has adopted a policy imposing any monetary penalty, including any fee, on any association member for a violation of the governing documents or rules of the association, including any monetary penalty relating to the activities of a guest or invitee of a member, the board of directors shall adopt and distribute to each member, by personal delivery or first-class mail, a schedule of the monetary penalties that may be assessed for those violations, which shall be in accordance with authorization for member discipline contained in the governing documents. The board of directors shall not be required to distribute any additional schedules of monetary penalties unless there are changes from the schedule that was adopted and distributed to the members pursuant to this subdivision.

(h) When the board of directors is to meet to consider or impose discipline upon a member, the board shall notify the member in writing, by either personal delivery or first-class mail, at least 10 days prior to the meeting. The notification shall contain, at a minimum, the date, time and place of the meeting, the nature of the alleged violation for which a member may be disciplined, and a statement that the member has a right to attend and may address the board at the meeting. The board of directors of the association shall meet in executive session if requested by the member being disciplined.

If the board imposes discipline on a member, the board shall provide the member a written notification of the disciplinary action, by either personal delivery or first-class mail, within 15 days following the action. A disciplinary action shall not be effective against a member unless the board fulfills the requirements of this subdivision.

(i) Whenever two or more associations have consolidated any of their functions under a joint neighborhood association or similar organization, members of each participating association shall be (1) entitled to attend all meetings of the joint association other than executive sessions, (2) given reasonable opportunity for participation in those meetings, and (3) entitled to the same access to the joint association's records as they are to the participating association's records.

(j) Nothing in this section shall be construed to create, expand, or reduce the authority of the board of directors of an association to impose monetary penalties on an association member for a violation of the governing documents or rules of the association.

Civ. Code § 1363.001. On-line Education Course.

To the extent existing funds are available, the Department of Consumer

Affairs and the Department of Real Estate shall develop an on-line education course for the board of directors of an association regarding the role, duties, laws, and responsibilities of board members and prospective board members, and the nonjudicial foreclosure process.

Civ. Code § 1363.005. Distribution Of Disclosure Documents.

The association shall, at the request of any member, distribute to the member, in the manner described in Section 1350.7, the following Disclosure Documents Index:

Disclosure Documents Index

Item	Description	Reference Code
1	Assessment and Reserve Funding Disclosure Summary (form)	Civil Code Sec. 1365.2.5
2	Pro Forma Operating Budget or Pro Pro Forma Operating Budget Summary	Civil Code Sec. 1365(a)
3	Assessment Collection Policy	Civil Code Sec. 1365(e) and 1367.1(a)
4	Notice/Assessments and Foreclosure (form)	Civil Code Sec. 1365.1
5	Insurance Coverage Summary	Civil Code Sec. 1365(f)
6	Board Minutes Access	Civil Code Sec. 1363.05(e)
7	Alternative Dispute Resolution (ADR) Rights (summary)	Civil Code Sec. 1369.590
8	Internal Dispute Resolution (IDR) Rights (summary)	Civil Code Sec. 1363.850
9	Architectural Changes Notice	Civil Code Sec. 1378(c)
10	Secondary Address Notification Request	Civil Code Sec. 1367.1(k)
11	Monetary Penalties Schedule	Civil Code Sec. 1363(g)
12	Reserve Funding Plan (summary)	Civil Code Sec. 1365(b)
13	Review of Financial Statement	Civil Code Sec. 1365(c)
14	Annual Update of Reserve Study	Civil Code Sec. 1365(a)

Elections and Meetings

Civ. Code § 1363.03. Adoption Of Rules Regarding Election Procedures; Appointment Of Election Inspectors; Voting By Secret Ballot; Proxy And Ballot Instructions; Publication Of Election Results; Retention Of Ballots; Application Of Article.

(a) An association shall adopt rules, in accordance with the procedures prescribed by Article 4 (commencing with Section 1357.100) of Chapter 2, that do all of the following:

(1) Ensure that if any candidate or member advocating a point of view is provided access to association media, newsletters, or Internet Web sites during a campaign, for purposes that are reasonably related to that election, equal access shall be provided to all candidates and members advocating a point of view, including those not endorsed by the board, for purposes that are reasonably related to the election. The association shall not edit or redact any content from these communications, but may include a statement specifying that the candidate or member, and not the association, is responsible for that content.

(2) Ensure access to the common area meeting space, if any exists, during a campaign, at no cost, to all candidates, including those who are not incumbents, and to all members advocating a point of view, including those not endorsed by the board, for purposes reasonably related to the election.

(3) Specify the qualifications for candidates for the board of directors and any other elected position, and procedures for the nomination of candidates, consistent with the governing documents. A nomination or election procedure shall not be deemed reasonable if it disallows any member of the association from nominating himself or herself for election to the board of directors.

(4) Specify the qualifications for voting, the voting power of each membership, the authenticity, validity, and effect of proxies, and the voting period for elections, including the times at which polls will open and close, consistent with the governing documents.

(5) Specify a method of selecting one or three independent third parties as inspector, or inspectors, of election utilizing one of the following methods:

(A) Appointment of the inspector or inspectors by the board.

(B) Election of the inspector or inspectors by the members of the association.

(C) Any other method for selecting the inspector or inspectors.

(6) Allow the inspector, or inspectors, to appoint and oversee additional persons to verify signatures and to count and tabulate votes as the inspector or inspectors deem appropriate, provided that the persons are independent third parties.

(b) Notwithstanding any other law or provision of the governing documents, elections regarding assessments legally requiring a vote, election and removal of members of the association board of directors, amendments to the governing documents, or the grant of exclusive use of common area property pursuant to Section 1363.07 shall be held by secret ballot in accordance with the procedures set forth in this section. A quorum shall be required only if so stated in the governing documents of the association or other provisions of law. If a quorum is required by the governing documents, each ballot received by the inspector of elections shall be treated as a member present at a meeting for purposes of establishing a quorum. An association shall allow for cumulative voting using the secret ballot procedures provided in this section, if cumulative voting is provided for in the governing documents.

(c) (1) The association shall select an independent third party or parties as an inspector of elections. The number of inspectors of elections shall be one or three.

(2) For the purposes of this section, an independent third party includes, but is not limited to, a volunteer poll worker with the county registrar of voters, a licensee of the California Board of Accountancy, or a notary public. An independent third party may be a member of the association, but may not be a member of the board of directors or a candidate for the board of directors or related to a member of the board of directors or a candidate for the board of directors. An independent third party may not be a person, business entity, or subdivision of a business entity who is currently employed or under contract to the association for any compensable services unless expressly authorized by rules of the association adopted pursuant to paragraph (5) of subdivision (a).

(3) The inspector or inspectors of elections shall do all of the following:

(A) Determine the number of memberships entitled to vote and the voting power of each.

(B) Determine the authenticity, validity, and effect of proxies, if any.

(C) Receive ballots.

(D) Hear and determine all challenges and questions in any way arising out of or in connection with the right to vote.

(E) Count and tabulate all votes.

(F) Determine when the polls shall close, consistent with the governing documents.

(G) Determine the tabulated results of the election.

(H) Perform any acts as may be proper to conduct the election with fairness to all members in accordance with this section, the Corporations Code, and all applicable rules of the association regarding the conduct of the election that are not in conflict with this section.

(4) An inspector of elections shall perform his or her duties impartially, in good faith, to the best of his or her ability, and as expeditiously as is practical. If there are three inspectors of elections, the decision or act of a majority shall be effective in all respects as the decision or act of all. Any report made by the inspector or inspectors of elections is prima facie evidence of the facts stated in the report.

(d) (1) For purposes of this section, the following definitions shall apply:

(A) "Proxy" means a written authorization signed by a member or the authorized representative of the member that gives another member or members the power to vote on behalf of that member.

(B) "Signed" means the placing of the member's name on the proxy (whether by manual signature, typewriting, telegraphic transmission, or otherwise) by the member or authorized representative of the member.

(2) Proxies shall not be construed or used in lieu of a ballot. An association may use proxies if permitted or required by the bylaws of the association and if those proxies meet the requirements of this article, other laws, and the association's governing documents, but the association shall not be required to prepare or distribute proxies pursuant to this section.

(3) Any instruction given in a proxy issued for an election that directs the manner in which the proxyholder is to cast the vote shall be set forth on a separate page of the proxy that can be detached and given to the proxyholder to retain. The proxyholder shall cast the member's vote by secret ballot. The proxy may be revoked by the member prior to the receipt of the ballot by the inspector of elections as described in Section 7613 of the Corporations Code.

(e) Ballots and two preaddressed envelopes with instructions on how to return ballots shall be mailed by first-class mail or delivered by the association to every member not less than 30 days prior to the deadline for voting. In order to preserve confidentiality, a voter may not be identified by name, address, or lot, parcel, or unit number on the ballot. The association shall use as a model those procedures used by California counties for ensuring confidentiality of vote by mail ballots, including all of the following:

(1) The ballot itself is not signed by the voter, but is inserted into an envelope that is sealed. This envelope is inserted into a second envelope that is sealed. In the upper left hand corner of the second envelope, the voter shall sign his or her name, indicate his or her name, and indicate the address or separate interest identifier that entitles him or her to vote.

(2) The second envelope is addressed to the inspector or inspectors of elections, who will be tallying the votes. The envelope may be mailed or delivered by hand to a location specified by the inspector or inspectors of elections. The member may request a receipt for delivery.

(f) All votes shall be counted and tabulated by the inspector or inspectors of elections or his or her designee in public at a properly noticed open meeting of the board of directors or members. Any candidate or other member of the association may witness the counting and tabulation of the votes. No person, including a member of the association or an employee of the management company, shall open or otherwise review any ballot prior to the time and place at which the ballots are counted and tabulated. The inspector of elections, or his or her designee, may verify the member's information and signature on the outer envelope prior to the meeting at which ballots are tabulated. Once a secret ballot is received by the inspector of elections, it shall be irrevocable.

(g) The tabulated results of the election shall be promptly reported to the board of directors of the association and shall be recorded in the minutes of the next meeting of the board of directors and shall be available for review by members of the association. Within 15 days of the election, the board shall publicize the tabulated results of the election in a communication directed to all members.

(h) The sealed ballots at all times shall be in the custody of the inspector or inspectors of elections or at a location designated by the inspector or inspectors until after the tabulation of the vote and until the time allowed by Section 7527 of the Corporations Code for challenging the election has expired, at which time custody shall be transferred to the association. If there is a recount or other challenge to the election process, the inspector or inspectors of elections shall, upon written request, make the ballots available for inspection and review by an association member or his or her authorized representative. Any recount shall be conducted in a manner that preserves the confidentiality of the vote.

(i) After the transfer of the ballots to the association, the ballots shall be stored by the association in a secure place for no less than one year after the date of the election.

(j) Notwithstanding any other provision of law, the rules adopted pursuant to this section may provide for the nomination of candidates from the floor of membership meetings or nomination by any other manner. Those rules may permit write-in candidates for ballots.

(k) Except for the meeting to count the votes required in subdivision (f), an election may be conducted entirely by mail unless otherwise specified in the governing documents.

(l) The provisions of this section apply to both incorporated and unincorporated associations, notwithstanding any contrary provision of the governing documents.

(m) The procedures set forth in this section shall apply to votes cast directly by the membership, but do not apply to votes cast by delegates or other elected representatives.

(n) In the event of a conflict between this section and the provisions of the Nonprofit Mutual Benefit Corporation Law (Part 3 (commencing with Section 7110) of Division 2 of Title 1 of the Corporations Code) relating to elections, the provisions of this section shall prevail.

(o) The amendments made to this section by the act adding this subdivision shall become operative on July 1, 2006.

Civ. Code § 1363.04. Use Of Association Funds For Campaign Purposes Prohibited.

(a) Association funds shall not be used for campaign purposes in connection with any association board election. Funds of the association shall not be used for campaign purposes in connection with any other association election except to the extent necessary to comply with duties of the association imposed by law.

(b) For the purposes of this section "campaign purposes" includes, but is not limited to, the following:

(1) Expressly advocating the election or defeat of any candidate that is on the association election ballot.

(2) Including the photograph or prominently featuring the name of any candidate on a communication from the association or its board, excepting the ballot and ballot materials, within 30 days of an election. This is not a campaign purpose if the communication is one for which subdivision (a) of Section 1363.03 requires that equal access be provided to another candidate or advocate.

Civ. Code § 1363.05. Member Attendance At Board Meetings; Executive Sessions; Emergency Meetings; Availability Of Board Minutes; Notice Of Meetings; Owner Right To Speak At Meetings.

(a) This section shall be known and may be cited as the Common Interest Development Open Meeting Act.

(b) Any member of the association may attend meetings of the board of directors of the association, except when the board adjourns to executive session to consider litigation, matters relating to the formation of contracts with third parties, member discipline, personnel matters, or to meet with a member, upon the member's request, regarding the member's payment of assessments, as specified in Section 1367 or 1367.1. The board of directors of the association shall meet in executive session, if requested by a member who may be subject to a fine, penalty, or other form of discipline, and the member shall be entitled to attend the executive session.

(c) Any matter discussed in executive session shall be generally noted in the minutes of the immediately following meeting that is open to the entire membership.

(d) The minutes, minutes proposed for adoption that are marked to indicate draft status, or a summary of the minutes, of any meeting of the board of directors of an association, other than an executive session, shall be available to members within 30 days of the meeting. The minutes, proposed minutes, or summary minutes shall be distributed to any member of the association upon request and upon reimbursement of the association's costs for making that distribution.

(e) Members of the association shall be notified in writing at the time that the *pro forma* budget required in Section 1365 is distributed, or at the time of any general mailing to the entire membership of the association, of their right to have copies of the minutes of meetings of the board of directors, and how and where those minutes may be obtained.

(f) Unless the time and place of meeting is fixed by the bylaws, or unless the bylaws provide for a longer period of notice, members shall be given notice of the time and place of a meeting as defined in subdivision (j), except for an emergency meeting, at least four days prior to the meeting. Notice shall be given by posting the notice in a prominent place or places within the common area and by mail to any owner who had requested notification of board meetings by mail, at the address requested by the owner. Notice may also be given, by mail or delivery of the notice to each unit in the development or by newsletter or similar means of communication. The notice shall contain the agenda for the meeting.

(g) An emergency meeting of the board may be called by the president of the association, or by any two members of the governing body other than the president, if there are circumstances that could not have been reasonably foreseen which require immediate attention and possible action by the board, and which of necessity make it impracticable to provide notice as required by this section.

(h) The board of directors of the association shall permit any member of the association to speak at any meeting of the association or the board of directors, except for meetings of the board held in executive session. A reasonable time limit for all members of the association to speak to the board of directors or before a meeting of the association shall be established by the board of directors.

(i) (1) Except as described in paragraphs (2) to (4), inclusive, the board of directors of the association may not discuss or take action on any item at a nonemergency meeting unless the item was placed on the agenda included in the notice that was posted and distributed pursuant to subdivision (f). This subdivision does not prohibit a resident who is not a member of the board from speaking on issues not on the agenda.

(2) Notwithstanding paragraph (1), a member of the board of directors, a managing agent or other agent of the board of directors, or a member of the staff of the board of directors, may do any of the following:

(A) Briefly respond to statements made or questions posed by a person speaking at a meeting as described in subdivision (h).

(B) Ask a question for clarification, make a brief announcement, or make a brief report on his or her own activities, whether in response to questions posed by a member of the association or based upon his or her own initiative.

(3) Notwithstanding paragraph (1), the board of directors or a member of the board of directors, subject to rules or procedures of the board of directors, may do any of the following:

(A) Provide a reference to, or provide other resources for factual information to, its managing agent or other agents or staff.

(B) Request its managing agent or other agents or staff to report back to the board of directors at a subsequent meeting concerning any matter, or take action to direct its managing agent or other agents or staff to place a matter of business on a future agenda.

(C) Direct its managing agent or other agents or staff to perform administrative tasks that are necessary to carry out this subdivision.

(4) (A) Notwithstanding paragraph (1), the board of directors may take action on any item of business not appearing on the agenda posted

and distributed pursuant to subdivision (f) under any of the following conditions:

(i) Upon a determination made by a majority of the board of directors present at the meeting that an emergency situation exists. An emergency situation exists if there are circumstances that could not have been reasonably foreseen by the board, that require immediate attention and possible action by the board, and that, of necessity, make it impracticable to provide notice.

(ii) Upon a determination made by the board by a vote of two-thirds of the members present at the meeting, or, if less than two-thirds of total membership of the board is present at the meeting, by a unanimous vote of the members present, that there is a need to take immediate action and that the need for action came to the attention of the board after the agenda was posted and distributed pursuant to subdivision (f).

(iii) The item appeared on an agenda that was posted and distributed pursuant to subdivision (f) for a prior meeting of the board of directors that occurred not more than 30 calendar days before the date that action is taken on the item and, at the prior meeting, action on the item was continued to the meeting at which the action is taken.

(B) Before discussing any item pursuant to this paragraph, the board of directors shall openly identify the item to the members in attendance at the meeting.

(j) As used in this section, "meeting" includes any congregation of a majority of the members of the board at the same time and place to hear, discuss, or deliberate upon any item of business scheduled to be heard by the board, except those matters that may be discussed in executive session.

Civ. Code § 1363.07. Membership Approval Required For Grant Of Exclusive Use Common Area; Exceptions.

(a) After an association acquires fee title to, or any easement right over, a common area, unless the association's governing documents specify a different percentage, the affirmative vote of members owning at least 67 percent of the separate interests in the common interest development shall be required before the board of directors may grant exclusive use of any portion of that common area to any member, except for any of the following:

(1) A reconveyance of all or any portion of that common area to the subdivider to enable the continuation of development that is in

substantial conformance with a detailed plan of phased development submitted to the Real Estate Commissioner with the application for a public report;

(2) Any grant of exclusive use that is in substantial conformance with a detailed plan of phased development submitted to the Real Estate Commissioner with the application for a public report or in accordance with the governing documents approved by the Real Estate Commissioner.

(3) Any grant of exclusive use that is for any of the following reasons:

(A) To eliminate or correct engineering errors in documents recorded with the county recorder or on file with a public agency or utility company.

(B) To eliminate or correct encroachments due to errors in construction of any improvements.

(C) To permit changes in the plan of development submitted to the Real Estate Commissioner in circumstances where the changes are the result of topography, obstruction, hardship, aesthetic considerations, or environmental conditions.

(D) To fulfill the requirement of a public agency.

(E) To transfer the burden of management and maintenance of any common area that is generally inaccessible and is not of general use to the membership at large of the association.

(F) Any grant in connection with an expressly zoned industrial or commercial development, or any grant within a subdivision of the type defined in Section 1373.

(b) Any measure placed before the members requesting that the board of directors grant exclusive use of any portion of the common area shall specify whether the association will receive any monetary consideration for the grant and whether the association or the transferee will be responsible for providing any insurance coverage for exclusive use of the common area.

Civ. Code § 1363.09. One Year Statute of Limitations - Action For Violation Of Article; Penalties; Small Claims Court Option.

(a) A member of an association may bring a civil action for declaratory or equitable relief for a violation of this article by an association of which he or she is a member, including, but not limited to, injunctive relief, restitution, or a combination thereof, within one year of the date the cause of action accrues. Upon a finding that the election procedures of this article, or the adoption of and adherence to rules provided by Article

4 (commencing with Section 1357.100) of Chapter 2, were not followed, a court may void any results of the election.

(b) A member who prevails in a civil action to enforce his or her rights pursuant to this article shall be entitled to reasonable attorney's fees and court costs, and the court may impose a civil penalty of up to five hundred dollars ($500) for each violation, except that each identical violation shall be subject to only one penalty if the violation affects each member of the association equally. A prevailing association shall not recover any costs, unless the court finds the action to be frivolous, unreasonable, or without foundation.

(c) A cause of action under Section 1363.03 with respect to access to association resources by a candidate or member advocating a point of view, the receipt of a ballot by a member, or the counting, tabulation, or reporting of, or access to, ballots for inspection and review after tabulation may be brought in small claims court if the amount of the demand does not exceed the jurisdiction of that court.

Managing Agents

Civ. Code § 1363.1. Prospective Managing Agent Disclosure.

(a) A prospective managing agent of a common interest development shall provide a written statement to the board of directors of the association of a common interest development as soon as practicable, but in no event more than 90 days, before entering into a management agreement which shall contain all of the following information concerning the managing agent:

(1) The names and business addresses of the owners or general partners of the managing agent. If the managing agent is a corporation, the written statement shall include the names and business addresses of the directors and officers and shareholders holding greater than 10 percent of the shares of the corporation.

(2) Whether or not any relevant licenses such as architectural design, construction, engineering, real estate, or accounting have been issued by this state and are currently held by the persons specified in paragraph (1). If a license is currently held by any of those persons, the statement shall contain the following information:

(A) What license is held.

(B) The dates the license is valid.

(C) The name of the licensee appearing on that license.

(3) Whether or not any relevant professional certifications or

designations such as architectural design, construction, engineering, real property management, or accounting are currently held by any of the persons specified in paragraph (1), including, but not limited to, a professional common interest development manager. If any certification or designation is held, the statement shall include the following information:

    (A) What the certification or designation is and what entity issued it.

    (B) The dates the certification or designation is valid.

    (C) The names in which the certification or designation is held.

  (b) As used in this section, a "managing agent" is a person or entity who, for compensation or in expectation of compensation, exercises control over the assets of a common interest development. A "managing agent" does not include either of the following:

    (1) A full-time employee of the association.

    (2) Any regulated financial institution operating within the normal course of its regulated business practice.

Civ. Code § 1363.2. Managing Agent Duties; Deposition Of Association Funds.

  (a) A managing agent of a common interest development who accepts or receives funds belonging to the association shall deposit all such funds that are not placed into an escrow account with a bank, savings association, or credit union, or into an account under the control of the association, into a trust fund account maintained by the managing agent in a bank, savings association, or credit union in this state. All funds deposited by the managing agent in the trust fund account shall be kept in this state in a financial institution, as defined in Section 31041 of the Financial Code, which is insured by the federal government, and shall be maintained there until dispersed in accordance with written instructions from the association entitled to the funds.

  (b) At the written request of the board of directors of the association, the funds the managing agent accepts or receives on behalf of the association shall be deposited into an interest-bearing account in a bank, savings association, or credit union in this state, provided all of the following requirements are met:

    (1) The account is in the name of the managing agent as trustee for the association or in the name of the association.

    (2) All of the funds in the account are covered by insurance provided by an agency of the federal government.

(3) The funds in the account are kept separate, distinct, and apart from the funds belonging to the managing agent or to any other person or entity for whom the managing agent holds funds in trust except that the funds of various associations may be commingled as permitted pursuant to subdivision (d).

(4) The managing agent discloses to the board of directors of the association the nature of the account, how interest will be calculated and paid, whether service charges will be paid to the depository and by whom, and any notice requirements or penalties for withdrawal of funds from the account.

(5) No interest earned on funds in the account shall inure directly or indirectly to the benefit of the managing agent or his or her employees.

(c) The managing agent shall maintain a separate record of the receipt and disposition of all funds described in this section, including any interest earned on the funds.

(d) The managing agent shall not commingle the funds of the association with his or her own money or with the money of others that he or she receives or accepts, unless all of the following requirements are met:

(1) The managing agent commingled the funds of various associations on or before February 26, 1990, and has obtained a written agreement with the board of directors of each association that he or she will maintain a fidelity and surety bond in an amount that provides adequate protection to the associations as agreed upon by the managing agent and the board of directors of each association.

(2) The managing agent discloses in the written agreement whether he or she is deriving benefits from the commingled account or the bank, credit union, or savings institution where the monies will be on deposit.

(3) The written agreement provided pursuant to this subdivision includes, but is not limited to, the name and address of the bonding companies, the amount of the bonds, and the expiration dates of the bonds.

(4) If there are any changes in the bond coverage or the companies providing the coverage, the managing agent discloses that fact to the board of directors of each affected association as soon as practical, but in no event more than 10 days after the change.

(5) The bonds assure the protection of the association and provide the association at least 10 days' notice prior to cancellation.

(6) Completed payments on the behalf of the association are deposited within 24 hours or the next business day and do not remain commingled for more than 10 calendar days.

(e) The prevailing party in an action to enforce this section shall be entitled to recover reasonable legal fees and court costs.

(f) As used in this section, a "managing agent" is a person or entity, who for compensation or, in expectation of compensation, exercises control over the assets of the association. However, a "managing agent" does not include a full-time employee of the association or a regulated financial institution operating within the normal course of business, or an attorney at law acting within the scope of his or her license.

(g) As used in this section, "completed payment" means funds received which clearly identify the account to which the funds are to be credited.

Public Information

Civ. Code § 1363.5. Articles Of Incorporation Disclosure Statement.

(a) The articles of incorporation of a common interest development association filed with the Secretary of State on or after January 1, 1995, shall include a statement, which shall be in addition to the statement of purposes of the corporation, that does all of the following:

(1) Identifies the corporation as an association formed to manage a common interest development under the Davis-Stirling Common Interest Development Act.

(2) States the business or corporate office of the association, if any, and, if the office is not on the site of the common interest development, states the nine-digit ZIP Code, front street, and nearest cross street for the physical location of the common interests development.

(3) States the name and address of the association's managing agent, as defined in Section 1363.1, if any.

(b) The statement of principal business activity contained in the annual statement filed by an incorporated association with the Secretary of State pursuant to Section 1502 of the Corporations Code shall also contain the statement specified in subdivision (a).

Civ. Code § 1363.6. Association Information Statement Submitted To Secretary Of State; Penalty For Non-Compliance.

(a) To assist with the identification of common interest developments, each association, whether incorporated or unincorporated, shall submit to the Secretary of State, on a form and for a fee not to exceed thirty dollars ($30) that the Secretary of State shall prescribe, the following information concerning the association and the development that it manages:

    (1) A statement that the association is formed to manage a common interest development under the Davis-Stirling Common Interest Development Act.

    (2) The name of the association.

    (3) The street address of the association's onsite office, or, if none, of the responsible officer or managing agent of the association.

    (4) The name, address and either the daytime telephone number or e-mail address of the president of the association, other than the address, telephone number, or e-mail address of the association's onsite office or managing agent of the association.

    (5) The name, street address, and daytime telephone number of the association's managing agent, if any.

    (6) The county, and if in an incorporated area, the city in which the development is physically located. If the boundaries of the development are physically located in more than one county, each of the counties in which it is located.

    (7) If the development is in an unincorporated area, the city closest in proximity to the development.

    (8) The nine-digit ZIP Code, front street, and nearest cross street of the physical location of the development.

    (9) The type of common interest development, as defined in subdivision (c) of Section 1351, managed by the association.

    (10) The number of separate interests, as defined in subdivision (l) of Section 1351, in the development.

  (b) The association shall submit the information required by this section as follows:

    (1) By incorporated associations, within 90 days after the filing of its original articles of incorporation, and thereafter at the time the association files its biennial statement of principal business activity with the Secretary of State pursuant to Section 8210 of the Corporations Code.

    (2) By unincorporated associations, in July of 2003, and in that same month biennially thereafter. Upon changing its status to that of a corporation, the association shall comply with the filing deadlines in paragraph (1).

  (c) The association shall notify the Secretary of State of any change in the street address of the association's onsite office or of the responsible officer or managing agent of the association in the form and for a fee prescribed by the Secretary of State, within 60 days of the change.

(d) On and after January 1, 2006, the penalty for an incorporated association's noncompliance with the initial or biennial filing requirements of this section shall be suspension of the association's rights, privileges, and powers as a corporation and monetary penalties, to the same extent and in the same manner as suspension and monetary penalties imposed pursuant to Section 8810 of the Corporations Code.

(e) The Secretary of State shall make the information submitted pursuant to paragraph (4) of subdivision (a) available only for governmental purposes and only to Members of the Legislature and the Business, Transportation and Housing Agency, upon written request. All other information submitted pursuant to this section shall be subject to public inspection pursuant to the California Public Records Act, Chapter 3.5 (commencing with Section 6250) of Division 7 of Title 1 of the Government Code. The information submitted pursuant to this section shall be made available for governmental or public inspection, as the case may be, on or before July 1, 2004, and thereafter.

Dispute Resolution Procedures

Civ. Code § 1363.810. Application Of Article.

(a) This article applies to a dispute between an association and a member involving their rights, duties, or liabilities under this title, under the Nonprofit Mutual Benefit Corporation Law (Part 3 (commencing with Section 7110) of Division 2 of Title 1 of the Corporations Code), or under the governing documents of the common interest development or association.

(b) This article supplements, and does not replace, Article 2 (commencing with Section 1369.510) of Chapter 7, relating to alternative dispute resolution as a prerequisite to an enforcement action.

Civ. Code § 1363.820. Dispute Resolution Procedure Required.

(a) An association shall provide a fair, reasonable, and expeditious procedure for resolving a dispute within the scope of this article.

(b) In developing a procedure pursuant to this article, an association shall make maximum, reasonable use of available local dispute resolution programs involving a neutral third party, including low-cost mediation programs such as those listed on the Internet Web sites of the Department of Consumer Affairs and the United States Department of Housing and

Urban Development.

(c) If an association does not provide a fair, reasonable, and expeditious procedure for resolving a dispute within the scope of this article, the procedure provided in Section 1363.840 applies and satisfies the requirement of subdivision (a).

Civ. Code § 1363.830. Dispute Resolution Procedure Minimum Requirements.

A fair, reasonable, and expeditious dispute resolution procedure shall at a minimum satisfy all of the following requirements:

(a) The procedure may be invoked by either party to the dispute. A request invoking the procedure shall be in writing.

(b) The procedure shall provide for prompt deadlines. The procedure shall state the maximum time for the association to act on a request invoking the procedure.

(c) If the procedure is invoked by a member, the association shall participate in the procedure.

(d) If the procedure is invoked by the association, the member may elect not to participate in the procedure. If the member participates but the dispute is resolved other than by agreement of the member, the member shall have a right of appeal to the association's board of directors.

(e) A resolution of a dispute pursuant to the procedure, that is not in conflict with the law or the governing documents, binds the association and is judicially enforceable. An agreement reached pursuant to the procedure, that is not in conflict with the law or the governing documents, binds the parties and is judicially enforceable.

(f) The procedure shall provide a means by which the member and the association may explain their positions.

(g) A member of the association shall not be charged a fee to participate in the process.

Civ. Code § 1363.840. Statutory Dispute Resolution Procedure.

(a) This section applies in an association that does not otherwise provide a fair, reasonable, and expeditious dispute resolution procedure. The procedure provided in this section is fair, reasonable, and expeditious, within the meaning of this article.

(b) Either party to a dispute within the scope of this article may invoke the following procedure:

(1) The party may request the other party to meet and confer in an effort to resolve the dispute. The request shall be in writing.

(2) A member of an association may refuse a request to meet and confer. The association may not refuse a request to meet and confer.

(3) The association's board of directors shall designate a member of the board to meet and confer.

(4) The parties shall meet promptly at a mutually convenient time and place, explain their positions to each other, and confer in good faith in an effort to resolve the dispute.

(5) A resolution of the dispute agreed to by the parties shall be memorialized in writing and signed by the parties, including the board designee on behalf of the association.

(c) An agreement reached under this section binds the parties and is judicially enforceable if both of the following conditions are satisfied:

(1) The agreement is not in conflict with law or the governing documents of the common interest development or association.

(2) The agreement is either consistent with the authority granted by the board of directors to its designee or the agreement is ratified by the board of directors.

(d) A member of the association may not be charged a fee to participate in the process.

Civ. Code § 1363.850. Notice Of Dispute Resolution Procedure.

The notice provided pursuant to Section 1369.590 shall include a description of the internal dispute resolution process provided pursuant to this article.

OPERATIONS
Common Areas

Civ. Code § 1364. Responsibility For Maintenance Of Common Area; Damage By Wood-Destroying Pests Or Organisms; Relocation Costs; Notice Of Repair; Access To Telephone Wiring.

(a) Unless otherwise provided in the declaration of a common interest development, the association is responsible for repairing, replacing, or maintaining the common areas, other than exclusive use common area, and the owner of each separate interest is responsible for maintaining that separate interest and any exclusive use common area appurtenant to the separate interest.

(b) (1) In a community apartment project, condominium project, or stock cooperative, as defined in Section 1351, unless otherwise provided in the declaration, the association is responsible for the repair and maintenance of the common area occasioned by the presence of wood-destroying pests or organisms.

(2) In a planned development as defined in Section 1351, unless a different maintenance scheme is provided in the declaration, each owner of a separate interest is responsible for the repair and maintenance of that separate interest as may be occasioned by the presence of wood-destroying pests or organisms. Upon approval of the majority of all members of the association, the responsibility for such repair and maintenance may be delegated to the association, which shall be entitled to recover the cost thereof as a special assessment.

(c) The costs of temporary relocation during the repair and maintenance of the areas within the responsibility of the association shall be borne by the owner of the separate interest affected.

(d) (1) The association may cause the temporary, summary removal of any occupant of a common interest development for such periods and at such times as may be necessary for prompt, effective treatment of wood-destroying pests or organisms.

(2) The association shall give notice of the need to temporarily vacate a separate interest to the occupants and to the owners, not less than 15 days nor more than 30 days prior to the date of the temporary relocation. The notice shall state the reason for the temporary relocation, the date and time of the beginning of treatment, the anticipated date and time of termination of treatment, and that the occupants will be responsible for their own accommodations during the temporary relocation.

(3) Notice by the association shall be deemed complete upon either:

(A) Personal delivery of a copy of the notice to the occupants, and sending a copy of the notice to the owners, if different than the occupants, by first-class mail, postage prepaid at the most current address shown on the books of the association.

(B) By sending a copy of the notice to the occupants at the separate interest address and a copy of the notice to the owners, if different than the occupants, by first-class mail, postage prepaid, at the most current address shown on the books of the association.

(e) For purposes of this section, "occupant" means an owner, resident, guest, invitee, tenant, lessee, sublessee, or other person in possession of the separate interest.

(f) Notwithstanding the provisions of the declaration, the owner of a separate interest is entitled to reasonable access to the common areas for the purpose of maintaining the internal and external telephone wiring made part of the exclusive use common areas of a separate interest pursuant to paragraph (2) of subdivision (1) of Section 1351. The access shall be subject to the consent of the association, whose approval shall not be unreasonably withheld, and which may include the association's approval of telephone wiring upon the exterior of the common areas, and other conditions as the association determines reasonable.

Fiscal Matters

Civ. Code § 1365. Financial Documents.

Unless the governing documents impose more stringent standards, the association shall prepare and distribute to all of its members the following documents:

(a) A *pro forma* operating budget, which shall include all of the following:

(1) The estimated revenue and expenses on an accrual basis.

(2) A summary of the association's reserves based upon the most recent review or study conducted pursuant to Section 1365.5, based only on assets held in cash or cash equivalents, which shall be printed in boldface type and include all of the following:

(A) The current estimated replacement cost, estimated remaining life, and estimated useful life of each major component.

(B) As of the end of the fiscal year for which the study is prepared:

(i) The current estimate of the amount of cash reserves necessary to repair, replace, restore, or maintain the major components.

(ii) The current amount of accumulated cash reserves actually set aside to repair, replace, restore, or maintain major components.

(iii) If applicable, the amount of funds received from either a compensatory damage award or settlement to an association from any person or entity for injuries to property, real or personal, arising out of any construction or design defects, and the expenditure or disposition of funds, including the amounts expended for the direct and indirect costs of repair of construction or design defects. These amounts shall be reported at the end of the fiscal year for which the study is prepared as separate line items under cash reserves pursuant to clause (ii). Instead of complying with the requirements set forth in this clause, an association that is obligated to issue a review of their financial statement pursuant to subdivision (b) may include in the review a statement containing all of the information required by this clause.

(C) The percentage that the amount determined for purposes of clause (ii) subparagraph (B) equals the amount determined for purposes of clause (i) of subparagraph (B).

(D) The current deficiency in reserve funding expressed on a per unit basis. The figure shall be calculated by subtracting the amount determined for purposes of clause (ii) of subparagraph (B) from the amount determined for purposes of clause (i) of subparagraph (B) and then dividing the result by the number of separate interests within the association, except that if assessments vary by the size or type of ownership interest, then the association shall calculate the current deficiency in a manner that reflects the variation.

(3) A statement as to all of the following:

(A) Whether the board of directors of the association has determined to defer or not undertake repairs or replacement of any major component with a remaining life of 30 years or less, including a justification for the deferral or decision not to undertake the repairs or replacement.

(B) Whether the board of directors of the association, consistent with the reserve funding plan adopted pursuant to subdivision (e) of Section 1365.5, has determined or anticipates that the levy of one or more special assessments will be required to repair, replace, or restore any major component or to provide adequate reserves therefor. If so, the statement shall also set out the estimated amount, commencement date, and duration of the assessment.

(C) The mechanism or mechanisms by which the board of directors will fund reserves to repair or replace major components, including assessments, borrowing, use of other assets, deferral of selected replacements or repairs, or alternative mechanisms.

(D) Whether the association has any outstanding loans with an original term of more than one year, including the payee, interest rate, amount outstanding, annual payment, and when the loan is scheduled to be retired.

(4) A general statement addressing the procedures used for the calculation and establishment of those reserves to defray the future repair, replacement, or additions to those major components that the association is obligated to maintain. The report shall include, but need not be limited to, reserve calculations made using the formula described in paragraph (4) of subdivision (b) of Section 1365.2.5, and may not assume a rate

of return on cash reserves in excess of 2 percent above the discount rate published by the Federal Reserve Bank of San Francisco at the time the calculation was made.

The summary of the association's reserves disclosed pursuant to paragraph (2) shall not be admissible in evidence to show improper financial management of an association, provided that other relevant and competent evidence of the financial condition of the association is not made inadmissible by this provision.

Notwithstanding a contrary provision in the governing documents, a copy of the operating budget shall be annually distributed not less than 30 days nor more than 90 days prior to the beginning of the association's fiscal year.

(b) Commencing January 1, 2009, a summary of the reserve funding plan adopted by the board of directors of the association, as specified in paragraph (4) of subdivision (e) of Section 1365.5. The summary shall include notice to members that the full reserve study plan is available upon request, and the association shall provide the full reserve plan to any member upon request.

(c) A review of the financial statement of the association shall be prepared in accordance with generally accepted accounting principles by a licensee of the California Board of Accountancy for any fiscal year in which the gross income to the association exceeds seventy-five thousand dollars ($75,000). A copy of the review of the financial statement shall be distributed within 120 days after the close of each fiscal year.

(d) Instead of the distribution of the pro forma operating budget required by subdivision (a), the board of directors may elect to distribute a summary of the pro forma operating budget to all of its members with a written notice that the pro forma operating budget is available at the business office of the association or at another suitable location within the boundaries of the development, and that copies will be provided upon request and at the expense of the association. If any member requests that a copy of the pro forma operating budget required by subdivision (a) be mailed to the member, the association shall provide the copy to the member by first-class United States mail at the expense of the association and delivered within five days. The written notice that is distributed to each of the association members shall be in at least 10-point boldface type on the front page of the summary of the budget.

(e) A statement describing the association's policies and practices in enforcing lien rights or other legal remedies for default in payment of its assessments against its members shall be annually delivered to the members not less than 30 days nor more than 90 days immediately preceding the beginning of the association's fiscal year.

(f) (1) A summary of the association's property, general liability, and earthquake, flood and fidelity insurance policies, which shall be distributed not less than 30 days nor more than 90 days preceding the beginning of the association's fiscal year, that includes all of the following information about each policy:

(A) The name of the insurer.

(B) The type of insurance.

(C) The policy limits of the insurance.

(D) The amount of deductibles, if any.

(2) The association shall, as soon as reasonably practicable, notify its members by first-class mail if any of the policies described in paragraph (1) have lapsed, been canceled, and are not immediately renewed, restored, or replaced, or if there is a significant change, such as a reduction in coverage or limits or an increase in the deductible, as to any of those policies. If the association receives any notice of nonrenewal of a policy described in paragraph (1), the association shall immediately notify its members if replacement coverage will not be in effect by the date the existing coverage will lapse.

(3) To the extent that any of the information required to be disclosed pursuant to paragraph (1) is specified in the insurance policy declaration page, the association may meet its obligation to disclose that information by making copies of that page and distributing it to all of its members.

(4) The summary distributed pursuant to paragraph (1) shall contain, in at least 10-point boldface type, the following statement: "This summary of the association's policies of insurance provides only certain information, as required by subdivision (f) of Section 1365 of the Civil Code, and should not be considered a substitute for the complete policy terms and conditions contained in the actual policies of insurance. Any association member may, upon request and provision of reasonable notice, review the association's insurance policies and, upon request and payment of reasonable duplication charges, obtain copies of those policies. Although the association maintains the policies of insurance specified in this summary, the association's policies of insurance may not cover your property, including personal property or, real property improvements to or around your dwelling, or personal injuries or other losses that occur within or around your dwelling. Even if a loss is covered, you may nevertheless be responsible for paying all or a portion of any deductible

that applies. Association members should consult with their individual insurance broker or agent for appropriate additional coverage."

Civ. Code § 1365.1. Distribution Of Written Notice of Assessments, Foreclosure, And Payment Plans.

(a) The association shall distribute the written notice described in subdivision (b) to each member of the association during the 60-day period immediately preceding the beginning of the association's fiscal year. The notice shall be printed in at least 12-point type. An association distributing the notice to an owner of an interest that is described in Section 11212 of the Business and Professions Code that is not otherwise exempt from this section pursuant to subdivision (a) of Section 11211.7, may delete from the notice described in subdivision (b) the portion regarding meetings and payment plans.

(b) The notice required by this section shall read as follows:

"NOTICE ASSESSMENTS AND FORECLOSURE

This notice outlines some of the rights and responsibilities of owners of property in common interest developments and the associations that manage them. Please refer to the sections of the Civil Code indicated for further information. A portion of the information in this notice applies only to liens recorded on or after January 1, 2003. You may wish to consult a lawyer if you dispute an assessment.

ASSESSMENTS AND FORECLOSURE

Assessments become delinquent 15 days after they are due, unless the governing documents provide for a longer time. The failure to pay association assessments may result in the loss of an owner's property through foreclosure. Foreclosure may occur either as a result of a court action, known as judicial foreclosure or without court action, often referred to as nonjudicial foreclosure. For liens recorded on and after January 1, 2006, an association may not use judicial or nonjudicial foreclosure to enforce that lien if the amount of the delinquent assessments or dues, exclusive of any accelerated assessments, late charges, fees, attorney's fees, interest, and costs of collection, is less than one thousand eight hundred dollars ($1,800). For delinquent assessments or dues in excess of one thousand eight hundred dollars ($1,800) or more than 12 months delinquent, an association may use judicial or nonjudicial foreclosure subject to the conditions set forth in Section 1367.4 of the Civil Code.

When using judicial or nonjudicial foreclosure, the association records a lien on the owner's property. The owner's property may be sold to satisfy the lien if the amounts secured by the lien are not paid. (Sections 1366, 1367.1, and 1367.4 of the Civil Code)

In a judicial or nonjudicial foreclosure, the association may recover assessments, reasonable costs of collection, reasonable attorney's fees, late charges, and interest. The association may not use nonjudicial foreclosure to collect fines or penalties, except for costs to repair common areas damaged by a member or a member's guests, if the governing documents provide for this. (Sections 1366 and 1367.1 of the Civil Code)

The association must comply with the requirements of Section 1367.1 of the Civil Code when collecting delinquent assessments. If the association fails to follow these requirements, it may not record a lien on the owner's property until it has satisfied those requirements. Any additional costs that result from satisfying the requirements are the responsibility of the association. (Section 1367.1 of the Civil Code)

At least 30 days prior to recording a lien on an owner's separate interest, the association must provide the owner of record with certain documents by certified mail, including a description of its collection and lien enforcement procedures and the method of calculating the amount. It must also provide an itemized statement of the charges owed by the owner. An owner has a right to review the association's records to verify the debt. (Section 1367.1 of the Civil Code)

If a lien is recorded against an owner's property in error, the person who recorded the lien is required to record a lien release within 21 days, and to provide an owner certain documents in this regard. (Section 1367.1 of the Civil Code)

The collection practices of the association may be governed by state and federal laws regarding fair debt collection. Penalties can be imposed for debt collection practices that violate these laws.

PAYMENTS

When an owner makes a payment, he or she may request a receipt, and the association is required to provide it. On the receipt, the association must indicate the date of payment and the person who received it. The association must inform owners of a mailing address for overnight payments. (Sections 1367.1 of the Civil Code)

An owner may, but is not obligated to, pay under protest any disputed charge or sum levied by the association, including, but not limited to, an assessment, fine, penalty, late fee, collection cost, or monetary penalty imposed as a disciplinary measure, and by so doing, specifically reserve the right to contest the disputed charge or sum in court or otherwise.

An owner may dispute an assessment debt by submitting a written request for dispute resolution to the association as set forth in Article 5 (commencing with Section 1363.810) of Chapter 4 of Title 6 of Division 2 of the Civil Code. In addition, an association may not initiate a foreclosure without participating in alternative dispute resolution with a neutral third party as set forth in Article 2 (commencing with Section 1369.510) of Chapter 7 of Title 6 of Division 2 of the Civil Code, if so requested by the owner. Binding arbitration shall not be available if the association intends to initiate a judicial foreclosure.

An owner is not liable for charges, interest, and costs of collection, if it is established that the assessment was paid properly on time. (Section 1367.1 of the Civil Code)

MEETINGS AND PAYMENT PLANS

An owner of a separate interest that is not a timeshare may request the association to consider a payment plan to satisfy a delinquent assessment. The association must inform owners of the standards for payment plans, if any exist. (Section 1367.1 of the Civil Code)

The board of the directors must meet with an owner who makes a proper written request for a meeting to discuss a payment plan when the owner has received a notice of a delinquent assessment. These payment plans must conform with the payment plan standards of the association, if they exist. (Section 1367.1 of the Civil Code)"

(c) A member of an association may provide written notice by facsimile transmission or United States mail to the association of a secondary address. If a secondary address is provided, the association shall send any and all correspondence and legal notices required pursuant to this article to both the primary and the secondary address.

Civ. Code § 1365.2. Right To Inspect And Copy Association Records; Restriction On Use; Cost Of Production; Redaction Of Information To Prevent Identity Theft; Penalties For Non-Compliance.

(a) For the purposes of this section, the following definitions shall apply:

(1) "Association records" means all of the following:

(A) Any financial document required to be provided to a member in Section 1365.

(B) Any financial document or statement required to be provided in Section 1368.

(C) Interim financial statements, periodic or as compiled, containing any of the following:

(i) Balance sheet.

(ii) Income and expense statement.

(iii) Budget comparison.

(iv) General ledger. A "general ledger" is a report that shows all transactions that occurred in an association account over a specified period of time. The records described in this subparagraph shall be prepared in accordance with an accrual or modified accrual basis of accounting.

(D) Executed contracts not otherwise privileged under law.

(E) Written board approval of vendor or contractor proposals or invoices.

(F) State and federal tax returns.

(G) Reserve account balances and records of payments made from reserve accounts.

(H) Agendas and minutes of meetings of the members, the board of directors and any committees appointed by the board of directors pursuant to Section 7212 of the Corporations Code; excluding, however, agendas, minutes, and other information from executive sessions of the board of directors as described in Section 1363.05.

(I) (i) Membership lists, including name, property address, and mailing address, if the conditions set forth in clause (ii) are met and except as otherwise provided in clause (iii).

(ii) The member requesting the list shall state the purpose for which the list is requested which purpose shall be reasonably related to the requester's interest as a member. If the association reasonably believes that the information in the list will be used for another purpose, it may deny the member access to the list. If the request is denied, in any subsequent action brought by the member under subdivision (f), the association shall have the burden to prove that the member would have allowed use of the information for purposes unrelated to his or her interest as a member.

(iii) A member of the association may opt out of the sharing of his or her name, property address, and mailing address by notifying the association in writing that he or she prefers to be contacted via the alternative process described in subdivision (c) of Section 8330 of the Corporations Code. This opt-out shall remain in effect until changed by the member.

(J) Check registers.

(2) "Enhanced association records" means invoices, receipts and canceled checks for payments made by the association, purchase orders approved by the association, credit card statements for credit cards issued in the name of the association, statements for services rendered, and reimbursement requests submitted to the association, provided that the person submitting the reimbursement request shall be solely responsible for removing all personal identification information from the request.

(b) (1) The association shall make available association records and enhanced association records for the time periods and within the timeframes provided in subdivisions (i) and (j) for inspection and copying by a member of the association, or the member's designated representative. The association may bill the requesting member for the direct and actual cost of copying requested documents. The association shall inform the member of the amount of the copying costs before copying the requested documents.

(2) A member of the association may designate another person to inspect and copy the specified association records on the member's behalf. The member shall make this designation in writing.

(c) (1) The association shall make the specified association records available for inspection and copying in the association's business office within the common interest development.

(2) If the association does not have a business office within the development, the association shall make the specified association records available for inspection and copying at a place that the requesting member and the association agree upon.

(3) If the association and the requesting member cannot agree upon a place for inspection and copying pursuant to paragraph (2), or if the requesting member submits a written request directly to the association for copies of specifically identified records, the association may satisfy the requirement to make the association records available for inspection and copying by mailing copies of the specifically identified records to the member by first-class mail within the timeframes set forth in subdivision (j).

(4) The association may bill the requesting member for the direct and actual cost of copying and mailing requested documents. The association shall inform the member of the amount of the copying and mailing costs, and the member shall agree to pay those costs, before copying and sending the requested documents.

(5) In addition to the direct and actual costs of copying and mailing, the association may bill the requesting member an amount not in excess of ten dollars ($10) per hour, and not to exceed two hundred dollars ($200) total per written request, for the time actually and reasonably involved in redacting the enhanced association records as provided in paragraph (2) of subdivision (a). The association shall inform the member of the estimated costs, and the member shall agree to pay those costs, before retrieving the requested documents.

(d) (1) Except as provided in paragraph (2), the association may withhold or redact information from the association records for any of the following reasons:

(A) The release of the information is reasonably likely to lead to identity theft. For the purposes of this section, "identity theft" means the unauthorized use of another person's personal identifying information to obtain credit, goods, services, money, or property. Examples of information that may be withheld or redacted pursuant to this paragraph include bank account numbers of members or vendors, social security or tax identification numbers, and check, stock, and credit card numbers.

(B) The release of the information is reasonably likely to lead to fraud in connection with the association.

(C) The information is privileged under law. Examples include documents subject to attorney-client privilege or relating to litigation in which the association is or may become involved, and confidential settlement agreements.

(D) The release of the information is reasonably likely to compromise the privacy of an individual member of the association.

(E) The information contains any of the following:

(i) Records of a-la-carte goods or services provided to individual members of the association for which the association received monetary consideration other than assessments.

(ii) Records of disciplinary actions, collection activities, or payment plans of members other than the member requesting the records.

(iii) Any person's personal identification information, including, without limitation, social security number, tax identification number, driver's license number, credit card account numbers, bank account number, and bank routing number.

(iv) Agendas, minutes, and other information from executive sessions of the board of directors as described in Section 1363.05, except for executed contracts not otherwise privileged. Privileged contracts shall not include contracts for maintenance, management, or legal services.

(v) Personnel records other than the payroll records required to be provided under paragraph (2).

(vi) Interior architectural plans, including security features, for individual homes.

(2) Except as provided by the attorney-client privilege, the association may not withhold or redact information concerning the compensation paid to employees, vendors, or contractors. Compensation information for individual employees shall be set forth by job classification or title, not by the employee's name, social security number, or other personal information.

(3) No association, officer, director, employee, agent or volunteer of an association shall be liable for damages to a member of the association or any third party as the result of identity theft or other breach of privacy because of the failure to withhold or redact that member's information under this subdivision unless the failure to withhold or redact the information was intentional, willful, or negligent.

(4) If requested by the requesting member, an association that denies or redacts records shall provide a written explanation specifying the legal basis for withholding or redacting the requested records.

(e) (1) The association records, and any information from them, may not be sold, used for a commercial purpose, or used for any other purpose not reasonably related to a member's interest as a member. An association may bring an action against any person who violates this section for injunctive relief and for actual damages to the association caused by the violation.

(2) This section may not be construed to limit the right of an association to damages for misuse of information obtained from the association records pursuant to this section or to limit the right of an association to injunctive relief to stop the misuse of this information.

(3) An association shall be entitled to recover reasonable costs and expenses, including reasonable attorney's fees, in a successful action to enforce its rights under this section.

(f) A member of an association may bring an action to enforce the member's right to inspect and copy the association records. If a court finds that the association unreasonably withheld access to the association records, the court shall award the member reasonable costs and expenses, including reasonable attorney's fees, and may assess a civil penalty of up to five hundred dollars ($500) for the denial of each separate written request. A cause of action under this section may be brought in small claims court if the amount of the demand does not exceed the jurisdiction of that court. A prevailing association may recover any costs if the court finds the action to be frivolous, unreasonable, or without foundation.

(g) The provisions of this section apply to any community service organization or similar entity, as defined in paragraph (3) of subdivision (c) of Section 1368, that is related to the association, *and to any nonprofit entity that provides services to a common interest development under a declaration of trust.* This section shall operate to give a member of the organization or entity a right to inspect and copy the records of that organization or entity equivalent to that granted to association members by this section.

(h) Requesting parties shall have the option of receiving specifically identified records by electronic transmission or machine-readable storage media as long as those records can be transmitted in a redacted format that does not allow the records to be altered. The cost of duplication shall be limited to the direct cost of producing the copy of a record in that electronic format. The association may deliver specifically indentified records by electronic transmission or machine-readable storage media as long as those records can be transmitted in a redacted format that prevents the records from being altered.

(i) The time periods for which specified records shall be provided is as follows:

(1) Association records shall be made available for the current fiscal year and for each of the previous two fiscal years.

(2) Minutes of member and board meetings shall be permanently made available. If a committee has decisionmaking authority, minutes of the meetings of that committee shall be made available commencing January 1, 2007, and shall thereafter be permanently made available.

(j) The timeframes in which access to specified records shall be provided to a requesting member are as follows:

(1) Association records prepared during the current fiscal year, within 10 business days following the association's receipt of the request.

(2) Association records prepared during the previous two fiscal years, within 30 calendar days following the association's receipt of the request.

(3) Any record or statement available pursuant to Section 1365 or 1368, within the timeframe specified therein.

(4) Minutes of member and board meetings, within the timeframe specified in subdivision (d) of Section 1363.05.

(5) Minutes of meetings of committees with decisionmaking authority for meetings commencing on or after January 1, 2007, within 15 calendar days following approval.

(6) Membership list, within the timeframe specified in Section 8330 of the Corporations Code.

(k) There shall be no liability pursuant to this section for an association that fails to retain records for the periods specified in subdivision (i) that were created prior to January 1, 2006.

(l) As applied to an association and its members, the provisions of this section are intended to supersede the provisions of Sections 8330 and 8333 of the Corporations Code to the extent those sections are inconsistent.

(m) The provisions of this section shall not apply to any common interest development in which separate interests are being offered for sale by a subdivider under the authority of a public report issued by the Department of Real Estate so long as the subdivider or all subdividers offering those separate interests for sale, or any employees of those subdividers or any other person who receives direct or indirect compensation from any of those subdividers, comprise a majority of the members of the board of directors of the association. Notwithstanding the foregoing, this section shall apply to that common interest development no later than 10 years after the close of escrow for the first sale of a separate interest to a member of the general public pursuant to the public report issued for the first phase of the development.

(n) This section shall become operative on July 1, 2006.

Civ. Code § 1365.2.5. Assessment And Reserve Funding Disclosure Summary.

(a) The disclosures required by this article with regard to an association or a property shall be summarized on the following form:

Assessment and Reserve Funding Disclosure Summary For the Fiscal Year Ending _____

(1) The current regular assessment per ownership interest is $_____ per _____. Note: If assessments vary by the size or type of ownership interest, the assessment applicable to this ownership interest may be found on page _____ of the attached summary.

(2) Additional regular or special assessments that have already been scheduled to be imposed or charged, regardless of the purpose, if they have been approved by the board and/or members:

Date assessment will be due:	Amount per ownership interest per month or year (If assessments are variable, see note immediately below):	Purpose of the assessment:
_____	_____	_____
_____	_____	_____
_____	_____	_____
_____	_____	_____
	Total: _____	

Note: If assessments vary by the size or type of ownership interest, the assessment applicable to this ownership interest may be found on page ____ of the attached report.

(3) Based upon the most recent reserve study and other information available to the board of directors, will currently projected reserve account balances be sufficient at the end of each year to meet the association's obligation for repair and/or replacement of major components during the next 30 years?   Yes _____   No _____

(4) If the answer to (3) is no, what additional assessments or other contributions to reserves would be necessary to ensure that sufficient reserve funds will be available each year during the next 30 years that have not yet been approved by the board or the members?

Approximate date assessment will be due:	Amount per ownership interest per month or year:
_____	_____
_____	_____
_____	_____
	Total: _____

(5) All major components are included in the reserve study and are included in its calculations.

(6) Based on the method of calculation in paragraph (4) of subdivision (b) of Section 1365.2.5, the estimated amount required in the reserve fund at the end of the current fiscal year is $_____, based in whole or in part on the last reserve study or update prepared by ____ as of ____ (month), ____ (year). The projected reserve fund cash balance at the end of the current fiscal year is $____, resulting in reserves being ____ percent funded at this date. If an alternate, but generally accepted, method of calculation is also used, the required reserve amount is $_____. (See attached explanation.)

(7) Based on the method of calculation in paragraph (4) of subdivision (b) of Section 1365.2.5 of the Civil Code, the estimated amount required in the reserve fund at the end of each of the next five budget years is $_____, and the projected reserve fund cash balance in each of those years, taking into account only assessments already approved and other known revenues, is $_____, leaving the reserve at _____ percent

Civil

funding. If the reserve funding plan approved by the association is implemented, the projected reserve fund cash balance in each of those years will be $_____, leaving the reserve at _____ percent funding. Note: The financial representations set forth in this summary are based on the best estimates of the preparer at that time. The estimates are subject to change. At the time this summary was prepared, the assumed long-term before-tax interest rate earned on reserve funds was ____percent per year, and the assumed long-term inflation rate to be applied to major component repair and replacement costs was ____ percent per year.

(b) For the purposes of preparing a summary pursuant to this section:

(1) "Estimated remaining useful life" means the time reasonably calculated to remain before a major component will require replacement.

(2) "Major component" has the meaning used in Section 1365.5. Components with an estimated remaining useful life of more than 30 years may be included in a study as a capital asset or disregarded from the reserve calculation, so long as the decision is revealed in the reserve study report and reported in the Assessment and Reserve Funding Disclosure Summary.

(3) The form set out in subdivision (a) shall accompany each pro forma operating budget or summary thereof that is delivered pursuant to this article. The form may be supplemented or modified to clarify the information delivered, so long as the minimum information set out in subdivision (a) is provided.

(4) For the purpose of the report and summary, the amount of reserves needed to be accumulated for a component at a given time shall be computed as the current cost of replacement or repair multiplied by the number of years the component has been in service divided by the useful life of the component. This shall not be construed to require the board to fund reserves in accordance with this calculation.

Civ. Code § 1365.3. Association Report Required To Meet Standards Of Corp. Code § 5012.

Unless the governing documents impose more stringent standards, any community service organization as defined in paragraph (3) of subdivision (c) of Section 1368 whose funding from the association or its members exceeds 10 percent of the organization's annual budget shall prepare and distribute to the association a report that meets the requirements of Section 5012 of the Corporations Code, and that describes in detail administrative costs and identifies the payees of those costs in a manner consistent with the provisions of Section 1365.2. If the community service organization does not comply with the standards, the report shall disclose the noncompliance in detail. If a community service organization is responsible for the maintenance of major components for which an association would otherwise be responsible, the community service organization shall supply to the association the information regarding those components that the association would use to complete disclosures and reserve reports required under this article. An association may rely upon information received from a community service organization, and shall provide access to the information pursuant to the provisions of Section 1365.2.

Civ. Code § 1365.5. Board Of Directors; Duties; Reserve Accounts.

(a) Unless the governing documents impose more stringent standards, the board of directors of the association shall do all of the following:

(1) Review a current reconciliation of the association's operating accounts on at least a quarterly basis.

(2) Review a current reconciliation of the association's reserve accounts on at least a quarterly basis.

(3) Review, on at least a quarterly basis, the current year's actual reserve revenues and expenses compared to the current year's budget.

(4) Review the latest account statements prepared by the financial institutions where the association has its operating and reserve accounts.

(5) Review an income and expense statement for the association's operating and reserve accounts on at least a quarterly basis.

(b) The signatures of at least two persons, who shall be members of the association's board of directors, or one officer who is not a member of the board of directors and a member of the board of directors, shall be required for the withdrawal of moneys from the association's reserve accounts.

(c) (1) The board of directors shall not expend funds designated as reserve funds for any purpose other than the repair, restoration, replacement, or maintenance of, or litigation involving the repair, restoration, replacement, or maintenance of, major components that the association is obligated to repair, restore, replace, or maintain and for which the reserve fund was established.

(2) However, the board may authorize the temporary transfer of moneys from a reserve fund to the association's general operating fund to meet short-term cash-flow requirements or other expenses, if the board has provided notice of the intent to consider the transfer in a notice of

meeting, which shall be provided as specified in Section 1363.05. The notice shall include the reasons the transfer is needed, some of the options for repayment, and whether a special assessment may be considered. If the board authorizes the transfer, the board shall issue a written finding, recorded in the board's minutes, explaining the reasons that the transfer is needed, and describing when and how the money will be repaid to the reserve fund. The transferred funds shall be restored to the reserve fund within one year of the date of the initial transfer, except that the board may, after giving the same notice required for considering a transfer, and, upon making a finding supported by documentation that a temporary delay would be in the best interests of the common interest development, temporarily delay the restoration. The board shall exercise prudent fiscal management in maintaining the integrity of the reserve account, and shall, if necessary, levy a special assessment to recover the full amount of the expended funds within the time limits required by this section. This special assessment is subject to the limitation imposed by Section 1366. The board may, at its discretion, extend the date the payment on the special assessment is due. Any extension shall not prevent the board from pursuing any legal remedy to enforce the collection of an unpaid special assessment.

(d) When the decision is made to use reserve funds or to temporarily transfer moneys from the reserve fund to pay for litigation, the association shall notify the members of the association of that decision in the next available mailing to all members pursuant to Section 5016 of the Corporations Code, and of the availability of an accounting of those expenses. Unless the governing documents impose more stringent standards, the association shall make an accounting of expenses related to the litigation on at least a quarterly basis. The accounting shall be made available for inspection by members of the association at the association's office.

(e) At least once every three years, the board of directors shall cause to be conducted a reasonably competent and diligent visual inspection of the accessible areas of the major components that the association is obligated to repair, replace, restore, or maintain as part of a study of the reserve account requirements of the common interest development, if the current replacement value of the major components is equal to or greater than one-half of the gross budget of the association excluding the association's reserve account for that period. The board shall review this study, or cause it to be reviewed, annually and shall consider and implement necessary adjustments to the board's analysis of the reserve account requirements as a result of that review.

The study required by this subdivision shall at a minimum include:

(1) Identification of the major components that the association is obligated to repair, replace, restore, or maintain that, as of the date of the study, have a remaining useful life of less than 30 years.

(2) Identification of the probable remaining useful life of the components identified in paragraph (1) as of the date of the study.

(3) An estimate of the cost of repair, replacement, restoration, or maintenance of the components identified in paragraph (1).

(4) An estimate of the total annual contribution necessary to defray the cost to repair, replace, restore, or maintain the components identified in paragraph (1) during and at the end of their useful life, after subtracting total reserve funds as of the date of the study.

(5) A reserve funding plan that indicates how the association plans to fund the contribution identified in paragraph (4) to meet the association's obligation for the repair and replacement of all major components with an expected remaining life of 30 years or less, not including those components that the board has determined will not be replaced or repaired. The plan shall include a schedule of the date and amount of any change in regular or special assessments that would be needed to sufficiently fund the reserve funding plan. The plan shall be adopted by the board of directors at an open meeting before the membership of the association as described in Section 1363.05. If the board of directors determines that an assessment increase is necessary to fund the reserve funding plan, any increase shall be approved in a separate action of the board that is consistent with the procedure described in Section 1366.

(f) As used in this section, "reserve accounts" means both of the following:

(1) Moneys that the association's board of directors has identified for use to defray the future repair or replacement of, or additions to, those major components that the association is obligated to maintain.

(2) The funds received, and not yet expended or disposed of, from either a compensatory damage award or settlement to an association from any person or entity for injuries to property, real or personal, arising from any construction or design defects. These funds shall be separately itemized from funds described in paragraph (1).

(g) As used in this section, "reserve account requirements" means the estimated funds that the association's board of directors has determined are required to be available at a specified point in time to repair, replace, or restore those major components that the association is obligated to maintain.

(h) This section does not apply to an association that does not have a "common area" as defined in Section 1351.

Civ. Code § 1365.6. Application Of Corp. Code § 310.

Notwithstanding any other law, and regardless of whether an association is a corporation, as defined in Section 162 of the Corporations Code, the provisions of Section 310 of the Corporations Code shall apply to any contract or other transaction authorized, approved, or ratified by the board or a committee of the board.

Insurance

Civ. Code § 1365.7. Liability Of Volunteer Officer Or Director; Criteria; Limitations.

(a) A volunteer officer or volunteer director of an association, as defined in subdivision (a) of Section 1351, which manages a common interest development that is exclusively residential, shall not be personally liable in excess of the coverage of insurance specified in paragraph (4) to any person who suffers injury, including, but not limited to, bodily injury, emotional distress, wrongful death, or property damage or loss as a result of the tortious act or omission of the volunteer officer or volunteer director if all of the following criteria are met:

(1) The act or omission was performed within the scope of the officer's or director's association duties.

(2) The act or omission was performed in good faith.

(3) The act or omission was not willful, wanton, or grossly negligent.

(4) The association maintained and had in effect at the time the act or omission occurred and at the time a claim is made one or more policies of insurance which shall include coverage for (A) general liability of the association and (B) individual liability of officers and directors of the association for negligent acts or omissions in that capacity; provided, that both types of coverage are in the following minimum amount:

(A) At least five hundred thousand dollars ($500,000) if the common interest development consists of 100 or fewer separate interests.

(B) At least one million dollars ($1,000,000) if the common interest development consists of more than 100 separate interests.

(b) The payment of actual expenses incurred by a director or officer in the execution of the duties of that position does not affect the director's or officer's status as a volunteer within the meaning of this section.

(c) An officer or director who at the time of the act or omission was a declarant, as defined in subdivision (g) of Section 1351, or who received either direct or indirect compensation as an employee from the declarant, or from a financial institution that purchased a separate interest, as defined in subdivision (l) of Section 1351, at a judicial or nonjudicial foreclosure of a mortgage or deed of trust on real property, is not a volunteer for the purposes of this section.

(d) Nothing in this section shall be construed to limit the liability of the association for its negligent act or omission or for any negligent act or omission of an officer or director of the association.

(e) This section shall only apply to a volunteer officer or director who is a tenant of a separate interest in the common interest development or is an owner of no more than two separate interests in the common interest development.

(f) (1) For purposes of paragraph (1) of subdivision (a), the scope of the officer's or director's association duties shall include, but shall not be limited to, both of the following decisions:

(A) Whether to conduct an investigation of the common interest development for latent deficiencies prior to the expiration of the applicable statute of limitations.

(B) Whether to commence a civil action against the builder for defects in design or construction.

(2) It is the intent of the Legislature that this section clarify the scope of association duties to which the protections against personal liability in this section apply. It is not the intent of the Legislature that these clarifications be construed to expand, or limit, the fiduciary duties owed by the directors or officers.

Civ. Code § 1365.9. Liability For Common Areas; Action Against Association; Insurance Requirements.

(a) It is the intent of the Legislature to offer civil liability protection to owners of the separate interests in a common interest development that have common areas owned in tenancy-in-common if the association carries a certain level of prescribed insurance that covers a cause of action in tort.

(b) Any cause of action in tort against any owner of a separate interest arising solely by reason of an ownership interest as a tenant in common in the common area of a common interest development shall be brought only against the association and not against the individual owners of the separate interests, as defined in subdivision (l) of Section 1351, if both of the insurance requirements in paragraphs (1) and (2) are met:

(1) The association maintained and has in effect for this cause of action, one or more policies of insurance which include coverage for general liability of the association.

(2) The coverage described in paragraph (1) is in the following minimum amounts:

(A) At least two million dollars ($2,000,000) if the common interest development consists of 100 or fewer separate interests.

(B) At least three million dollars ($3,000,000) if the common interest development consists of more than 100 separate interests.

Assessments

Civ. Code § 1366. Regular And Special Assessments; Limitation On Increases; Delinquent Assessments; Interest.

(a) Except as provided in this section, the association shall levy regular and special assessments sufficient to perform its obligations under the governing documents and this title. However, annual increases in regular assessments for any fiscal year, as authorized by subdivision (b), shall not be imposed unless the board has complied with subdivision (a) of Section 1365 with respect to that fiscal year, or has obtained the approval of owners, constituting a quorum, casting a majority of the votes at a meeting or election of the association conducted in accordance with Chapter 5 (commencing with Section 7510) of Part 3 of Division 2 of Title 1 of the Corporations Code and Section 7613 of the Corporations Code. For the purposes of this section, "quorum" means more than 50 percent of the owners of an association.

(b) Notwithstanding more restrictive limitations placed on the board by the governing documents, the board of directors may not impose a regular assessment that is more than 20 percent greater than the regular assessment for the association's preceding fiscal year or impose special assessments which in the aggregate exceed 5 percent of the budgeted gross expenses of the association for that fiscal year without the approval of owners, constituting a quorum, casting a majority of the votes at a meeting or election of the association conducted in accordance with Chapter 5 (commencing with Section 7510) of Part 3 of Division 2 of Title 1 of the Corporations Code and Section 7613 of the Corporations Code. For the purposes of this section, quorum means more than 50 percent of the owners of an association. This section does not limit assessment increases necessary for emergency situations. For purposes of this section, an emergency situation is any one of the following:

(1) An extraordinary expense required by an order of a court.

(2) An extraordinary expense necessary to repair or maintain the common interest development or any part of it for which the association is responsible where a threat to personal safety on the property is discovered.

(3) An extraordinary expense necessary to repair or maintain the common interest development or any part of it for which the association is responsible that could not have been reasonably foreseen by the board in preparing and distributing the *pro forma* operating budget under Section 1365. However, prior to the imposition or collection of an assessment under this subdivision, the board shall pass a resolution containing written findings as to the necessity of the extraordinary expense involved and why the expense was not or could not have been reasonably foreseen in the budgeting process, and the resolution shall be distributed to the members with the notice of assessment.

(c) Regular assessments imposed or collected to perform the obligations of an association under the governing documents or this title shall be exempt from execution by a judgment creditor of the association only to the extent necessary for the association to perform essential services, such as paying for utilities and insurance. In determining the appropriateness of an exemption, a court shall ensure that only essential services are protected under this subdivision.

This exemption shall not apply to any consensual pledges, liens, or encumbrances that have been approved by the owners of an association, constituting a quorum, casting a majority of the votes at a meeting or election of the association, or to any state tax lien, or to any lien for labor or materials supplied to the common area.

(d) The association shall provide notice by first-class mail to the owners of the separate interests of any increase in the regular or special assessments of the association, not less than 30 nor more than 60 days prior to the increased assessment becoming due.

(e) Regular and special assessments levied pursuant to the governing documents are delinquent 15 days after they become due, unless the declaration provides a longer time period, in which case the longer time period shall apply. If an assessment is delinquent, the association may recover all of the following:

(1) Reasonable costs incurred in collecting the delinquent

assessment, including reasonable attorneys' fees.

(2) A late charge not exceeding 10 percent of the delinquent assessment or ten dollars ($10), whichever is greater, unless the declaration specifies a late charge in a smaller amount, in which case any late charge imposed shall not exceed the amount specified in the declaration.

(3) Interest on all sums imposed in accordance with this section, including the delinquent assessments, reasonable fees and costs of collection, and reasonable attorney's fees, at an annual interest rate not to exceed 12 percent, commencing 30 days after the assessment becomes due, unless the declaration specifies the recovery of interest at a rate of a lesser amount, in which case the lesser rate of interest shall apply.

(f) Associations are hereby exempted from interest-rate limitations imposed by Article XV of the California Constitution, subject to the limitations of this section.

Civ. Code § 1366.1. Excessive Assessments Or Fees.

An association shall not impose or collect an assessment or fee that exceeds the amount necessary to defray the costs for which it is levied.

Civ. Code § 1366.2. Collection Of Assessments; Recording Of Identifying Statement.

(a) In order to facilitate the collection of regular assessments, special assessments, transfer fees, and similar charges, the board of directors of any association is authorized to record a statement or amended statement identifying relevant information for the association. This statement may include any or all of the following information:

(1) The name of the association as shown in the conditions, covenants, and restrictions or the current name of the association, if different.

(2) The name and address of a managing agent or treasurer of the association or other individual or entity authorized to receive assessments and fees imposed by the association.

(3) A daytime telephone number of the authorized party identified in paragraph (2) if a telephone number is available.

(4) A list of separate interests subject to assessment by the association, showing the assessor's parcel number or legal description, or both, of the separate interests.

(5) The recording information identifying the declaration or declarations of covenants, conditions, and restrictions governing the association.

Civil

(6) If an amended statement is being recorded, the recording information identifying the prior statement or statements which the amendment is superseding.

(b) The county recorder is authorized to charge a fee for recording the document described in subdivision (a), which fee shall be based upon the number of pages in the document and the recorder's per-page recording fee.

Civ. Code § 1366.4. Assessments Based On Taxable Value.

(a) Except as provided in subdivision (b), notwithstanding any provision of this title or the governing documents to the contrary, an association shall not levy assessments on separate interests within the common interest development based on the taxable value of the separate interests unless the association, on or before December 31, 2009, in accordance with its governing documents, levied assessments on those separate interests based on their taxable value, as determined by the tax assessor of the county in which the separate interests are located.

(b) An association that is responsible for paying taxes on the separate interests within the common interest development may levy that portion of assessments on separate interests that is related to the payment of taxes based on the taxable value of the separate interest, as determined by the tax assessor.

Civ. Code § 1367. Lien For Delinquent Assessments.

(a) A regular or special assessment and any late charges, reasonable costs of collection, and interest, as assessed in accordance with Section 1366, shall be a debt of the owner of the separate interest at the time the assessment or other sums are levied. Before an association may place a lien upon the separate interest of an owner to collect a debt which is past due under this subdivision, the association shall notify the owner in writing by certified mail of the fee and penalty procedures of the association, provide an itemized statement of the charges owed by the owner, including items on the statement which indicate the assessments owed, any late charges and the method of calculation, any attorney's fees, and the collection practices used by the association, including the right of the association to the reasonable costs of collection. In addition, any payments towards such a debt shall first be applied to the assessments owed, and only after the principal owed is paid in full shall such payments be applied to interest or collection expenses.

(b) The amount of the assessment, plus any costs of collection, late charges, and interest assessed in accordance with Section 1366, shall be a lien on the owner's interest in the common interest development from and after the time the association causes to be recorded with the county recorder of the county in which the separate interest is located, a notice of delinquent assessment, which shall state the amount of the assessment and other sums imposed in accordance with Section 1366, a legal description of the owner's interest in the common interest development against which the assessment and other sums are levied, the name of the record owner of the owner's interest in the common interest development against which the lien is imposed, and, in order for the lien to be enforced by nonjudicial foreclosure as provided in subdivision (e) the name and address of the trustee authorized by the association to enforce the lien by sale. The notice of delinquent assessment shall be signed by the person designated in the declaration or by the association for that purpose, or if no one is designated, by the president of the association, and mailed in the manner set forth in Section 2924b, to all record owners of the owner's interest in the common interest development no later than 10 calendar days after recordation. Upon payment of the sums specified in the notice of delinquent assessment, the association shall cause to be recorded a further notice stating the satisfaction and release of the lien thereof. A monetary penalty imposed by the association as a means of reimbursing the association for costs incurred by the association in the repair of damage to common areas and facilities for which the member or the member's guests or tenants were responsible may become a lien against the member's separate interest enforceable by the sale of the interest under Sections 2924, 2924b, and 2924c, provided the authority to impose a lien is set forth in the governing documents. It is the intent of the Legislature not to contravene Section 2792.26 of Title 10 of the California Code of Regulations, as that section appeared on January 1, 1996, for associations of subdivisions that are being sold under authority of a subdivision public report, pursuant to Part 2 (commencing with Section 11000) of Division 4 of the Business and Professions Code.

(c) Except as indicated in subdivision (b), a monetary penalty imposed by the association as a disciplinary measure for failure of a member to comply with the governing instruments, except for the late payments, may not be characterized nor treated in the governing instruments as an assessment which may become a lien against the member's subdivision interest enforceable by the sale of the interest under Sections 2924, 2924b, and 2924c.

(d) A lien created pursuant to subdivision (b) shall be prior to all other liens recorded subsequent to the notice of assessment, except that the declaration may provide for the subordination thereof to any other liens and encumbrances.

(e) After the expiration of 30 days following the recording of a lien created pursuant to subdivision (b), the lien may be enforced in any manner permitted by law, including sale by the court, sale by the trustee designated in the notice of delinquent assessment, or sale by a trustee substituted pursuant to Section 2934a. Any sale by the trustee shall be conducted in accordance with the provisions of Sections 2924, 2924b, and 2924c applicable to the exercise of powers of sale in mortgages and deeds of trusts.

(f) Nothing in this section or in subdivision (a) of Section 726 of the Code of Civil Procedure prohibits actions against the owner of a separate interest to recover sums for which a lien is created pursuant to this section or prohibits an association from taking a deed in lieu of foreclosure.

(g) This section only applies to liens recorded on or after January 1, 1986 and prior to January 1, 2003.

Civ. Code § 1367.1. Lien For Delinquent Assessments Recorded After January 1, 2003.

(a) A regular or special assessment and any late charges, reasonable fees and costs of collection, reasonable attorney's fees, if any, and interest, if any, as determined in accordance with Section 1366, shall be a debt of the owner of the separate interest at the time the assessment or other sums are levied. At least 30 days prior to recording a lien upon the separate interest of the owner of record to collect a debt that is past due under this subdivision, the association shall notify the owner of record in writing by certified mail of the following:

(1) A general description of the collection and lien enforcement procedures of the association and the method of calculation of the amount, a statement that the owner of the separate interest has the right to inspect the association records, pursuant to Section 8333 of the Corporations Code, and the following statement in 14-point boldface type, if printed, or in capital letters, if typed: "IMPORTANT NOTICE: IF YOUR SEPARATE INTEREST IS PLACED IN FORECLOSURE BECAUSE YOU ARE BEHIND IN YOUR ASSESSMENTS, IT MAY BE SOLD WITHOUT COURT ACTION".

(2) An itemized statement of the charges owed by the owner, including items on the statement which indicate the amount of any delinquent assessments, the fees and reasonable costs of collection,

reasonable attorney's fees, any late charges, and interest, if any.

(3) A statement that the owner shall not be liable to pay the charges, interest, and costs of collection, if it is determined the assessment was paid on time to the association.

(4) The right to request a meeting with the board as provided by subdivision (c).

(5) The right to dispute the assessment debt by submitting a written request for dispute resolution to the association pursuant to the association's "meet and confer" program required in Article 5 (commencing with Section 1363.810) of Chapter 4.

(6) The right to request alternative dispute resolution with a neutral third party pursuant to Article 2 (commencing with Section 1369.510) of Chapter 7 before the association may initiate foreclosure against the owner's separate interest, except that binding arbitration shall not be available if the association intends to initiate a judicial foreclosure.

(b) Any payments made by the owner of a separate interest toward the debt set forth, as required in subdivision (a), shall first be applied to the assessments owed, and, only after the assessments owed are paid in full shall the payments be applied to the fees and costs of collection, attorney's fees, late charges, or interest. When an owner makes a payment, the owner may request a receipt and the association shall provide it. The receipt shall indicate the date of payment and the person who received it. The association shall provide a mailing address for overnight payment of assessments.

(c) (1) (A) Prior to recording a lien for delinquent assessments, an association shall offer the owner and, if so requested by the owner, participate in dispute resolution pursuant to the association's "meet and confer" program required in Article 5 (commencing with Section 1363.810) of Chapter 4.

(B) Prior to initiating a foreclosure for delinquent assessments, an association shall offer the owner and, if so requested by the owner, shall participate in dispute resolution pursuant to the association's "meet and confer" program required in Article 5 (commencing with Section 1363.810) of Chapter 4 or alternative dispute resolution with a neutral third party pursuant to Article 2 (commencing with Section 1369.510) of Chapter 7. The decision to pursue dispute resolution or a particular type of alternative dispute resolution shall be the choice of the owner, except that binding arbitration shall not be available if the association intends to initiate a judicial foreclosure.

(2) For liens recorded on or after January 1, 2006, the decision to

record a lien for delinquent assessments shall be made only by the board of directors of the association and may not be delegated to an agent of the association. The board shall approve the decision by a majority vote of the board members in an open meeting. The board shall record the vote in the minutes of that meeting.

(3) An owner, other than an owner of any interest that is described in Section 11212 of the Business and Professions Code that is not otherwise exempt from this section pursuant to subdivision (a) of Section 11211.7, may submit a written request to meet with the board to discuss a payment plan for the debt noticed pursuant to subdivision (a). The association shall provide the owners the standards for payment plans, if any exist. The board shall meet with the owner in executive session within 45 days of the postmark of the request, if the request is mailed within 15 days of the date of the postmark of the notice, unless there is no regularly scheduled board meeting within that period, in which case the board may designate a committee of one or more members to meet with the owner. Payment plans may incorporate any assessments that accrue during the payment plan period. Payment plans shall not impede an association's ability to record a lien on the owner's separate interest to secure payment of delinquent assessments. Additional late fees shall not accrue during the payment plan period if the owner is in compliance with the terms of the payment plan. In the event of a default on any payment plan, the association may resume its efforts to collect the delinquent assessments from the time prior to entering into the payment plan.

(d) The amount of the assessment, plus any costs of collection, late charges, and interest assessed in accordance with Section 1366, shall be a lien on the owner's separate interest in the common interest development from and after the time the association causes to be recorded with the county recorder of the county in which the separate interest is located, a notice of delinquent assessment, which shall state the amount of the assessment and other sums imposed in accordance with Section 1366, a legal description of the owner's separate interest in the common interest development against which the assessment and other sums are levied, the name of the record owner of the owner's interest in the common interest development against which the lien is imposed. The itemized statement of the charges owed by the owner described in paragraph (2) of subdivision (a) shall be recorded together with the notice of delinquent assessment. In order for the lien to be enforced by nonjudicial foreclosure as provided in subdivision (g), the notice of delinquent assessment shall state the name and address of the trustee authorized by the association to enforce the lien by sale. The notice of delinquent assessment shall be signed by the person designated in the declaration or by the association for that purpose, or if no one is designated, by the president of the association. A copy of the recorded notice of delinquent assessment shall be mailed by certified mail to every person whose name is shown as an owner of the separate interest in the association's records, and the notice shall be mailed no later than 10 calendar days after recordation. Within 21 days of the payment of the sums specified in the notice of delinquent assessment, the association shall record or cause to be recorded in the office of the county recorder in which the notice of delinquent assessment is recorded a lien release or notice of rescission and provide the owner of the separate interest a copy of the lien release or notice that the delinquent assessment has been satisfied. A monetary charge imposed by the association as a means of reimbursing the association for costs incurred by the association in the repair of damage to common areas and facilities for which the member or the member's guests or tenants were responsible may become a lien against the member's separate interest enforceable by the sale of the interest under Sections 2924, 2924b, and 2924c, provided the authority to impose a lien is set forth in the governing documents. It is the intent of the Legislature not to contravene Section 2792.26 of Title 10 of the California Code of Regulations, as that section appeared on January 1, 1996, for associations of subdivisions that are being sold under authority of a subdivision public report, pursuant to Part 2 (commencing with Section 11000) of Division 4 of the Business and Professions Code.

(e) Except as indicated in subdivision (d), a monetary penalty imposed by the association as a disciplinary measure for failure of a member to comply with the governing instruments, except for the late payments, may not be characterized nor treated in the governing instruments as an assessment that may become a lien against the member's subdivision separate interest enforceable by the sale of the interest under Sections 2924, 2924b, and 2924c.

(f) A lien created pursuant to subdivision (d) shall be prior to all other liens recorded subsequent to the notice of assessment, except that the declaration may provide for the subordination thereof to any other liens and encumbrances.

(g) An association may not voluntarily assign or pledge the association's right to collect payments or assessments, or to enforce or foreclose a lien to a third party, except when the assignment or pledge is made to a financial institution or lender chartered or licensed under federal or state law, when acting within the scope of that charter or license, as security for a loan obtained by the association; however, the foregoing provision may not restrict the right or ability of an association to assign any unpaid obligations of a former member to a third party for purposes of collection. Subject to the limitations of this subdivision, after the expiration of 30 days following the recording of a lien created pursuant to subdivision (d), the lien may be enforced in any manner permitted by law, including sale by the court, sale by the trustee designated in the notice of delinquent assessment, or sale by a trustee substituted pursuant to Section 2934a. Any sale by the trustee shall be conducted in accordance with Sections 2924, 2924b, and 2924c applicable to the exercise of powers of sale in mortgages and deeds of trusts. The fees of a trustee may not exceed the amounts prescribed in Sections 2924c and 2924d, plus the cost of service for either of the following:

(1) The notice of default pursuant to subdivision (j) of Section 1367.1.

(2) The decision of the board to foreclose upon the separate interest of an owner as described in paragraph (3) of subdivision (c) of Section 1367.4.

(h) Nothing in this section or in subdivision (a) of Section 726 of the Code of Civil Procedure prohibits actions against the owner of a separate interest to recover sums for which a lien is created pursuant to this section or prohibits an association from taking a deed in lieu of foreclosure.

(i) If it is determined that a lien previously recorded against the separate interest was recorded in error, the party who recorded the lien shall, within 21 calendar days, record or cause to be recorded in the office of the county recorder in which the notice of delinquent assessment is recorded a lien release or notice of rescission and provide the owner of the separate interest with a declaration that the lien filing or recording was in error and a copy of the lien release or notice of rescission.

(j) In addition to the requirements of Section 2924, a notice of default shall be served by the association on the owner's legal representative in accordance with the manner of service of summons in Article 3 (commencing with Section 415.10) of Chapter 4 of Title 5 of Part 2 of the Code of Civil Procedure. The owner's legal representative shall be the person whose name is shown as the owner of a separate interest in the association's records, unless another person has been previously designated by the owner as his or her legal representative in writing and mailed to the association in a manner that indicates that the association has received it.

(k) Upon receipt of a written request by an owner identifying a secondary address for purposes of collection notices, the association shall send additional copies of any notices required by this section to the secondary address provided. The association shall notify owners of their right to submit secondary addresses to the association, at the time the association issues the *pro forma* operating budget pursuant to Section 1365. The owner's request shall be in writing and shall be mailed to the association in a manner that shall indicate the association has received it. The owner may identify or change a secondary address at any time, provided that, if a secondary address is identified or changed during the collection process, the association shall only be required to send notices to the indicated secondary address from the point the association receives the request.

(l) (1) An association that fails to comply with the procedures set forth in this section shall, prior to recording a lien, recommence the required notice process.

(2) Any costs associated with recommencing the notice process shall be borne by the association and not by the owner of a separate interest.

(m) This section only applies to liens recorded on or after January 1, 2003.

(n) This section is subordinate to, and shall be interpreted in conformity with, Section 1367.4.

Civ. Code § 1367.4. Limitations On Collection Of Delinquent Assessments Through Foreclosure; Right Of Redemption.

(a) Notwithstanding any law or any provisions of the governing documents to the contrary, this section shall apply to debts for assessments that arise on and after January 1, 2006.

(b) An association that seeks to collect delinquent regular or special assessments of an amount less than one thousand eight hundred dollars ($1,800), not including any accelerated assessments, late charges, fees and costs of collection, attorney's fees, or interest, may not collect that debt through judicial or nonjudicial foreclosure, but may attempt to collect or secure that debt in any of the following ways:

(1) By a civil action in small claims court, pursuant to Chapter 5.5 (commencing with Section 116.110) of Title 1 of the Code of Civil Procedure. An association that chooses to proceed by an action in small claims court, and prevails, may enforce the judgment as permitted under Article 8 (commencing with Section 116.810) of Title 1 of the Code of Civil Procedure. The amount that may be recovered in small claims court to collect upon a debt for delinquent assessments may not exceed the

jurisdictional limits of the small claims court and shall be the sum of the following:

(A) The amount owed as of the date of filing the complaint in the small claims court proceeding.

(B) In the discretion of the court, an additional amount to that described in subparagraph (A) equal to the amount owed for the period from the date the complaint is filed until satisfaction of the judgment, which total amount may include accruing unpaid assessments and any reasonable late charges, fees and costs of collection, attorney's fees, and interest, up to the jurisdictional limits of the small claims court.

(2) By recording a lien on the owner's separate interest upon which the association may not foreclose until the amount of the delinquent assessments secured by the lien, exclusive of any accelerated assessments, late charges, fees and costs of collection, attorney's fees, or interest, equals or exceeds one thousand eight hundred dollars ($1,800) or the assessments secured by the lien are more than 12 months delinquent. An association that chooses to record a lien under these provisions, prior to recording the lien, shall offer the owner and, if so requested by the owner, participate in dispute resolution as set forth in Article 5 (commencing with Section 1363.810) of Chapter 4.

(3) Any other manner provided by law, except for judicial or nonjudicial foreclosure.

(c) An association that seeks to collect delinquent regular or special assessments of an amount of one thousand eight hundred dollars ($1,800) or more, not including any accelerated assessments, late charges, fees and costs of collection, attorney's fees, or interest, or any assessments secured by the lien that are more than 12 months delinquent, may use judicial or nonjudicial foreclosure subject to the following conditions:

(1) Prior to initiating a foreclosure on an owner's separate interest, the association shall offer the owner and, if so requested by the owner, participate in dispute resolution pursuant to the association's "meet and confer" program required in Article 5 (commencing with Section 1363.810) of Chapter 4 or alternative dispute resolution as set forth in Article 2 (commencing with Section 1369.510) of Chapter 7. The decision to pursue dispute resolution or a particular type of alternative dispute resolution shall be the choice of the owner, except that binding arbitration shall not be available if the association intends to initiate a judicial foreclosure.

(2) The decision to initiate foreclosure of a lien for delinquent assessments that has been validly recorded shall be made only by the board

Civil

of directors of the association and may not be delegated to an agent of the association. The board shall approve the decision by a majority vote of the board members in an executive session. The board shall record the vote in the minutes of the next meeting of the board open to all members. The board shall maintain the confidentiality of the owner or owners of the separate interest by identifying the matter in the minutes by the parcel number of the property, rather than the name of the owner or owners. A board vote to approve foreclosure of a lien shall take place at least 30 days prior to any public sale.

(3) The board shall provide notice by personal service in accordance with the manner of service of summons in Article 3 (commencing with Section 415.10) of Chapter 4 of Title 5 of Part 2 of the Code of Civil Procedure to an owner of a separate interest who occupies the separate interest or to the owner's legal representative, if the board votes to foreclose upon the separate interest. The board shall provide written notice to an owner of a separate interest who does not occupy the separate interest by first-class mail, postage prepaid, at the most current address shown on the books of the association. In the absence of written notification by the owner to the association, the address of the owner's separate interest may be treated as the owner's mailing address.

(4) A nonjudicial foreclosure by an association to collect upon a debt for delinquent assessments shall be subject to a right of redemption. The redemption period within which the separate interest may be redeemed from a foreclosure sale under this paragraph ends 90 days after the sale. In addition to the requirements of Section 2924f, a notice of sale in connection with an association's foreclosure of a separate interest in a common interest development shall include a statement that the property is being sold subject to the right of redemption created in this paragraph.

(d) The limitation on foreclosure of assessment liens for amounts under the stated minimum in this section does not apply to assessments owed by owners of separate interests in timeshare estates, as defined in subdivision (x) of Section 11112 of the Business and Professions Code, or to assessments owed by developers.

Civ. Code § 1367.5. Lien Filed In Error; Reversal Of Costs And Fees.
If it is determined through dispute resolution pursuant to the association's "meet and confer" program required in Article 5 (commencing with Section 1363.810) of Chapter 4 or alternative dispute resolution with a neutral third party pursuant to Article 2 (commencing with Section 1369.510) of Chapter 7 that an association has recorded a

lien for a delinquent assessment in error, the association shall promptly reverse all late charges, fees, interest, attorney's fees, costs of collection, costs imposed for the notice prescribed in subdivision (a) of Section 1367.1, and costs of recordation and release of the lien authorized under subdivision (b) of Section 1367.4, and pay all costs related to the dispute resolution or alternative dispute resolution.

Civ. Code § 1367.6. Payment Of Assessments Under Protest; Small Claims Option.

(a) If a dispute exists between the owner of a separate interest and the association regarding any disputed charge or sum levied by the association, including, but not limited to, an assessment, fine, penalty, late fee, collection cost, or monetary penalty imposed as a disciplinary measure, and the amount in dispute does not exceed the jurisdictional limits stated in Sections 116.220 and 116.221 of the Code of Civil Procedure, the owner of the separate interest may, in addition to pursuing dispute resolution pursuant to Article 5 (commencing with Section 1363.810) of Chapter 4, pay under protest the disputed amount and all other amounts levied, including any fees and reasonable costs of collection, reasonable attorney's fees, late charges, and interest, if any, pursuant to subdivision (e) of Section 1366, and commence an action in small claims court pursuant to Chapter 5.5 (commencing with Section 116.110) of Title 1 of the Code of Civil Procedure.

(b) Nothing in this section shall impede an association's ability to collect delinquent assessments as provided in Sections 1367.1 and 1367.4.

TRANSFER OF OWNERSHIP RIGHTS

Civ. Code § 1368. Documents Provided To Prospective Purchaser.

(a) The owner of a separate interest, other than an owner subject to the requirements of Section 11018.6 of the Business and Professions Code, shall, as soon as practicable before transfer of title to the separate interest or execution of a real property sales contract therefor, as defined in Section 2985, provide the following to the prospective purchaser:

(1) A copy of the governing documents of the common interest development, including any operating rules, and including a copy of the association's articles of incorporation, or, if not incorporated, a statement in writing from an authorized respresentative of the association that the association is not incorporated.

(2) If there is a restriction in the governing documents limiting

the occupancy, residency, or use of a separate interest on the basis of age in a manner different from that provided in Section 51.3, a statement that the restriction is only enforceable to the extent permitted by Section 51.3 and a statement specifying the applicable provisions of Section 51.3.

(3) A copy of the most recent documents distributed pursuant to Section 1365.

(4) A true statement in writing obtained from an authorized representative of the association as to the amount of the association's current regular and special assessments and fees, any assessments levied upon the owner's interest in the common interest development that are unpaid on the date of the statement, and any monetary fines or penalties levied upon the owner's interest and unpaid on the date of the statement. The statement obtained from an authorized representative shall also include true information on late charges, interest, and costs of collection which, as of the date of the statement, are or may be made a lien upon the owner's interest in a common interest development pursuant to Section 1367 or 1367.1.

(5) A copy or a summary of any notice previously sent to the owner pursuant to subdivision (h) of Section 1363 that sets forth any alleged violation of the governing documents that remains unresolved at the time of the request. The notice shall not be deemed a waiver of the association's right to enforce the governing documents against the owner or the prospective purchaser of the separate interest with respect to any violation. This paragraph shall not be construed to require an association to inspect an owner's separate interest.

(6) A copy of the preliminary list of defects provided to each member of the association pursuant to Section 1375, unless the association and the builder subsequently enter into a settlement agreement or otherwise resolve the matter and the association complies with Section 1375.1. Disclosure of the preliminary list of defects pursuant to this paragraph does not waive any privilege attached to the document. The preliminary list of defects shall also include a statement that a final determination as to whether the list of defects is accurate and complete has not been made.

(7) A copy of the latest information provided for in Section 1375.1.

(8) Any change in the association's current regular and special assessments and fees which have been approved by the association's board of directors, but have not become due and payable as of the date disclosure is provided pursuant to this subdivision.

(b) Upon written request, an association shall, within 10 days of the mailing or delivery of the request, provide the owner of a separate interest with a copy of the requested items specified in paragraphs (1) to (8), inclusive, of subdivision (a). The items required to be made available pursuant to this section may be maintained in electronic form and requesting parties shall have the option of receiving them by electronic transmission or machine readable storage media if the association maintains these items in electronic form. The association may charge a reasonable fee for this service based upon the association's actual cost to procure, prepare, and reproduce the requested items.

(c) (1) *Except as provided in* paragraph (2), neither an association nor a community service organization or similar entity may impose or collect any assessment, penalty, or fee in connection with a transfer of title or any other interest except for the following:

(A) An amount not to exceed the association's actual costs to change its records.

(B) An amount authorized by subdivision (b).

(2) *The prohibition in paragraph (1) does not apply to a community service organization or similar entity, or to a nonprofit entity that provides services to a common interest development under a declaration of trust, that is described in subparagraph (A) or (B):*

(A) The community service organization or similar entity satisfies both of the following requirements:

(i) The community service organization or similar entity was established prior to February 20, 2003.

(ii) The community service organization or similar entity exists and operates, in whole or in part, to fund or perform environmental mitigation or to restore or maintain wetlands or native habitat, as required by the state or local government as an express written condition of development.

(B) The community service organization or similar entity, *or to a nonprofit entity that provides services to a common interest development under a declaration of trust,* satisfies all of the following requirements:

(i) The organization or entity is not an organization or entity described in subparagraph (A).

(ii) The organization or entity was established and received a transfer fee prior to January 1, 2004.

(iii) On and after January 1, 2006, the organization or entity offers a purchaser the following payment options for the fee or charge it collects at time of transfer:

(I) Paying the fee or charge at the time of transfer.

(II) Paying the fee or charge pursuant to an installment payment plan for a period of not less than seven years. If the purchaser elects to pay the fee or charge in installment payments, the organization or entity may also collect additional amounts that do not exceed the actual costs for billing and financing on the amount owed. If the purchaser sells the separate interest before the end of the installment payment plan period, he or she shall pay the remaining balance prior to transfer.

(3) For the purposes of this subdivision, a "community service organization or similar entity" means a nonprofit entity, other than an association, that is organized to provide services to residents of the common interest development or to the public in addition to the residents, to the extent community common areas or facilities are available to the public. A "community service organization or similar entity" does not include an entity that has been organized solely to raise moneys and contribute to other nonprofit organizations that are qualified as tax exempt under Section 501(c)(3) of the Internal Revenue Code and that provide housing or housing assistance.

(d) Any person or entity who willfully violates this section is liable to the purchaser of a separate interest that is subject to this section for actual damages occasioned thereby and, in addition, shall pay a civil penalty in an amount not to exceed five hundred dollars ($500). In an action to enforce this liability, the prevailing party shall be awarded reasonable attorneys' fees.

(e) Nothing in this section affects the validity of title to real property transferred in violation of this section.

(f) In addition to the requirements of this section, an owner transferring title to a separate interest shall comply with applicable requirements of Sections 1133 and 1134.

(g) For the purposes of this section, a person who acts as a community association manager is an agent, as defined in Section 2297, of the association.

Civ. Code § 1368.1. Arbitrary Or Unreasonable Restriction On Owner's Ability To Market Unit Void.

(a) Any rule or regulation of an association that arbitrarily or unreasonably restricts an owner's ability to market his or her interest in a common interest development is void.

(b) No association may adopt, enforce, or otherwise impose any rule or regulation that does either of the following:

(1) Imposes an assessment or fee in connection with the marketing of an owner's interest in an amount that exceeds the association's actual or direct costs. That assessment or fee shall be deemed to violate the limitation set forth in Section 1366.1.

(2) Establishes an exclusive relationship with a real estate broker through which the sale or marketing of interests in the development is required to occur. The limitation set forth in this paragraph does not apply to the sale or marketing of separate interests owned by the association or to the sale or marketing of common areas by the association.

(c) For purposes of this section, "market" and "marketing" mean listing, advertising, or obtaining or providing access to show the owner's interest in the development.

(d) This section does not apply to rules or regulations made pursuant to Section 712 or 713 regarding real estate signs.

CIVIL ACTIONS AND LIENS
Miscellaneous Provisions

Civ. Code § 1368.3. Association Standing As Real Party In Interest.

An association established to manage a common interest development has standing to institute, defend, settle, or intervene in litigation, arbitration, mediation, or administrative proceedings in its own name as the real party in interest and without joining with it the individual owners of the common interest development, in matters pertaining to the following:

(a) Enforcement of the governing documents.

(b) Damage to the common area.

(c) Damage to a separate interest that the association is obligated to maintain or repair.

(d) Damage to a separate interest that arises out of, or is integrally related to, damage to the common area or a separate interest that the association is obligated to maintain or repair.

Civ. Code § 1368.4. Damages Allocated By Comparative Fault.

(a) In an action maintained by an association pursuant to subdivision (b), (c), or (d) of Section 1368.3, the amount of damages recovered by the association shall be reduced by the amount of damages allocated to the association or its managing agents in direct proportion to their percentage of fault based upon principles of comparative fault. The comparative fault of the association or its managing agents may be raised by way of defense,

Civil

but shall not be the basis for a cross-action or separate action against the association or its managing agents for contribution or implied indemnity, where the only damage was sustained by the association or its members. It is the intent of the Legislature in enacting this subdivision to require that comparative fault be pleaded as an affirmative defense, rather than a separate cause of action, where the only damage was sustained by the association or its members.

(b) In an action involving damages described in subdivision (b), (c), or (d) of Section 1368.3, the defendant or cross-defendant may allege and prove the comparative fault of the association or its managing agents as a setoff to the liability of the defendant or cross-defendant even if the association is not a party to the litigation or is no longer a party whether by reason of settlement, dismissal, or otherwise.

(c) Subdivisions (a) and (b) apply to actions commenced on or after January 1, 1993.

(d) Nothing in this section affects a person's liability under Section 1431, or the liability of the association or its managing agent for an act or omission which causes damages to another.

Civ. Code § 1368.5. Civil Action By Association; Notice Prior To Filing.

(a) Not later than 30 days prior to the filing of any civil action by the association against the declarant or other developer of a common interest development for alleged damage to the common areas, alleged damage to the separate interests that the association is obligated to maintain or repair, or alleged damage to the separate interests that arises out of, or is integrally related to, damage to the common areas or separate interests that the association is obligated to maintain or repair, the board of directors of the association shall provide written notice to each member of the association who appears on the records of the association when the notice is provided. This notice shall specify all of the following:

(1) That a meeting will take place to discuss problems that may lead to the filing of a civil action.

(2) The options, including civil actions, that are available to address the problems.

(3) The time and place of this meeting.

(b) Notwithstanding subdivision (a), if the association has reason to believe that the applicable statute of limitations will expire before the association files the civil action, the association may give the notice, as described above, within 30 days after the filing of the action.

Civ. Code § 1369. Liens For Labor And Materials.

In a condominium project, no labor performed or services or materials furnished with the consent of, or at the request of, an owner in the condominium project or his or her agent or his or her contractor shall be the basis for the filing of a lien against any other property of any other owner in the condominium project unless that other owner has expressly consented to or requested the performance of the labor or furnishing of the materials or services. However, express consent shall be deemed to have been given by the owner of any condominium in the case of emergency repairs thereto. Labor performed or services or materials furnished for the common areas, if duly authorized by the association, shall be deemed to be performed or furnished with the express consent of each condominium owner. The owner of any condominium may remove his or her condominium from a lien against two or more condominiums or any part thereof by payment to the holder of the lien of the fraction of the total sum secured by the lien which is attributable to his or her condominium.

Alternative Dispute Resolution

Civ. Code § 1369.510. "Alternative Dispute Resolution" And "Enforcement Action" Defined.

As used in this article:

(a) "Alternative dispute resolution" means mediation, arbitration, conciliation, or other nonjudicial procedure that involves a neutral party in the decisionmaking process. The form of alternative dispute resolution chosen pursuant to this article may be binding or nonbinding, with the voluntary consent of the parties.

(b) "Enforcement action" means a civil action or proceeding, other than a cross-complaint, for any of the following purposes:

(1) Enforcement of this title.

(2) Enforcement of the Nonprofit Mutual Benefit Corporation Law (Part 3 (commencing with Section 7110) of Division 2 of Title 1 of the Corporations Code).

(3) Enforcement of the governing documents of a common interest development.

Civ. Code § 1369.520. Alternative Dispute Resolution Required Prior To Filing An Enforcement Action.

(a) An association or an owner or a member of a common interest development may not file an enforcement action in the superior court unless the parties have endeavored to submit their dispute to alternative dispute resolution pursuant to this article.

(b) This section applies only to an enforcement action that is solely for declaratory, injunctive, or writ relief, or for that relief in conjunction with a claim for monetary damages not in excess of the jurisdictional limits stated in Sections 116.220 and 116.221 of the Code of Civil Procedure.

(c) This section does not apply to a small claims action.

(d) Except as otherwise provided by law, this section does not apply to an assessment dispute.

Civ. Code § 1369.530. Service Of Request For Resolution.

(a) Any party to a dispute may initiate the process required by Section 1369.520 by serving on all other parties to the dispute a Request for Resolution. The Request for Resolution shall include all of the following:

(1) A brief description of the dispute between the parties.

(2) A request for alternative dispute resolution.

(3) A notice that the party receiving the Request for Resolution is required to respond within 30 days of receipt or the request will be deemed rejected.

(4) If the party on whom the request is served is the owner of a separate interest, a copy of this article.

(b) Service of the Request for Resolution shall be by personal delivery, first-class mail, express mail, facsimile transmission, or other means reasonably calculated to provide the party on whom the request is served actual notice of the request.

(c) A party on whom a Request for Resolution is served has 30 days following service to accept or reject the request. If a party does not accept the request within that period, the request is deemed rejected by the party.

Civ. Code § 1369.540. Completion Of Resolution Process Within 90 Days.

(a) If the party on whom a Request for Resolution is served accepts the request, the parties shall complete the alternative dispute resolution within 90 days after the party initiating the request receives the acceptance, unless this period is extended by written stipulation signed by both parties.

(b) Chapter 2 (commencing with Section 1115) of Division 9 of the Evidence Code applies to any form of alternative dispute resolution initiated by a Request for Resolution under this article, other than arbitration.

(c) The costs of the alternative dispute resolution shall be borne by the parties.

Civ. Code § 1369.550. Tolling Of Time Limitation For Commencing An Enforcement Action.

If a Request for Resolution is served before the end of the applicable time limitation for commencing an enforcement action, the time limitation is tolled during the following periods:

(a) The period provided in Section 1369.530 for response to a Request for Resolution.

(b) If the Request for Resolution is accepted, the period provided by Section 1369.540 for completion of alternative dispute resolution, including any extension of time stipulated to by the parties pursuant to Section 1369.540.

Civ. Code § 1369.560. Filing Certification Of Compliance.

(a) At the time of commencement of an enforcement action, the party commencing the action shall file with the initial pleading a certificate stating that one or more of the following conditions is satisfied:

(1) Alternative dispute resolution has been completed in compliance with this article.

(2) One of the other parties to the dispute did not accept the terms offered for alternative dispute resolution.

(3) Preliminary or temporary injunctive relief is necessary.

(b) Failure to file a certificate pursuant to subdivision (a) is grounds for a demurrer or a motion to strike unless the court finds that dismissal of the action for failure to comply with this article would result in substantial prejudice to one of the parties.

Civ. Code § 1369.570. Stipulated Agreement To Pursue Alternative Dispute Resolution After Commencement Of Enforcement Action.

(a) After an enforcement action is commenced, on written stipulation of the parties, the matter may be referred to alternative dispute resolution. The referred action is stayed. During the stay, the action is not subject to the rules implementing subdivision (c) of Section 68603 of the Government Code.

(b) The costs of the alternative dispute resolution shall be borne by the parties.

Civ. Code § 1369.580. Court Discretion In Awarding Fees And Costs Based Upon Participation In Alternative Dispute Resolution.

In an enforcement action in which fees and costs may be awarded pursuant to subdivision (c) of Section 1354, the court, in determining the amount of the award, may consider whether a party's refusal to participate in alternative dispute resolution before commencement of the action was reasonable.

Civ. Code § 1369.590. Annual Distribution Of Summary Of Alternative Dispute Resolution Procedures Required.

(a) An association shall annually provide its members a summary of the provisions of this article that specifically references this article. The summary shall include the following language:

"Failure of a member of the association to comply with the alternative dispute resolution requirements of Section 1369.520 of the Civil Code may result in the loss of your right to sue the association or another member of the association regarding enforcement of the governing documents or the applicable law."

(b) The summary shall be provided either at the time the *pro forma* budget required by Section 1365 is distributed or in the manner prescribed in Section 5016 of the Corporations Code. The summary shall include a description of the association's internal dispute resolution process, as required by Section 1363.850.

CONSTRUCTION OF INSTRUMENTS AND ZONING

Civ. Code § 1370. Liberal Construction Of Governing Documents.

Any deed, declaration, or condominium plan for a common interest development shall be liberally construed to facilitate the operation of the common interest development, and its provisions shall be presumed to be independent and severable. Nothing in Article 3 (commencing with Section 715) of Chapter 2 of Title 2 of Part 1 of this division shall operate to invalidate any provisions of the governing documents of a common interest development.

Civ. Code § 1371. Boundaries Of Unit.

In interpreting deeds and condominium plans, the existing physical boundaries of a unit in a condominium project, when the boundaries of the unit are contained within a building, or of a unit reconstructed in substantial accordance with the original plans thereof, shall be conclusively presumed to be its boundaries rather than the metes and bounds expressed in the deed or condominium plan, if any exists, regardless of settling or lateral movement of the building and regardless of minor variance between boundaries shown on the plan or in the deed and those of the building.

Civ. Code § 1372. Construction Of Local Zoning Ordinances.

Unless a contrary intent is clearly expressed, local zoning ordinances shall be construed to treat like structures, lots, parcels, areas, or spaces in like manner regardless of whether the common interest development is a community apartment project, condominium project, planned development, or stock cooperative.

Civ. Code § 1373. Developments Expressly Zoned As Industrial Or Commercial And Limited To Such Purposes.

(a) The following provisions do not apply to a common interest development that is limited to industrial or commercial uses by zoning or by a declaration of covenants, conditions, and restrictions that has been recorded in the official records of each county in which the common interest development is located:

　　(1) Section 1356.

　　(2) Article 4 (commencing with Section 1357.100) of Chapter 2 of Title 6 of Part 4 of Division 2.

　　(3) Subdivision (b) of Section 1363.

　　(4) Section 1365.

　　(5) Section 1365.5.

　　(6) Subdivision (b) of Section 1366.

　　(7) Section 1366.1.

　　(8) Section 1368.

　　(9) Section 1378.

(b) The Legislature finds that the provisions listed in subdivision (a) are appropriate to protect purchasers in residential common interest developments, however, the provisions may not be necessary to protect purchasers in commercial or industrial developments since the application of those provisions could result in unnecessary burdens and costs for these types of developments.

Civ. Code § 1374. Inapplicability Of Law To Developments Without Common Area.

Nothing in this title may be construed to apply to a development wherein there does not exist a common area as defined in subdivision (b) of Section 1351. This section is declaratory of existing law.

CONSTRUCTION DEFECT LITIGATION

Civ. Code § 1375. Construction Defect Litigation; Prefiling; Dispute Resolution Process.

(a) Before an association files a complaint for damages against a builder, developer, or general contractor ("respondent") of a common interest development based upon a claim for defects in the design or construction of the common interest development, all of the requirements of this section shall be satisfied with respect to the builder, developer, or general contractor.

(b) The association shall serve upon the respondent a "Notice of Commencement of Legal Proceeding." The notice shall be served by certified mail to the registered agent of the respondent, or if there is no registered agent, then to any officer of the respondent. If there are no current officers of the respondent, service shall be upon the person or entity otherwise authorized by law to receive service of process. Service upon the general contractor shall be sufficient to initiate the process set forth in this section with regard to any builder or developer, if the builder or developer is not amendable to service of process by the foregoing methods. This notice shall toll all applicable statutes of limitation and repose, whether contractual or statutory, by and against all potentially responsible parties, regardless of whether they were named in the notice, including claims for indemnity applicable to the claim for the period set forth in subdivision (c). The notice shall include all of the following:

(1) The name and location of the project.

(2) An initial list of defects sufficient to apprise the respondent of the general nature of the defects at issue.

(3) A description of the results of the defects, if known.

(4) A summary of the results of a survey or questionnaire distributed to homeowners to determine the nature and extent of defects, if a survey has been conducted or a questionnaire has been distributed.

(5) Either a summary of the results of testing conducted to determine the nature and extent of defects or the actual test results, if that testing has been conducted.

(c) Service of the notice shall commence a period, not to exceed 180 days, during which the association, the respondent, and all other participating parties shall try to resolve the dispute through the processes set forth in this section. This 180-day period may be extended for one additional period, not to exceed 180 days, only upon the mutual agreement of the association, the respondent, and any parties not deemed peripheral pursuant to paragraph (3) of subdivision (e). Any extensions beyond the first extension shall require the agreement of all participating parties. Unless extended, the dispute resolution process prescribed by this section shall be deemed completed. All extensions shall continue the tolling period described in subdivision (b).

(d) Within 25 days of the date the association serves the Notice of Commencement of Legal Proceedings, the respondent may request in writing to meet and confer with the board of directors of the association. Unless the respondent and the association otherwise agree, there shall be not more than one meeting, which shall take place no later than 10 days from the date of the respondent's written request, at a mutually agreeable time and place. The meeting shall be subject to subdivision (b) of Section 1363.05. The discussions at the meeting are privileged communications and are not admissible in evidence in any civil action, unless the association and the respondent consent in writing to their admission.

(e) Upon receipt of the notice, the respondent shall, within 60 days, comply with the following:

(1) The respondent shall provide the association with access to, for inspection and copying of, all plans and specifications, subcontracts, and other construction files for the project that are reasonably calculated to lead to the discovery of admissible evidence regarding the defects claimed. The association shall provide the respondent with access to, for inspection and copying of, all files reasonably calculated to lead to the discovery of admissible evidence regarding the defects claimed, including all reserve studies, maintenance records and any survey questionnaires, or results of testing to determine the nature and extent of defects. To the extent any of the above documents are withheld based on privilege, a privilege log shall be prepared and submitted to all other parties. All other potentially responsible parties shall have the same rights as the respondent regarding the production of documents upon receipt of written notice of the claim, and shall produce all relevant documents within 60 days of receipt of the notice of the claim.

(2) The respondent shall provide written notice by certified mail to all subcontractors, design professionals, their insurers, and the insurers of any additional insured whose identities are known to the respondent or readily ascertainable by review of the project files or other similar sources and whose potential responsibility appears on the face of the notice. This notice to subcontractors, design professionals, and insurers shall include

a copy of the Notice of Commencement of Legal Proceeding, and shall specify the date and manner by which the parties shall meet and confer to select a dispute resolution facilitator pursuant to paragraph (1) of subdivision (f), advise the recipient of its obligation to participate in the meet and confer or serve a written acknowledgment of receipt regarding this notice, advise the recipient that it will waive any challenge to selection of the dispute resolution facilitator if it elects not to participate in the meet and confer, advise the recipient that it may be bound by any settlement reached pursuant to subdivision (d) of Section 1375.05, advise the recipient that it may be deemed to have waived rights to conduct inspection and testing pursuant to subdivision (c) of Section 1375.05, advise the recipient that it may seek the assistance of an attorney, and advise the recipient that it should contact its insurer, if any. Any subcontractor or design professional, or insurer for that subcontractor, design professional, or additional insured, who receives written notice from the respondent regarding the meet and confer shall, prior to the meet and confer, serve on the respondent a written acknowledgment of receipt. That subcontractor or design professional shall, within 10 days of service of the written acknowledgment of receipt, provide to the association and the respondent a Statement of Insurance that includes both of the following:

(A) The names, addresses, and contact persons, if known, of all insurance carriers, whether primary or excess and regardless of whether a deductible or self-insured retention applies, whose policies were in effect from the commencement of construction of the subject project to the present and which potentially cover the subject claims.

(B) The applicable policy numbers for each such policy of insurance.

(3) Any subcontractor or design professional, or insurer for that subcontractor, design professional, or additional insured, who so chooses, may, at any time, make a written request to the dispute resolution facility for designation as a peripheral party. That request shall be served contemporaneously on the association and the respondent. If no objection to that designation is received within 15 days, or upon rejection of that objection, the dispute resolution facilitator shall designate that subcontractor or design professional as a peripheral party, and shall thereafter seek to limit the attendance of that subcontractor or design professional only to those dispute resolution sessions deemed peripheral party sessions or to those sessions during which the dispute resolution facilitator believes settlement as to peripheral parties may be finalized.

Nothing in this subdivision shall preclude a party who has been designated a peripheral party from being reclassified as a nonperipheral party, nor shall this subdivision preclude a party designated as a nonperipheral party from being reclassified as a peripheral party after notice to all parties and an opportunity to object. For purposes of this subdivision, a peripheral party is a party having total claimed exposure of less than twenty-five thousand dollars ($25,000).

(f) (1) Within 20 days of sending the notice set forth in paragraph (2) of subdivision (e), the association, respondent, subcontractors, design professionals, and their insurers who have been sent a notice as described in paragraph (2) of subdivision (e) shall meet and confer in an effort to select a dispute resolution facilitator to preside over the mandatory dispute resolution process prescribed by this section. Any subcontractor or design professional who has been given timely notice of this meeting but who does not participate, waives any challenge he or she may have as to the selection of the dispute resolution facilitator. The role of the dispute resolution facilitator is to attempt to resolve the conflict in a fair manner. The dispute resolution facilitator shall be sufficiently knowledgeable in the subject matter and be able to devote sufficient time to the case. The dispute resolution facilitator shall not be required to reside in or have an office in the county in which the project is located. The dispute resolution facilitator and the participating parties shall agree to a date, time, and location to hold a case management meeting of all parties and the dispute resolution facilitator, to discuss the claims being asserted and the scheduling of events under this section. The case management meeting with the dispute resolution facilitator shall be held within 100 days of service of the Notice of Commencement of Legal Proceedings at a location in the county where the project is located. Written notice of the case management meeting with the dispute resolution facilitator shall be sent by the respondent to the association, subcontractors and design professionals, and their insurers who are known to the respondent to be on notice of the claim, no later than 10 days prior to the case management meeting, and shall specify its date, time, and location. The dispute resolution facilitator in consultation with the respondent, shall maintain a contact list of the participating parties.

(2) No later than 10 days prior to the case management meeting, the dispute resolution facilitator shall disclose to the parties all matters that could cause a person aware of the facts to reasonably entertain a doubt that the proposed dispute resolution facilitator would be able to resolve the conflict in a fair manner. The facilitator's disclosure shall include the existence of any ground specified in Section 170.1 of the Code of Civil

Procedure for disqualification of a judge, any attorney-client relationship the facilitator has or had with any party or lawyer for a party to the dispute resolution process, and any professional or significant personal relationship the facilitator or his or her spouse or minor child living in the household has or had with any party to the dispute resolution process. The disclosure shall also be provided to any subsequently noticed subcontractor or design professional within 10 days of the notice.

(3) A dispute resolution facilitator shall be disqualified by the court if he or she fails to comply with this paragraph and any party to the dispute resolution process serves a notice of disqualification prior to the case management meeting. If the dispute resolution facilitator complies with this paragraph, he or she shall be disqualified by the court on the basis of the disclosure if any party to the dispute resolution process serves a notice of disqualification prior to the case management meeting.

(4) If the parties cannot mutually agree to a dispute resolution facilitator, then each party shall submit a list of three dispute resolution facilitators. Each party may then strike one nominee from the other parties' list, and petition the court, pursuant to the procedure described in subdivisions (n) and (o), for final selection of the dispute resolution facilitator. The court may issue an order for final selection of the dispute resolution facilitator pursuant to this paragraph.

(5) Any subcontractor or design professional who receives notice of the association's claim without having previously received timely notice of the meet and confer to select the dispute resolution facilitator shall be notified by the respondent regarding the name, address, and telephone number of the dispute resolution facilitator. Any such subcontractor or design professional may serve upon the parties and the dispute resolution facilitator a written objection to the dispute resolution facilitator within 15 days of receiving notice of the claim. Within seven days after service of this objection, the subcontractor or design professional may petition the superior court to replace the dispute resolution facilitator. The court may replace the dispute resolution facilitator only upon a showing of good cause, liberally construed. Failure to satisfy the deadlines set forth in this subdivision shall constitute a waiver of the right to challenge the dispute resolution facilitator.

(6) The costs of the dispute resolution facilitator shall be apportioned in the following manner: one-third to be paid by the association; one-third to be paid by the respondent; and one-third to be paid by the subcontractors and design professionals, as allocated among them by the dispute resolution facilitator. The costs of the dispute

resolution facilitator shall be recoverable by the prevailing party in any subsequent litigation pursuant to Section 1032 of the Code of Civil Procedure, provided however that any nonsettling party may, prior to the filing of the complaint, petition the facilitator to reallocate the costs of the dispute resolution facilitator as they apply to any nonsettling party. The determination of the dispute resolution facilitator with respect to the allocation of these costs shall be binding in any subsequent litigation. The dispute resolution facilitator shall take into account all relevant factors and equities between all parties in the dispute resolution process when reallocating costs.

(7) In the event the dispute resolution facilitator is replaced at any time, the case management statement created pursuant to subdivision (h) shall remain in full force and effect.

(8) The dispute resolution facilitator shall be empowered to enforce all provisions of this section.

(g) (1) No later than the case management meeting, the parties shall begin to generate a data compilation showing the following information regarding the alleged defects at issue:

(A) The scope of the work performed by each potentially responsible subcontractor.

(B) The tract or phase number in which each subcontractor provided goods or services, or both.

(C) The units, either by address, unit number, or lot number, at which each subcontractor provided goods or services, or both.

(2) This data compilation shall be updated as needed to reflect additional information. Each party attending the case management meeting, and any subsequent meeting pursuant to this section, shall provide all information available to that party relevant to this data compilation.

(h) At the case management meeting, the parties shall, with the assistance of the dispute resolution facilitator, reach agreement on a case management statement, which shall set forth all of the elements set forth in paragraphs (1) to (8), inclusive, except that the parties may dispense with one or more of these elements if they agree that it is appropriate to do so. The case management statement shall provide that the following elements shall take place in the following order:

(1) Establishment of a document depository, located in the county where the project is located, for deposit of documents, defect lists, demands, and other information provided for under this section. All documents exchanged by the parties and all documents created pursuant to this subdivision shall be deposited in the document depository, which

shall be available to all parties throughout the prefiling dispute resolution process and in any subsequent litigation. When any document is deposited in the document depository, the party depositing the document shall provide written notice identifying the document to all other parties. The costs of maintaining the document depository shall be apportioned among the parties in the same manner as the costs of the dispute resolution facilitator.

(2) Provision of a more detailed list of defects by the association to the respondent after the association completes a visual inspection of the project. This list of defects shall provide sufficient detail for the respondent to ensure that all potentially responsible subcontractors and design professionals are provided with notice of the dispute resolution process. If not already completed prior to the case management meeting, the Notice of Commencement of Legal Proceeding shall be served by the respondent on all additional subcontractors and design professionals whose potential responsibility appears on the face of the more detailed list of defects within seven days of receipt of the more detailed list. The respondent shall serve a copy of the case management statement, including the name, address, and telephone number of the dispute resolution facilitator, to all the potentially responsible subcontractors and design professionals at the same time.

(3) Nonintrusive visual inspection of the project by the respondent, subcontractors, and design professionals.

(4) Invasive testing conducted by the association, if the association deems appropriate. All parties may observe and photograph any testing conducted by the association pursuant to this paragraph, but may not take samples or direct testing unless, by mutual agreement, costs of testing are shared by the parties.

(5) Provision by the association of a comprehensive demand which provides sufficient detail for the parties to engage in meaningful dispute resolution as contemplated under this section.

(6) Invasive testing conducted by the respondent, subcontractors, and design professionals, if they deem appropriate.

(7) Allowance for modification of the demand by the association if new issues arise during the testing conducted by the respondent, subcontractor, or design professionals.

(8) Facilitated dispute resolution of the claim, with all parties, including peripheral parties, as appropriate, and insurers, if any, present and having settlement authority. The dispute resolution facilitators shall endeavor to set specific times for the attendance of specific parties at dispute resolution sessions. If the dispute resolution facilitator does not set

specific times for the attendance of parties at dispute resolution sessions, the dispute resolution facilitator shall permit those parties to participate in dispute resolution sessions by telephone.

(i) In addition to the foregoing elements of the case management statement described in subdivision (h), upon mutual agreement of the parties, the dispute resolution facilitator may include any or all of the following elements in a case management statement: the exchange of consultant or expert photographs; expert presentations; expert meetings; or any other mechanism deemed appropriate by the parties in the interest of resolving the dispute.

(j) The dispute resolution facilitator, with the guidance of the parties, shall at the time the case management statement is established, set deadlines for the occurrence of each event set forth in the case management statement, taking into account such factors as the size and complexity of the case, and the requirement of this section that this dispute resolution process not exceed 180 days absent agreement of the parties to an extension of time.

(k) (1) (A) At a time to be determined by the dispute resolution facilitator, the respondent may submit to the association all of the following:

(i) A request to meet with the board to discuss a written settlement offer.

(ii) A written settlement offer, and a concise explanation of the reasons for the terms of the offer.

(iii) A statement that the respondent has access to sufficient funds to satisfy the conditions of the settlement offer.

(iv) A summary of the results of testing conducted for the purposes of determining the nature and extent of defects, if this testing has been conducted, unless the association provided the respondent with actual test results.

(B) If the respondent does not timely submit the items required by this subdivision, the association shall be relieved of any further obligation to satisfy the requirements of this subdivision only.

(C) No less than 10 days after the respondent submits the items required by this paragraph, the respondent and the board of directors of the association shall meet and confer about the respondent's settlement offer.

(D) If the association's board of directors rejects a settlement offer presented at the meeting held pursuant to this subdivision, the board shall hold a meeting open to each member of the association.

The meeting shall be held no less than 15 days before the association commences an action for damages against the respondent.

(E) No less than 15 days before this meeting is held, a written notice shall be sent to each member of the association specifying all of the following:

(i) That a meeting will take place to discuss problems that may lead to the filing of a civil action, and the time and place of this meeting.

(ii) The options that are available to address the problems, including the filing of a civil action and a statement of the various alternatives that are reasonably foreseeable by the association to pay for those options and whether these payments are expected to be made from the use of reserve account funds or the imposition of regular or special assessments, or emergency assessment increases.

(iii) The complete text of any written settlement offer, and a concise explanation of the specific reasons for the terms of the offer submitted to the board at the meeting held pursuant to subdivision (d) that was received from the respondent.

(F) The respondent shall pay all expenses attributable to sending the settlement offer to all members of the association. The respondent shall also pay the expense of holding the meeting, not to exceed three dollars ($3) per association member.

(G) The discussions at the meeting and the contents of the notice and the items required to be specified in the notice pursuant to paragraph (E) are privileged communications and are not admissible in evidence in any civil action, unless the association consents to their admission.

(H) No more than one request to meet and discuss a written settlement offer may be made by the respondent pursuant to this subdivision.

(l) Except for the purpose of in camera review as provided in subdivision (c) of Section 1375.05, all defect lists and demands, communications, negotiations, and settlement offers made in the course of the prelitigation dispute resolution process provided by this section shall be inadmissible pursuant to Sections 1119 to 1124, inclusive, of the Evidence Code and all applicable decisional law. This inadmissibility shall not be extended to any other documents or communications which would not otherwise be deemed inadmissible.

(m) Any subcontractor or design professional may, at any time, petition the dispute resolution facilitator to release that party from the dispute resolution process upon a showing that the subcontractor or design professional is not potentially responsible for the defect claims at issue. The petition shall be served contemporaneously on all other parties, who shall have 15 days from the date of service to object. If a subcontractor or design professional is released, and it later appears to the dispute resolution facilitator that it may be a responsible party in light of the current defect list or demand, the respondent shall renotice the party as provided by paragraph (2) of subdivision (e), provide a copy of the current defect list or demand, and direct the party to attend a dispute resolution session at a stated time and location. A party who subsequently appears after having been released by the dispute resolution facilitator shall not be prejudiced by its absence from the dispute resolution process as the result of having been previously released by the dispute resolution facilitator.

(n) Any party may, at any time, petition the superior court in the county where the project is located, upon a showing of good cause, and the court may issue an order, for any of the following, or for appointment of a referee to resolve a dispute regarding any of the following:

(1) To take a deposition of any party to the process, or subpoena a third party for deposition or production of documents, which is necessary to further prelitigation resolution of the dispute.

(2) To resolve any disputes concerning inspection, testing, production of documents, or exchange of information provided for under this section.

(3) To resolve any disagreements relative to the timing or contents of the case management statement.

(4) To authorize internal extensions of timeframes set forth in the case management statement.

(5) To seek a determination that a settlement is a good faith settlement pursuant to Section 877.6 of the Code of Civil Procedure and all related authorities. The page limitations and meet and confer requirements specified in this section shall not apply to these motions, which may be made on shortened notice. Instead, these motions shall be subject to other applicable state law, rules of court, and local rules. A determination made by the court pursuant to this motion shall have the same force and effect as the determination of a postfiling application or motion for good faith settlement.

(6) To ensure compliance, on shortened notice, with the obligation to provide a Statement of Insurance pursuant to paragraph (2) of subdivision (e).

(7) For any other relief appropriate to the enforcement of the

provisions of this section, including the ordering of parties, and insurers, if any, to the dispute resolution process with settlement authority.

(o) (1)   A petition filed pursuant to subdivision (n) shall be filed in the superior court in the county in which the project is located. The court shall hear and decide the petition within 10 days after filing. The petitioning party shall serve the petition on all parties, including the date, time, and location of the hearing no later than five business days prior to the hearing. Any responsive papers shall be filed and served no later than three business days prior to the hearing. Any petition or response filed under this section shall be no more than three pages in length.

(2)   All parties shall meet with the dispute resolution facilitator, if one has been appointed and confer in person or by the telephone prior to the filing of that petition to attempt to resolve the matter without requiring court intervention.

(p) As used in this section:

(1)   "Association" shall have the same meaning as defined in subdivision (a) of Section 1351.

(2)   "Builder" means the declarant, as defined in subdivision (g) of Section 1351.

(3)   "Common interest development" shall have the same meaning as in subdivision (c) of Section 1351, except that it shall not include developments or projects with less than 20 units.

(q) The alternative dispute resolution process and procedures described in this section shall have no application or legal effect other than as described in this section.

(r) This section shall become operative on July 1, 2002, however it shall not apply to any pending suit or claim for which notice has previously been given.

(s) This section shall become inoperative on July 1, 2017, and as of January 1, 2018, is repealed, unless a later enacted statute, that is enacted before January 1, 2018, deletes or extends the dates on which it becomes inoperative and is repealed.

Civ. Code § 1375.05. Construction Defect Litigation; Filing Of Complaint; Inspection Process; Expert Witness Depositions.

(a) Upon the completion of the mandatory prefiling dispute resolution process described in Section 1375, if the parties have not settled the matter, the association or its assignee may file a complaint in the superior court in the county in which the project is located. Those matters shall be given trial priority.

(b) In assigning trial priority, the court shall assign the earliest possible trial date, taking into consideration the pretrial preparation completed pursuant to Section 1375, and shall deem the complaint to have been filed on the date of service of the Notice of Commencement of Legal Proceeding described under Section 1375.

(c) Any respondent, subcontractor, or design professional who received timely prior notice of the inspections and testing conducted under Section 1375 shall be prohibited from engaging in additional inspection or testing, except if all of the following specific conditions are met, upon motion to the court:

(1) There is an insurer for a subcontractor or design professional, that did not have timely notice that legal proceedings were commenced under Section 1375 at least 30 days prior to the commencement of inspections or testing pursuant to paragraph (6) of subdivision (h) of Section 1375.

(2) The insurer's insured did not participate in any inspections or testing conducted under the provisions of paragraph (6) of subdivision (h) of Section 1375.

(3) The insurer has, after receiving notice of a complaint filed in superior court under subdivision (a), retained separate counsel, who did not participate in the Section 1375 dispute resolution process, to defend its insured as to the allegations in the complaint.

(4) It is reasonably likely that the insured would suffer prejudice if additional inspections or testing are not permitted.

(5) The information obtainable through the proposed additional inspections or testing is not available through any reasonable alternative sources.

If the court permits additional inspections or testing upon finding that these requirements are met, any additional inspections or testing shall be limited to the extent reasonably necessary to avoid the likelihood of prejudice and shall be coordinated among all similarly situated parties to ensure that they occur without unnecessary duplication. For purposes of providing notice to an insurer prior to inspections or testing under paragraph (6) of subdivision (h) of Section 1375, if notice of the proceedings was not provided by the insurer's insured, notice may be made via certified mail either by the subcontractor, design professional, association, or respondent to the address specified in the Statement of Insurance provided under paragraph (2) of subdivision (e) of Section 1375. Nothing herein shall affect the rights of an intervenor who files a complaint in intervention. If the association alleges defects that were not specified in the prefiling dispute resolution process under Section 1375, the respondent, subcontractor, and design professionals shall be permitted to engage in testing or inspection necessary to respond to the additional claims. A party who seeks additional inspections or testing based upon the amendment of claims shall apply to the court for leave to conduct those inspections or that testing.

If the court determines that it must review the defect claims alleged by the association in the prefiling dispute resolution process in order to determine whether the association alleges new or additional defects, this review shall be conducted in camera. Upon objection of any party, the court shall refer the matter to a judge other than the assigned trial judge to determine if the claim has been amended in such a way as to require additional testing or inspection.

(d) Any subcontractor or design professional who had notice of the facilitated dispute resolution conducted under Section 1375 but failed to attend, or attended without settlement authority, shall be bound by the amount of any settlement reached in the facilitated dispute resolution in any subsequent trial, although the affected party may introduce evidence as to the allocation of the settlement. Any party who failed to participate in the facilitated dispute resolution because the party did not receive timely notice of the mediation shall be relieved of any obligation to participate in the settlement. Notwithstanding any privilege applicable to the prefiling dispute resolution process provided by Section 1375, evidence may be introduced by any party to show whether a subcontractor or design professional failed to attend or attended without settlement authority. The binding effect of this subdivision shall in no way diminish or reduce a nonsettling subcontractor or design professional's right to defend itself or assert all available defenses relevant to its liability in any subsequent trial. For purposes of this subdivision, a subcontractor or design professional shall not be deemed to have attended without settlement authority because it asserted defenses to its potential liability.

(e) Notice of the facilitated dispute resolution conducted under Section 1375 must be mailed by the respondent no later than 20 days prior to the date of the first facilitated dispute resolution session to all parties. Notice shall also be mailed to each of these parties' known insurance carriers. Mailing of this notice shall be by certified mail. Any subsequent facilitated dispute resolution notices shall be served by any means reasonably calculated to provide those parties actual notice.

(f) As to the complaint, the order of discovery shall, at the request of any defendant, except upon a showing of good cause, permit the association's expert witnesses to be deposed prior to any percipient party depositions. The depositions shall, at the request of the association be followed immediately by the defendant's experts and then by the subcontractors' and design professionals' experts, except on a showing of good cause. For purposes of this section, in determining what constitutes "good cause," the court shall consider, among other things, the goal of early disclosure of defects and whether the expert is prepared to render a final opinion, except that the court may modify the scope of any expert's deposition to address those concerns.

(g) (1) The only method of seeking judicial relief for the failure of the association or the respondent to complete the dispute resolution process under Section 1375 shall be the assertion, as provided for in this subdivision, of a procedural deficiency to an action for damages by the association against the respondent after that action has been filed. A verified application asserting a procedural deficiency shall be filed with the court no later than 90 days after the answer to the plaintiff's complaint has been served, unless the court finds that extraordinary conditions exist.

(2) Upon the verified application of the association or the respondent alleging substantial noncompliance with Section 1375, the court shall schedule a hearing within 21 days of the application to determine whether the association or respondent has substantially complied with this section. The issue may be determined upon affidavits or upon oral testimony, in the discretion of the court.

(3) (A) If the court finds that the association or the respondent did not substantially comply with this paragraph, the court shall stay the action for up to 90 days to allow the noncomplying party to establish substantial compliance. The court shall set a hearing within 90 days to determine substantial compliance. At any time, the court may, for good cause shown, extend the period of the stay upon application of the noncomplying party.

(B) If, within the time set by the court pursuant to this paragraph, the association or the respondent has not established that it has substantially complied with this section, the court shall determine if, in the interest of justice, the action should be dismissed without prejudice, or if another remedy should be fashioned. Under no circumstances shall the court dismiss the action with prejudice as a result of the association's failure to substantially comply with this section. In determining the appropriate remedy, the court shall consider the extent to which the respondent has complied with this section.

(h) This section shall become operative on July 1, 2002, however it shall not apply to any pending action or proceeding.

(i) This section shall become inoperative on July 1, 2010, and, as of January 1, 2011, is repealed, unless a later enacted statute that is enacted before January 1, 2011, deletes or extends the dates on which it becomes inoperative and is repealed.

Civ. Code § 1375.1. Disclosure To Association Members Of Settlement Agreement Regarding Defects.

(a) As soon as is reasonably practicable after the association and the builder have entered into a settlement agreement or the matter has otherwise been resolved regarding alleged defects in the common areas, alleged defects in the separate interests that the association is obligated to maintain or repair, or alleged defects in the separate interests that arise out of, or are integrally related to, defects in the common areas or separate interests that the association is obligated to maintain or repair, where the defects giving rise to the dispute have not been corrected, the association shall, in writing, inform only the members of the association whose names appear on the records of the association that the matter has been resolved, by settlement agreement or other means, and disclose all of the following:

(1) A general description of the defects that the association reasonably believes, as of the date of the disclosure, will be corrected or replaced.

(2) A good faith estimate, as of the date of the disclosure, of when the association believes that the defects identified in paragraph (1) will be corrected or replaced. The association may state that the estimate may be modified.

(3) The status of the claims for defects in the design or construction of the common interest development that were not identified in paragraph (1) whether expressed in a preliminary list of defects sent to each member of the association or otherwise claimed and disclosed to the members of the association.

(b) Nothing in this section shall preclude an association from amending the disclosures required pursuant to subdivision (a), and any amendments shall supersede any prior conflicting information disclosed to the members of the association and shall retain any privilege attached to the original disclosures.

(c) Disclosure of the information required pursuant to subdivision (a) or authorized by subdivision (b) shall not waive any privilege attached to the information.

(d) For the purposes of the disclosures required pursuant to this section, the term "defects" shall be defined to include any damage resulting from defects.

IMPROVEMENTS

Civ. Code § 1376. Installation Of Video And Television Antenna.

(a) Any covenant, condition, or restriction contained in any deed, contract, security instrument, or other instrument affecting the transfer or sale of, or any interest in, a common interest development that effectively prohibits or restricts the installation or use of a video or television antenna, including a satellite dish, or that effectively prohibits or restricts the attachment of that antenna to a structure within that development where the antenna is not visible from any street or common area, except as otherwise prohibited or restricted by law, is void and unenforceable as to its application to the installation or use of a video or television antenna that has a diameter or diagonal measurement of 36 inches or less.

(b) This section shall not apply to any covenant, condition, or restriction, as described in subdivision (a), that imposes reasonable restrictions on the installation or use of a video or television antenna, including a satellite dish, that has a diameter or diagonal measurement of 36 inches or less. For purposes of this section, "reasonable restrictions" means those restrictions that do not significantly increase the cost of the video or television antenna system, including all related equipment, or significantly decrease its efficiency or performance and include all of the following:

(1) Requirements for application and notice to the association prior to the installation.

(2) Requirement of the owner of a separate interest, as defined in Section 1351, to obtain the approval of the association for the installation of a video or television antenna that has a diameter or diagonal measurement of 36 inches or less on a separate interest owned by another.

(3) Provision for the maintenance, repair, or replacement of roofs or other building components.

(4) Requirements for installers of a video or television antenna to indemnify or reimburse the association or its members for loss or damage caused by the installation, maintenance, or use of a video or television antenna that has a diameter or diagonal measurement of 36 inches or less.

(c) Whenever approval is required for the installation or use of a video or television antenna, including a satellite dish, the application for approval shall be processed by the appropriate approving entity for the common interest development in the same manner as an application for approval of an architectural modification to the property, and the issuance of a decision on the application shall not be willfully delayed.

(d) In any action to enforce compliance with this section, the prevailing party shall be awarded reasonable attorney's fees.

Civ. Code § 1378. Required Architectural Review Procedures; Exemptions.

(a) This section applies if an association's governing documents require association approval before an owner of a separate interest may make a physical change to the owner's separate interest or to the common area. In reviewing and approving or disapproving a proposed change, the association shall satisfy the following requirements:

(1) The association shall provide a fair, reasonable, and expeditious procedure for making its decision. The procedure shall be included in the association's governing documents. The procedure shall provide for prompt deadlines. The procedure shall state the maximum time for response to an application or a request for reconsideration by the board of directors.

(2) A decision on a proposed change shall be made in good faith and may not be unreasonable, arbitrary, or capricious.

(3) Notwithstanding a contrary provision of the governing documents, a decision on a proposed change may not violate any governing provision of law, including, but not limited to, the Fair Employment and Housing Act (Part 2.8 (commencing with Section 12900) of Division 3 of Title 2 of the Government Code), or a building code or other applicable law governing land use or public safety.

(4) A decision on a proposed change shall be in writing. If a proposed change is disapproved, the written decision shall include both an explanation of why the proposed change is disapproved and a description of the procedure for reconsideration of the decision by the board of directors.

(5) If a proposed change is disapproved, the applicant is entitled to reconsideration by the board of directors of the association that made the decision, at an open meeting of the board. This paragraph does not require reconsideration of a decision that is made by the board of directors or a body that has the same membership as the board of directors, at a meeting that satisfies the requirements of Section 1363.05. Reconsideration by the board does not constitute dispute resolution within the meaning of Section

1363.820.

(b)   Nothing in this section authorizes a physical change to the common area in a manner that is inconsistent with an association's governing documents, unless the change is required by law.

(c)   An association shall annually provide its members with notice of any requirements for association approval of physical changes to property. The notice shall describe the types of changes that require association approval and shall include a copy of the procedure used to review and approve or disapprove a proposed change.

CHAPTER 3

ORGANIZATION AND MANAGEMENT OF NONPROFIT MUTUAL BENEFIT CORPORATIONS
(Corporations Code §§ 7110-7160 and 7210-7238)

Corp. Code § 7110. Title Of Part.

This part shall be known and may be cited as the Nonprofit Mutual Benefit Corporation Law.

Corp. Code § 7111. Lawful Purposes Of Nonprofit Mutual Benefit Corporations.

Subject to any other provision of law of this state applying to the particular class of corporation or line of activity, a corporation may be formed under this part for any lawful purpose; provided that a corporation all of the assets of which are irrevocably dedicated to charitable, religious, or public purposes and which as a matter of law or according to its articles or bylaws must, upon dissolution, distribute its assets to a person or persons carrying on a charitable, religious, or public purpose or purposes may not be formed under this part.

Corp. Code § 7120. Corporation Formed By Execution And Filing Of Articles; Signatures Required.

(a) One or more persons may form a corporation under this part by executing and filing articles of incorporation.

(b) If initial directors are named in the articles, each director named in the articles shall sign and acknowledge the articles; if initial directors are not named in the articles, the articles shall be signed by one or more persons who thereupon are the incorporators of the corporation.

(c) The corporate existence begins upon the filing of the articles and continues perpetually, unless otherwise expressly provided by law or in the articles.

Corp. Code § 7121. Change Of Unincorporated Association To

Corporation.

(a) In the case of an existing unincorporated association, the association may change its status to that of a corporation upon a proper authorization for such by the association in accordance with its rules and procedures.

(b) In addition to the matters required to be set forth in the articles pursuant to Section 7130, the articles in the case an incorporation authorized by subdivision (a) shall set forth that an existing unincorporated association, stating its name, is being incorporated by the filing of the articles.

(c) The articles filed pursuant to this section shall be accompanied by a verified statement of any two officers or governing board members of the association stating that the incorporation of the association by means of the articles to which the verified statement is attached has been approved by the association in accordance with its rules and procedures.

(d) Upon the change of status of an unincorporated association to a corporation pursuant to subdivision (a), the property of the association becomes the property of the corporation and the members of the association who had any voting rights of the type referred to in Section 5056 become members of the corporation.

(e) The filing for record in the office of the county recorder of any county in this state in which any of the real property of the association is located, of a copy of the articles of incorporation filed pursuant to this section, certified by the Secretary of State, shall evidence record ownership in the corporation of all interests of the association in and to the real property located in that county.

(f) All rights of creditors and all liens upon the property of the association shall be preserved unimpaired. Any action or proceeding pending by or against the unincorporated association may be prosecuted to judgment, which shall bind the corporation, or the corporation may be proceeded against or substituted in its place.

(g) If a corporation is organized by a person who is or was an officer, director or member of an unincorporated association and such corporation is not organized pursuant to subdivision (a), the unincorporated association may continue to use its name and the corporation may not use a name which is the same as or similar to the name of the unincorporated association.

Corp. Code § 7122. Prohibited Names; Reservation Of Names.

(a) The Secretary of State shall not file articles setting forth a name in which "bank," "trust," "trustee" or related words appear, unless the certificate of approval of the Superintendent of Banks is attached thereto.

(b) The Secretary of State shall not file articles pursuant to this part setting forth a name which may create the impression that the purpose of the corporation is public, charitable or religious or that it is a charitable foundation.

(c) The Secretary of State shall not file articles which set forth a name which is likely to mislead the public or which is the same as, or resembles so closely as to tend to deceive, the name of a domestic corporation, the name of a foreign corporation which is authorized to transact intrastate business or has registered its name pursuant to Section 2101, a name which a foreign corporation has assumed under subdivision (b) of Section 2106, a name which will become the record name of a domestic or foreign corporation upon the effective date of a filed corporate instrument where there is a delayed effective date pursuant to subdivision (c) of Section 110, or subdivision (c) of Section 5008, or a name which is under reservation pursuant to this section, Section 201, Section 5122, or Section 9122 except that a corporation may adopt a name that is substantially the same as an existing domestic or foreign corporation which is authorized to transact intrastate business or has registered its name pursuant to Section 2101, upon proof of consent by such corporation and a finding by the Secretary of State that under the circumstances the public is not likely to be misled.

The use by a corporation of a name in violation of this section may be enjoined notwithstanding the filing of its articles by the Secretary of State.

(d) Any applicant may, upon payment of the fee prescribed therefor in the Government Code, obtain from the Secretary of State a certificate of reservation of any name not prohibited by subdivision (c), and upon the issuance of the certificate the name stated therein shall be reserved for a period of 60 days. The Secretary of State shall not, however, issue certificates reserving the same name for two or more consecutive 60-day periods to the same applicant or for the use or benefit of the same person; nor shall consecutive reservations be made by or for the use or benefit of the same person of names so similar as to fall within the prohibitions of subdivision (c).

Corp. Code § 7130. Required Provisions.

The articles of incorporation of a corporation formed under this part shall set forth the following:

(a) The name of the corporation.

(b)(1) Except as provided in paragraph (2),the following statement:

"This corporation is a nonprofit mutual benefit corporation organized under the Nonprofit Mutual Benefit Corporation Law. The purpose of this corporation is to engage in any lawful act or activity for which a corporation may be organized under such law."

(2) In the case of a corporation formed under this part that is subject to the California Credit Union Law, the articles shall set forth a statement of purpose that is prescribed in the applicable provisions of the California Credit Union Law.

(3) The articles may include a further definition of the corporation's purposes.

(c) The name and address in this state of the corporation's initial agent for service of process in accordance with subdivision (b) of Section 8210.

Corp. Code § 7131. Statement Limiting Purposes Or Powers.

The articles of incorporation may set forth a further statement limiting the purposes or powers of the corporation.

Corp. Code § 7132. Optional Provisions.

(a) The articles of incorporation may set forth any or all of the following provisions, which shall not be effective unless expressly provided in the articles:

(1) A provision limiting the duration of the corporation's existence to a specified date.

(2) A provision conferring upon the holders of any evidences of indebtedness, issued or to be issued by a corporation the right to vote in the election of directors and on any other matters on which members may vote under this part even if the corporation does not have members.

(3) A provision conferring upon members the right to determine the consideration for which memberships shall be issued.

(4) In the case of a subordinate corporation instituted or created under the authority of a head organization, a provision setting forth either or both of the following:

(A) That the subordinate corporation shall dissolve whenever its charter is surrendered to, taken away by, or revoked by the head organization granting it.

(B) That in the event of its dissolution pursuant to an article provision allowed by subparagraph (A) or in the event of its dissolution for any reason, any assets of the corporation after compliance with the applicable provisions of Chapters 15 (commencing with Section 8510), 16 (commencing with Section 8610), and 17 (commencing with Section 8710) shall be distributed to the head organization.

(b) Nothing contained in subdivision (a) shall affect the enforceability, as between the parties thereto, of any lawful agreement not otherwise contrary to public policy.

(c) The articles of incorporation may set forth any or all of the following provisions:

(1) The names and addresses of the persons appointed to act as initial directors.

(2) Provisions concerning the transfer of memberships, in accordance with Section 7320.

(3) The classes of members, if any, and if there are two or more classes, the rights, privileges, preferences, restrictions and conditions attaching to each class.

(4) A provision which would allow any member to have more or less than one vote in any election or other matter presented to the members for a vote.

(5) A provision that requires an amendment to the articles, as provided in subdivision (a) of Section 7812, or to the bylaws, and any amendment or repeal of that amendment, to be approved in writing by a specified person or persons other than the board or the members. However, this approval requirement, unless the articles specify otherwise, shall not apply if any of the following circumstances exist:

(A) The specified person or persons have died or ceased to exist.

(B) If the right of the specified person or persons to approve is in the capacity of an officer, trustee, or other status and the office, trust, or status has ceased to exist.

(C) If the corporation has a specific proposal for amendment or repeal, and the corporation has provided written notice of that proposal, including a copy of the proposal, to the specified person or persons at the most recent address for each of them, based on the corporation's records, and the corporation has not received written approval or nonapproval within the period specified in the notice, which shall not be less than 10 nor more than 30 days commencing at least 20 days after the notice has been provided.

(6) Any other provision, not in conflict with law, for the management of the activities and for the conduct of the affairs of the corporation, including any provision which is required or permitted by this part to be stated in the bylaws.

Corp. Code § 7133. Articles As Proof Of Corporate Existence.

For all purposes other than an action in the nature of *quo warranto*, a copy of the articles of a corporation duly certified by the Secretary of State is conclusive evidence of the formation of the corporation and *prima facie* evidence of its corporate existence.

Corp. Code § 7134. Powers of Incorporators When Directors Not Named.

If initial directors have not been named in the articles, the incorporator or incorporators, until the directors are elected, may do whatever is necessary and proper to perfect the organization of the corporation, including the adoption and amendment of bylaws of the corporation and the election of directors and officers.

Corp. Code § 7135. Sections 7130 And 7131 As Not Limiting Court Power Over Corporation.

Nothing in Sections 7130 or 7131 or in any provision of the articles of a mutual benefit corporation shall be construed to limit the equitable power of a court to impress a charitable trust upon any or all of the assets of a mutual benefit corporation or otherwise treat it as a public benefit corporation.

Corp. Code § 7140. Powers Of Corporation.

Subject to any limitations contained in the articles or bylaws and to compliance with other provisions of this division and any other applicable laws, a corporation, in carrying out its activities, shall have all of the powers of a natural person, including, without limitation, the power to:

(a) Adopt, use, and at will alter a corporate seal, but failure to affix a seal does not affect the validity of any instrument.

(b) Adopt, amend, and repeal bylaws.

(c) Qualify to conduct its activities in any other state, territory, dependency or foreign country.

(d) Issue, purchase, redeem, receive, take or otherwise acquire, own, sell, lend, exchange, transfer or otherwise dispose of, pledge, use and otherwise deal in and with its own memberships bonds, debentures, notes and debt securities.

(e) Pay pensions, and establish and carry out pension, deferred compensation, saving, thrift and other retirement, incentive and benefit plans, trusts and provisions for any or all of its directors, officers, employees and persons providing services to it or any of its subsidiary or related or associated corporations, and to indemnify and purchase and maintain insurance on behalf of any fiduciary of such plans, trusts, or provisions.

(f) Issue certificates evidencing membership in accordance with the provisions of Section 7313 and issue identity cards.

(g) Levy dues, assessments, and admission and transfer fees.

(h) Make donations for the public welfare or for community funds, hospital, charitable, educational, scientific, civic, religious or similar purposes.

(i) Assume obligations, enter into contracts, including contracts of guarantee or suretyship, incur liabilities, borrow or lend money or otherwise use its credit, and secure any of its obligations, contracts or liabilities by mortgage, pledge or other encumbrance of all or any part of its property and income.

(j) Participate with others in any partnership, joint venture or other association, transaction or arrangement of any kind whether or not such participation involves sharing or delegation of control with or to others.

(k) Act as trustee under any trust incidental to the principal objects of the corporation, and receive, hold, administer, exchange, and expend funds and property subject to such trust.

(l) Carry on a business at a profit and apply any profit that results from the business activity to any activity in which it may lawfully engage.

Corp. Code § 7141. Ultra Vires Acts; Corporation Bound By Authorized Or Ratified Contract.

Subject to Section 7142:

(a) No limitation upon the activities, purposes, or powers of the corporation or upon the powers of the members, officers, or directors, or the manner of exercise of such powers, contained in or implied by the articles or by Chapters 15 (commencing with Section 8510), 16 (commencing with Section 8610), and 17 (commencing with Section 8710) shall be asserted as between the corporation or member, officer or director and any third person, except in a proceeding: (1) by a member or the state to enjoin the doing or continuation of unauthorized activities by the corporation or its officers, or both, in cases where third parties have not acquired rights thereby, (2) to dissolve the corporation, or (3) by the corporation or by a member suing in a representative suit against the officers or directors of the corporation for violation of their authority.

(b) Any contract or conveyance made in the name of a corporation which is authorized or ratified by the board, or is done within the scope of authority, actual or apparent, conferred by the board or within the agency power of the officer executing it, except as the board's authority is limited by law other than this part, binds the corporation, and the corporation acquires rights thereunder whether the contract is executed or wholly or in part executory.

Corp. Code § 7142. Action For Breach Of Charitable Trust; Who May Bring; Remedies.

(a) Notwithstanding Section 7141, in the case of a corporation holding assets in charitable trust, any of the following may bring an action to enjoin, correct, obtain damages for or to otherwise remedy a breach of the charitable trust:

(1) The corporation, or a member in the name of the corporation pursuant to Section 7710.

(2) An officer of the corporation.

(3) A director of the corporation.

(4) A person with a reversionary, contractual, or property interest in the assets subject to such charitable trust.

(5) The Attorney General, or any person granted relator status by the Attorney General. The Attorney General shall be given notice of any action brought by the persons specified in paragraphs (1) through (4), and may intervene.

(b) In an action under this section, the court may not rescind or enjoin the performance of a contract unless:

(1) All of the parties to the contract are parties to the action;or

(2) No party to the contract has, in good faith, and without actual notice of the trust restriction, parted with value, under the contract or in reliance upon it; and

(3) It is equitable to do so.

Corp. Code § 7150. Adoption, Amendment Or Repeal.

(a) Except as provided in subdivision (c) and Sections 7151, 7220, 7224, 7512, 7613, and 7615, bylaws may be adopted, amended or repealed by the board unless the action would:

(1) Materially and adversely affect the rights of members as to voting, dissolution, redemption, or transfer;

(2) Increase or decrease the number of members authorized in total or for any class;

(3) Effect an exchange, reclassification or cancellation of all or part of the memberships; or

(4) Authorize a new class of membership.

(b) Bylaws may be adopted, amended or repealed by approval of the members (Section 5034); provided, however, that such adoption, amendment or repeal also requires approval by the members of a class if such action would:

(1) Materially and adversely affect the rights, privileges, preferences, restrictions or conditions of that class as to voting, dissolution, redemption, or transfer in a manner different than such action affects another class;

(2) Materially and adversely affect such class as to voting, dissolution, redemption, or transfer by changing the rights, privileges, preferences, restrictions or conditions of another class;

(3) Increase or decrease the number of memberships authorized for such class;

(4) Increase the number of memberships authorized for another class;

(5) Effect an exchange, reclassification or cancellation of all or part of the memberships of such class; or

(6) Authorize a new class of memberships.

(c) The articles or bylaws may restrict or eliminate the power of the board to adopt, amend or repeal any or all bylaws, subject to subdivision (e) of Section 7151.

(d) Bylaws may also provide that the repeal or amendment of those bylaws, or the repeal or amendment of specified portions of those bylaws, may occur only with the approval in writing of a specified person or persons other than the board or members. However, this approval requirement, unless the bylaws specify otherwise, shall not apply if any of the following circumstances exist:

(1) The specified person or persons have died or ceased to exist.

(2) If the right of the specified person or persons to approve is in the capacity of an officer, trustee, or other status and the office, trust, or status has ceased to exist.

(3) If the corporation has a specific proposal for amendment or repeal, and the corporation has provided written notice of that proposal, including a copy of the proposal, to the specified person or persons at the most recent address for each of them, based on the corporation's records, and the corporation has not received written approval or nonapproval within the period specified in the notice, which shall not be less than 10 nor more than 30 days commencing at least 20 days after the notice has been provided.

Corp. Code § 7151. Required And Optional Provisions; Number Of Directors.

(a) The bylaws shall set forth (unless such provision is contained in the articles, in which case it may only be changed by an amendment of the articles) the number of directors of the corporation, or the method of determining the number of directors of the corporation, or that the number of directors shall be not less than a stated minimum nor more than a stated maximum with the exact number of directors to be fixed, within the limits specified, by approval of the board or the members (Section 5034), in the manner provided in the bylaws, subject to subdivision (e). The number or minimum number of directors may be one or more.

(b) Once members have been admitted, a bylaw specifying or changing a fixed number of directors or the maximum or minimum number or changing from a fixed to a variable board or vice versa may only be adopted by approval of the members (Section 5034).

(c) The bylaws may contain any provision, not in conflict with law or the articles, for the management of the activities and for the conduct of the affairs of the corporation, including but not limited to:

(1) Any provision referred to in subdivision (c) of Section 7132.

(2) The time, place and manner of calling, conducting and giving notice of members', directors' and committee meetings, or of conducting mail ballots.

(3) The qualifications, duties and compensation of directors; the time of their election; and the requirements of a quorum for directors' and committee meetings.

(4) The appointment of committees, composed of directors or nondirectors or both, by the board or any officer and the authority of any such committees.

(5) The appointment, duties, compensation and tenure of officers.

(6) The mode of determination of members of record.

(7) The making of reports and financial statements to members.

(8) Setting, imposing and collecting dues, assessments, and admission and transfer fees.

(d) The bylaws may provide for the manner of admission, withdrawal, suspension, and expulsion of members, consistent with the requirements of Section 7341.

(e) The bylaws may require, for any or all corporate actions (except as provided in paragraphs (1) and (2) of subdivision (a) of Section 7222, subdivision (c) of Section 7615, and Section 8610) the vote of a larger proportion of, or all of, the members or the members of any class, unit, or grouping of members or the vote of a larger proportion of, or all of, the directors, than is otherwise required by this part. Such a provision in the bylaws requiring such greater vote shall not be altered, amended or repealed except by such greater vote, unless otherwise provided in the bylaws.

(f) The bylaws may contain a provision limiting the number of members, in total or of any class, which the corporation is authorized to admit.

Corp. Code § 7152. Provisions For Delegates.

A corporation may provide in its bylaws for delegates having some or all of the authority of members. Where delegates are provided for, the bylaws shall set forth delegates' terms of office, any reasonable method for delegates' selection and removal, and any reasonable method for calling, noticing and holding meetings of delegates and may set forth the manner in which delegates may act by written ballot similar to Section 7513 for written ballot of members. Delegates may only act personally at a meeting or by written ballot and may not act by proxy. Delegates may be given a name other than "delegates."

Corp. Code § 7160. Location And Inspection Of Articles And Bylaws.

Every corporation shall keep at its principal office in this state the original or a copy of its articles and bylaws as amended to date, which shall be open to inspection by the members at all reasonable times during office hours. If the corporation has no office in this state, it shall upon the written request of any member furnish to such member a copy of the articles or bylaws as amended to date.

Corp. Code § 7210. Corporate Powers Exercised By Board; Delegation.

Each corporation shall have a board of directors. Subject to the provisions of this part and any limitations in the articles or bylaws relating to action required to be approved by the members (Section 5034), or by a majority of all members (Section 5033), the activities and affairs of a corporation shall be conducted and all corporate powers shall be exercised by or under the direction of the board. The board may delegate the

Corporations

management of the activities of the corporation to any person or persons, management company, or committee however composed, provided that the activities and affairs of the corporation shall be managed and all corporate powers shall be exercised under the ultimate direction of the board.

Corp. Code § 7211. Board Meetings; Notice; Quorum; Consent To Act Without Meeting.

(a) Unless otherwise provided in the articles or in the bylaws, all of the following apply:

(1) Meetings of the board may be called by the chair of the board or the president or any vice president or the secretary or any two directors.

(2) Regular meetings of the board may be held without notice if the time and place of the meetings are fixed by the bylaws or the board. Special meetings of the board shall be held upon four days' notice by first-class mail or 48 hours' notice delivered personally or by telephone, including a voice messaging system or by electronic transmission by the corporation (Section 20). The articles or bylaws may not dispense with notice of a special meeting. A notice, or waiver of notice, need not specify the purpose of any regular or special meeting of the board.

(3) Notice of a meeting need not be given to a director who provided a waiver of notice or consent to holding the meeting or an approval of the minutes thereof in writing, whether before or after the meeting, or who attends the meeting without protesting, prior thereto or at its commencement, the lack of notice to that director. These waivers, consents and approvals shall be filed with the corporate records or made a part of the minutes of the meetings.

(4) A majority of the directors present, whether or not a quorum is present, may adjourn any meeting to another time and place. If the meeting is adjourned for more than 24 hours, notice of an adjournment to another time and place shall be given prior to time of the adjourned meeting to the directors who were not present at the time of the adjournment.

(5) Meetings of the board may be held at a place within or without the state that has been designated in the notice of the meeting or, if not stated in the notice or if there is no notice, designated in the bylaws or by resolution of the board.

(6) Members of the board may participate in a meeting through use of conference telephone, electronic video screen communication, or electronic transmission by and to the corporation (Sections 20 and 21). Participation in a meeting through the use of conference telephone

or electronic video screen communication pursuant to this subdivision constitutes presence in person at that meeting as long as all members participating in the meeting are able to hear one another. Participation in a meeting through use of electronic transmission by and to the corporation, other than conference telephone and electronic video screen communication, pursuant to this subdivision constitutes presence in person at the meeting if both of the following apply:

(A) Each member participating in the meeting can communicate with all of the other members concurrently.

(B) Each member is provided the means of participating in all matters before the board, including, without limitation, the capacity to propose, or to interpose an objection to, a specific action to be taken by the corporation.

(7) A majority of the number of directors authorized in or pursuant to the articles or bylaws constitutes a quorum of the board for the transaction of business. The articles or bylaws may require the presence of one or more specified directors in order to constitute a quorum of the board to transact business, as long as the death of a director or the death or nonexistence of the person or persons otherwise authorized to appoint or designate that director does not prevent the corporation from transacting business in the normal course of events. The articles or bylaws may not provide that a quorum shall be less than one-fifth the number of directors authorized in the articles or bylaws, or less than two, whichever is larger, unless the number of directors authorized in the articles or bylaws is one, in which case one director constitutes a quorum.

(8) Subject to the provisions of Sections 7212, 7233, 7234, and subdivision (e) of Section 7237 and Section 5233, insofar as it is made applicable pursuant to Section 7238, an act or decision done or made by a majority of the directors present at a meeting duly held at which a quorum is present is the act of the board. The articles or bylaws may not provide that a lesser vote than a majority of the directors present at a meeting is the act of the board. A meeting at which a quorum is initially present may continue to transact business notwithstanding the withdrawal of directors, if any action taken is approved by at least a majority of the required quorum for the meeting, or a greater number required by this division, the articles or bylaws.

(b) An action required or permitted to be taken by the board may be taken without a meeting, if all members of the board shall individually or collectively consent in writing to that action. The written consent or consents shall be filed with the minutes of the proceedings of the board.

The action by written consent shall have the same force and effect as a unanimous vote of the directors. For the purposes of this section only, "all members of the board" does not include an "interested director" as defined in Section 5233, insofar as it is made applicable pursuant to Section 7238.

(c) Each director present and voting at a meeting shall have one vote on each matter presented to the board of directors for action at that meeting. No director may vote at any meeting by proxy.

(d) This section applies also to incorporators, to committees of the board, and to action by those incorporators or committees mutatis mutandis.

Corp. Code § 7212. Executive Committees; Creation; Authority To Act.

(a) The board may, by resolution adopted by a majority of the number of directors then in office, provided that a quorum is present, create one or more committees, each consisting of two or more directors, to serve at the pleasure of the board. Appointments to such committees shall be by a majority vote of the directors then in office, unless the articles or bylaws require a majority vote of the number of directors authorized in the articles or bylaws. The bylaws may authorize one or more committees, each consisting of two or more directors, and may provide that a specified officer or officers who are also directors of the corporation shall be a member or members of such committee or committees. The board may appoint one or more directors as alternate members of such committee, who may replace any absent member at any meeting of the committee. Such committee, to the extent provided in the resolution of the board or in the bylaws, shall have all of the authority of the board, except with respect to:

(1) The approval of any action for which this part also requires approval of the members (Section 5034) or approval of a majority of all members (Section 5033), regardless of whether the corporation has members.

(2) The filling of vacancies on the board or in any committee which has the authority of the board.

(3) The fixing of compensation of the directors for serving on the board or on any committee.

(4) The amendment or repeal of bylaws or the adoption of new bylaws.

(5) The amendment or repeal of any resolution of the board which by its express terms is not amendable or repealable.

(6)   The appointment of committees of the board or the members thereof.

(7)   The expenditure of corporate funds to support a nominee for director after there are more people nominated for director than can be elected.

(8)   With respect to any assets held in charitable trust, the approval of any self-dealing transaction except as provided in paragraph (3) of subdivision (d) of Section 5233.

(b)   A committee exercising the authority of the board shall not include as members persons who are not directors. However, the board may create other committees that do not exercise the authority of the board and these other committees may include persons who are not directors.

(c)   Unless the bylaws otherwise provide, the board may delegate to any committee, appointed pursuant to paragraph (4) of subdivision (c) of Section 7151 or otherwise, powers as authorized by Section 7210, but may not delegate the powers set forth in paragraphs (1) to (8), inclusive, of subdivision (a).

Corp. Code § 7213. Corporate Officers Required; Selection; Resignation.

(a)   A corporation shall have a chairman of the board, who may be given the title chair of the board, chairperson of the board, chairman of the board, or chairwoman of the board, or a president or both, a secretary, a treasurer or a chief financial officer and any other officers with any titles and duties as shall be stated in the bylaws or determined by the board and as may be necessary to enable it to sign instruments. The president, or if there is no president the chair of the board, is the general manager and chief executive officer of the corporation, unless otherwise provided in the articles or bylaws. Unless otherwise specified in the articles or the bylaws, if there is no chief financial officer, the treasurer is the chief financial officer of the corporation. Any number of offices may be held by the same person unless the articles or bylaws provide otherwise.

(b)   Except as otherwise provided by the articles or bylaws, officers shall be chosen by the board and serve at the pleasure of the board, subject to the rights, if any, of an officer under any contract of employment. Any officer may resign at any time upon written notice to the corporation without prejudice to the rights, if any, of the corporation under any contract to which the officer is a party.

Corp. Code § 7214. Validity Of Instrument Signed By Officers.

Subject to the provisions of subdivision (a) of Section 7141 and Section 7142, any note, mortgage, evidence of indebtedness, contract, conveyance or other instrument in writing, and any assignment or endorsement thereof, executed or entered into between any corporation and any other person, when signed by any one of the chairman of the board, the president or any vice president and by any one of the secretary, any assistant secretary, the chief financial officer or any assistant treasurer of such corporation, is not invalidated as to the corporation by any lack of authority of the signing officers in the absence of actual knowledge on the part of the other person that the signing officers had no authority to execute the same.

Corp. Code § 7215. Proof Of Corporate Bylaws; Resolutions.

The original or a copy in writing or in any other form capable of being converted into clearly legible tangible form of the bylaws or of the minutes of any incorporators', members', directors', committee or other meeting or of any resolution adopted by the board or a committee thereof, or members, certified to be a true copy by a person purporting to be the secretary or an assistant secretary of the corporation, is *prima facie* evidence of the adoption of such bylaws or resolution or of the due holding of such meeting and of the matters stated therein.

Corp. Code § 7220. Term Of Office; Manner Of Selection.

(a) Except as provided in subdivision (d), directors shall be elected for such terms, not longer than four years, as are fixed in the articles or bylaws. However, the terms of directors of a corporation without members may be up to six years. In the absence of any provision in the articles or bylaws, the term shall be one year. The articles or bylaws may provide for staggering the terms of directors by dividing the total number of directors into groups of one or more directors. The terms of office of the several groups and the number of directors in each group need not be uniform. No amendment of the articles or bylaws may extend the term of a director beyond that for which the director was elected, nor may any bylaw provision increasing the terms of directors be adopted without approval of the members (Section 5034).

(b) Unless the articles or bylaws otherwise provide, each director, including a director elected to fill a vacancy, shall hold office until the expiration of the term for which elected and until a successor has been elected and qualified, unless the director has been removed from office.

(c) The articles or bylaws may provide for the election of one or more directors by the members of any class voting as a class.

(d) For the purposes of this subdivision, "designator" means one or more designators. Subdivisions (a) through (c) notwithstanding, all or any portion of the directors authorized in the articles or bylaws of a corporation may hold office by virtue of designation or selection as provided by the articles or bylaws rather than by election. Such directors shall continue in office for the term prescribed by the governing article or bylaw provision, or, if there is no term prescribed, until the governing article or bylaw provision is duly amended or repealed, except as provided in subdivision (e) of Section 7222. A bylaw provision authorized by this subdivision may be adopted, amended, or repealed only by approval of the members (Section 5034), except as provided in subdivision (d) of Section 7150. Unless otherwise provided in the articles or bylaws, the entitlement to designate or select a director or directors shall cease if any of the following circumstances exist:

(1) The specified designator of that director or directors has died or ceased to exist.

(2) If the entitlement of the specified designator of that director or directors to designate is in the capacity of an officer, trustee, or other status and the office, trust, or status has ceased to exist.

(e) If a corporation has not issued memberships and (1) all the directors resign, die, or become incompetent, or (2) a corporation's initial directors have not been named in the articles and all incorporators resign, die, or become incompetent before the election of the initial directors, the superior court of any county may appoint directors of the corporation upon application by any party in interest.

Corp. Code § 7221. Removal Of Director For Cause.

(a) The board may declare vacant the office of a director who has been declared of unsound mind by a final order of court, or convicted of a felony, or, in the case of a corporation holding assets in charitable trust, has been found by a final order or judgment of any court to have breached any duty arising as a result of Section 7238, or, if at the time a director is elected, the bylaws provide that a director may be removed for missing a specified number of board meetings, fails to attend the specified number of meetings.

(b) As provided in paragraph (3) of subdivision (c) of Section 7151, the articles or bylaws may prescribe the qualifications of the directors. The board, by a majority vote of the directors who meet all of the required qualifications to be a director, may declare vacant the office of any director who fails or ceases to meet any required qualification that was in effect at the beginning of that director's current term of office.

Corp. Code § 7222. Removal Of Director Without Cause.

(a) Subject to subdivisions (b) and (f), any or all directors may be removed without cause if:

(1) In a corporation with fewer than 50 members, the removal is approved by a majority of all members (Section 5033).

(2) In a corporation with 50 or more members, the removal is approved by the members (Section 5034).

(3) In a corporation with no members, the removal is approved by a majority of the directors then in office.

(b) Except for a corporation having no members, pursuant to Section 7310:

(1) In a corporation in which the articles or bylaws authorize members to cumulate their votes pursuant to subdivision (a) of Section 7615, no director may be removed (unless the entire board is removed) when the votes cast against removal, or not consenting in writing to the removal, would be sufficient to elect the director if voted cumulatively at an election at which the same total number of votes were cast (or, if the action is taken by written ballot, all memberships entitled to vote were voted) and the entire number of directors authorized at the time of the director's most recent election were then being elected.

(2) When by the provisions of the articles or bylaws the members of any class, voting as a class, are entitled to elect one or more directors, any director so elected may be removed only by the applicable vote of the members of that class.

(3) When by the provisions of the articles or bylaws the members within a chapter or other organizational unit, or region or other geographic grouping, voting as such, are entitled to elect one or more directors, any director so elected may be removed only by the applicable vote of the members within the organizational unit or geographic grouping.

(c) Any reduction of the number of directors or any amendment reducing the number of classes of directors does not remove any director prior to the expiration of the director's term of office unless the reduction or amendment also provides for the removal of one or more specified directors.

(d) Except as provided in this section and Sections 7221 and 7223, a director may not be removed prior to the expiration of the director's term of office.

(e) Where a director removed under this section or Section 7221 or Section 7223 was chosen by designation pursuant to subdivision (d) of Section 7220, then:

(1) Where a different person may be designated pursuant to the governing article or bylaw provision, the new designation shall be made.

(2) Where the governing article or bylaw provision contains no provision under which a different person may be designated, the governing article or bylaw provision shall be deemed repealed.

(f) For the purposes of this subdivision, "designator" means one or more designators. If by the provisions of the articles or bylaws a designator is entitled to designate one or more directors, then:

(1) Unless otherwise provided in the articles or bylaws at the time of designation, any director so designated may be removed without cause by the designator of that director.

(2) Any director so designated may only be removed under subdivision (a) with the written consent of the designator of that director.

(3) Unless otherwise provided in the articles or bylaws, the right to remove shall not apply if any of the following circumstances exist:

(A) The designator entitled to that right has died or ceased to exist.

(B) If that right is in the capacity of an officer, trustee, or other status, and the office, trust, or status has ceased to exist.

Corp. Code § 7223. Removal Of Director By Director's Or Members' Suit; Role Of Attorney General.

(a) The superior court of the proper county may, at the suit of one of the parties specified in subdivision (b), remove from office any director in case of fraudulent or dishonest acts or gross abuse of authority or discretion with reference to the corporation or breach of any duty arising as a result of Section 7238 and may bar from reelection any director so removed for a period prescribed by the court. The corporation shall be made a party to such action.

(b) An action under subdivision (a) may be instituted by any of the following:

(1) A director.

(2) In the case of a corporation where the total number of votes entitled to be cast for a director is less than 5,000, twice the authorized number (Section 5036) of members, or 20 members, whichever is less.

(3) In the case of a corporation where the total number of votes entitled to be cast for a director is 5,000 or more, twice the authorized number (Section 5036) of members, or 100 members, whichever is less.

Corporations

(c) In the case of a corporation holding assets in charitable trust, the Attorney General may bring an action under subdivision (a), may intervene in such an action brought by any other party and shall be given notice of any such action brought by any other party.

Corp. Code § 7224. Filling Vacancies; Resignation.

(a) Unless otherwise provided in the articles or bylaws and except for a vacancy created by the removal of a director, vacancies on the board may be filled by approval of the board (Section 5032) or, if the number of directors then in office is less than a quorum, by (1) the unanimous written consent of the directors then in office, (2) the affirmative vote of a majority of the directors then in office at a meeting held pursuant to notice or waivers of notice complying with Section 7211, or (3) a sole remaining director. Unless the articles or a bylaw approved by the members (Section 5034) provide that the board may fill vacancies occurring in the board by reason of the removal of directors, or unless the corporation has no members pursuant to Section 7310, such vacancies may be filled only by approval of the members (Section 5034).

(b) The members may elect a director at any time to fill any vacancy not filled by the directors.

(c) Any director may resign effective upon giving written notice to the chairman of the board, the president, the secretary or the board of directors of the corporation, unless the notice specifies a later time for the effectiveness of such resignation. If the resignation is effective at a future time, a successor may be elected to take office when the resignation becomes effective.

Corp. Code § 7225. Provisional Director.

(a) If a corporation has an even number of directors who are equally divided and cannot agree as to the management of its affairs, so that its activities can no longer be conducted to advantage or so that there is danger that its property, activities or business will be impaired or lost, the superior court of the proper county may, notwithstanding any provisions of the articles or bylaws and whether or not an action is pending for an involuntary winding up or dissolution of the corporation, appoint a provisional director pursuant to this section. Action for such appointment may be brought by any director or by members holding not less than 33 1/3 percent of the voting power.

(b) If the members of a corporation are deadlocked so that they cannot elect the directors to be elected at the time prescribed therefor, the superior court of the proper county may, notwithstanding any provisions of the articles or bylaws, upon petition of members holding 50 percent of the voting power, appoint a provisional director or directors pursuant to this section or order such other equitable relief as the court deems appropriate.

(c) In the case of a corporation holding assets in charitable trust:

(1) Any person bringing an action under subdivision (a) or (b) shall give notice to the Attorney General, who may intervene; and

(2) The Attorney General may bring an action under subdivision (a) or (b).

(d) A provisional director shall be an impartial person, who is neither a member nor a creditor of the corporation, nor related by consanguinity or affinity within the third degree according to the common law to any of the other directors of the corporation or to any judge of the court by which such provisional director is appointed. A provisional director shall have all the rights and powers of a director until the deadlock in the board or among members is broken or until such provisional director is removed by order of the court or by approval of a majority of all members (Section 5033). Such person shall be entitled to such compensation as shall be fixed by the court unless otherwise agreed with the corporation.

Corp. Code § 7230. Application Of Article To All Directors.

(a) Any duties and liabilities set forth in this article shall apply without regard to whether a director is compensated by the corporation.

(b) Part 4 (commencing with Section 16000) of Division 9 of the Probate Code does not apply to the directors of any corporation.

Corp. Code § 7231. Duties And Liabilities Of Directors.

(a) A director shall perform the duties of a director, including duties as a member of any committee of the board upon which the director may serve, in good faith, in a manner such director believes to be in the best interests of the corporation and with such care, including reasonable inquiry, as an ordinarily prudent person in a like position would use under similar circumstances.

(b) In performing the duties of a director, a director shall be entitled to rely on information, opinions, reports or statements, including financial statements and other financial data, in each case prepared or presented by:

(1) One or more officers or employees of the corporation whom the director believes to be reliable and competent in the matters

presented;

(2) Counsel, independent accountants or other persons as to matters which the director believes to be within such person's professional or expert competence; or

(3) A committee upon which the director does not serve that is composed exclusively of any or any combination of directors, persons described in paragraph (1), or persons described in paragraph (2), as to matters within the committee's designated authority, which committee the director believes to merit confidence, so long as, in any case, the director acts in good faith, after reasonable inquiry when the need therefor is indicated by the circumstances and without knowledge that would cause such reliance to be unwarranted.

(c) A person who performs the duties of a director in accordance with subdivisions (a) and (b) shall have no liability based upon any alleged failure to discharge the person's obligations as a director, including, without limiting the generality of the foregoing, any actions or omissions which exceed or defeat a public or charitable purpose to which assets held by a corporation are dedicated.

Corp. Code § 7231.5. Liability Of Volunteer Director Or Officer Failure To Discharge Duties.

(a) Except as provided in Section 7233 or 7236, there is no monetary liability on the part of, and no cause of action for damages shall arise against, any volunteer director or volunteer executive officer of a nonprofit corporation subject to this part based upon any alleged failure to discharge the person's duties as a director or officer if the duties are performed in a manner that meets all of the following criteria:

(1) The duties are performed in good faith.

(2) The duties are performed in a manner such director or officer believes to be in the best interests of the corporation.

(3) The duties are performed with such care, including reasonable inquiry as an ordinarily prudent person in a like position would use under similar circumstances.

(b) "Volunteer" means the rendering of services without compensation. "Compensation" means remuneration whether by way of salary, fee, or other consideration for services rendered. However, the payment of per diem, mileage, or other reimbursement expenses to a director or executive officer does not affect that person's status as a volunteer within the meaning of this section.

(c) "Executive officer" means the president, vice president, secretary, or treasurer of a corporation or other individual serving in like capacity who assists in establishing the policy of the corporation.

(d) This section shall apply only to trade, professional, and labor organizations incorporated pursuant to this part which operate exclusively for fraternal, educational, and other nonprofit purposes, and under the provisions of Section 501(c) of the United States Internal Revenue Code.

(e) This section shall not be construed to limit the provisions of Section 7231.

Corp. Code § 7232. Applicability Of § 7231 To Selection Of Directors.

(a) Section 7231 governs the duties of directors as to any acts or omissions in connection with the election, selection, or nomination of directors.

(b) This section shall not be construed to limit the generality of Section 7231.

Corp. Code § 7233. Transactions Involving Director.

(a) No contract or other transaction between a corporation and one or more of its directors, or between a corporation and any domestic or foreign corporation, firm or association in which one or more of its directors has a material financial interest, is either void or voidable because such director or directors or such other corporation, business corporation, firm or association are parties or because such director or directors are present at the meeting of the board or a committee thereof which authorizes, approves or ratifies the contract or transaction, if:

(1) The material facts as to the transaction and as to such director's interest are fully disclosed or known to the members and such contract or transaction is approved by the members (Section 5034) in good faith, with any membership owned by any interested director not being entitled to vote thereon;

(2) The material facts as to the transaction and as to such director's interest are fully disclosed or known to the board or committee, and the board or committee authorizes, approves or ratifies the contract or transaction in good faith by a vote sufficient without counting the vote of the interested director or directors and the contract or transaction is just and reasonable as to the corporation at the time it is authorized, approved or ratified; or

(3) As to contracts or transactions not approved as provided in

paragraph (1) or (2) of this subdivision, the person asserting the validity of the contract or transaction sustains the burden of proving that the contract or transaction was just and reasonable as to the corporation at the time it was authorized, approved or ratified.

A mere common directorship does not constitute a material financial interest within the meaning of this subdivision. A director is not interested within the meaning of this subdivision in a resolution fixing the compensation of another director as a director, officer or employee of the corporation, notwithstanding the fact that the first director is also receiving compensation from the corporation.

(b) No contract or other transaction between a corporation and any corporation, business corporation or association of which one or more of its directors are directors is either void or voidable because such director or directors are present at the meeting of the board or a committee thereof which authorizes, approves or ratifies the contract or transaction, if:

(1) The material facts as to the transaction and as to such director's other directorship are fully disclosed or known to the board or committee, and the board or committee authorizes, approves or ratifies the contract or transaction in good faith by a vote sufficient without counting the vote of the common director or directors or the contract or transaction is approved by the members (Section 5034) in good faith; or

(2) As to contracts or transactions not approved as provided in paragraph (1) of this subdivision, the contract or transaction is just and reasonable as to the corporation at the time it is authorized, approved or ratified.

This subdivision does not apply to contracts or transactions covered by subdivision (a).

Corp. Code § 7234. Quorum For Purposes Of § 7233.

Interested or common directors may be counted in determining the presence of a quorum at a meeting of the board or a committee thereof which authorizes, approves or ratifies a contract or transaction as provided in Section 7233.

Corp. Code § 7235. Corporate Loans, Guaranties, And Advances.

(a) Unless prohibited by the articles or bylaws, a corporation may loan money or property to, or guarantee the obligation of, any director or officer of the corporation or of its parent, affiliate or subsidiary, provided:

(1) The board determines the loan or guaranty may reasonably be expected to benefit the corporation.

(2) Prior to consummating the transaction or any part thereof, the loan or guaranty is either:

(A) Approved by the members (Section 5034), without counting the vote of the director or officer, if a member, or

(B) Approved by the vote of a majority of the directors then in office, without counting the vote of the director who is to receive the loan or the benefit of the guaranty.

(b) Notwithstanding subdivision (a), a corporation may advance money to a director or officer of the corporation or of its parent, affiliate or subsidiary, for any expenses reasonably anticipated to be incurred in the performance of the duties of the director or officer of the corporation or of its parent, affiliate or subsidiary, provided that in the absence of such an advance the director or officer would be entitled to be reimbursed for these expenses by the corporation, its parent, affiliate or subsidiary.

(c) The provisions of subdivisions (a) and (b) do not apply to credit unions, or to the payment of premiums in whole or in part by a corporation on a life insurance policy on the life of a director or officer, so long as repayment to the corporation of the amount paid by it is secured by the proceeds of the policy and its cash surrender value, or to loans permitted under any statute regulating any special class of corporations.

Corp. Code § 7236. Directors' Liability For Distributions, Loans And Guaranties.

(a) Subject to the provisions of Section 7231, directors of a corporation who approve any of the following corporate actions shall be jointly and severally liable to the corporation for the benefit of all of the creditors entitled to institute an action under paragraph (1) or (2) of subdivision (c) or to the corporation in an action by the head organization or members under paragraph (1) or (3) of subdivision (c):

(1) The making of any distribution contrary to Chapter 4 (commencing with Section 7410).

(2) The distribution of assets after institution of dissolution proceedings of the corporation, without paying or adequately providing for all known liabilities of the corporation, excluding any claims not filed by creditors within the time limit set by the court in a notice given to creditors under Chapter 15 (commencing with Section 8510), Chapter 16 (commencing with Section 8610), and Chapter 17 (commencing with Section 8710).

(3) The making of any loan or guaranty contrary to Section 7235.

Corporations

(b) A director who is present at a meeting of the board, or any committee thereof, at which action specified in subdivision (a) is taken and who abstains from voting shall be considered to have approved the action.

(c) Suit may be brought in the name of the corporation to enforce the liability:

(1) Under paragraph (1) of subdivision (a) against any or all directors liable by the persons entitled to sue under subdivision (c) of Section 7420.

(2) Under paragraph (2) or (3) of subdivision (a) against any or all directors liable by any one or more creditors of the corporation whose debts or claims arose prior to the time of the corporate action who have not consented to the corporate action, whether or not they have reduced their claims to judgment.

(3) Under paragraph (3) of subdivision (a) against any or all directors liable by any one or more members at the time of any corporate action specified in paragraph (3) of subdivision (a) who have not consented to the corporate action, without regard to the provisions of Section 7710.

(d) The damages recoverable from a director under this section shall be the amount of the illegal distribution, or the loss suffered by the corporation as a result of the illegal loan or guaranty, but not exceeding, in the case of an action for the benefit of creditors, the liabilities of the corporation owed to nonconsenting creditors at the time of the violation.

(e) Any director sued under this section may implead all other directors liable and may compel contribution, either in that action or in an independent action against directors not joined in that action.

(f) Directors liable under this section shall also be entitled to be subrogated to the rights of the corporation:

(1) With respect to paragraph (1) of subdivision (a), against the persons who received the distribution.

(2) With respect to paragraph (2) of subdivision (a), against the persons who received the distribution.

(3) With respect to paragraph (3) of subdivision (a), against the person who received the loan or guaranty.

Any director sued under this section may file a cross-complaint against the person or persons who are liable to the director as a result of the subrogation provided for in this subdivision or may proceed against them in an independent action.

Corp. Code § 7237. Indemnification Of Corporate "Agent".

(a) For the purposes of this section, "agent" means any person who is or was a director, officer, employee or other agent of the corporation, or is or was serving at the request of the corporation as a director, officer, employee or agent of another foreign or domestic corporation, partnership, joint venture, trust or other enterprise, or was a director, officer, employee or agent of a foreign or domestic corporation which was a predecessor corporation of the corporation or of another enterprise at the request of such predecessor corporation; "proceeding" means any threatened, pending or completed action or proceeding, whether civil, criminal, administrative or investigative; and "expenses" includes without limitation attorneys' fees and any expenses of establishing a right to indemnification under subdivision (d) or paragraph (3) of subdivision (e).

(b) A corporation shall have power to indemnify any person who was or is a party or is threatened to be made a party to any proceeding (other than an action by or in the right of the corporation to procure a judgment in its favor, an action brought under Section 5233 of Part 2 (commencing with Section 5110) made applicable pursuant to Section 7238, or an action brought by the Attorney General or a person granted relator status by the Attorney General for any breach of duty relating to assets held in charitable trust) by reason of the fact that such person is or was an agent of the corporation, against expenses, judgments, fines, settlements and other amounts actually and reasonably incurred in connection with such proceeding if such person acted in good faith and in a manner such person reasonably believed to be in the best interests of the corporation and, in the case of a criminal proceeding, had no reasonable cause to believe the conduct of such person was unlawful. The termination of any proceeding by judgment, order, settlement, conviction or upon a plea of *nolo contendere* or its equivalent shall not, of itself, create a presumption that the person did not act in good faith and in a manner which the person reasonably believed to be in the best interests of the corporation or that the person had reasonable cause to believe that the person's conduct was unlawful.

(c) A corporation shall have power to indemnify any person who was or is a party or is threatened to be made a party to any threatened, pending or completed action by or in the right of the corporation, or brought under Section 5233 of Part 2 (commencing with Section 5110) made applicable pursuant to Section 7238, or brought by the Attorney General or a person granted relator status by the Attorney General for breach of duty relating to assets held in charitable trust, to procure a judgment in its favor by reason of the fact that such person is or was an agent of the corporation, against expenses actually and reasonably incurred by such person in connection with the defense or settlement of such action if such person acted in good faith, in a manner such person believed to be in the best interests of the corporation and with such care, including reasonable inquiry, as an ordinarily prudent person in a like position would use under similar circumstances. No indemnification shall be made under this subdivision:

(1) In respect of any claim, issue or matter as to which such person shall have been adjudged to be liable to the corporation in the performance of such person's duty to the corporation, unless and only to the extent that the court in which such proceeding is or was pending shall determine upon application that, in view of all the circumstances of the case, such person is fairly and reasonably entitled to indemnity for the expenses which such court shall determine;

(2) Of amounts paid in settling or otherwise disposing of a threatened or pending action, with or without court approval; or

(3) Of expenses incurred in defending a threatened or pending action which is settled or otherwise disposed of without court approval unless such action concerns assets held in charitable trust and is settled with the approval of the Attorney General.

(d) To the extent that an agent of a corporation has been successful on the merits in defense of any proceeding referred to in subdivision (b) or (c) or in defense of any claim, issue or matter therein, the agent shall be indemnified against expenses actually and reasonably incurred by the agent in connection therewith.

(e) Except as provided in subdivision (d), any indemnification under this section shall be made by the corporation only if authorized in the specific case, upon a determination that indemnification of the agent is proper in the circumstances because the agent has met the applicable standard of conduct set forth in subdivision (b) or (c) by:

(1) A majority vote of a quorum consisting of directors who are not parties to such proceeding;

(2) Approval of the members (Section 5034), with the persons to be indemnified not being entitled to vote thereon; or

(3) The court in which such proceeding is or was pending upon application made by the corporation or the agent or the attorney or other person rendering services in connection with the defense, whether or not such application by the agent, attorney or other person is opposed by the corporation.

(f)   Expenses incurred in defending any proceeding may be advanced by the corporation prior to the final disposition of such proceeding upon receipt of an undertaking by or on behalf of the agent to repay such amount unless it shall be determined ultimately that the agent is entitled to be indemnified as authorized in this section. The provisions of subdivision (a) of Section 7235 do not apply to advances made pursuant to this subdivision.

(g)   No provision made by a corporation to indemnify its or its subsidiary's directors or officers for the defense of any proceeding, whether contained in the articles, bylaws, a resolution of members or directors, an agreement or otherwise, shall be valid unless consistent with this section. Nothing contained in this section shall affect any right to indemnification to which persons other than such directors and officers may be entitled by contract or otherwise.

(h)   No indemnification or advance shall be made under this section, except as provided in subdivision (d) or paragraph (3) of subdivision (e), in any circumstance where it appears:

(1)   That it would be inconsistent with a provision of the articles, bylaws, a resolution of the members or an agreement in effect at the time of the accrual of the alleged cause of action asserted in the proceeding in which the expenses were incurred or other amounts were paid, which prohibits or otherwise limits indemnification; or

(2)   That it would be inconsistent with any condition expressly imposed by a court in approving a settlement.

(i)   A corporation shall have power to purchase and maintain insurance on behalf of any agent of the corporation against any liability asserted against or incurred by the agent in such capacity or arising out of the agent's status as such whether or not the corporation would have the power to indemnify the agent against such liability under the provisions of this section.

(j)   This section does not apply to any proceeding against any trustee, investment manager or other fiduciary of an employee benefit plan in such person's capacity as such, even though such person may also be an agent as defined in subdivision (a) of the employer corporation. A corporation shall have power to indemnify such trustee, investment manager or other fiduciary to the extent permitted by subdivision (f) of Section 207.

Corp. Code § 7238. Law Governing Assets In Charitable Trust.

Where a corporation holds assets in charitable trust, the conduct of its directors or of any person performing functions similar to those performed

by a director, shall, in respect to the assets held in charitable trust, be
governed by the standards of conduct set forth in Article 3 (commencing
with Section 5230) of Chapter 2 of Part 2 for directors of nonprofit public
benefit corporations. This does not limit any additional requirements
which may be specifically set forth in this part regarding corporations
holding assets in charitable trust.

CHAPTER 4

MEMBERSHIP IN NONPROFIT MUTUAL BENEFIT CORPORATIONS & ELECTRONIC TRANSMISSION

(Corporations Code §§ 20, 21, 310, 5009, 5012, 5016, 5032-5034, 5069, 7312, 7341, 7510-7527, and 7610-7616)

Corp. Code § 20. "Electronic Transmission" Defined.

"Electronic transmission by the corporation" means a communication

(a) delivered by (1) facsimile telecommunication or electronic mail when directed to the facsimile number or electronic mail address, respectively, for that recipient on record with the corporation, (2) posting on an electronic message board or network which the corporation has designated for those communications, together with a separate notice to the recipient of the posting, which transmission shall be validly delivered upon the later of the posting or delivery of the separate notice thereof, or (3) other means of electronic communication,

(b) to a recipient who has provided an unrevoked consent to the use of those means of transmission for communications under or pursuant to this code, and

(c) that creates a record that is capable of retention, retrieval, and review, and that may thereafter be rendered into clearly legible tangible form.

However, an electronic transmission under this code by a corporation to an individual shareholder or member of the corporation who is a natural person, and if an officer or director of the corporation, only if communicated to the recipient in that person's capacity as a shareholder or member, is not authorized unless, in addition to satisfying the requirements of this section, the consent to the transmission has been preceded by or includes a clear written statement to the recipient as to (a) any right of the recipient to have the record provided or made available on paper or in nonelectronic form, (b) whether the consent applies only to that transmission, to specified categories of communications, or to all communications from the corporation, and (c) the procedures the recipient must use to withdraw consent.

Corp. Code § 21. Construction - Electronic Transmission.

"Electronic transmission to the corporation" means a communication
(a) delivered by (1) facsimile telecommunication or electronic mail when directed to the facsimile number or electronic mail address, respectively, which the corporation has provided from time to time to shareholders or members and directors for sending communications to the corporation, (2) posting on an electronic message board or network which the corporation has designated for those communications, and which transmission shall be validly delivered upon the posting, or (3) other means of electronic communication,
(b) as to which the corporation has placed in effect reasonable measures to verify that the sender is the shareholder or member (in person or by proxy) or director purporting to send the transmission, and
(c) that creates a record that is capable of retention, retrieval, and review, and that may thereafter be rendered into clearly legible tangible form.

Corp. Code § 310. Transactions Between Corporations And Directors Or Corporations Having Interrelated Directors.

(a) No contract or other transaction between a corporation and one or more of its directors, or between a corporation and any corporation, firm or association in which one or more of its directors has a material financial interest, is either void or voidable because such director or directors or such other corporation, firm or association are parties or because such director or directors are present at the meeting of the board or a committee thereof which authorizes, approves or ratifies the contract or transaction, if

(1) The material facts as to the transaction and as to such director's interest are fully disclosed or known to the shareholders and such contract or transaction is approved by the shareholders (Section 153) in good faith, with the shares owned by the interested director or directors not being entitled to vote thereon, or

(2) The material facts as to the transaction and as to such director's interest are fully disclosed or known to the board or committee, and the board or committee authorizes, approves or ratifies the contract or transaction in good faith by a vote sufficient without counting the vote of the interested director or directors and the contract or transaction is just and reasonable as to the corporation at the time it is authorized, approved or ratified, or

(3) As to contracts or transactions not approved as provided in paragraph (1) or (2) of this subdivision, the person asserting the validity of

the contract or transaction sustains the burden of proving that the contract or transaction was just and reasonable as to the corporation at the time it was authorized, approved or ratified. A mere common directorship does not constitute a material financial interest within the meaning of this subdivision. A director is not interested within the meaning of this subdivision in a resolution fixing the compensation of another director as a director, officer or employee of the corporation, notwithstanding the fact that the first director is also receiving compensation from the corporation.

(b) No contract or other transaction between a corporation and any corporation or association of which one or more of its directors are directors is either void or voidable because such director or directors are present at the meeting of the board or a committee thereof which authorizes, approves or ratifies the contract or transaction, if

(1) The material facts as to the transaction and as to such director's other directorship are fully disclosed or known to the board or committee, and the board or committee authorizes, approves or ratifies the contract or transaction in good faith by a vote sufficient without counting the vote of the common director or directors or the contract or transaction is approved by the shareholders (Section 153) in good faith, or

(2) As to contracts or transactions not approved as provided in paragraph (1) of this subdivision, the contract or transaction is just and reasonable as to the corporation at the time it is authorized, approved or ratified. This subdivision does not apply to contracts or transactions covered by subdivision (a).

(c) Interested or common directors may be counted in determining the presence of a quorum at a meeting of the board or a committee thereof which authorizes, approves or ratifies a contract or transaction.

Corp. Code § 5009. Mailings.

Except as otherwise required, any reference in this part, Part 2, Part 3, Part 4 or Part 5 to mailing means first-, second-, or third-class mail, postage prepaid, unless registered mail is specified. Registered mail includes certified mail.

Corp. Code § 5012. "Financial Statements" Defined.

All references in this part, Part 2 (commencing with Section 5110), Part 3 (commencing with Section 7110), or Part 4 (commencing with Section 9110) to financial statements of a corporation mean statements prepared in conformity with generally accepted accounting principles or some other basis of accounting which reasonably sets forth the assets and liabilities and the income and expenses of the corporation and discloses the accounting basis used in their preparation.

Corp. Code § 5016. Notices Or Reports Mailed Or Delivered As Part Of Newsletter Or Magazine.

A notice or report mailed or delivered as part of a newsletter, magazine or other organ regularly sent to members shall constitute written notice or report pursuant to this division when addressed and mailed or delivered to the member, or in the case of members who are residents of the same household and who have the same address on the books of the corporation, when addressed and mailed or delivered to one of such members, at the address appearing on the books of the corporation.

Corp. Code § 5032. Approval By The Board.

"Approved by the board" means approved or ratified by the vote of the board or by the vote of a committee authorized to exercise the powers of the board, except as to matters not within the competence of the committee under Section 5212, Section 7212, or Section 92121.

Corp. Code § 5033. Approval By Majority Of Members.

"Approval by (or approval of) a majority of all members" means approval by an affirmative vote (or written ballot in conformity with Section 5513, Section 7513, or Section 9413) of a majority of the votes entitled to be cast. Such approval shall include the affirmative vote of a majority of the outstanding memberships of each class, unit, or grouping of members entitled, by any provision of the articles or bylaws or of Part 2, Part 3, Part 4 or Part 5 to vote as a class, unit, or grouping of members on the subject matter being voted upon and shall also include the affirmative vote of such greater proportion, including all, of the votes of the memberships of any class, unit, or grouping of members if such greater proportion is required by the bylaws (subdivision (e) of Section 5151, subdivision (e) of Section 7151, or subdivision (e) of Section 9151) or Part 2, Part 3, Part 4 or Part 5.

Corp. Code § 5034. Approval Of Members.

"Approval by (or approval of) the members" means approved or ratified by the affirmative vote of a majority of the votes represented and voting at a duly held meeting at which a quorum is present (which affirmative votes also constitute a majority of the required quorum) or written ballot in conformity with Section 5513, 7513, or 9413 or by the affirmative vote or written ballot of such greater proportion, including all of the votes of the memberships of any class, unit, or grouping of members as may be provided in the bylaws (subdivision (e) of Section 5151, subdivision (e) of Section 7151, or subdivision (e) of Section 9151) or in Part 2, Part 3, Part 4 or Part 5 for all or any specified member action.

Corp. Code § 5069. Proxy.

"Proxy" means a written authorization signed by a member or the member's attorney in fact giving another person or persons power to vote on behalf of such member. "Signed" for the purpose of this section means the placing of the member's name on the proxy (whether by manual signature, typewriting, telegraphic transmission or otherwise) by the member or such member's attorney in fact.

Corp. Code § 7312. Multiple And Fractional Memberships.

No person may hold more than one membership, and no fractional memberships may be held, except as follows:

(a) Two or more persons may have an indivisible interest in a single membership when authorized by, and in a manner or under the circumstances prescribed by, the articles or bylaws subject to Section 7612.

(b) If the articles or bylaws provide for classes of membership and if the articles or bylaws permit a person to be a member of more than one class, a person may hold a membership in one or more classes.

(c) Any branch, division, or office of any person, which is not formed primarily to be a member, may hold a separate membership.

(d) In the case of membership in an owners' association, created in connection with any of the forms of development referred to in Section 11004.5 of the Business and Professions Code, the articles or bylaws may permit a person who owns an interest, or who has a right of exclusive occupancy, in more than one lot, parcel, area, apartment, or unit to hold a separate membership in the owners' association for each such lot, parcel, area, apartment, or unit.

(e) In the case of membership in a mutual water company, as defined in Section 14300, the articles or bylaws may permit a person entitled to membership by reason of the ownership, lease, or right of occupancy of more than one lot, parcel, or other service unit to hold a separate membership in the mutual water company for each lot, parcel, or other service unit.

(f) In the case of membership in a mobilehome park acquisition

Corporations

corporation, as described in Section 11010.8 of the Business and Professions Code, a bona fide secured party who has, pursuant to a security interest in a membership, taken title to the membership by way of foreclosure, repossession or voluntary repossession, and who is actively attempting to resell the membership to a prospective homeowner or resident of the mobilehome park, may own more than one membership.

Corp. Code § 7341. Expulsion, Suspension, Or Termination; Fairness And Reasonableness; Procedure.

(a) No member may be expelled or suspended, and no membership or memberships may be terminated or suspended, except according to procedures satisfying the requirements of this section. An expulsion, termination or suspension not in accord with this section shall be void and without effect.

(b) Any expulsion, suspension, or termination must be done in good faith and in a fair and reasonable manner. Any procedure which conforms to the requirements of subdivision (c) is fair and reasonable, but a court may also find other procedures to be fair and reasonable when the full circumstances of the suspension, termination, or expulsion are considered.

(c) A procedure is fair and reasonable when:

(1) The provisions of the procedure have been set forth in the articles or bylaws, or copies of such provisions are sent annually to all the members as required by the articles or bylaws;

(2) It provides the giving of 15 days' prior notice of the expulsion, suspension or termination and the reasons therefor; and

(3) It provides an opportunity for the member to be heard, orally or in writing, not less than five days before the effective date of the expulsion, suspension or termination by a person or body authorized to decide that the proposed expulsion, termination or suspension not take place.

(d) Any notice required under this section may be given by any method reasonably calculated to provide actual notice. Any notice given by mail must be given by first-class or registered mail sent to the last address of the members shown on the corporation's records.

(e) Any action challenging an expulsion, suspension or termination of membership, including any claim alleging defective notice, must be commenced within one year after the date of the expulsion, suspension or termination. In the event such an action is successful the court may order any relief, including reinstatement, it finds equitable under the circumstances, but no vote of the members or of the board may be set aside solely because a person was at the time of the vote wrongfully excluded by virtue of the challenged expulsion, suspension or termination, unless the court finds further that the wrongful expulsion, suspension or termination was in bad faith and for the purpose, and with the effect, of wrongfully excluding the member from the vote or from the meeting at which the vote took place, so as to affect the outcome of the vote.

(f)   This section governs only the procedures for expulsion, suspension or termination and not the substantive grounds therefor. An expulsion, suspension or termination based upon substantive grounds which violate contractual or other rights of the member or are otherwise unlawful is not made valid by compliance with this section.

(g)   A member who is expelled or suspended or whose membership is terminated shall be liable for any charges incurred, services or benefits actually rendered, dues, assessments or fees incurred before the expulsion, suspension or termination or arising from contract or otherwise.

Corp. Code § 7510. Place, Date, And Time; Failure To Hold Meetings; Quorum; Special Meetings.

(a)   Meetings of members may be held at a place within or without the state that is stated in or fixed in accordance with the bylaws. If no other place is stated or so fixed, meetings of members shall be held at the principal office of the corporation. Unless prohibited by the bylaws of the corporation, if authorized by the board of directors in its sole discretion, and subject to the requirement of consent in clause (b) of Section 20 and those guidelines and procedures as the board of directors may adopt, members not physically present in person (or, if proxies are allowed, by proxy) at a meeting of members may, by electronic transmission by and to the corporation (Sections 20 and 21) or by electronic video screen communication, participate in a meeting of members, be deemed present in person (or, if proxies are allowed, by proxy), and vote at a meeting of members whether that meeting is to be held at a designated place or in whole or in part by means of electronic transmission by and to the corporation or by electronic video screen communication, in accordance with subdivision (f).

(b)   A regular meeting of members shall be held on a date and time, and with the frequency stated in or fixed in accordance with the bylaws, but in any event in each year in which directors are to be elected at that meeting for the purpose of conducting such election, and to transact any other proper business which may be brought before the meeting.

(c)   If a corporation with members is required by subdivision (b) to hold a regular meeting and fails to hold the regular meeting for a period of 60 days after the date designated therefor or, if no date has been designated, for a period of 15 months after the formation of the corporation or after its last regular meeting, or if the corporation fails to hold a written ballot for a period of 60 days after the date designated therefor, then the superior court of the proper county may summarily order the meeting to be held or the ballot to be conducted upon the application of a member or the Attorney General, after notice to the corporation giving it an opportunity to be heard.

(d) The votes represented, either in person (or, if proxies are allowed, by proxy), at a meeting called or by written ballot ordered pursuant to the subdivision (c) and entitled to be cast on the business to be transacted shall constitute a quorum, notwithstanding any provision of the articles or bylaws or in this part to the contrary. The court may issue such orders as may be appropriate including, without limitation, orders designating the time and place of the meeting, the record date for determination of members entitled to vote, and the form of notice of the meeting.

(e) Special meetings of members for any lawful purpose may be called by the board, the chairman of the board, the president, or such other persons, if any, as are specified in the bylaws. In addition, special meetings of members for any lawful purpose may be called by 5 percent or more of the members.

(f) A meeting of the members may be conducted, in whole or in part, by electronic transmission by and to the corporation or by electronic video screen communication (1) if the corporation implements reasonable measures to provide members in person (or, if proxies are allowed, by proxy) a reasonable opportunity to participate in the meeting and to vote on matters submitted to the members, including an opportunity to read or hear the proceedings of the meeting substantially concurrently with those proceedings, and (2) if any member votes or takes other action at the meeting by means of electronic transmission to the corporation or electronic video screen communication, a record of that vote or action is maintained by the corporation. Any request by a corporation to a member pursuant to clause (b) of Section 20 for consent to conduct a meeting of members by electronic transmission by and to the corporation, shall include a notice that absent consent of the member pursuant to clause (b) of Section 20, the meeting shall be held at a physical location in accordance with subdivision (a).

Corp. Code § 7511. Notice To Members; Waiver.

(a) Whenever members are required or permitted to take any action at a meeting, a written notice of the meeting shall be given not less than 10 nor more than 90 days before the date of the meeting to each member who, on the record date for notice of the meeting, is entitled to vote thereat; provided, however, that if notice is given by mail, and the notice is not mailed by first-class, registered, or certified mail, that notice shall be given not less than 20 days before the meeting. Subject to subdivision (f), and subdivision (b) of Section 7512, the notice shall state the place, date and time of the meeting, the means of electronic transmission by and to the corporation (Sections 20 and 21) or electronic video screen communication, if any, by which members may participate in that meeting, and (1) in the case of a special meeting, the general nature of the business to be transacted, and no other business may be transacted, or (2) in the case of the regular meeting, those matters which the board, at the time the notice is given, intends to present for action by the members, but, except as provided in subdivision (b) of Section 7512, any proper matter may be presented at the meeting for the action. The notice of any meeting at which directors are to be elected shall include the names of all those who are nominees at the time the notice is given to members.

(b) Notice of a members' meeting or any report shall be given either personally, by electronic transmission by a corporation, or by mail or other means of written communication, addressed to a member at the address of the member appearing on the books of the corporation or given by the member to the corporation for purpose of notice; or if no such address appears or is given, at the place where the principal office of the corporation is located or by publication at least once in a newspaper of general circulation in the county in which the principal office is located. An affidavit of giving of any notice or report in accordance with the provisions of this part, executed by the secretary, assistant secretary or any transfer agent, shall be prima facie evidence of the giving of the notice or report.

If any notice or report addressed to the member at the address of the member appearing on the books of the corporation is returned to the corporation by the United States Postal Service marked to indicate that the United States Postal Service is unable to deliver the notice or report to the member at the address, all future notices or reports shall be deemed to have been duly given without further mailing if the same shall be available for the member upon written demand of the member at the principal office of the corporation for a period of one year from the date of the giving of the notice or report to all other members.

Notice given by electronic transmission by the corporation under this subdivision shall be valid only if it complies with Section 20. Notwithstanding the foregoing, notice shall not be given by electronic transmission by the corporation under this subdivision after either of the following:

(1) The corporation is unable to deliver two consecutive notices to the member by that means.

(2) The inability to so deliver the notices to the member becomes known to the secretary, any assistant secretary, the transfer agent, or other person responsible for the giving of the notice.

(c) Upon request in writing to the corporation addressed to the attention of the chairman of the board, president, vice president, or secretary by any person (other than the board) entitled to call a special meeting of members, the officer forthwith shall cause notice to be given to the members entitled to vote that a meeting will be held at a time fixed by the board not less than 35 nor more than 90 days after the receipt of the request. If the notice is not given within 20 days after receipt of the request, the persons entitled to call the meeting may give the notice or the superior court of the proper county shall summarily order the giving of the notice, after notice to the corporation giving it an opportunity to be heard. The court may issue such orders as may be appropriate, including, without limitation, orders designating the time and place of the meeting, the record date for determination of members entitled to vote, and the form of notice.

(d) When a members' meeting is adjourned to another time or place, unless the bylaws otherwise require and except as provided in this subdivision, notice need not be given of the adjourned meeting if the time and place thereof (or the means of electronic transmission by and to the corporation or electronic video screen communication, if any, by which members may participate) are announced at the meeting at which the adjournment is taken. No meeting may be adjourned for more than 45 days. At the adjourned meeting the corporation may transact any business which might have been transacted at the original meeting. If after the adjournment a new record date is fixed for notice or voting, a notice of the adjourned meeting shall be given to each member who, on the record date for notice of the meeting, is entitled to vote at the meeting.

(e) The transactions of any meeting of members however called and noticed, and wherever held, are as valid as though had at a meeting duly held after regular call and notice, if a quorum is present either in person or by proxy, and if, either before or after the meeting, each of the persons entitled to vote, not present in person (or, if proxies are allowed, by proxy), signs a written waiver of notice or a consent to the holding of the meeting or an approval of the minutes thereof in writing. All such waivers, consents and approvals shall be filed with the corporate records or made a part of the minutes of the meeting. Attendance of a person at a meeting shall constitute a waiver of notice of and presence at the meeting, except when the person objects, at the beginning of the meeting, to the transaction of any business because the meeting is not lawfully called or convened and except that attendance at a meeting is not a waiver of any right to object to the consideration of matters required by this part to be included in the notice but not so included, if the objection is expressly made at the meeting. Neither the business to be transacted at nor the purpose of any regular or special meeting of members need be specified in any written waiver of notice, consent to the holding of the meeting or approval of the minutes thereof, unless otherwise provided in the articles or bylaws, except as provided in subdivision (f).

(f) Any approval of the members required under Sections 7222, 7224, 7233, 7812, 8610, or 8719, other than unanimous approval by those entitled to vote, shall be valid only if the general nature of the proposal so approved was stated in the notice of meeting or in any written waiver of notice.

(g) A court may find that notice not given in conformity with this section is still valid, if it was given in a fair and reasonable manner.

Corp. Code § 7512. Quorum.

(a) One-third of the voting power, represented in person or by proxy, shall constitute a quorum at a meeting of members, but, subject to subdivisions (b) and (c), a bylaw may set a different quorum. Any bylaw amendment to increase the quorum may be adopted only by approval of the members (Section 5034). If a quorum is present, the affirmative vote of the majority of the voting power represented at the meeting, entitled to vote, and voting on any matter shall be the act of the members unless the vote of a greater number or voting by classes is required by this part or the articles or bylaws.

(b) Where a bylaw authorizes a corporation to conduct a meeting with a quorum of less than one-third of the voting power, then the only matters that may be voted upon at any regular meeting actually attended, in person or by proxy, by less than one-third of the voting power are matters notice of the general nature of which was given, pursuant to the first sentence of subdivision (a) of Section 7511.

(c) Subject to subdivision (b), the members present at a duly called or held meeting at which a quorum is present may continue to transact business until adjournment notwithstanding the withdrawal of enough members to leave less than a quorum, if any action taken (other than adjournment) is approved by at least a majority of the members required to constitute a quorum or, if required by this division, or by the articles or the bylaws,the vote of the greater number or voting by classes.

(d) In the absence of a quorum, any meeting of members may be adjourned from time to time by the vote of a majority of the votes represented either in person or by proxy, but no other business may be transacted except as provided in subdivision (c).

Corp. Code § 7513. Acts Without Meeting; Written Ballot.

(a) Subject to subdivision (e), and unless prohibited in the articles or bylaws, any action which may be taken at any regular or special meeting of members may be taken without a meeting if the corporation distributes a written ballot to every member entitled to vote on the matter. Unless otherwise provided by the articles or bylaws and if approved by the board of directors, that ballot and any related material may be sent by electronic transmission by the corporation (Section 20)[1] and responses may be returned to the corporation by electronic transmission to the corporation (Section 21)[1]. That ballot shall set forth the proposed action, provide an opportunity to specify approval or disapproval of any proposal, and provide a reasonable time within which to return the ballot to the corporation.

(b) Approval by written ballot pursuant to this section shall be valid only when the number of votes cast by ballot within the time period specified equals or exceeds the quorum required to be present at a meeting authorizing the action, and the number of approvals equals or exceeds the number of votes that would be required to approve at a meeting at which the total number of votes cast was the same as the number of votes cast by ballot.

(c) Ballots shall be solicited in a manner consistent with the requirements of subdivision (b) of Section 7511 and Section 7514. All such solicitations shall indicate the number of responses needed to meet the quorum requirement and, with respect to ballots other than for the election of directors, shall state the percentage of approvals necessary to pass the measure submitted. The solicitation must specify the time by which the ballot must be received in order to be counted.

(d) Unless otherwise provided in the articles or bylaws, a written ballot may not be revoked.

(e) Directors may be elected by written ballot under this section, where authorized by the articles or bylaws, except that election by written ballot may not be authorized where the directors are elected by cumulative voting pursuant to Section 7615.

(f) When directors are to be elected by written ballot and the articles or bylaws prescribe a nomination procedure, the procedure may provide for a date for the close of nominations prior to the printing and distributing of the written ballots.

Corp. Code § 7514. Voting By Proxy Or Written Ballot.

(a) Any form of proxy or written ballot distributed to 10 or more members of a corporation with 100 or more members shall afford an opportunity on the proxy or form of written ballot to specify a choice between approval and disapproval of each matter or group of related matters intended, at the time the written ballot or proxy is distributed, to be acted upon at the meeting for which the proxy is solicited or by such written ballot, and shall provide, subject to reasonable specified conditions, that where the person solicited specifies a choice with respect to any such matter the vote shall be cast in accordance therewith.

(b) In any election of directors, any form of proxy or written ballot in which the directors to be voted upon are named therein as candidates and which is marked by a member "withhold" or otherwise marked in a manner indicating that the authority to vote for the election of directors is withheld shall not be voted either for or against the election of a director.

(c) Failure to comply with this section shall not invalidate any corporate action taken, but may be the basis for challenging any proxy at a meeting or written ballot and the superior court may compel compliance therewith at the suit of any member.

Corp. Code § 7515. Court Order For Meeting Or Written Ballot.

(a) If for any reason it is impractical or unduly difficult for any corporation to call or conduct a meeting of its members, delegates or directors, or otherwise obtain their consent, in the manner prescribed by its articles or bylaws, or this part, then the superior court of the proper county, upon petition of a director, officer, delegate or member, may order that such a meeting be called or that a written ballot or other form of obtaining the vote of members, delegates or directors be authorized, in such a manner as the court finds fair and equitable under the circumstances.

(b) The court shall, in an order issued pursuant to this section, provide for a method of notice reasonably designed to give actual notice to all parties who would be entitled to notice of a meeting held pursuant to the articles, bylaws and this part, whether or not the method results in actual notice to every such person, or conforms to the notice requirements that would otherwise apply. In a proceeding under this section the court may determine who the members or directors are.

(c) The order issued pursuant to this section may dispense with any requirement relating to the holding of and voting at meetings or obtaining of votes, including any requirement as to quorums or as to the number or percentage of votes needed for approval, that would otherwise be imposed by the articles, bylaws, or this part.

(d) Wherever practical any order issued pursuant to this section shall limit the subject matter of the meetings or other forms of consent authorized to items, including amendments to the articles or bylaws, the resolution of which will or may enable the corporation to continue managing its affairs without further resort to this section; provided, however, that an order under this section may also authorize the obtaining of whatever votes and approvals are necessary for the dissolution, merger, sale of assets or reorganization of the corporation.

(e) Any meeting or other method of obtaining the vote of members, delegates or directors conducted pursuant to an order issued under this section, and which complies with all the provisions of such order, is for all purposes a valid meeting or vote, as the case may be, and shall have the same force and effect as if it complied with every requirement imposed by the articles, bylaws, and this part.

Corp. Code § 7516. Written Consent Of Members.

Any action required or permitted to be taken by the members may be taken without a meeting, if all members shall individually or collectively consent in writing to the action. The written consent or consents shall be filed with the minutes of the proceedings of the members. The action by written consent shall have the same force and effect as the unanimous vote of the members.

Corp. Code § 7517. Acceptance Or Rejection Of Ballot, Consent, Waiver, Or Proxy Appointment.

(a) If the name signed on a ballot, consent, waiver, or proxy appointment corresponds to the name of a member, the corporation if acting in good faith is entitled to accept the ballot, consent, waiver or proxy appointment and give it effect as the act of the member.

(b) If the name signed on a ballot, consent, waiver, or proxy appointment does not correspond to the record name of a member, the corporation if acting in good faith is nevertheless entitled to accept the ballot, consent, waiver, or proxy appointment and give it effect as the act of the member if any of the following occur:

(1) The member is an entity and the name signed purports to be that of an officer or agent of the entity.

(2) The name signed purports to be that of an attorney-in-fact of the member and if the corporation requests, evidence acceptable to the corporation of the signatory's authority to sign for the member has been presented with respect to the ballot, consent, waiver, or proxy appointment.

(3) Two or more persons hold the membership as cotenants or fiduciaries and the name signed purports to be the name of at least one of the coholders, and the person signing appears to be acting on behalf of all the coholders.

(4) The name signed purports to be that of an administrator, executor, guardian, or conservator representing the member and, if the corporation requests, evidence of fiduciary status acceptable to the corporation has been presented with respect to the ballot, consent, waiver, or proxy appointment.

(5) The name signed purports to be that of a receiver or trustee in bankruptcy of the member, and, if the corporation requests, evidence of this status acceptable to the corporation has been presented with respect to the ballot, consent, waiver, or proxy appointment.

(c) The corporation is entitled to reject a ballot, consent, waiver, or proxy appointment if the secretary or other officer or agent authorized to tabulate votes, acting in good faith, has a reasonable basis for doubt concerning the validity of the signature or the signatory's authority to sign for the member.

(d) The corporation and any officer or agent thereof who accepts or rejects a ballot, consent, waiver, or proxy appointment in good faith and in accordance with the standards of this section shall not be liable in damages to the member for the consequences of the acceptance or rejection.

(e) Corporate action based on the acceptance or rejection of a ballot, consent, waiver, or proxy appointment under this section is valid unless a court of competent jurisdiction determines otherwise.

Corp. Code § 7520. Election Of Directors By Members; Procedure.

(a) As to directors elected by members, there shall be available to the members reasonable nomination and election procedures given the nature, size and operations of the corporation.

(b) If a corporation complies with all of the provisions of Sections 7521, 7522, 7523, and 7524 applicable to a corporation with the same number of members, the nomination and election procedures of that corporation, shall be deemed reasonable. However, those sections do not prescribe the exclusive means of making available to the members reasonable procedures for nomination and election of directors. A corporation may make available to the members other reasonable nomination and election procedures given the nature, size, and operations of the corporation.

(c) Subject to the provisions of subdivisions (a), (b), and (d) of Section 7616, the superior court of the proper county shall enforce the provisions of this section.

Corp. Code § 7521. Nomination.

A corporation with 500 or more members may provide that, except for directors who are elected as authorized by Section 7152 or 7153, and except as provided in Section 7522, any person who is qualified to be elected to the board of directors of a corporation may be nominated:

(a) By any method authorized by the bylaws, or if no method is set forth in the bylaws by any method authorized by the board.

(b) By petition delivered to an officer of the corporation, signed within 11 months preceding the next time directors will be elected, by members representing the following number of votes:

Number of Votes Eligible to be Cast for Director Disregarding Any Provision for Cumulative Voting	Number of Votes
Under 5,000	2% of voting power
5,000 or more	1/20 of 1% of voting power but not less than 100

This subdivision does not apply to a corporation described in subdivision (c).

(c) In corporations with one million or more members engaged primarily in the business of retail merchandising of consumer goods, by petition delivered to an officer of the corporation, signed within 11 months preceding the next time directors will be elected, by such reasonable number of members as is set forth in the bylaws, or if no number is set forth in the bylaws, by such reasonable number of members as is determined by the directors.

(d) If there is a meeting to elect directors, by any member present at the meeting in person or by proxy if proxies are permitted.

Corp. Code § 7522. Close Of Nominations; When Election Not Required.

A corporation with 5,000 or more members may provide that, in any election of a director or directors by members of the corporation except for an election authorized by Section 7152 or 7153:

(a) The corporation's articles or bylaws shall set a date for the close of nominations for the board. The date shall not be less than 50 nor more than 120 days before the day directors are to be elected. No nominations for the board can be made after the date set for the close of nominations.

(b) If more people are nominated for the board than can be elected, the election shall take place by means of a procedure which allows all nominees a reasonable opportunity to solicit votes and all members a reasonable opportunity to choose among the nominees.

(c) A nominee shall have a reasonable opportunity to communicate to the members the nominee's qualifications and the reasons for the nominee's candidacy.

(d) If after the close of nominations the number of people nominated for the board is not more than the number of directors to be elected, the corporation may without further action declare that those nominated and qualified to be elected have been elected.

Corp. Code § 7523. Publication Of Material Soliciting Votes; Nominees' Rights.

Where a corporation with 500 or more members publishes any material soliciting a vote for any nominee for director in any publication owned or controlled by the corporation, the corporation may provide that it shall make available to all other nominees, in the same issue of the publication, an equal amount of space, with equal prominence, to be used by the nominee for a purpose reasonably related to the election.

Corp. Code § 7524. Request To Corporation To Mail Election Material.

A corporation with 500 or more members may provide that upon written request by any nominee for election to the board and the payment of the reasonable costs of mailing (including postage), the corporation shall within 10 business days after such request (provided payment has been made) mail to all members, or such portion of them as the nominee may reasonably specify, any material, which the nominee may furnish and which is reasonably related to the election, unless the corporation within five business days after the request allows the nominee, at the corporation's option, the rights set forth in either paragraph (1) or (2) of subdivision (a) of Section 8330.

Corp. Code § 7525. Refusal To Publish Or Mail Material; Liability For Contents.

(a) This section shall apply to corporations publishing or mailing materials on behalf of any nominee in connection with procedures for the nomination and election of directors.

(b) Neither the corporation, nor its agents, officers, directors, or employees, may be held criminally liable, liable for any negligence (active or passive) or otherwise liable for damages to any person on account of any material which is supplied by a nominee for director and which it mails or publishes in procedures intended to comply with Section 7520 or pursuant to Section 7523 or 7524 but the nominee on whose behalf such material was published or mailed shall be liable and shall indemnify and hold the corporation, its agents, officers, directors, and employees and each of them harmless from all demands, costs, including reasonable legal fees and expenses, claims, damages and causes of action arising out of such material or any such mailing or publication.

(c) Nothing in this section shall prevent a corporation or any of its agents, officers, directors, or employees from seeking a court order providing that the corporation need not mail or publish material tendered by or on behalf of a nominee under this article on the ground the material will expose the moving party to liability.

Corp. Code § 7526. Use Of Corporate Funds To Support Nominee.

Without authorization of the board, no corporation funds may be expended to support a nominee for director after there are more people nominated for director than can be elected.

Corp. Code § 7527. Time To Contest Election, Appointment, Or Removal Of Director; Defect In Notice.

An action challenging the validity of any election, appointment or removal of a director or directors must be commenced within nine months after the election, appointment or removal. If no such action is commenced, in the absence of fraud, any election, appointment or removal of a director is conclusively presumed valid nine months thereafter.

Corp. Code § 7610. One Vote Per Member; Exceptions.

Except as provided in a corporation's articles or bylaws or Section 7615, each member shall be entitled to one vote on each matter submitted to a vote of the members. Single memberships in which two or more persons have an indivisible interest shall be voted as provided in Section 7612.

Corp. Code § 7611. Record Date; Determining Voting Eligibility.

(a) The bylaws may provide or, in the absence of such provision, the board may fix, in advance, a date as the record date for the purpose of determining the members entitled to notice of any meeting of members. Such record date shall not be more than 90 nor less than 10 days before the date of the meeting. If no record date is fixed, members at the close of business on the business day preceding the day on which notice is given or, if notice is waived, at the close of business on the business day preceding the day on which the meeting is held are entitled to notice of a meeting of members. A determination of members entitled to notice of a meeting of members shall apply to any adjournment of the meeting unless the board fixes a new record date for the adjourned meeting.

(b) The bylaws may provide or, in the absence of such provision, the board may fix, in advance, a date as the record date for the purpose of determining the members entitled to vote at a meeting of members. Such record date shall not be more than 60 days before the date of the meeting. Such record date shall also apply in the case of an adjournment of the meeting unless the board fixes a new record date for the adjourned meeting. If no record date is fixed, members on the day of the meeting who are otherwise eligible to vote are entitled to vote at the meeting of members or, in the case of an adjourned meeting, members on the day of the adjourned meeting who are otherwise eligible to vote are entitled to vote at the adjourned meeting of members.

(c) The bylaws may provide or, in the absence of such provision, the board may fix, in advance, a date as the record date for the purpose of determining the members entitled to cast written ballots (Section 7513). Such record date shall not be more than 60 days before the day on which the first written ballot is mailed or solicited. If no record date is fixed, members on the day the first written ballot is mailed or solicited who are otherwise eligible to vote are entitled to cast written ballots.

(d) The bylaws may provide or, in the absence of such provision, the board may fix, in advance, a date as the record date for the purpose of determining the members entitled to exercise any rights in respect of

Corporations

any other lawful action. Such record date shall not be more than 60 days prior to such other action. If no record date is fixed, members at the close of business on the day on which the board adopts the resolution relating thereto, or the 60th day prior to the date of such other action, whichever is later, are entitled to exercise such rights.

Corp. Code § 7612. Memberships In Two Or More Names.

If a membership stands of record in the names of two or more persons, whether fiduciaries, members of a partnership, joint tenants, tenants in common, husband and wife as community property, tenants by the entirety, persons entitled to vote under a voting agreement or otherwise, or if two or more persons (including proxyholders) have the same fiduciary relationship respecting the same membership, unless the secretary of the corporation is given written notice to the contrary and is furnished with a copy of the instrument or order appointing them or creating the relationship wherein it is so provided, their acts with respect to voting shall have the following effect:

   (a) If only one votes, such act binds all; or

   (b) If more than one vote, the act of the majority so voting binds all.

Corp. Code § 7613. Proxies.

   (a) Any member may authorize another person or persons to act by proxy with respect to such membership except that this right may be limited or withdrawn by the articles or bylaws, subject to subdivision (f). Any proxy purported to be executed in accordance with the provisions of this part shall be presumptively valid.

   (b) No proxy shall be valid after the expiration of 11 months from the date thereof unless otherwise provided in the proxy, except that the maximum term of any proxy shall be three years from the date of execution. Every proxy continues in full force and effect until revoked by the person executing it prior to the vote pursuant thereto, except as otherwise provided in this section. Such revocation may be effected by a writing delivered to the corporation stating that the proxy is revoked or by a subsequent proxy executed by the person executing the prior proxy and presented to the meeting, or as to any meeting by attendance at such meeting and voting in person by the person executing the proxy. The dates contained on the forms of proxy presumptively determine the order of execution, regardless of the postmark dates on the envelopes in which they are mailed.

   (c) A proxy is not revoked by the death or incapacity of the maker or the termination of a membership as a result thereof unless, before the vote is counted, written notice of such death or incapacity is received by the corporation.

(d) Unless otherwise provided in the articles or bylaws, the proxy of a member which states that it is irrevocable for the period specified therein (notwithstanding subdivisions (b) and (c)) when it is held by any of the following or a nominee of any of the following:

(1) A person who has purchased or who has agreed to purchase the membership;

(2) A creditor or creditors of the corporation or the member who extended or continued credit to the corporation or the member in consideration of the proxy if the proxy states that it was given in consideration of such extension or continuation of credit and the name of the person extending or continuing the credit; or

(3) A person who has contracted to perform services as an employee of the corporation, if the proxy is required by the contract of employment and if the proxy states that it was given in consideration of such contract of employment, the name of the employee and the period of employment contracted for.

Notwithstanding the period of irrevocability specified, the proxy becomes revocable when the agreement to purchase is terminated; the debt of the corporation or the member is paid; or the period of employment provided for in the contract of employment has terminated. In addition to the foregoing paragraphs (1) through (3), a proxy of a member may be made irrevocable (notwithstanding subdivision (c)) if it is given to secure the performance of a duty or to protect a title, either legal or equitable, until the happening of events which, by its terms, discharge the obligations secured by it.

(e) A proxy may be revoked, notwithstanding a provision making it irrevocable by a transferee of a membership without knowledge of the existence of the provision unless the existence of the proxy and its irrevocability appears on the certificate representing the membership.

(f) Subdivision (a) notwithstanding;

(1) No amendment of the articles or bylaws repealing, restricting, creating or expanding proxy rights may be adopted without approval by the members (Section 5034); and

(2) No amendment of the articles or bylaws restricting or limiting the use of proxies may affect the validity of a previously issued irrevocable proxy during the term of its irrevocability, so long as it complied with applicable provisions, if any, of the articles or bylaws at the time of its

issuance, and is otherwise valid under this section.

(g) Anything to the contrary notwithstanding, any revocable proxy covering matters requiring a vote of the members pursuant to Section 7222; Section 7224; Section 7233; paragraph (1) of subdivision (f) of this section; Section 7812; paragraph (2) of subdivision (a) of Section 7911; Section 8012; subdivision (a) of Section 8015; Section 8610; or subdivision (a) of Section 8719 is not valid as to such matters unless it sets forth the general nature of the matter to be voted on.

Corp. Code § 7614. Inspectors Of Election.

(a) In advance of any meeting of members, the board may appoint inspectors of election to act at the meeting and any adjournment thereof. If inspectors of election are not so appointed, or if any persons so appointed fail to appear or refuse to act, the chairman of any meeting of members may, and on the request of any member or a member's proxy shall, appoint inspectors of election (or persons to replace those who so fail or refuse) at the meeting. The number of inspectors shall be either one or three. If appointed at a meeting on the request of one or more members or proxies, the majority of members represented in person or by proxy shall determine whether one or three inspectors are to be appointed. In the case of any action by written ballot (Section 7513), the board may similarly appoint inspectors of election to act with powers and duties as set forth in this section.

(b) The inspectors of election shall determine the number of memberships outstanding and the voting power of each, the number represented at the meeting, the existence of a quorum, and the authenticity, validity and effect of proxies, receive votes, ballots or consents, hear and determine all challenges and questions in any way arising in connection with the right to vote, count and tabulate all votes or consents, determine when the polls shall close, determine the result and do such acts as may be proper to conduct the election or vote with fairness to all members.

(c) The inspectors of election shall perform their duties impartially, in good faith, to the best of their ability and as expeditiously as is practical. If there are three inspectors of election, the decision, act or certificate of a majority is effective in all respects as the decision, act or certificate of all. Any report or certificate made by the inspectors of election is *prima facie* evidence of the facts stated therein.

Corp. Code § 7615. Cumulative Voting; Determining Winner; When Ballots Are Required.

(a) If the articles or bylaws authorize cumulative voting, but not otherwise, every member entitled to vote at any election of directors may cumulate the member's votes and give one candidate a number of votes equal to the number of directors to be elected multiplied by the number of votes to which the member is entitled, or distribute the member's votes on the same principle among as many candidates as the member thinks fit. An article or bylaw provision authorizing cumulative voting may be repealed or amended only by approval of the members (Section 5034), except that the governing article or bylaw provision may require the vote of a greater proportion of the members, or of the members of any class, for its repeal.

(b) No member shall be entitled to cumulate votes for a candidate or candidates unless the candidate's name or candidates' names have been placed in nomination prior to the voting and the member has given notice at the meeting prior to the voting of the member's intention to cumulate votes. If any one member has given this notice, all members may cumulate their votes for candidates in nomination.

(c) In any election of directors by cumulative voting, the candidates receiving the highest number of votes are elected, subject to any lawful provision specifying election by classes.

(d) In any election of directors not governed by subdivision (c), unless otherwise provided in the articles or bylaws, the candidates receiving the highest number of votes are elected.

(e) Elections for directors need not be by ballot unless a member demands election by ballot at the meeting and before the voting begins or unless the bylaws so require.

Corp. Code § 7616. Action To Determine Validity Of Election Or Appointment Of Director; Notice To Attorney General.

(a) Upon the filing of an action therefor by any director or member or by any person who had the right to vote in the election at issue, the superior court of the proper county shall determine the validity of any election or appointment of any director of any corporation.

(b) In the case of a corporation holding assets in charitable trust, any person bringing an action under this section shall give notice of the action to the Attorney General, who may intervene.

(c) Upon the filing of the complaint, and before any further proceedings are had, the court shall enter an order fixing a date for the hearing, which shall be within five days unless for good cause shown a later date is fixed, and requiring notice of the date for the hearing and a copy of the complaint to be served upon the corporation and upon the person whose purported election or appointment is questioned and upon any person (other than the plaintiff) whom the plaintiff alleges to have been elected or appointed, in the manner in which a summons is required to be served, or, if the court so directs, by registered mail; and the court may make such further requirements as to notice as appear to be proper under the circumstances.

(d) The court, consistent with the provisions of this part and in conformity with the articles and bylaws to the extent feasible, may determine the person entitled to the office of director or may order a new election to be held or appointment to be made, may determine the validity, effectiveness and construction of voting agreements and voting trusts, the validity of the issuance of memberships and the right of persons to vote and may direct such other relief as may be just and proper.

CHAPTER 5

NONPROFIT MUTUAL BENEFIT CORPORATION GOVERNING DOCUMENTS
(Corporations Code §§ 7810-7820, 8210-8338 and Government Code § 66469-66472.1)

Corp. Code § 7810. Permissible Amendments To Articles Of Incorporation.

(a) By complying with the provisions of this chapter, a corporation may amend its articles from time to time, in any and as many respects as may be desired, so long as its articles as amended contain only such provisions as it would be lawful to insert in original articles filed at the time of the filing of the amendment or as authorized by Section 7813.5 and, if a change in the rights of members or an exchange, reclassification or cancellation of memberships is to be made, such provisions as may be necessary to effect such change, exchange, reclassification or cancellation. It is the intent of the Legislature in adopting this section to exercise to the fullest extent the reserve power of the state over corporations and to authorize any amendment of the articles covered by the preceding sentence regardless of whether any provision contained in the amendment was permissible at the time of the original incorporation of the corporation.

(b) A corporation shall not amend its articles to alter any statement which may appear in the original articles of the names and addresses of the first directors, nor the name and address of the initial agent, except to correct an error in the statement or to delete either after the corporation has filed a statement under Section 8210.

Corp. Code § 7811. Amendment By Incorporators.

Any amendment of the articles may be adopted by a writing signed by a majority of the incorporators, so long as:

(a) No directors were named in the original articles;

(b) No directors have been elected; and

(c) The corporation has no members.

Corp. Code § 7812. Approval Of Board And Members Required; Exceptions.

(a) Except as provided in this section or Section 7813, amendments may be adopted if approved by the board and approved by the members (Section 5034) and approved by such other person or persons, if any, as required by the articles. The approval by the members or other person or persons may be before or after the approval by the board.

(b) Notwithstanding subdivision (a), the following amendments may be adopted by approval of the board alone:

(1) An amendment extending the corporate existence or making the corporate existence perpetual, if the corporation was organized prior to August 14, 1929.

(2) An amendment deleting the names and addresses of the first directors or the name and address of the initial agent.

(3) Any amendment, at a time the corporation has no members; provided, however, that if the articles require approval by any person for an amendment, an amendment may not be adopted without such approval.

(4) An amendment adopted pursuant to Section 9913.

(c) Whenever the articles require for corporate action the approval of a particular class of members or of a larger proportion of, or all of, the votes of any class, or of a larger proportion of, or all of, the directors, than is otherwise required by this part, the provision in the articles requiring such greater vote shall not be altered, amended or repealed except by such class or such greater vote, unless otherwise provided in the articles.

Corp. Code § 7813. Amendments Affecting Rights Of Class.

An amendment must also be approved by the members (Section 5034) of a class, whether or not such class is entitled to vote thereon by the provisions of the articles or bylaws, if the amendment would:

(a) Materially and adversely affect the rights, privileges, preferences, restrictions or conditions of that class as to voting, dissolution, redemption or transfer in a manner different than such action affects another class;

(b) Materially and adversely affect such class as to voting, dissolution, redemption or transfer by changing the rights, privileges, preferences, restrictions or conditions of another class;

(c) Increase or decrease the number of memberships authorized for such class;

(d) Increase the number of memberships authorized for another class;

(e) Effect an exchange, reclassification or cancellation of all or part of the memberships of such class; or

(f)   Authorize a new class of memberships.

Corp. Code § 7813.5. Amendments To Change Status.

(a)   A mutual benefit corporation may amend its articles to change its status to that of a public benefit corporation, a religious corporation, a business corporation, or a cooperative corporation by complying with this section and the other sections of this chapter.

(b)   Except as authorized by Section 7811 or unless the corporation has no members, an amendment to change its status to a public benefit corporation or religious corporation shall: (i) be approved by the members (Section 5034), and the fairness of the amendment to the members shall be approved by the Commissioner of Corporations pursuant to Section 25142; (ii) be approved by the members (Section 5034) in an election conducted by written ballot pursuant to Section 7513 in which no negative votes are cast; or (iii) be approved by 100 percent of the voting power.

(c)   Amended articles authorized by this section shall include the provisions which would have been required (other than the name of the initial agent for service of process if a statement has been filed pursuant to Section 8210), and may in addition only include those provisions which would have been permitted, in original articles filed by the type of corporation (public benefit, religious, business, or cooperative) into which the mutual benefit corporation is changing its status.

(d)   At the time of filing a certificate of amendment to change status to a public benefit corporation, a corporation shall furnish an additional copy of the certificate of amendment to the Secretary of State who shall forward that copy to the Attorney General.

(e)   In the case of a change of status to a business corporation or a cooperative corporation, if the Franchise Tax Board has issued a determination exempting the corporation from tax as provided in Section 23701 of the Revenue and Taxation Code, the corporation shall be subject to Section 23221 of the Revenue and Taxation Code upon filing the certificate of amendment.

Corp. Code § 7814. Filing Certificate Of Amendment.

(a)   Except for amendments adopted by the incorporators pursuant to Section 7811, upon adoption of an amendment, the corporation shall file a certificate of amendment, which shall consist of an officers' certificate stating:

(1)   The wording of the amendment or amended articles in

accordance with Section 7816;

(2) That the amendment has been approved by the board;

(3) If the amendment is one for which the approval of the members (Section 5034) or the approval of 100 percent of the voting power is required, that the amendment was approved by the required vote of members; and

(4) If the amendment is one which may be adopted with approval by the board alone, a statement of the facts entitling the board alone to adopt the amendment.

(5) If the amendment is one for which the approval of a person or persons other than the incorporators, directors or members is required, that the approval of such person or persons has been obtained.

(b) In the event of an amendment of the articles pursuant to a merger, the filing of the officers' certificate and agreement pursuant to Section 8014 shall be in lieu of any filing required under this chapter.

Corp. Code § 7815. Filing Of Amendment By Incorporators.

In the case of amendments adopted by the incorporators under Section 7811, the corporation shall file a certificate of amendment signed and verified by a majority of the incorporators which shall state that the signers thereof constitute at least a majority of the incorporators, that directors were not named in the original articles and have not been elected, that the corporation has no members and that they adopt the amendment or amendments therein set forth.

Corp. Code § 7816. Contents Of Certificate Of Amendment.

The certificate of amendment shall establish the wording of the amendment or amended articles by one or more of the following means:

(a) By stating that the articles shall be amended to read as therein set forth in full.

(b) By stating that any provision of the articles, which shall be identified by the numerical or other designation given it in the articles or by stating the wording thereof, shall be stricken from the articles or shall be amended to read as set forth in the certificate.

(c) By stating that the provisions set forth therein shall be added to the articles. If the purpose of the amendment is to reclassify, cancel, exchange, or otherwise change outstanding memberships the amended articles shall state the effect thereof on outstanding memberships.

Corp. Code § 7817. Effect Of Filing Certificate Of Amendment.

Upon the filing of the certificate of amendment, the articles shall be amended in accordance with the certificate and any change, reclassification or cancellation of memberships shall be effected, and a copy of the certificate, certified by the Secretary of State, is prima facie evidence of the performance of the conditions necessary to the adoption of the amendment.

Corp. Code § 7818. Extension Of Term Of Corporate Existence By Amendment.

Upon the filing of the certificate of amendment, the articles shall be amended in accordance with the certificate and any change, reclassification or cancellation of memberships shall be effected, and a copy of the certificate, certified by the Secretary of State, is prima facie evidence of the performance of the conditions necessary to the adoption of the amendment. 7818. A corporation formed for a limited period may at any time subsequent to the expiration of the term of its corporate existence, extend the term of its existence by an amendment to its articles removing any provision limiting the term of its existence and providing for perpetual existence. If the filing of the certificate of amendment providing for perpetual existence would be prohibited if it were original articles by the provisions of Section 7122, the Secretary of State shall not file such certificate unless, by the same or a concurrently filed certificate of amendment, the articles of such corporation are amended to adopt a new available name. For the purpose of the adoption of any such amendment, persons who have been functioning as directors of such corporation shall be considered to have been validly elected even though their election may have occurred after the expiration of the original term of the corporate existence.

Corp. Code § 7819. Restated Articles Of Incorporation.

(a) A corporation may restate in a single certificate the entire text of its articles as amended by filing an officers' certificate or, in circumstances where incorporators or the board may amend a corporation's articles pursuant to Sections 7811 and 7815, a certificate signed and verified by a majority of the incorporators or the board, as applicable, entitled "Restated Articles of Incorporation of (insert name of corporation)" which shall set forth the articles as amended to the date of filing of the certificate, except that the signatures and acknowledgments of the articles by the incorporators and any statements regarding the effect of any prior amendment upon memberships and any provisions of agreements of merger (other than amendments to the articles of the surviving corporation) and the names and addresses of the first directors and of the initial agent for service of process shall be omitted (except that the names and addresses of the initial agent for service of process and, if previously set forth in the articles, the initial directors, shall not be omitted prior to the time that the corporation has filed a statement under Section 8210). Such omissions are not alterations or amendments of the articles. The certificate may also itself alter or amend the articles in any respect, in which case the certificate must comply with Section 7814 or 7815, as the case may be, and Section 7816.

(b) If the certificate does not itself alter or amend the articles in any respect, it shall be approved by the board or, prior to the issuance of any memberships and the naming and election of directors, by a majority of the incorporators, and shall be subject to the provisions of this chapter relating to an amendment of the articles not requiring approval of the members (Section 5034). If the certificate does itself alter or amend the articles, it shall be subject to the provisions of this chapter relating to the amendment or amendments so made.

(c) Restated articles of incorporation filed pursuant to this section shall supersede for all purposes the original articles and all amendments filed prior thereto.

Corp. Code § 7820. Effect Of Limitations Of Charitable Trust.

(a) Amendment of the articles of a corporation holding property in charitable trust, pursuant to this chapter, does not, of itself, abrogate any requirement or limitation imposed upon the corporation, or any property held by it, by virtue of the trust under which such property is held by the corporation.

(b) The Attorney General may, at the corporation's request, and pursuant to such regulations as the Attorney General may issue, give rulings as to whether the Attorney General will or may oppose a proposed action, or article amendment, as inconsistent with or proscribed by the requirements of a charitable trust.

Corp. Code § 8210. Articles Of Incorporation; Biennial Updating.

(a) Every corporation shall, within 90 days after the filing of its original articles and biennially thereafter during the applicable filing period, file, on a form prescribed by the Secretary of State, a statement containing: (1) the names and complete business or residence addresses of its chief executive officer, secretary, and chief financial officer; (2) the street address of its principal office in this state, if any; (3) the mailing address of the corporation, if different from the street address of its principal executive office or if the corporation has no principal office address in this state.

(b) The statement required by subdivision (a) shall also designate, as the agent of the corporation for the purpose of service of process, a natural person residing in this state or any domestic or foreign or foreign business corporation that has complied with Section 1505 and whose capacity to act as an agent has not terminated. If a natural person is designated, the statement shall set forth the person's complete business or residence *street* address. If a corporate agent is designated, no address for it shall be set forth.

(c) For the purposes of this section, the applicable filing period for a corporation shall be the calendar month during which its original articles were filed and the immediately preceding five calendar months. The Secretary of State shall mail a notice for compliance with this section to each corporation approximately three months prior to the close of the applicable filing period. The notice shall state the due date for compliance and shall be mailed to the last address of the corporation according to the records of the Secretary of State. Neither the failure of the Secretary of State to mail the notice nor the failure of the corporation to receive it is an excuse for failure to comply with this section.

(d) Whenever any of the information required by subdivision (a) is changed, the corporation may file a current statement containing all the information required by subdivisions (a) and (b). In order to change its agent for service of process or the address of the agent, the corporation must file a current statement containing all the information required by subdivisions (a) and (b). Whenever any statement is filed pursuant to this section, it supersedes any previously filed statement and the statement in the articles as to the agent for service of process and the address of the agent.

(e) The Secretary of State may destroy or otherwise dispose of any statement filed pursuant to this section after it has been superseded by the filing of a new statement.

(f) This section shall not be construed to place any person dealing with the corporation on notice of, or under any duty to inquire about, the existence or content of a statement filed pursuant to this section.

Corp. Code § 8310. Subject To Inspection To Be Written.

If any record subject to inspection pursuant to this chapter is not maintained in written form, a request for inspection is not complied with unless and until the corporation at its expense makes such records available in written form. For the purposes of this chapter "written" or "in writing" also includes cathode ray tube and similar electronic communications methods.

Corp. Code § 8311. Inspection By Agent Or Attorneys; Right To Copy.

Any inspection under this chapter may be made in person or by agent or attorney and the right of inspection includes the right to copy and make extracts.

Corp. Code § 8313. No Limitation On Inspection Rights.

The rights of members provided in this chapter may not be limited by contract or the articles or bylaws.

Corp. Code § 8320. Records Required To Be Kept; Form Of Records.

(a) Each corporation shall keep:

(1) Adequate and correct books and records of account:

(2) Minutes of the proceedings of its members, board and committees of the board; and

(3) A record of its members giving their names and addresses and the class of membership held by each.

(b) Those minutes and other books and records shall be kept either in written form or in any other form capable of being converted into clearly legible tangible form or in any combination of the foregoing. When minutes and other books and records are kept in a form capable of being converted into clearly legible paper form, the clearly legible paper form into which those minutes and other books and records are converted shall be admissible in evidence, and accepted for all other purposes, to the same extent as an original paper record of the same information would have been, provided that the paper form accurately portrays the record.

Corp. Code § 8321. Notice Of Annual Report.

(a) A corporation shall notify each member yearly of the member's right to receive a financial report pursuant to this subdivision. Except as provided in subdivision (c), upon written request of a member the board shall promptly cause the most recent annual report to be sent to the requesting member. An annual report shall be prepared not later than

120 days after the close of the corporation's fiscal year. Unless otherwise provided by the articles or bylaws and if approved by the board of directors, that report and any accompanying material may be sent by electronic transmission by the corporation (Section 20). That report shall contain in appropriate detail the following:

(1) A balance sheet as of the end of that fiscal year and an income statement and a statement of cashflow for that fiscal year.

(2) A statement of the place where the names and addresses of the current members are located.

(3) Any information required by Section 8322.

(b) The report required by subdivision (a) shall be accompanied by any report thereon of independent accountants, or, if there is no report, the certificate of an authorized officer of the corporation that the statements were prepared without audit from the books and records of the corporation.

(c) Subdivision (a) does not apply to any corporation which receives less than ten thousand dollars ($10,000) in gross revenues or receipts during the fiscal year.

Corp. Code § 8322. Annual Statements Of Transactions With Interested Persons And Of Indemnification.

(a) Any provision of the articles or bylaws notwithstanding, every corporation shall furnish annually to its members and directors a statement of any transaction or indemnification of a kind described in subdivision (d) or (e), if any such transaction or indemnification took place. If the corporation issues an annual report to all members, this subdivision shall be satisfied by including the required information in the annual report. A corporation which does not issue an annual report to all members, pursuant to subdivision (c) of Section 8321, shall satisfy this section by mailing or delivering to its members the required statement within 120 days after the close of the corporation's fiscal year. Unless otherwise provided by the articles or bylaws and if approved by the board of directors, that statement may be sent by electronic transmission by the corporation (Section 20).

(b) Except as provided in subdivision (c), a covered transaction under this section is a transaction in which the corporation, its parent, or its subsidiary was a party, and in which either of the following had a direct or indirect material financial interest:

(1) Any director or officer of the corporation, or its parent or subsidiary.

(2) Any holder of more than 10 percent of the voting power of

the corporation, its parent or its subsidiary.

For the purpose of subdivision (d), an "interested person" is any person described in paragraph (1) or (2) of this subdivision.

(c) Transactions approved by the members of a corporation (Section 5034), under subdivision (a) of Section 7233, are not covered transactions. For the purpose of subdivision (b), a mere common directorship is not a material financial interest.

(d) The statement required by subdivision (a) shall describe briefly:

(1) Any covered transaction (excluding compensation of officers and directors) during the previous fiscal year involving more than fifty thousand dollars ($50,000), or which was one of a number of covered transactions in which the same interested person had a direct or indirect material financial interest, and which transactions in the aggregate involved more than fifty thousand dollars ($50,000).

(2 The names of the interested persons involved in such transactions, stating such person's relationship to the corporation, the nature of such person's interest in the transaction and, where practicable, the amount of such interest; provided, that in the case of a transaction with a partnership of which such person is a partner, only the interest of the partnership need be stated.

(e) The statement required by subdivision (a) shall describe briefly the amount and circumstances of any loans, guaranties, indemnifications or advances aggregating more than ten thousand dollars ($10,000) paid or made during the fiscal year to any officer or director of the corporation pursuant to Section 7237; provided that no such report need be made in the case of a loan, guaranty, or indemnification approved by the members (Section 5034) or a loan or guaranty not subject to the provisions of subdivision (a) of Section 7235.

Corp. Code § 8325. Demand For Election Results.

For a period of 60 days following the conclusion of an annual, regular, or special meeting of members, a corporation shall, upon written request from a member, forthwith inform the member of the result of any particular vote of members taken at the meeting, including the number of memberships voting for, the number of memberships voting against, and the number of memberships abstaining or withheld from voting. If the matter voted on was the election of directors, the corporation shall report the number of memberships, or votes if voted cumulatively, cast for each nominee for director. If more than one class or series of memberships voted, the report shall state the appropriate numbers by class and series of memberships.

Corp. Code § 8330. Demand For Members' Names, Addresses, And Voting Rights By Member.

(a) Subject to Sections 8331 and 8332, and unless the corporation provides a reasonable alternative pursuant to subdivision (c), a member may do either or both of the following as permitted by subdivision (b):

(1) Inspect and copy the record of all the members' names, addresses and voting rights, at reasonable times, upon five business days' prior written demand upon the corporation which demand shall state the purpose for which the inspection rights are requested; or

(2) Obtain from the secretary of corporation, upon written demand and tender of a reasonable charge, a list of the names, addresses and voting rights of those members entitled to vote for the election of directors, as of the most recent record date for which it has been compiled or as of a date specified by the member subsequent to the date of demand. The demand shall state the purpose for which the list is requested. The membership list shall be made available on or before the later of ten business days after the demand is received or after the date specified therein as the date of which the list is to be compiled.

(b) The rights set for in subdivision (a) may be exercised by:

(1) Any member, for a purpose reasonably related to such person's interest as a member. Where the corporation reasonably believes that the information will be used for another purpose, or where it provides a reasonable alternative pursuant to subdivision (c), it may deny the member access to the list. In any subsequent action brought by the member under Section 8336, the court shall enforce the rights set forth in subdivision (a) unless the corporation proves that the member will allow use of the information for purposes unrelated to the person's interest as a member or that the alternative method offered reasonably achieves the proper purpose set forth in the demand.

(2) The authorized number of members for a purpose reasonably related to the members' interest as members.

(c) The corporation may, within ten business days after receiving a demand under subdivision (a), deliver to the person or persons making the demand a written offer of an alternative method of achieving the purpose identified in said demand without providing access to or a copy of the membership list. An alternative method which reasonably and in a timely manner accomplishes the proper purpose set forth in a demand made under subdivision (a) shall be deemed a reasonable alternative, unless within a reasonable time after acceptance of the offer the corporation fails to do those things which it offered to do. Any rejection of the offer shall be in writing and shall indicate the reasons the alternative proposed by the corporation does not meet the proper purpose of the demand made pursuant to subdivision (a).

Corp. Code § 8331. Petition By Corporation To Set Aside Demand; Time; Procedure; Grounds.

(a) Where the corporation, in good faith, and with a substantial basis, believes that the membership list, demanded under Section 8330 by the authorized number (Section 5036), will be used for a purpose not reasonably related to the interests as members of the person or persons making the demand (hereinafter called the requesting parties) as members or provides a reasonable alternative pursuant to subdivision (c) of Section 8330, it may petition the superior court of the proper county for an order setting aside the demand.

(b) Except as provided in subdivision (c), a petition for an order to show cause why a protective order pursuant to subdivision (d) should not issue shall be filed within 10 business days after the demand by the authorized number under Section 8330 or receipt of a written rejection by the authorized number of an offer made pursuant to subdivision (c) of Section 8330, whichever is later. The petition shall be accompanied by an application for a hearing on the petition. Upon the filing of the petition, the court shall issue a protective order staying production of the list demanded until the hearing on the order to show cause. The court shall set the hearing on the order to show cause not more than 20 days from the date of the filing of the petition. The order to show cause shall be granted unless the court finds that there is no reasonable probability that the corporation will make the showing required under subdivision (f).

(c) A corporation may file a petition under this section more than 10 business days after the demand or rejection under Section 8330, but only upon a showing the delay was caused by excusable neglect. In no event, however, may any petition under this section be considered if filed more than 30 days after the requesting parties' demand or rejection, whichever is later.

(d) Upon the return day of the order to show cause, the court may issue a protective order staying production of the list demanded until final adjudication of the petition filed pursuant to this section. No protective order shall issue under this subdivision unless the court finds that the rights of the requesting parties can reasonably be preserved and that the corporation is likely to make the showing required by subdivision (f) or the court is likely to issue a protective order pursuant to subdivision (g).

(e) If the corporation fails to file a petition within the time allowed by subdivision (b) or (c), whichever is applicable, or fails to obtain a protective order under subdivision (d), then the corporation shall comply with the demand, and no further action may be brought by the corporation under this section.

(f) The court shall issue the final order setting aside the demand only if the corporation proves:

(1) That there is a reasonable probability that the requesting parties will permit use of the membership list for a purpose unrelated to their interests as members; or

(2) That the method offered by the corporation is a reasonable alternative in that it reasonably achieves the proper purpose set forth in the requesting parties' demand and that the corporation intends and is able to effectuate the reasonable alternative.

(g) In the final order, the court may, in its discretion, order an alternate mechanism for achieving the proper purposes of the requesting parties, or impose just and proper conditions upon the use of the membership list which reasonably assures compliance with Section 8330 and section 8338.

(h) The court shall award reasonable costs and expenses including reasonable attorneys' fees, to requesting parties who successfully oppose any petition or application filed pursuant to this section.

(i) Where the corporation has neither, within the time allowed, complied with a demand by the authorized number (Section 5036) under Section 8330, nor obtained a protective order staying production of the list, or a final order setting aside the demand, which is then in effect, the requesting parties may petition the superior court of the proper county for a writ of mandamus pursuant to Section 1085 of the Code of Civil Procedure compelling the corporation to comply with the demand. At the hearing, the court shall hear the parties summarily, by affidavit or otherwise, and shall issue a peremptory writ of mandamus unless it appears that the demand was not made by an authorized number (Section 5036), that the demand has been complied with, that the corporation, pursuant to subdivision (c) of Section 8330, made an offer which was not rejected in writing within a reanoable time, or that a protective or final order properly issued under subdivision (d), (f) or (g) is then in effect. No inquiry may be made in such proceeding into the use for which the authorized number seek the list. The court shall award reasonable attorneys' fees to persons granted an order under this subdivision.

(j) Nothing in this section shall be construed to limit the right of the corporation to obtain damages for any misuse of a membership list obtained under Section 8330, or otherwise, or to obtain injunctive relief necessary to restrain misuse of a member list. A corporation shall be entitled to recover reasonable costs and expenses, including reasonable attorneys' fees, incurred in successfully bringing any such action.

Corp. Code § 8332. Power Of Court To Limit Rights Under Section 8330; Temporary Order Suspending Time Limit.

(a) Upon petition of the corporation or any member, the superior court of the proper county may limit or restrict the rights set forth in Section 8330 where, and only where, such limitation or restriction is necessary to protect the rights of any member under the Constitution of the United States or the Constitution of the State of California. An order issued pursuant to this subdivision shall provide, insofar as possible, for alternative mechanisms by which the persons seeking to exercise rights under Section 8330 may communicate with members for purposes reasonably related to their interests as members.

(b) Upon the filing of a petition under subdivision (a), the court may, if requested by the person making the petition, issue a temporary order suspending the running of any time limit specified in Section 8330 for compliance with that section. Such an order may be extended, after notice and hearing, until final adjudication of the petition, wherever it appears that the petitioner may prevail on the merits, and it is otherwise equitable to do so.

Corp. Code § 8333. Inspection Of Accounting Books, Records, And Minutes By Member.

The accounting books and records and minutes of proceedings of the members and the board and committees of the board shall be open to inspection upon the written demand on the corporation of any member at any reasonable time, for a purpose reasonably related to such person's interests as a member.

Corp. Code § 8334. Director's Right Of Inspection.

Every director shall have the absolute right at any reasonable time to inspect and copy all books, records and documents of every kind and to inspect the physical properties of the corporation of which such person is a director.

Corp. Code § 8335. Court Order Postponing Meeting When Records Not Obtained.

Where the proper purpose of the person or persons making a demand pursuant to Section 8330 is frustrated by (1) any delay by the corporation in complying with a demand under Section 8330 beyond the time limits specified therein, or (2) any delay caused by the filing of a petition under Section 8331 or Section 8332, or (3) any delay caused by the alternative proposed under subdivision (c) of Section 8330, the person or persons properly making the demand shall have, in the discretion of the court, a right to obtain from the superior court an order postponing any members' meeting previously noticed for a period equal to the period of such delay. The members may obtain such an order in a proceeding brought pursuant to Section 8331 upon the filing of a verified complaint in the proper county and after a hearing, notice of which shall be given to such persons and in such manner as the court may direct. Such right shall be in addition to any other legal or equitable remedies to which the member may be entitled.

Corp. Code § 8336. Power Of Superior Court To Enforce Inspection Rights Or Appoint Inspectors Or Accountants.

(a) Upon refusal of a lawful demand for inspection under this chapter, or a lawful demand pursuant to Section 8330 or Section 8333, the superior court of the proper county, or the county where the books or records in question are kept, may enforce the demand or right of inspection with just and proper conditions or may, for good cause shown, appoint one or more competent inspectors or independent accountants to audit the financial statements kept in this state and investigate the property, funds and affairs of any corporation and of any subsidiary corporation thereof, domestic or foreign, keeping records in this state and to report thereon in such manner as the court may direct.

(b) All officers and agents of the corporation shall produce to the inspectors or accountants so appointed all books and documents in their custody or power, under penalty of punishment for contempt of court.

(c) All expenses of the investigation or audit shall be defrayed by the applicant unless the court orders them to be paid or shared by the corporation.

Corp. Code § 8337. Award Of Costs, Expenses, Attorneys' Fees.

In any action or proceeding under this article, and except as required by Section 8331, if the court finds the failure of the corporation to comply with a proper demand thereunder was without justification, the court may award the member reasonable costs and expenses, including reasonable attorneys' fees, in connection with such action or proceeding.

Corp. Code § 8338. Prohibited Uses Of Membership Lists; Damages For Misuse.

(a) A membership list is a corporate asset. Without consent of the board a membership list or any part thereof may not be obtained or used by any person for any purpose not reasonably related to a member's interest as a member. Without limiting the generality of the foregoing, without the consent of the board a membership list or any part thereof may not be:

(1) Used to solicit money or property unless such money or property will be used solely to solicit the vote of the members in an election to be held by their corporation.

(2) Used for any purpose which the user does not reasonably and in good faith believe will benefit the corporation.

(3) Used for any commercial purpose or purpose in competition with the corporation.

(4) Sold to or purchased by any person.

(b) Any person who violates the provisions of subdivision (a) shall be liable for any damages such violation causes the corporation and shall account for and pay to the corporation any profit derived as a result of said violation. In addition, a court in its discretion may award exemplary damages for a fraudulent or malicious violation of subdivision (a).

(c) Nothing in this article shall be construed to limit the right of a corporation to obtain injunctive relief necessary to restrain misuse of a membership list or any part thereof.

(d) In any action or proceeding under this section, a court may award the corporation reasonable costs and expenses, including reasonable attorneys' fees, in connection with such action or proceeding.

(e) As used in this section, the term "membership list" means the record of the members' names and addresses.

Gov't Code § 66469. Amendment Of Parcel Map.

After a final map or parcel map is filed in the office of the county recorder, it may be amended by a certificate of correction or an amending map for any of the following purposes:

(a) To correct an error in any course or distance shown thereon.

(b) To show any course or distance that was omitted therefrom.

(c) To correct an error in the description of the real property shown on the map.

(d) To indicate monuments set after the death, disability, retirement from practice, or replacement of the engineer or surveyor charged with responsibilities for setting monuments.

(e) To show the proper location or character of any monument which has been changed in location or character originally was shown at the wrong location or incorrectly as to its character.

(f) To correct any additional information filed or recorded pursuant to Section 66434.2, if the correction does not impose any additional burden on the present fee owners of the real property and does not alter any right, title, or interest in the real property reflected on the recorded map.

(g) To correct any other type of map error or omission as approved by the county surveyor or city engineer that does not affect any property right, including, but not limited to, lot numbers, acreage, street names, and identification of adjacent record maps. As used in this section, "error" does not include changes in courses or distances from which an error is not ascertainable from the data shown on the final or parcel map.

Gov't Code § 66470. Recording Of Certificate Of Correction.

The amending map or certificate of correction shall be prepared and signed by a registered civil engineer or licensed land surveyor. An amending map shall conform to the requirements of Section 66434, if a final map, or subdivisions (a) to (d), inclusive, and (f) to (i), inclusive, of Section 66445, if a parcel map. The amending map or certificate of correction shall set forth in detail the corrections made and show the names of the fee owners of the real property affected by the correction or omission on the date of the filing or recording of the original recorded map. Upon recordation of a certificate of correction, the county recorder shall within 60 days of recording transmit a certified copy to the county surveyor or county engineer who shall maintain an index of recorded certificates of correction. The county recorder may charge a fee, in addition to the fee charged for recording the certificate of correction, which shall be transmitted to the county surveyor or the county engineer, as compensation for the cost of maintaining an index of recorded certificates of correction. The amount of this additional fee shall not exceed the fee which is charged for recording the certificate of correction. If the property affected by a map is located within a city, the county recorder shall, upon request of the city engineer, provide copies of recorded certificates of correction to the city engineer.

Gov't Code § 66471. Time Limitations On Approval And Recording Of Certificate Of Correction.

(a) If the subdivision is in unincorporated territory, the county surveyor shall examine the amending map or certificate of correction and if the only changes made are those set forth in Section 66469, he or she shall certify to this fact on the amending map or certificate of correction. If the subdivision is in the city, such examination and certification shall be by the city surveyor or city engineer.

(b) As to a certificate of correction, the county surveyor, city surveyor, or city engineer shall have 20 working days in which to examine the certificate of correction for compliance with Sections 66469 and 66470, endorse a statement on it of his or her examination and certification, and present it to the county recorder for recordation. In the event the submitted certificate of correction fails to comply with Sections 66469 and 66470, the county surveyor, city surveyor, or city engineer shall return it within the same 20 working days to the person who presented it, together with a written statement of the changes necessary to make it conform to the requirements of Sections 66469 and 66470. The licensed land surveyor or registered civil engineer submitting the certificate of correction may then make the changes in compliance with Sections 66469 and 66470 and resubmit the certificate of correction to the county surveyor, city surveyor, or city engineer for approval. The county surveyor, city surveyor, or city engineer shall have 10 working days after resubmission and approval of the certificate of correction to present it to the county recorder for recordation. 66472. The amending map or certificate of correction certified by the county surveyor, city surveyor, or city engineer shall be filed or recorded in the office of the county recorder in which the original map was filed. Upon that filing or recordation, the county recorder shall index the names of the fee owners of the real property reflected on the original recorded map, and the appropriate tract designation shown on the amending map or certificate of correction in the general index and map index respectively. Thereupon, the original map shall be deemed to have been conclusively so corrected, and thereafter shall impart constructive notice of all those corrections in the same manner as though set forth upon the original map.

Gov't Code § 66472.1. Modification Of Parcel Map By Local Agency; Public Hearing.

In addition to the amendments authorized by Section 66469, after a final map or parcel map is filed in the office of the county recorder, the recorded final map may be modified by a certificate of correction or an amending map, if authorized by local ordinance, if the local agency finds that there are changes in circumstances that make any or all of the conditions of the map no longer appropriate or necessary and that the modifications do not impose any additional burden on the fee owners of the real property, and if the modifications do not alter any right, title, or interest in the real property reflected on the recorded map, and the local agency finds that the map as modified conforms to Section 66474. Any modification shall be set for public hearing as provided for in Section 66451.3. The local agency shall confine the hearing to consideration of, and action on, the proposed modification.

CHAPTER 6

TAXATION OF COMMON INTEREST DEVELOPMENTS
(United States Internal Revenue Code § 528 and IRS Revenue Ruling 70-604) (California Revenue & Taxation Code §§ 2188.3, 2188.5, 2188.6, 23701& 23701t)

Federal

I.R.C. § 528. Taxation Of Homeowner Associations.

(a) General rule. A homeowners association [as defined in subsection (c)] shall be subject to taxation under this subtitle only to the extent provided in this section. A homeowners association shall be considered an organization exempt from income taxes for the purpose of any law which refers to organizations exempt from income taxes.

(b) Tax imposed. A tax is hereby imposed for each taxable year on the owners association taxable income of every homeowners association. Such tax shall be equal to 30 percent of the homeowners association taxable income.

(c) Homeowners association defined. For purposes of this section

(1) Homeowners association. The term "homeowners association" means: an organization which is a condominium management association or a residential real estate management association if

(A) such organization is organized and operated to provide for the acquisition, construction, management, maintenance, and care of association property,

(B) sixty percent or more of the gross income of such organization for the taxable year consists solely of amounts received as membership dues, fees, or assessments from (i) owners of residential units in the case of a condominium management association, or (ii) owners of residences or residential lots in the case of a residential real estate management association.

(C) ninety percent or more of the expenditures of the organization for the taxable year are expenditures for the acquisition, construction, management, maintenance, and care of association property,

(D) no part of the net earnings of such organization inures (other than by acquiring, constructing, or providing management, maintenance, and care of association property, and other than by a rebate of excess membership dues, fees, or assessments) to the benefit of any private shareholder or individual, and

(E) such organization elects (at such time and in such manner as the Secretary by regulations prescribes) to have this section apply for the taxable year.

(2) Condominium management association. The term "condominium management association" means any organization meeting the requirement of subparagraph (A) of paragraph (1) with respect to a condominium project substantially all of the units of which are used by individuals for residences.

(3) Residential real estate management association. The term "residential real estate management association" means any organization meeting the requirements of subparagraph (A) of paragraph (1) with respect to a subdivision, development, or similar area substantially all the lots or buildings of which may only be used by individuals for residences.

(4) Association property. The term "association property" means:

(A) property held by the organization

(B) property commonly held by the members of the organization

(C) property within the organization privately held by the members of the organization, and

(D) property owned by a governmental unit and used for the benefit of residents of such unit.

(d) Homeowners association taxable income defined.

(1) Taxable income defined. For purposes of this section, the homeowners association taxable income of any organization for any taxable year is an amount equal to the excess (if any) of

(A) the gross amount for the taxable year (excluding any exempt function income), over

(B) the deductions allowed by this chapter which are directly connected with the production of the gross income (excluding exempt function income), computed with the modifications provided in paragraph (2).

(2) Modifications. For purposes of this subsection

(A) there shall be allowed a specific deduction of $100,

(B) no net operating loss deduction shall be allowed under Section 172, and

(C) no deduction shall be allowed under part VIII of subchapter B (relating to special deductions for corporations).

(3) Exempt function income. For purposes of this subsection, the term "exempt function income" means any amount received as membership dues, fees, or assessments from

(A) owners of condominium housing units in the case of a condominium management association, or

(B) owners of real property in the case of a residential real estate management association.

IRS Revenue Ruling 70-604. Excess Assessments.

A condominium management corporation assesses its stockholder-owners for the purposes of managing, operating, maintaining, and replacing the common elements of the condominium property. This is the sole activity of the corporation and its by-laws do not authorize it to engage in any other activity.

A meeting is held each year by the stockholder-owners of the corporation, at which they decide what is to be done with any excess assessments not actually used for the purposes described above, i.e., they decide either to return the excess to themselves or to have the excess applied against the following year's assessments.

Held, the excess assessments for the taxable year over and above the actual expenses paid or incurred for the purposes described above are not taxable income to the corporation, since such excess, in effect, has been returned to the stockholder-owners.

California

Rev. & Tax. Code § 2188.3. Condominiums.

Whenever real property has been divided into condominiums, as defined in Section 783 of the Civil Code, (a) each condominium owned in fee shall be separately assessed to the owner thereof, and the tax on each such condominium shall constitute a lien solely thereon; (b) each condominium not owned in fee shall be separately assessed, as if it were owned in fee, to the owner of the condominium or the owner of the fee or both (and the tax on each such condominium shall be a lien solely on the interest of the owner of the fee in the real property included in such condominium and on such condominium), if so agreed by the assessor in a writing of record; such an agreement shall be binding upon such assessor and his successors in office with respect to such project so long as it continues to be divided into condominiums in the same manner as that in effect when the agreement was made.

Rev. & Tax. Code § 2188.5. Planned Developments; Assessment; Application Of Amendment To Subd. (b).

(a) (1) Subject to the limitations set forth in subdivision (b), whenever real property has been divided into planned developments as defined in Section 11003 of the Business and Professions Code, the interests therein shall be presumed to be the value of each separately owned lot, parcel or area, and the assessment shall reflect this value which includes all of the following:

(A) The assessment attributable to the value of the separately owned lot, parcel or area and the improvements thereon.

(B) The assessment attributable to the share in the common area reserved as an appurtenance of the separately owned lot, parcel or area.

(C) The new base year value of the common area resulting from any change in ownership pursuant to Chapter 2 (commencing with Section 60) or new construction pursuant to Chapter 3 (commencing with Section 70) attributable to the share in the common area reserved as an appurtenance of the separately owned lot, parcel or area.

(2) For the purpose of this section, "common area" shall mean the land and improvements within a lot, parcel or area, the beneficial use and enjoyment of which is reserved in whole or in part as an appurtenance to the separately owned lots, parcels or area, whether this common area is held in common or through ownership of share of stock or membership in an owners' association. The tax on each separately owned lot, parcel or area shall constitute a lien solely thereon and upon the proportionate interest in the common area appurtenant thereto.

(b) Assessment in accordance with the provisions of subdivision (a) shall only be required with respect to those planned developments which satisfy both of the following conditions:

(1) The development is located entirely within a single tax code area.

(2) The entire beneficial ownership of the common area is reserved as an appurtenance to the separately owned lots, parcels or areas.

(c) The amendment to subdivision (b) made by the act Chapter 407 of the Statutes of 1984 shall apply to real property which has been divided into planned developments as defined in Sections 11003 and 11003.1 of the Business and Professions Code, on and after the effective date of Chapter 407 of the Statutes of 1984.

Rev. & Tax. Code § 2188.6. Separate Unit Assessment And Tax Bill; Lien On Unit Only.

(a) Unless a request for exemption has been recorded pursuant to subdivision (d), prior to the creation of a condominium as defined in Section 783 of the Civil Code, the county assessor may separately assess each individual unit which is shown on the condominium plan of a proposed condominium project when all of the following documents have been recorded as required by law:

(1) A subdivision final map or parcel map, as described in Sections 66434 and 66445, respectively, of the Government Code.

(2) A condominium plan, as defined in subdivision (e) of Section 1351 of the Civil Code.

(3) A declaration, as defined in subdivision (h) of Section 1351 of the Civil Code.

(b) The tax due on each individual unit shall constitute a lien solely on that unit.

(c) The lien created pursuant to this section shall be a lien on an undivided interest in a portion of real property coupled with a separate interest in space called a unit as described in subdivision (f) of Section 1351 of the Civil Code.

(d) The record owner of the real property may record with the condominium plan a request that the real property be exempt from separate assessment pursuant to this section. If a request for exemption is recorded, separate assessment of a condominium unit shall be made only in accordance with Section 2188.3.

(e) This section shall become operative on January 1, 1990, and shall apply to condominium projects for which a condominium plan is recorded after that date.

Rev. & Tax. Code § 23701. Exemption Of Specified Organizations.

Organizations which are organized and operated for nonprofit purposes within the provisions of a specific section of this article, or are defined in Section 23701h (relating to certain title-holding companies) or Section 23701x (relating to certain title-holding companies), are exempt from taxes imposed under this part, except as provided in this article or in Article 2 (commencing with Section 23731) of this chapter, if:

(a) An application for exemption is submitted in the form prescribed by the Franchise Tax Board; and

(b) A filing fee of twenty-five dollars ($25) is paid with each application for exemption filed with the Franchise Tax Board after December 31, 1969; and

(c) The Franchise Tax Board issues a determination exempting the organization from tax.

This section shall not prevent a determination from having a retroactive effect and does not prevent the issuance of a determination with respect to a domestic organization which was in existence prior to January 1, 1970, and exempt under prior law without the submission of a formal application or payment of a filing fee. For the purposes of this section, the term "domestic" means created or organized under the laws of this state.

The Franchise Tax Board may issue rulings and regulations as are necessary and reasonable to carry out the provisions of this article.

Rev. & Tax. Code § 23701t. Homeowners' Association Conditions; Definitions.

(a) A homeowners' association organized and operated to provide for the acquisition, construction, management, maintenance, and care of residential association property if all of the following apply:

(1) Sixty percent or more of the gross income of the organization for the taxable year consists solely of amounts received as membership dues, fees and assessments from either of the following:

(A) Tenant-stockholders or owners of residential units, residences, or lots.

(B) Owners of time-share rights to use, or time-share ownership interests in, association property in the case of a time-share association.

(2) Ninety percent or more of the expenditures of the organization for the taxable year are expenditures for the acquisition, construction, management, maintenance, and care of association property and, in the case of a time-share association, for activities provided to or on behalf of members of the association.

(3) No part of the net earnings inures (other than by providing management, maintenance and care of association property or by a rebate of excess membership dues, fees or assessments) to the benefit of any private shareholder or individual.

(4) Amounts received as membership dues, fees and assessments not expended for association purposes during the taxable year are transferred to and held in trust to provide for the management, maintenance, and care of association property and common areas.

(b) The term "association property" means:

(1) Property held by the organization.

(2) Property held in common by the members of the organization.

(3) Property within the organization privately held by the members of the organization.

In the case of a time-share association, "association property" includes property in which the time-share association, or members of the association, have rights arising out of recorded easements, covenants, or other recorded instruments to use property related to the time-share project.

(c) A homeowners association shall be subject to tax under this part with respect to its "homeowners association taxable income," and that income shall be subject to tax as provided by Chapter 3 (commencing with Section 23501).

(1) For purposes of this section, the term "homeowners' association taxable income" of any organization for any taxable year means an amount equal to the excess over one hundred dollars ($100) (if any) of-

(A) The gross income for the taxable year (excluding any exempt function income), over

(B) The deductions allowed by this part which are directly connected with the production of the gross income (excluding exempt function income).

(2) For purposes of this section, the term "exempt function income" means any amount received as membership fees, dues and assessments from tenant-shareholders or owners of residential units, residences or lots, or owners of time-share rights to use, or time-share ownership interests in, association property in the case of a time-share association.

(d) The term "homeowners' association" includes a condominium management association, a residential real estate management association,

a time-share association, and a cooperative housing corporation.

(e) "Cooperative housing corporation" includes, but is not limited to, a limited-equity housing cooperative, as defined in Section 33007.5 of the Health and Safety Code, organized either as a nonprofit public benefit corporation pursuant to Part 2 (commencing with Section 5110) of Division 2 of Title 1 of the Corporations Code, or a nonprofit mutual benefit corporation pursuant to Part 3 (commencing with Section 7110) of Division 2 of Title 1 of the Corporations Code.

(f) The term "time-share association" means any organization (other than a condominium management association) organized and operated to provide for the acquisition, construction, management, maintenance, and care of association property if any member thereof holds a time-share right to use, or a time-share ownership interest in, real property constituting association property.

(g) The amendments made to this section by the act adding this subdivision shall apply to taxable years beginning on or after January 1, 1998.

CHAPTER 7

FILING CIVIL ACTIONS
(Code of Civil Procedure §§ 336-339.5, 415.10, 415.20, 415.21, 425.15 & 425.16)

Statutes of Limitation

Civ. Proc. § 336. Five Year Statute Of Limitation On Violation Of Restriction On Use Of Real Property.

Within five years:

(a) An action for mesne profits of real property.

(b) An action for violation of a restriction, as defined in Section 784 of the Civil Code. The period prescribed in this subdivision runs from the time the person seeking to enforce the restriction discovered or, through the exercise of reasonable diligence, should have discovered the violation. A failure to commence an action for violation of a restriction within the period prescribed in this subdivision does not waive the right to commence an action for any other violation of the restriction and does not, in itself, create an implication that the restriction is abandoned, obsolete, or otherwise unenforceable. This subdivision shall not bar commencement of an action for violation of a restriction before January 1, 2001, and until January 1, 2001, any other applicable statutory or common law limitation shall continue to apply to that action.

Civ. Proc. § 337. Four Year Statute Of Limitation On Written Contract And Accounts.

Within four years:

1.   An action upon any contract, obligation or liability founded upon an instrument in writing, except as provided in Section 336a of this code; provided, that the time within which any action for a money judgment for the balance due upon an obligation for the payment of which a deed of trust or mortgage with power of sale upon real property or any interest therein was given as security, following the exercise of the power of sale in such deed of trust or mortgage, may be brought shall not extend beyond three

months after the time of sale under such deed of trust or mortgage.

2.　　An action to recover (1) upon a book account whether consisting of one or more entries; (2) upon an account stated based upon an account in writing, but the acknowledgment of the account stated need not be in writing; (3) a balance due upon a mutual, open and current account, the items of which are in writing; provided, however, that where an account stated is based upon an account of one item, the time shall begin to run from the date of said item, and where an account stated is based upon an account of more than one item, the time shall begin to run from the date of the last item.

3.　　An action based upon the rescission of a contract in writing. The time begins to run from the date upon which the facts that entitle the aggrieved party to rescind occurred. Where the ground for rescission is fraud or mistake, the time does not begin to run until the discovery by the aggrieved party of the facts constituting the fraud or mistake. Where the ground for rescission is misrepresentation under Section 359 of the Insurance Code, the time does not begin to run until the representation becomes false.

Civ. Proc. § 337.1. Four Year Statute Of Limitation On Injury Or Death From Deficient Planning Or Construction.

(a)　Except as otherwise provided in this section, no action shall be brought to recover damages from any person performing or furnishing the design, specifications, surveying, planning, supervision or observation of construction or construction of an improvement to real property more than four years after the substantial completion of such improvement for any of the following:

(1)　Any patent deficiency in the design, specifications, surveying, planning, supervision or observation of construction or construction of an improvement to, or survey of, real property;

(2)　Injury to property, real or personal, arising out of any such patent deficiency; or

(3)　Injury to the person or for wrongful death arising out of any such patent deficiency.

(b)　If by reason of such patent deficiency, an injury to property or the person or an injury causing wrongful death occurs during the fourth year after such substantial completion, an action in tort to recover damages for such an injury or wrongful death may be brought within one year after the date on which such injury occurred, irrespective of the date of death, but in no event may such an action be brought more than five years after

Litigation

the substantial completion of construction of such improvement.

(c) Nothing in this section shall be construed as extending the period prescribed by the laws of this state for the bringing of any action.

(d) The limitation prescribed by this section shall not be asserted by way of defense by any person in actual possession or the control, as owner, tenant or otherwise, of such an improvement at the time any deficiency in such an improvement constitutes the proximate cause of the injury or death for which it is proposed to bring an action.

(e) As used in this section, "patent deficiency" means a deficiency which is apparent by reasonable inspection.

(f) Subdivisions (a) and (b) shall not apply to any owner-occupied single-unit residence.

Civ. Proc. § 337.15. Ten Year Statute of Limitation On Actions To Recover Damages From Latent Defects In Planning Or Construction.

(a) No action may be brought to recover damages from any person, or the surety of a person, who develops real property or performs or furnishes the design, specifications, surveying, planning, supervision, testing, or observation of construction or construction of an improvement to real property more than 10 years after the substantial completion of the development or improvement for any of the following:

(1) Any latent deficiency in the design, specification, surveying, planning, supervision, or observation of construction or construction of an improvement to, or survey of, real property.

(2) Injury to property, real or personal, arising out of any such latent deficiency.

(b) As used in this section, "latent deficiency" means a deficiency which is not apparent by reasonable inspection.

(c) As used in this section, "action" includes an action for indemnity brought against a person arising out of that person's performance or furnishing of services or materials referred to in this section, except that a cross-complaint for indemnity may be filed pursuant to subdivision (b) of Section 428.10 in an action which has been brought within the time period set forth in subdivision (a) of this section.

(d) Nothing in this section shall be construed as extending the period prescribed by the laws of this state for bringing any action.

(e) The limitation prescribed by this section shall not be asserted by way of defense by any person in actual possession or the control, as owner, tenant or otherwise, of such an improvement, at the time any deficiency in

Litigation

the improvement constitutes the proximate cause for which it is proposed to bring an action.

(f)   This section shall not apply to actions based on willful misconduct or fraudulent concealment.

(g)   The 10-year period specified in subdivision (a) shall commence upon substantial completion of the improvement, but not later than the date of one of the following, whichever first occurs:

(1)   The date of final inspection by the applicable public agency.

(2)   The date of recordation of a valid notice of completion.

(3)   The date of use or occupation of the improvement.

(4)   One year after termination or cessation of work on the improvement.

The date of substantial completion shall relate specifically to the performance or furnishing design, specifications, surveying, planning, supervision, testing, observation of construction or construction services by each profession or trade rendering services to the improvement.

Civ. Proc. § 338. Three Year Statute of Limitation On Statutory Suit, Trespass Or Injury To Real Property, Fraud And Mistake, Official Bonds, Slander Of Title, False Advertising, Water Quality Control Or Physical Damage To Private Property.

Within three years:

(a)   An action upon a liability created by statute, other than a penalty or forfeiture.

(b)   An action for trespass upon or injury to real property.

(c)(1) An action for taking, detaining, or injuring any goods or chattels, including actions for the specific recovery of personal property.

(2) The cause of action in the case of theft, as described in Section 484 of the Penal Code, of any article of historical, interpretative, scientific, or artistic significance is not deemed to have accrued until the discovery of the whereabouts of the article by the aggrieved party, his or her agent, or the law enforcement agency that originally investigated the theft.

(3)(A) Notwithstanding paragraphs (1) and (2), an action for the specific recovery of a work of fine art brought against a museum, gallery, auctioneer, or dealer, in the case of an unlawful taking or theft, as described in Section 484 of the Penal Code, of a work of fine art, including a taking or theft by means of fraud or duress, shall be commenced within six years of the actual discovery by the claimant or his or her agent, of both of the following:

(i) The identity and the whereabouts of the work of fine art. In the case where there is a possibility of misidentification of the object of fine art in question, the identity can be satisfied by the identification of facts sufficient to determine that the work of fine art is likely to be the work of fine art that was unlawfully taken or stolen.

(ii) Information or facts that are sufficient to indicate that the claimant has a claim for a possessory interest in the work of fine art that was unlawfully taken or stolen.

(B) The provisions of this paragraph shall apply to all pending and future actions commenced on or before December 31, 2017, including any actions dismissed based on the expiration of statutes of limitation in effect prior to the date of enactment of this statute if the judgment in that action is not yet final or if the time for filing an appeal from a decision on that action has not expired, provided that the action concerns a work of fine art that was taken within 100 years prior to the date of enactment of this statute.

(C) For purposes of this paragraph:

(i) "Actual discovery," notwithstanding Section 19 of the Civil Code, does not include any constructive knowledge imputed by law.

(ii) "Auctioneer" means any individual who is engaged in, or who by advertising or otherwise holds himself or herself out as being available to engage in, the calling for, the recognition of, and the acceptance of, offers for the purchase of goods at an auction as defined in subdivision (b) of Section 1812.601 of the Civil Code.

(iii) "Dealer" means a person who holds a valid seller's permit and who is actively and principally engaged in, or conducting the business of, selling works of fine art.

(iv) "Duress" means a threat of force, violence, danger, or retribution against an owner of the work of fine art in question, or his or her family member, sufficient to coerce a reasonable person of ordinary susceptibilities to perform an act that otherwise would not have been performed or to acquiesce to an act to which he or she would otherwise not have acquiesced.

(v) "Fine art" has the same meaning as defined in paragraph (1) of subdivision (d) of Section 982 of the Civil Code.

(vi) "Museum or gallery" shall include any public or private organization or foundation operating as a museum or gallery.

(4) Section 361 shall not apply to an action brought pursuant to

paragraph (3).

(5) A party in an action to which paragraph (3) applies may raise all equitable and legal affirmative defenses and doctrines, including, without limitation, laches and unclean hands.

(d)   An action for relief on the ground of fraud or mistake. The cause of action in that case is not to be deemed to have accrued until the discovery, by the aggrieved party, of the facts constituting the fraud or mistake.

(e)   An action upon a bond of a public official except any cause of action based on fraud or embezzlement is not to be deemed to have accrued until the discovery, by the aggrieved party or his or her agent, of the facts constituting the cause of action upon the bond.

(f) *(1)*   An action against a notary public on his or her bond or in his or her official capacity except that any cause of action based on malfeasance or misfeasance is not deemed to have accrued until discovery, by the aggrieved party or his or her agent, of the facts, constituting the cause of action

(2)   Notwithstanding paragraph (1), an action based on malfeasance or misfeasance shall be commenced within one year from discovery, by the aggrieved party or his or her agent, of the facts constituting the cause of action or within three years from the performance of the notarial act giving rise to the action, whichever is later.

(3)   Notwithstanding paragraph (1), an action against a notary public on his or her bond or in his or her official capacity shall be commenced within six years.

(g)   An action for slander of title to real property.

(h)   An action commenced under Section 17536 of the Business and Professions Code. The cause of action in that case shall not be deemed to have accrued until the discovery by the aggrieved party, the Attorney General, the district attorney, the county counsel, the city prosecutor, or the city attorney of the facts constituting grounds for commencing such an action.

(i)   An action commenced under the Porter-Cologne Water Quality Control Act (Division 7 (commencing with Section 13000) of the Water Code). The cause of action in that case shall not be deemed to have accrued until the discovery by the State Water Resources Control Board or a regional water quality control board of the facts constituting grounds for commencing actions under their jurisdiction.

(j)   An action to recover for physical damage to private property under Section 19 of Article I of the California Constitution.

(k)   An action commenced under Division 26 (commencing with

Section 39000) of the Health and Safety Code. These causes of action shall not be deemed to have accrued until the discovery by the State Air Resources Board or by a district, as defined in Section 39025 of the Health and Safety Code, of the facts constituting grounds for commencing the action under its jurisdiction.

(l) An action commenced under Section 1603.1, 1615, or 5650.1 of the Fish and Game Code. These causes of action shall not be deemed to have accrued until discovery by the agency bringing the action of the facts constituting the grounds for commencing the action.

(m) An action challenging the validity of the levy upon a parcel of a special tax levied by a local agency on a per parcel basis.

(n) An action commencing under Section 51.7 of the Civil Code.

Civ. Proc. § 339. Two Year Statute of Limitation On Oral Contracts, Abstract Or Guaranty Of Title, Title Insurance Or Rescission.

Within two years:

1. An action upon a contract, obligation or liability not founded upon an instrument of writing, except as provided in Section 2725 of the Commercial Code or subdivision 2 of Section 337 of this code; or an action founded upon a contract, obligation or liability, evidenced by a certificate, or abstract or guaranty of title of real property, or by a policy of title insurance; provided, that the cause of action upon a contract, obligation or liability evidenced by a certificate, or abstract or guaranty of title of real property or policy of title insurance shall not be deemed to have accrued until the discovery of the loss or damage suffered by the aggrieved party thereunder.

2. An action against a sheriff or coroner upon a liability incurred by the doing of an act in an official capacity and in virtue of office, or by the omission of an official duty including the nonpayment of money collected in the enforcement of a judgment.

3. An action based upon the rescission of a contract not in writing. The time begins to run from the date upon which the facts that entitle the aggrieved party to rescind occurred. Where the ground for rescission is fraud or mistake, the time does not begin to run until the discovery by the aggrieved party of the facts constituting the fraud or mistake.

Civ. Proc. § 339.5. Lease Not In Writing; Period For Action After Breach.

Where a lease of real property is not in writing, no action shall be brought under Section 1951.2 of the Civil Code more than two years after the breach of the lease and abandonment of the property, or more than two years after the termination of the right of the lessee to possession of the property, whichever is the earlier time.

Service Of Summons

Civ. Proc. § 415.10. Personal Delivery of Summons.

A summons may be served by personal delivery of a copy of the summons and of the complaint to the person to be served. Service of a summons in this manner is deemed complete at the time of such delivery.

The date upon which personal delivery is made shall be entered on or affixed to the face of the copy of the summons at the time of its delivery. However, service of a summons without such date shall be valid and effective.

Civ. Proc. § 415.20. Service Of Summons In Lieu Of Personal Delivery.

(a) In lieu of personal delivery of a copy of the summons and complaint to the person to be served as specified in Section 416.10, 416.20, 416.30, 416.40, or 416.50, a summons may be served by leaving a copy of the summons and complaint during usual office hours in his or her office or, if no physical address is known, at his or her usual mailing address, other than a United States Postal Service post office box, with the person who is apparently in charge thereof, and by thereafter mailing a copy of the summons and complaint by first-class mail, postage prepaid to the person to be served at the place where a copy of the summons and complaint were left. When service is effected by leaving a copy of the summons and complaint at a mailing address, it shall be left with a person at least 18 years of age, who shall be informed of the contents thereof. Service of a summons in this manner is deemed complete on the 10th day after the mailing.

(b) If a copy of the summons and of the complaint cannot with reasonable diligence be personally delivered to the person to be served, as specified in Section 416.60, 416.70, 416.80, or 416.90, a summons may be served by leaving a copy of the summons and complaint at the person's dwelling house, usual place of abode, usual place of business, or usual mailing address other than a United States Postal Service post office box, in the presence of a competent member of the household or a person apparently in charge of his or her office, place of business, or usual mailing address other than a United States Postal Service post office box, at least 18 years of age, who shall be informed of the contents thereof, and by thereafter mailing a copy of the summons and complaint by first-class mail, postage prepaid to the person to be served at the place where a copy of the summons and of the complaint were left. Service of a summons in this manner is deemed complete on the 10th day after the mailing.

Civ. Proc. § 415.21. Access To Gated Community For Service Of Process.

(a) Notwithstanding any other provision of law any person shall be granted access to a gated community for a reasonable period of time for the purpose of performing lawful service of process or service of a subpoena, upon identifying to the guard the person or persons to be served, and upon displaying a current driver's license or other identification, and one of the following:

(1) A badge or other confirmation that the individual is acting in his or her capacity as a representative of a county sheriff or marshal.

(2) Evidence of current registration as a process server pursuant to Chapter 16 (commencing with Section 22350) of Division 8 of the Business and Professions Code.

(b) This section shall only apply to a gated community which is staffed at the time service of process is attempted by a guard or other security personnel assigned to control access to the community.

Claims Against Volunteer Director

Civ. Proc. § 425.15. Cause Of Action Against Volunteer Director Or Officer Of Nonprofit Corporation.

(a) No cause of action against a person serving without compensation as a director or officer of a nonprofit corporation described in this section, on account of any negligent act or omission by that person within the scope of that person's duties as a director acting in the capacity of a board member, or as an officer acting in the capacity of, and within the scope of the duties of, an officer, shall be included in a complaint or other pleading unless the court enters an order allowing the pleading that includes that claim to be filed after the court determines that the party seeking to file the pleading has established evidence that substantiates the claim. The court may allow the filing of a pleading that includes that claim following the filing of a verified petition therefor accompanied by the proposed pleading and supporting affidavits stating the facts upon which the liability is based.

The court shall order service of the petition upon the party against whom the action is proposed to be filed and permit that party to submit opposing affidavits prior to making its determination. The filing of the petition, proposed pleading, and accompanying affidavits shall toll the running of any applicable statute of limitations until the final determination of the matter, which ruling, if favorable to the petitioning party, shall permit the proposed pleading to be filed.

(b) Nothing in this section shall affect the right of the plaintiff to discover evidence on the issue of damages.

(c) Nothing in this section shall be construed to affect any action against a nonprofit corporation for any negligent action or omission of a volunteer director or officer occurring within the scope of the person's duties.

(d) For the purposes of this section, "compensation" means remuneration whether by way of salary, fee, or other consideration for services rendered. However, the payment of per diem, mileage, or other reimbursement expenses to a director or officer shall not constitute compensation.

(e) (1)   This section applies only to officers and directors of nonprofit corporations that are subject to Part 2 (commencing with Section 5110), Part 3 (commencing with Section 7110), or Part 4 (commencing with Section 9110) of Division 2 of Title 1 of the Corporations Code that are organized to provide charitable, educational, scientific, social, or other forms of public service and that are exempt from federal income taxation under Section 501(c)(1), except any credit union, or Section 501(c)(4), 501(c)(5), 501(c)(7), or 501(c)(19) of the Internal Revenue Code.

(2) This section does not apply to any corporation that unlawfully restricts membership, services, or benefits conferred on the basis of political affiliation, age, or any characteristic listed or defined in subdivision (b) or (e) of Section 51 of the Civil Code.

Civ. Proc. § 425.16. Motion To Strike Pusuant To Free Speech Clause Under California And U.S. Constitutions.

(a) The Legislature finds and declares that there has been a disturbing increase in lawsuits brought primarily to chill the valid exercise of the constitutional rights of freedom of speech and petition for the redress of grievances. The Legislature finds and declares that it is in the public interest to encourage continued participation in matters of public significance, and that this participation should not be chilled through abuse of the judicial process. To this end, this section shall be construed broadly.

(b) (1)   A cause of action against a person arising from any act of that person in furtherance of the person's right of petition or free speech under the United States or California Constitution in connection with a public issue shall be subject to a special motion to strike, unless the court determines that the plaintiff has established that there is a probability that the plaintiff will prevail on the claim.

(2) In making its determination, the court shall consider the pleadings, and supporting and opposing affidavits stating the facts upon which the liability or defense is based.

(3) If the court determines that the plaintiff has established a probability that he or she will prevail on the claim, neither that determination nor the fact of that determination shall be admissible in evidence at any later stage of the case, or in any subsequent action, and no burden of proof or degree of proof otherwise applicable shall be affected by that determination in any later stage of the case or in any subsequent proceeding.

(c) (1) Except as provided in paragraph (2), in any action subject to subdivision (b), a prevailing defendant on a special motion to strike shall be entitled to recover his or her attorney's fees and costs. If the court finds that a special motion to strike is frivolous or is solely intended to cause unnecessary delay, the court shall award costs and reasonable attorney's fees to a plaintiff prevailing on the motion, pursuant to Section 128.5.

(2) A defendant who prevails on a special motion to strike in an action subject to paragraph (1) shall not be entitled to attorney's fees and costs if that cause of action is brought pursuant to Section 6259, 11130, 11130.3, 54960, or 54960.1 of the Government Code. Nothing in this paragraph shall be construed to prevent a prevailing defendant from recovering attorney's fees and costs pursuant to subdivision (d) of Section 6259, 11130.5, or 54690.5.

(d)   This section shall not apply to any enforcement action brought in the name of the people of the State of California by the Attorney General, district attorney, or city attorney, acting as a public prosecutor.

(e)   As used in this section, "act in furtherance of a person's right of petition or free speech under the United States or California Constitution in connection with a public issue" includes:

(1) any written or oral statement or writing made before a legislative, executive, or judicial proceeding, or any other official proceeding authorized by law;

(2)   any written or oral statement or writing made in connection with an issue under consideration or review by a legislative, executive,

or judicial body, or any other official proceeding authorized by law;

(3) any written or oral statement or writing made in a place open to the public or a public forum in connection with an issue of public interest;

(4) or any other conduct in furtherance of the exercise of the constitutional right of petition or the constitutional right of free speech in connection with a public issue or an issue of public interest.

(f) The special motion may be filed within 60 days of the service of the complaint or, in the court's discretion, at any later time upon terms it deems proper. The motion shall be scheduled by the clerk of the court for a hearing not more than 30 days after the service of the motion unless the docket conditions of the court require a later hearing.

(g) All discovery proceedings in the action shall be stayed upon the filing of a notice of motion made pursuant to this section. The stay of discovery shall remain in effect until notice of entry of the order ruling on the motion. The court, on noticed motion and for good cause shown, may order that specified discovery be conducted notwithstanding this subdivision.

(h) For purposes of this section, "complaint" includes "cross-complaint" and "petition," "plaintiff" includes "cross-complainant" and "petitioner," and "defendant" includes "cross-defendant" and "respondent."

(i) An order granting or denying a special motion to strike shall be appealable under Section 904.1.

(j) (1)   Any party who files a special motion to strike pursuant to this section, and any party who files an opposition to a special motion to strike, shall, promptly upon so filing, transmit to the Judicial Council, by e-mail or facsimile, a copy of the endorsed, filed caption page of the motion or opposition, a copy of any related notice of appeal or petition for a writ, and a conformed copy of any order issued pursuant to this section, including any order granting or denying a special motion to strike, discovery, or fees.

(2) The Judicial Council shall maintain a public record of information transmitted pursuant to this subdivision for at least three years, and may store the information on microfilm or other appropriate electronic media.

CHAPTER 8

CONSTRUCTION DEFECT LITIGATION
(Civil Code §§ 895-945.5, 43.99 and 1134)

DEFINITIONS

Civ. Code § 895. Requirements For Actions For Construction Defects; Definitions.

(a) "Structure" means any residential dwelling, other building, or improvement located upon a lot or within a common area.

(b) "Designed moisture barrier" means an installed moisture barrier specified in the plans and specifications, contract documents, or manufacturer's recommendations.

(c) "Actual moisture barrier" means any component or material, actually installed, that serves to any degree as a barrier against moisture, whether or not intended as such.

(d) "Unintended water" means water that passes beyond, around, or through a component or the material that is designed to prevent that passage.

(e) "Close of escrow" means the date of the close of escrow between the builder and the original homeowner. With respect to claims by an association, as defined in subdivision (a) of Section 1351, "close of escrow" means the date of substantial completion, as defined in Section 337.15 of the Code of Civil Procedure, or the date the builder relinquishes control over the association's ability to decide whether to initiate a claim under this title, whichever is later.

(f) "Claimant" or "homeowner" includes the individual owners of single-family homes, individual unit owners of attached dwellings and, in the case of a common interest development, any association as defined in subdivision (a) of Section 1351.

ACTIONABLE DEFECTS

Civ. Code § 896. Standards For Original Construction.

In any action seeking recovery of damages arising out of, or related to deficiencies in, the residential construction, design, specifications, surveying, planning, supervision, testing, or observation of construction, a builder, and to the extent set forth in Chapter 4 (commencing with Section 910), a general contractor, subcontractor, material supplier, individual product manufacturer, or design professional, shall, except as specifically set forth in this title, be liable for, and the claimant's claims or causes of action shall be limited to violation of, the following standards, except as specifically set forth in this title. This title applies to original construction intended to be sold as an individual dwelling unit. As to condominium conversions, this title does not apply to or does not supersede any other statutory or common law.

(a) With respect to water issues:

(1) A door shall not allow unintended water to pass beyond, around, or through the door or its designed or actual moisture barriers, if any.

(2) Windows, patio doors, deck doors, and their systems shall not allow water to pass beyond, around, or through the window, patio door, or deck door or its designed or actual moisture barriers, including, without limitation, internal barriers within the systems themselves. For purposes of this paragraph, "systems" include, without limitation, windows, window assemblies, framing, substrate, flashings, and trim, if any.

(3) Windows, patio doors, deck doors, and their systems shall not allow excessive condensation to enter the structure and cause damage to another component. For purposes of this paragraph, "systems" include, without limitation, windows, window assemblies, framing, substrate, flashings, and trim, if any.

(4) Roofs, roofing systems, chimney caps, and ventilation components shall not allow water to enter the structure or to pass beyond, around, or through the designed or actual moisture barriers, including, without limitation, internal barriers located within the systems themselves. For purposes of this paragraph, "systems" include, without limitation, framing, substrate, and sheathing, if any.

(5) Decks, deck systems, balconies, balcony systems, exterior stairs, and stair systems shall not allow water to pass into the adjacent structure. For purposes of this paragraph, "systems" include, without limitation, framing, substrate, flashing, and sheathing, if any.

Litigation

(6) Decks, deck systems, balconies, balcony systems, exterior stairs, and stair systems shall not allow unintended water to pass within the systems themselves and cause damage to the systems. For purposes of this paragraph, "systems" include, without limitation, framing, substrate, flashing, and sheathing, if any.

(7) Foundation systems and slabs shall not allow water or vapor to enter into the structure so as to cause damage to another building component.

(8) Foundation systems and slabs shall not allow water or vapor to enter into the structure so as to limit the installation of the type of flooring materials typically used for the particular application.

(9) Hardscape, including paths and patios, irrigation systems, landscaping systems, and drainage systems, that are installed as part of the original construction, shall not be installed in such a way as to cause water or soil erosion to enter into or come in contact with the structure so as to cause damage to another building component.

(10) Stucco, exterior siding, exterior walls, including, without limitation, exterior framing, and other exterior wall finishes and fixtures and the systems of those components and fixtures, including, but not limited to, pot shelves, horizontal surfaces, columns, and plant-ons, shall be installed in such a way so as not to allow unintended water to pass into the structure or to pass beyond, around, or through the designed or actual moisture barriers of the system, including any internal barriers located within the system itself. For purposes of this paragraph, "systems" include, without limitation, framing, substrate, flashings, trim, wall assemblies, and internal wall cavities, if any.

(11) Stucco, exterior siding, and exterior walls shall not allow excessive condensation to enter the structure and cause damage to another component. For purposes of this paragraph, "systems" include, without limitation, framing, substrate, flashings, trim, wall assemblies, and internal wall cavities, if any.

(12) Retaining and site walls and their associated drainage systems shall not allow unintended water to pass beyond, around, or through its designed or actual moisture barriers including, without limitation, any internal barriers, so as to cause damage. This standard does not apply to those portions of any wall or drainage system that are designed to have water flow beyond, around, or through them.

(13) Retaining walls and site walls, and their associated drainage systems, shall only allow water to flow beyond, around, or through the areas designated by design.

(14) The lines and components of the plumbing system, sewer system, and utility systems shall not leak.

(15) Plumbing lines, sewer lines, and utility lines shall not corrode so as to impede the useful life of the systems.

(16) Sewer systems shall be installed in such a way as to allow the designated amount of sewage to flow through the system.

(17) Showers, baths, and related waterproofing systems shall not leak water into the interior of walls, flooring systems, or the interior of other components.

(18) The waterproofing systems behind or under ceramic tile and tile countertops shall not allow water into the interior of walls, flooring systems, or other components so as to cause damage. Ceramic tile systems shall be designed and installed so as to deflect intended water to the waterproofing system.

(b) With respect to structural issues:

(1) Foundations, load bearing components, and slabs, shall not contain significant cracks or significant vertical displacement.

(2) Foundations, load bearing components, and slabs shall not cause the structure, in whole or in part, to be structurally unsafe.

(3) Foundations, load bearing components, and slabs, and underlying soils shall be constructed so as to materially comply with the design criteria set by applicable government building codes, regulations, and ordinances for chemical deterioration or corrosion resistance in effect at the time of original construction.

(4) A structure shall be constructed so as to materially comply with the design criteria for earthquake and wind load resistance, as set forth in the applicable government building codes, regulations, and ordinances in effect at the time of original construction.

(c) With respect to soil issues:

(1) Soils and engineered retaining walls shall not cause, in whole or in part, damage to the structure built upon the soil or engineered retaining wall.

(2) Soils and engineered retaining walls shall not cause, in whole or in part, the structure to be structurally unsafe.

(3) Soils shall not cause, in whole or in part, the land upon which no structure is built to become unusable for the purpose represented at the time of original sale by the builder or for the purpose for which that land is commonly used.

(d) With respect to fire protection issues:

(1) A structure shall be constructed so as to materially comply

with the design criteria of the applicable government building codes, regulations, and ordinances for fire protection of the occupants in effect at the time of the original construction.

(2) Fireplaces, chimneys, chimney structures, and chimney termination caps shall be constructed and installed in such a way so as not to cause an unreasonable risk of fire outside the fireplace enclosure or chimney.

(3) Electrical and mechanical systems shall be constructed and installed in such a way so as not to cause an unreasonable risk of fire.

(e) With respect to plumbing and sewer issues: Plumbing and sewer systems shall be installed to operate properly and shall not materially impair the use of the structure by its inhabitants. However, no action may be brought for a violation of this subdivision more than four years after close of escrow.

(f) With respect to electrical system issues: Electrical systems shall operate properly and shall not materially impair the use of the structure by its inhabitants. However, no action shall be brought pursuant to this subdivision more than four years from close of escrow.

(g) With respect to issues regarding other areas of construction:

(1) Exterior pathways, driveways, hardscape, sidewalls, sidewalks, and patios installed by the original builder shall not contain cracks that display significant vertical displacement or that are excessive. However, no action shall be brought upon a violation of this paragraph more than four years from close of escrow.

(2) Stucco, exterior siding, and other exterior wall finishes and fixtures, including, but not limited to, pot shelves, horizontal surfaces, columns, and plant-ons, shall not contain significant cracks or separations.

(3) (A)   To the extent not otherwise covered by these standards, manufactured products, including, but not limited to, windows, doors, roofs, plumbing products and fixtures, fireplaces, electrical fixtures, HVAC units, countertops, cabinets, paint, and appliances shall be installed so as not to interfere with the products' useful life, if any.

(B) For purposes of this paragraph, "useful life" means a representation of how long a product is warranted or represented, through its limited warranty or any written representations, to last by its manufacturer, including recommended or required maintenance. If there is no representation by a manufacturer, a builder shall install manufactured products so as not to interfere with the product's utility.

(C) For purposes of this paragraph, "manufactured product" means a product that is completely manufactured offsite.

(D) If no useful life representation is made, or if the representation is less than one year, the period shall be no less than one year. If a manufactured product is damaged as a result of a violation of these standards, damage to the product is a recoverable element of damages. This subparagraph does not limit recovery if there has been damage to another building component caused by a manufactured product during the manufactured product's useful life.

(E) This title does not apply in any action seeking recovery solely for a defect in a manufactured product located within or adjacent to a structure.

(4) Heating, if any, shall be installed so as to be capable of maintaining a room temperature of 70 degrees Fahrenheit at a point three feet above the floor in any living space.

(5) Living space air-conditioning, if any, shall be provided in a manner consistent with the size and efficiency design criteria specified in Title 24 of the California Code of Regulations or its successor.

(6) Attached structures shall be constructed to comply with interunit noise transmission standards set by the applicable government building codes, ordinances, or regulations in effect at the time of the original construction. If there is no applicable code, ordinance, or regulation, this paragraph does not apply. However, no action shall be brought pursuant to this paragraph more than one year from the original occupancy of the adjacent unit.

(7) Irrigation systems and drainage shall operate properly so as not to damage landscaping or other external improvements. However, no action shall be brought pursuant to this paragraph more than one year from close of escrow.

(8) Untreated wood posts shall not be installed in contact with soil so as to cause unreasonable decay to the wood based upon the finish grade at the time of original construction. However, no action shall be brought pursuant to this paragraph more than two years from close of escrow.

(9) Untreated steel fences and adjacent components shall be installed so as to prevent unreasonable corrosion. However, no action shall be brought pursuant to this paragraph more than four years from close of escrow.

(10) Paint and stains shall be applied in such a manner so as not to cause deterioration of the building surfaces for the length of time specified

by the paint or stain manufacturers' representations, if any. However, no action shall be brought pursuant to this paragraph more than five years from close of escrow.

(11) Roofing materials shall be installed so as to avoid materials falling from the roof.

(12) The landscaping systems shall be installed in such a manner so as to survive for not less than one year. However, no action shall be brought pursuant to this paragraph more than two years from close of escrow.

(13) Ceramic tile and tile backing shall be installed in such a manner that the tile does not detach.

(14) Dryer ducts shall be installed and terminated pursuant to manufacturer installation requirements. However, no action shall be brought pursuant to this paragraph more than two years from close of escrow.

(15) Structures shall be constructed in such a manner so as not to impair the occupants' safety because they contain public health hazards as determined by a duly authorized public health official, health agency, or governmental entity having jurisdiction. This paragraph does not limit recovery for any damages caused by a violation of any other paragraph of this section on the grounds that the damages do not constitute a health hazard.

Civ. Code § 897.   Inclusion Of Items Not Addressed.

The standards set forth in this chapter are intended to address every function or component of a structure. To the extent that a function or component of a structure is not addressed by these standards, it shall be actionable if it causes damage.

OBLIGATIONS

Civ. Code § 900.   Warranty Covering Fit And Finish Items.

As to fit and finish items, a builder shall provide a homebuyer with a minimum one-year express written limited warranty covering the fit and finish of the following building components. Except as otherwise provided by the standards specified in Chapter 2 (commencing with Section 896), this warranty shall cover the fit and finish of cabinets, mirrors, flooring, interior and exterior walls, countertops, paint finishes, and trim, but shall not apply to damage to those components caused by defects in other components governed by the other provisions of this title. Any fit and finish matters covered by this warranty are not subject to the provisions of this title. If a builder fails to provide the express warranty required by this section, the warranty for these items shall be for a period of one year.

Civ. Code § 901. Enhanced Protection Agreement.

A builder may, but is not required to, offer greater protection or protection for longer time periods in its express contract with the homeowner than that set forth in Chapter 2 (commencing with Section 896). A builder may not limit the application of Chapter 2 (commencing with Section 896) or lower its protection through the express contract with the homeowner. This type of express contract constitutes an "enhanced protection agreement."

Civ. Code § 902. Applicability Of Civ. Code §§ 896 And 897 To Enhanced Protection Agreement.

If a builder offers an enhanced protection agreement, the builder may choose to be subject to its own express contractual provisions in place of the provisions set forth in Chapter 2 (commencing with Section 896). If an enhanced protection agreement is in place, Chapter 2 (commencing with Section 896) no longer applies other than to set forth minimum provisions by which to judge the enforceability of the particular provisions of the enhanced protection agreement.

Civ. Code § 903. Enhanced Protection Agreement; Builder Duties.

If a builder offers an enhanced protection agreement in place of the provisions set forth in Chapter 2 (commencing with Section 896), the election to do so shall be made in writing with the homeowner no later than the close of escrow. The builder shall provide the homeowner with a complete copy of Chapter 2 (commencing with Section 896) and advise the homeowner that the builder has elected not to be subject to its provisions. If any provision of an enhanced protection agreement is later found to be unenforceable as not meeting the minimum standards of Chapter 2 (commencing with Section 896), a builder may use this chapter in lieu of those provisions found to be unenforceable.

Civ. Code § 904. Enforcement Of Construction Standards.

If a builder has elected to use an enhanced protection agreement, and a homeowner disputes that the particular provision or time periods of the enhanced protection agreement are not greater than, or equal to, the provisions of Chapter 2 (commencing with Section 896) as they apply to the particular deficiency alleged by the homeowner, the homeowner may seek to enforce the application of the standards set forth in this chapter as to those claimed deficiencies. If a homeowner seeks to enforce a particular standard in lieu of a provision of the enhanced protection agreement, the homeowner shall give the builder written notice of that intent at the time the homeowner files a notice of claim pursuant to Chapter 4 (commencing with Section 910).

Civ. Code § 905. Action To Enforce Construction Standards.

If a homeowner seeks to enforce Chapter 2 (commencing with Section 896), in lieu of the enhanced protection agreement in a subsequent litigation or other legal action, the builder shall have the right to have the matter bifurcated, and to have an immediately binding determination of his or her responsive pleading within 60 days after the filing of that pleading, but in no event after the commencement of discovery, as to the application of either Chapter 2 (commencing with Section 896) or the enhanced protection agreement as to the deficiencies claimed by the homeowner. If the builder fails to seek that determination in the timeframe specified, the builder waives the right to do so and the standards set forth in this title shall apply. As to any nonoriginal homeowner, that homeowner shall be deemed in privity for purposes of an enhanced protection agreement only to the extent that the builder has recorded the enhanced protection agreement on title or provided actual notice to the nonoriginal homeowner of the enhanced protection agreement. If the enhanced protection agreement is not recorded on title or no actual notice has been provided, the standards set forth in this title apply to any nonoriginal homeowners' claims.

Civ. Code § 906. Builder's Election.

A builder's election to use an enhanced protection agreement addresses only the issues set forth in Chapter 2 (commencing with Section 896) and does not constitute an election to use or not use the provisions of Chapter 4 (commencing with Section 910). The decision to use or not use Chapter 4 (commencing with Section 910) is governed by the provisions of that chapter.

Civ. Code § 907. Homeowner Maintenance Obligations.

A homeowner is obligated to follow all reasonable maintenance obligations and schedules communicated in writing to the homeowner by the builder and product manufacturers, as well as commonly accepted maintenance practices. A failure by a homeowner to follow these obligations, schedules, and practices may subject the homeowner to the affirmative defenses contained in Section 944.

PRELITIGATION PROCEDURE

Civ. Code § 910. Required Procedures Prior To Filing Action For Violation Of Construction Standards.

Prior to filing an action against any party alleged to have contributed to a violation of the standards set forth in Chapter 2 (commencing with Section 896), the claimant shall initiate the following prelitigation procedures:

(a)   The claimant or his or her legal representative shall provide written notice via certified mail, overnight mail, or personal delivery to the builder, in the manner prescribed in this section, of the claimant's claim that the construction of his or her residence violates any of the standards set forth in Chapter 2 (commencing with Section 896). That notice shall provide the claimant's name, address, and preferred method of contact, and shall state that the claimant alleges a violation pursuant to this part against the builder, and shall describe the claim in reasonable detail sufficient to determine the nature and location, to the extent known, of the claimed violation. In the case of a group of homeowners or an association, the notice may identify the claimants solely by address or other description sufficient to apprise the builder of the locations of the subject residences. That document shall have the same force and effect as a notice of commencement of a legal proceeding.

(b)   The notice requirements of this section do not preclude a homeowner from seeking redress through any applicable normal customer service procedure as set forth in any contractual, warranty, or other builder-generated document; and, if a homeowner seeks to do so, that request shall not satisfy the notice requirements of this section.

Civ. Code § 911. "Builder" Defined.

(a) For purposes of this title, except as provided in subdivision (b), "builder" means any entity or individual, including, but not limited to a builder, developer, general contractor, contractor, or original seller, who, at the time of sale, was also in the business of selling residential units to the public for the property that is the subject of the homeowner's claim or was in the business of building, developing, or constructing residential units for public purchase for the property that is the subject of the homeowner's claim.

(b) For the purposes of this title, "builder" does not include any entity or individual whose involvement with a residential unit that is the subject of the homeowner's claim is limited to his or her capacity as general contractor or contractor and who is not a partner, member of, subsidiary of, or otherwise similarly affiliated with the builder. For purposes of this title, these nonaffiliated general contractors and nonaffiliated contractors shall be treated the same as subcontractors, material suppliers, individual product manufacturers, and design professionals.

Civ. Code § 912. Builder's Duties.

A builder shall do all of the following:

(a) Within 30 days of a written request by a homeowner or his or her legal representative, the builder shall provide copies of all relevant plans, specifications, mass or rough grading plans, final soils reports, Department of Real Estate public reports, and available engineering calculations, that pertain to a homeowner's residence specifically or as part of a larger development tract. The request shall be honored if it states that it is made relative to structural, fire safety, or soils provisions of this title. However, a builder is not obligated to provide a copying service, and reasonable copying costs shall be borne by the requesting party. A builder may require that the documents be copied onsite by the requesting party, except that the homeowner may, at his or her option, use his or her own copying service, which may include an offsite copy facility that is bonded and insured. If a builder can show that the builder maintained the documents, but that they later became unavailable due to loss or destruction that was not the fault of the builder, the builder may be excused from the requirements of this subdivision, in which case the builder shall act with reasonable diligence to assist the homeowner in obtaining those documents from any applicable government authority or from the source that generated the document. However, in that case, the time limits specified by this section do not apply.

(b) At the expense of the homeowner, who may opt to use an offsite copy facility that is bonded and insured, the builder shall provide to the homeowner or his or her legal representative copies of all maintenance and preventative maintenance recommendations that pertain to his or her residence within 30 days of service of a written request for those documents. Those documents shall also be provided to the homeowner in conjunction with the initial sale of the residence.

(c) At the expense of the homeowner, who may opt to use an offsite copy facility that is bonded and insured, a builder shall provide to the homeowner or his or her legal representative copies of all manufactured products maintenance, preventive maintenance, and limited warranty information within 30 days of a written request for those documents. These documents shall also be provided to the homeowner in conjunction with the initial sale of the residence.

(d) At the expense of the homeowner, who may opt to use an offsite copy facility that is bonded and insured, a builder shall provide to the homeowner or his or her legal representative copies of all of the builder's limited contractual warranties in accordance with this part in effect at the time of the original sale of the residence within 30 days of a written request for those documents. Those documents shall also be provided to the homeowner in conjunction with the initial sale of the residence.

(e) A builder shall maintain the name and address of an agent for notice pursuant to this chapter with the Secretary of State or, alternatively, elect to use a third party for that notice if the builder has notified the homeowner in writing of the third party's name and address, to whom claims and requests for information under this section may be mailed. The name and address of the agent for notice or third party shall be included with the original sales documentation and shall be initialed and acknowledged by the purchaser and the builder's sales representative.

This subdivision applies to instances in which a builder contracts with a third party to accept claims and act on the builder's behalf. A builder shall give actual notice to the homeowner that the builder has made such an election, and shall include the name and address of the third party.

(f) A builder shall record on title a notice of the existence of these procedures and a notice that these procedures impact the legal rights of the homeowner. This information shall also be included with the original sales documentation and shall be initialed and acknowledged by the purchaser and the builder's sales representative.

(g) A builder shall provide, with the original sales documentation, a written copy of this title, which shall be initialed and acknowledged by the purchaser and the builder's sales representative.

(h) As to any documents provided in conjunction with the original sale, the builder shall instruct the original purchaser to provide those documents to any subsequent purchaser.

(i) Any builder who fails to comply with any of these requirements within the time specified is not entitled to the protection of this chapter, and the homeowner is released from the requirements of this chapter and may proceed with the filing of an action, in which case the remaining chapters of this part shall continue to apply to the action.

Civ. Code § 913. Written Acknowledgment Of Receipt Of Notice.

A builder or his or her representative shall acknowledge, in writing, receipt of the notice of the claim within 14 days after receipt of the notice of the claim. If the notice of the claim is served by the claimant's legal representative, or if the builder receives a written representation letter from a homeowner's attorney, the builder shall include the attorney in all subsequent substantive communications, including, without limitation, all written communications occurring pursuant to this chapter, and all substantive and procedural communications, including all written communications, following the commencement of any subsequent complaint or other legal action, except that if the builder has retained or involved legal counsel to assist the builder in this process, all communications by the builder's counsel shall only be with the claimant's legal representative, if any.

Civ. Code § 914. Nonadversarial Procedure Established.

(a) This chapter establishes a nonadversarial procedure, including the remedies available under this chapter which, if the procedure does not resolve the dispute between the parties, may result in a subsequent action to enforce the other chapters of this title. A builder may attempt to commence nonadversarial contractual provisions other than the nonadversarial procedures and remedies set forth in this chapter, but may not, in addition to its own nonadversarial contractual provisions, require adherence to the nonadversarial procedures and remedies set forth in this chapter, regardless of whether the builder's own alternative nonadversarial contractual provisions are successful in resolving the dispute or ultimately deemed enforceable. At the time the sales agreement is executed, the builder shall notify the homeowner whether the builder intends to engage in the nonadversarial procedure of this section or attempt to enforce alternative nonadversarial contractual provisions. If the builder elects to use alternative nonadversarial contractual provisions in lieu of this chapter, the election is binding, regardless of whether the builder's alternative nonadversarial contractual provisions are successful in resolving the ultimate dispute or are ultimately deemed enforceable.

(b) Nothing in this title is intended to affect existing statutory or decisional law pertaining to the applicability, viability, or enforceability of alternative dispute resolution methods, alternative remedies, or contractual arbitration, judicial reference, or similar procedures requiring a binding resolution to enforce the other chapters of this title or any other disputes between homeowners and builders. Nothing in this title is intended to affect the applicability, viability, or enforceability, if any, of contractual arbitration or judicial reference after a nonadversarial procedure or provision has been completed.

Civ. Code § 915. Actions Resulting In Nonapplication Of Chapter.

If a builder fails to acknowledge receipt of the notice of a claim within the time specified, elects not to go through the process set forth in this chapter, or fails to request an inspection within the time specified, or at the conclusion or cessation of an alternative nonadversarial proceeding, this chapter does not apply and the homeowner is released from the requirements of this chapter and may proceed with the filing of an action. However, the standards set forth in the other chapters of this title shall continue to apply to the action.

Civ. Code § 916. Builder's Investigation Of Claimed Unmet Standards.

(a) If a builder elects to inspect the claimed unmet standards, the builder shall complete the initial inspection and testing within 14 days after acknowledgment of receipt of the notice of the claim, at a mutually convenient date and time. If the homeowner has retained legal representation, the inspection shall be scheduled with the legal representative's office at a mutually convenient date and time, unless the legal representative is unavailable during the relevant time periods. All costs of builder inspection and testing, including any damage caused by the builder inspection, shall be borne by the builder. The builder shall also provide written proof that the builder has liability insurance to cover any damages or injuries occurring during inspection and testing. The builder shall restore the property to its pretesting condition within 48 hours of the testing. The builder shall, upon request, allow the inspections to be observed and electronically recorded, video recorded, or photographed by the claimant or his or her legal representative.

(b) Nothing that occurs during a builder's or claimant's inspection or testing may be used or introduced as evidence to support a spoliation defense by any potential party in any subsequent litigation.

(c) If a builder deems a second inspection or testing reasonably necessary, and specifies the reasons therefor in writing within three days following the initial inspection, the builder may conduct a second inspection or testing. A second inspection or testing shall be completed within 40 days of the initial inspection or testing. All requirements concerning the initial inspection or testing shall also apply to the second inspection or testing.

(d) If the builder fails to inspect or test the property within the time specified, the claimant is released from the requirements of this section and may proceed with the filing of an action. However, the standards set forth in the other chapters of this title shall continue to apply to the action.

(e) If a builder intends to hold a subcontractor, design professional, individual product manufacturer, or material supplier, including an insurance carrier, warranty company, or service company, responsible for its contribution to the unmet standard, the builder shall provide notice to that person or entity sufficiently in advance to allow them to attend the initial, or if requested, second inspection of any alleged unmet standard and to participate in the repair process. The claimant and his or her legal representative, if any, shall be advised in a reasonable time prior to the inspection as to the identity of all persons or entities invited to attend. This subdivision does not apply to the builder's insurance company. Except with respect to any claims involving a repair actually conducted under this chapter, nothing in this subdivision shall be construed to relieve a subcontractor, design professional, individual product manufacturer, or material supplier of any liability under an action brought by a claimant.

Civ. Code § 917. Offer To Repair.

Within 30 days of the initial or, if requested, second inspection or testing, the builder may offer in writing to repair the violation. The offer to repair shall also compensate the homeowner for all applicable damages recoverable under Section 944, within the timeframe for the repair set forth in this chapter. Any such offer shall be accompanied by a detailed, specific, step-by-step statement identifying the particular violation that is being repaired, explaining the nature, scope, and location of the repair, and setting a reasonable completion date for the repair. The offer shall also include the names, addresses, telephone numbers, and license numbers of the contractors whom the builder intends to have perform the repair. Those contractors shall be fully insured for, and shall be responsible for, all damages or injuries that they may cause to occur during the repair, and evidence of that insurance shall be provided to the homeowner upon request. Upon written request by the homeowner or his or her legal representative, and within the timeframes set forth in this chapter, the builder shall also provide any available technical documentation, including, without limitation, plans and specifications, pertaining to the claimed violation within the particular home or development tract. The offer shall also advise the homeowner in writing of his or her right to request up to three additional contractors from which to select to do the repair pursuant to this chapter.

Civ. Code § 918. Homeowner Acceptance Of Offer To Repair.

Upon receipt of the offer to repair, the homeowner shall have 30 days to authorize the builder to proceed with the repair. The homeowner may alternatively request, at the homeowner's sole option and discretion, that the builder provide the names, addresses, telephone numbers, and license numbers for up to three alternative contractors who are not owned or financially controlled by the builder and who regularly conduct business in the county where the structure is located. If the homeowner so elects, the builder is entitled to an additional noninvasive inspection, to occur at a mutually convenient date and time within 20 days of the election, so as to permit the other proposed contractors to review the proposed site of the repair. Within 35 days after the request of the homeowner for alternative contractors, the builder shall present the homeowner with a choice of contractors. Within 20 days after that presentation, the homeowner shall authorize the builder or one of the alternative contractors to perform the repair.

Civ. Code § 919. Offer To Mediate.

The offer to repair shall also be accompanied by an offer to mediate the dispute if the homeowner so chooses. The mediation shall be limited to a four-hour mediation, except as otherwise mutually agreed before a nonaffiliated mediator selected and paid for by the builder. At the homeowner's sole option, the homeowner may agree to split the cost of the mediator, and if he or she does so, the mediator shall be selected jointly. The mediator shall have sufficient availability such that the mediation occurs within 15 days after the request to mediate is received and occurs at a mutually convenient location within the county where the action is pending. If a builder has made an offer to repair a violation, and the mediation has failed to resolve the dispute, the homeowner shall allow the repair to be performed either by the builder, its contractor, or the selected contractor.

Civ. Code § 920. Actions Resulting In Filing Of Action By Homeowner.

If the builder fails to make an offer to repair or otherwise strictly comply with this chapter within the times specified, the claimant is released from the requirements of this chapter and may proceed with the filing of an action. If the contractor performing the repair does not complete the repair in the time or manner specified, the claimant may file an action. If this occurs, the standards set forth in the other chapters of this part shall continue to apply to the action.

Civ. Code § 921. Procedure When Resolution Involves Repair By Builder.

(a) In the event that a resolution under this chapter involves a repair by the builder, the builder shall make an appointment with the claimant, make all appropriate arrangements to effectuate a repair of the claimed unmet standards, and compensate the homeowner for all damages resulting therefrom free of charge to the claimant. The repair shall be scheduled through the claimant's legal representative, if any, unless he or she is unavailable during the relevant time periods. The repair shall be commenced on a mutually convenient date within 14 days of acceptance or, if an alternative contractor is selected by the homeowner, within 14 days of the selection, or, if a mediation occurs, within seven days of the mediation, or within five days after a permit is obtained if one is required. The builder shall act with reasonable diligence in obtaining any such permit.

(b) The builder shall ensure that work done on the repairs is done with the utmost diligence, and that the repairs are completed as soon as reasonably possible, subject to the nature of the repair or some unforeseen event not caused by the builder or the contractor performing the repair. Every effort shall be made to complete the repair within 120 days.

Civ. Code § 922. Observation And Recording Of Repair Allowed.

The builder shall, upon request, allow the repair to be observed and electronically recorded, video recorded, or photographed by the claimant or his or her legal representative. Nothing that occurs during the repair process may be used or introduced as evidence to support a spoliation defense by any potential party in any subsequent litigation.

Civ. Code § 923. Full Disclosure Of Repairs.

The builder shall provide the homeowner or his or her legal representative, upon request, with copies of all correspondence, photographs, and other materials pertaining or relating in any manner to the repairs.

Civ. Code § 924. Written Explanation Of Unrepaired Items.

If the builder elects to repair some, but not all of, the claimed unmet standards, the builder shall, at the same time it makes its offer, set forth with particularity in writing the reasons, and the support for those reasons, for not repairing all claimed unmet standards.

Civ. Code § 925. Failure To Timely Complete Repairs.

If the builder fails to complete the repair within the time specified in the repair plan, the claimant is released from the requirements of this chapter and may proceed with the filing of an action. If this occurs, the standards set forth in the other chapters of this title shall continue to apply to the action.

Civ. Code § 926. Release Or Waiver In Exchange For Repair Work Prohibited.

The builder may not obtain a release or waiver of any kind in exchange for the repair work mandated by this chapter. At the conclusion of the repair, the claimant may proceed with filing an action for violation of the applicable standard or for a claim of inadequate repair, or both, including all applicable damages available under Section 944.

Civ. Code § 927. Statute Of Limitations.

If the applicable statute of limitations has otherwise run during this process, the time period for filing a complaint or other legal remedies for violation of any provision of this title, or for a claim of inadequate repair, is extended from the time of the original claim by the claimant to 100 days after the repair is completed, whether or not the particular violation is the one being repaired. If the builder fails to acknowledge the claim within the time specified, elects not to go through this statutory process, or fails to request an inspection within the time specified, the time period for filing a complaint or other legal remedies for violation of any provision of this title is extended from the time of the original claim by the claimant to 45 days after the time for responding to the notice of claim has expired. If the builder elects to attempt to enforce its own nonadversarial procedure in lieu of the procedure set forth in this chapter, the time period for filing a complaint or other legal remedies for violation of any provision of this part is extended from the time of the original claim by the claimant to 100 days after either the completion of the builder's alternative nonadversarial procedure, or 100 days after the builder's alternative nonadversarial procedure is deemed unenforceable, whichever is later.

Civ. Code § 928. Mediation Procedure.

If the builder has invoked this chapter and completed a repair, prior to filing an action, if there has been no previous mediation between the parties, the homeowner or his or her legal representative shall request mediation in writing. The mediation shall be limited to four hours, except as otherwise mutually agreed before a nonaffiliated mediator selected and paid for by the builder. At the homeowner's sole option, the homeowner may agree to split the cost of the mediator and if he or she does so, the mediator shall be selected jointly. The mediator shall have sufficient availability such that the mediation will occur within 15 days after the request for mediation is received and shall occur at a mutually convenient location within the county where the action is pending. In the event that a mediation is used at this point, any applicable statutes of limitations shall be tolled from the date of the request to mediate until the next court day after the mediation is completed, or the 100-day period, whichever is later.

Civ. Code § 929. Cash Offer In Lieu Of Repair.

(a) Nothing in this chapter prohibits the builder from making only a cash offer and no repair. In this situation, the homeowner is free to accept the offer, or he or she may reject the offer and proceed with the filing of an action. If the latter occurs, the standards of the other chapters of this title shall continue to apply to the action.

(b) The builder may obtain a reasonable release in exchange for the cash payment. The builder may negotiate the terms and conditions of any reasonable release in terms of scope and consideration in conjunction with a cash payment under this chapter.

Civ. Code § 930. Strict Construction Of Requirements; Failure To Conform.

(a) The time periods and all other requirements in this chapter are to be strictly construed, and, unless extended by the mutual agreement of the parties in accordance with this chapter, shall govern the rights and obligations under this title. If a builder fails to act in accordance with this section within the timeframes mandated, unless extended by the mutual agreement of the parties as evidenced by a postclaim written confirmation by the affected homeowner demonstrating that he or she has knowingly and voluntarily extended the statutory timeframe, the claimant may proceed with filing an action. If this occurs, the standards of the other chapters of this title shall continue to apply to the action.

Litigation

(b) If the claimant does not conform with the requirements of this chapter, the builder may bring a motion to stay any subsequent court action or other proceeding until the requirements of this chapter have been satisfied. The court, in its discretion, may award the prevailing party on such a motion, his or her attorney's fees and costs in bringing or opposing the motion.

Civ. Code § 931. Claim Combined With Other Causes Of Action.

If a claim combines causes of action or damages not covered by this part, including, without limitation, personal injuries, class actions, other statutory remedies, or fraud-based claims, the claimed unmet standards shall be administered according to this part, although evidence of the property in its unrepaired condition may be introduced to support the respective elements of any such cause of action. As to any fraud-based claim, if the fact that the property has been repaired under this chapter is deemed admissible, the trier of fact shall be informed that the repair was not voluntarily accepted by the homeowner. As to any class action claims that address solely the incorporation of a defective component into a residence, the named and unnamed class members need not comply with this chapter.

Civ. Code § 932. Subsequently Discovered Claims.

Subsequently discovered claims of unmet standards shall be administered separately under this chapter, unless otherwise agreed to by the parties. However, in the case of a detached single family residence, in the same home, if the subsequently discovered claim is for a violation of the same standard as that which has already been initiated by the same claimant and the subject of a currently pending action, the claimant need not reinitiate the process as to the same standard. In the case of an attached project, if the subsequently discovered claim is for a violation of the same standard for a connected component system in the same building as has already been initiated by the same claimant, and the subject of a currently pending action, the claimant need not reinitiate this process as to that standard.

Civ. Code § 933. Evidence Of Repair Work.

If any enforcement of these standards is commenced, the fact that a repair effort was made may be introduced to the trier of fact. However, the claimant may use the condition of the property prior to the repair as the basis for contending that the repair work was inappropriate, inadequate, or incomplete, or that the violation still exists. The claimant need not show that the repair work resulted in further damage nor that damage has continued to occur as a result of the violation.

Civ. Code § 934. Evidence Of Parties' Conduct.

Evidence of both parties' conduct during this process may be introduced during a subsequent enforcement action, if any, with the exception of any mediation. Any repair efforts undertaken by the builder, shall not be considered settlement communications or offers of settlement and are not inadmissible in evidence on such a basis.

Civ. Code § 935. Similar Requirements Of Civil Code § 1375.

To the extent that provisions of this chapter are enforced and those provisions are substantially similar to provisions in Section 1375 of the Civil Code, but an action is subsequently commenced under Section 1375 of the Civil Code, the parties are excused from performing the substantially similar requirements under Section 1375 of the Civil Code.

Civ. Code § 936. Liability Of Subcontractors.

Each and every provision of the other chapters of this title apply to general contractors, subcontractors, material suppliers, individual product manufacturers, and design professionals to the extent that the subcontractors, material suppliers, individual product manufacturers, and design professionals caused, in whole or in part, a violation of a particular standard as the result of a negligent act or omission or a breach of contract. In addition to the affirmative defenses set forth in Section 945.5, a general contractor, subcontractor, material supplier, design professional, individual product manufacturer, or other entity may also offer common law and contractual defenses as applicable to any claimed violation of a standard. All actions by a claimant or builder to enforce an express contract, or any provision thereof, against a general contractor, subcontractor, material supplier, individual product manufacturer, or design professional is preserved.

Nothing in this title modifies the law pertaining to joint and several liability for builders, general contractors, subcontractors, material suppliers, individual product manufacturer, and design professionals that contribute to any specific violation of this title. However, the negligence standard in this section does not apply to any general contractor, subcontractor, material supplier, individual product manufacturer, or design professional with respect to claims for which strict liability would apply.

Civ. Code § 937. Claims And Damages Not Covered By Title.

Nothing in this title shall be interpreted to eliminate or abrogate the requirement to comply with Section 411.35 of the Code of Civil Procedure or to affect the liability of design professionals, including architects and architectural firms, for claims and damages not covered by this title.

Civ. Code § 938. Application Of Title.

This title applies only to new residential units where the purchase agreement with the buyer was signed by the seller on or after January 1, 2003.

PROCEDURE

Civ. Code § 941. Time Limit For Bringing Action.

(a) Except as specifically set forth in this title, no action may be brought to recover under this title more than 10 years after substantial completion of the improvement but not later than the date of recordation of a valid notice of completion.

(b) As used in this section, "action" includes an action for indemnity brought against a person arising out of that person's performance or furnishing of services or materials referred to in this title, except that a cross-complaint for indemnity may be filed pursuant to subdivision (b) of Section 428.10 of the Code of Civil Procedure in an action which has been brought within the time period set forth in subdivision (a).

(c) The limitation prescribed by this section may not be asserted by way of defense by any person in actual possession or the control, as owner, tenant or otherwise, of such an improvement, at the time any deficiency in the improvement constitutes the proximate cause for which it is proposed to make a claim or bring an action.

(d) Sections 337.15 and 337.1 of the Code of Civil Procedure do not apply to actions under this title.

(e) Existing statutory and decisional law regarding tolling of the statute of limitations shall apply to the time periods for filing an action or making a claim under this title, except that repairs made pursuant to Chapter 4 (commencing with Section 910), with the exception of the tolling provision contained in Section 927, do not extend the period for filing an action, or restart the time limitations contained in subdivision (a) or (b) of Section 7091 of the Business and Professions Code. If a builder arranges for a contractor to perform a repair pursuant to Chapter 4 (commencing with Section 910), as to the builder the time period for calculating the statute of limitation in subdivision (a) or (b) of Section 7091 of the Business and Professions Code shall pertain to the substantial completion of the original construction and not to the date of repairs under this title. The time limitations established by this title do not apply to any action by a claimant for a contract or express contractual provision. Causes of action and damages to which this chapter does not apply are not limited by this section.

Civ. Code § 942. Claims Involving Residential Construction Standards.

In order to make a claim for violation of the standards set forth in Chapter 2 (commencing with Section 896), a homeowner need only demonstrate, in accordance with the applicable evidentiary standard, that the home does not meet the applicable standard, subject to the affirmative defenses set forth in Section 945.5. No further showing of causation or damages is required to meet the burden of proof regarding a violation of a standard set forth in Chapter 2 (commencing with Section 896), provided that the violation arises out of, pertains to, or is related to, the original construction.

Civ. Code § 943. Other Causes Of Action; Claims Involving Detached Single-Family Homes.

(a) Except as provided in this title, no other cause of action for a claim covered by this title or for damages recoverable under Section 944 is allowed. In addition to the rights under this title, this title does not apply to any action by a claimant to enforce a contract or express contractual provision, or any action for fraud, personal injury, or violation of a statute. Damages awarded for the items set forth in Section 944 in such other cause of action shall be reduced by the amounts recovered pursuant to Section 944 for violation of the standards set forth in this title.

(b) As to any claims involving a detached single-family home, the homeowner's right to the reasonable value of repairing any nonconformity is limited to the repair costs, or the diminution in current value of the home caused by the nonconformity, whichever is less, subject to the personal use exception as developed under common law.

Civ. Code § 944. Damages.

If a claim for damages is made under this title, the homeowner is only entitled to damages for the reasonable value of repairing any violation of the standards set forth in this title, the reasonable cost of repairing any damages caused by the repair efforts, the reasonable cost of repairing and rectifying any damages resulting from the failure of the home to meet the standards, the reasonable cost of removing and replacing any improper repair by the builder, reasonable relocation and storage expenses, lost business income if the home was used as a principal place of a business licensed to be operated from the home, reasonable investigative costs for each established violation, and all other costs or fees recoverable by contract or statute.

Civ. Code § 945. Original Purchasers And Successors-In-Interest.

The provisions, standards, rights, and obligations set forth in this title are binding upon all original purchasers and their successors-in-interest. For purposes of this title, associations and others having the rights set forth in Sections 1368.3 and 1368.4 shall be considered to be original purchasers and shall have standing to enforce the provisions, standards, rights, and obligations set forth in this title.

Civ. Code § 945.5. Affirmative Defenses.

A builder, general contractor, subcontractor, material supplier, individual product manufacturer, or design professional, under the principles of comparative fault pertaining to affirmative defenses, may be excused, in whole or in part, from any obligation, damage, loss, or liability if the builder, general contractor, subcontractor, material supplier, individual product manufacturer, or design professional, can demonstrate any of the following affirmative defenses in response to a claimed violation:

(a) To the extent it is caused by an unforeseen act of nature which caused the structure not to meet the standard. For purposes of this section an "unforeseen act of nature" means a weather condition, earthquake, or manmade event such as war, terrorism, or vandalism, in excess of the design criteria expressed by the applicable building codes, regulations, and ordinances in effect at the time of original construction.

(b) To the extent it is caused by a homeowner's unreasonable failure to minimize or prevent those damages in a timely manner, including the failure of the homeowner to allow reasonable and timely access for inspections and repairs under this title. This includes the failure to give timely notice to the builder after discovery of a violation, but does not include damages due to the untimely or inadequate response of a builder to the homeowner's claim.

(c) To the extent it is caused by the homeowner or his or her agent, employee, general contractor, subcontractor, independent contractor, or consultant by virtue of their failure to follow the builder's or manufacturer's recommendations, or commonly accepted homeowner maintenance obligations. In order to rely upon this defense as it relates to a builder's recommended maintenance schedule, the builder shall show that the homeowner had written notice of these schedules and recommendations and that the recommendations and schedules were reasonable at the time they were issued.

(d) To the extent it is caused by the homeowner or his or her agent's or an independent third party's alterations, ordinary wear and tear, misuse, abuse, or neglect, or by the structure's use for something other than its intended purpose.

(e) To the extent that the time period for filing actions bars the claimed violation.

(f) As to a particular violation for which the builder has obtained a valid release.

(g) To the extent that the builder's repair was successful in correcting the particular violation of the applicable standard.

(h) As to any causes of action to which this statute does not apply, all applicable affirmative defenses are preserved.

Civ. Code § 43.99. Liability Of Independent Quality Review Provider.

(a) There shall be no monetary liability on the part of, and no cause of action for damages shall arise against, any person or other legal entity that is under contract with an applicant for a residential building permit to provide independent quality review of the plans and specifications provided with the application in order to determine compliance with all applicable requirements imposed pursuant to the State Housing Law (Part 1.5 (commencing with Section 17910) of Division 13 of the Health and Safety Code), or any rules or regulations adopted pursuant to that law, or under contract with that applicant to provide independent quality review of the work of improvement to determine compliance with these plans and specifications, if the person or other legal entity meets the requirements of this section and one of the following applies:

(1) The person, or a person employed by any other legal entity, performing the work as described in this subdivision, has completed not less than five years of verifiable experience in the appropriate field and

has obtained certification as a building inspector, combination inspector, or combination dwelling inspector from the International Conference of Building Officials (ICBO) and has successfully passed the technical written examination promulgated by ICBO for those certification categories.

(2) The person, or a person employed by any other legal entity, performing the work as described in this subdivision, has completed not less than five years of verifiable experience in the appropriate field and is a registered professional engineer, licensed general contractor, or a licensed architect rendering independent quality review of the work of improvement or plan examination services within the scope of his or her registration or licensure.

(3) The immunity provided under this section does not apply to any action initiated by the applicant who retained the qualified person.

(4) A "qualified person" for purposes of this section means a person holding a valid certification as one of those inspectors.

(b) Except for qualified persons, this section shall not relieve from, excuse or lessen in any manner, the responsibility or liability of any person, company, contractor, builder, developer, architect, engineer, designer, or other individual or entity who develops, improves, owns, operates, or manages any residential building for any damages to persons or property caused by construction or design defects. The fact that an inspection by a qualified person has taken place may not be introduced as evidence in a construction defect action, including any reports or other items generated by the qualified person. This subdivision shall not apply in any action initiated by the applicant who retained the qualified person.

(c) Nothing in this section, as it relates to construction inspectors or plans examiners, shall be construed to alter the requirements for licensure, or the jurisdiction, authority, or scope of practice, of architects pursuant to Chapter 3 (commencing with Section 5500) of Division 3 of the Business and Professions Code, professional engineers pursuant to Chapter 7 (commencing with Section 6700) of Division 3 of the Business and Professions Code, or general contractors pursuant to Chapter 9 (commencing with Section 7000) of Division 3 of the Business and Professions Code.

(d) Nothing in this section shall be construed to alter the immunity of employees of the Department of Housing and Community Development under the Tort Claims Act (Division 3.6 (commencing with Section 810) of Title 1 of the Government Code) when acting pursuant to Section 17965 of the Health and Safety Code.

(e) The qualifying person shall engage in no other construction, design, planning, supervision, or activities of any kind on the work of improvement, nor provide quality review services for any other party on the work of improvement.

(f) The qualifying person, or other legal entity, shall maintain professional errors and omissions insurance coverage in an amount not less than two million dollars ($2,000,000).

(g) The immunity provided by subdivision (a) does not inure to the benefit of the qualified person for damages caused to the applicant solely by the negligence or willful misconduct of the qualified person resulting from the provision of services under the contract with the applicant.

Civ. Code § 1134. Required Disclosure Before Sale Of Newly Converted Condominium.

(a) As soon as practicable before transfer of title for the first sale of a unit in a residential condominium, community apartment project, or stock cooperative which was converted from an existing dwelling to a condominium project, community apartment project, or stock cooperative, the owner or subdivider, or agent of the owner or subdivider, shall deliver to a prospective buyer a written statement listing all substantial defects or malfunctions in the major systems in the unit and common areas of the premises, or a written statement disclaiming knowledge of any such substantial defects or malfunctions. The disclaimer may be delivered only after the owner or subdivider has inspected the unit and the common areas and has not discovered a substantial defect or malfunction which a reasonable inspection would have disclosed.

(b) If any disclosure required to be made by this section is delivered after the execution of an agreement to purchase, the buyer shall have three days after delivery in person or five days after delivery by deposit in the mail, to terminate his or her agreement by delivery of written notice of that termination to the owner, subdivider, or agent. Any disclosure delivered after the execution of an agreement to purchase shall contain a statement describing the buyer's right, method and time to rescind as prescribed by this subdivision.

(c) For the purposes of this section:

(1) "Major systems" includes, but is not limited to, the roof, walls, floors, heating, air conditioning, plumbing, electrical systems or components of a similar or comparable nature, and recreational facilities.

(2) Delivery to a prospective buyer of the written statement required by this section shall be deemed effected when delivered personally

or by mail to the prospective buyer or to an agent thereof, or to a spouse unless the agreement provides to the contrary. Delivery shall also be made to additional prospective buyers who have made a request therefor in writing.

(3) "Prospective buyer" includes any person who makes an offer to purchase a unit in the condominium, community apartment project, or stock cooperative.

(d) Any person who willfully fails to carry out the requirements of this section shall be liable in the amount of actual damages suffered by the buyer.

(e) Nothing in this section shall preclude the injured party from pursuing any remedy available under any other provision of law.

(f) No transfer of title to a unit subject to the provisions of this chapter shall be invalid solely because of the failure of any person to comply with the requirements of this section.

(g) The written statement required by this section shall not abridge or limit any other obligation of disclosure created by any other provision of law or which is or may be required to avoid fraud, deceit, or misrepresentation in the transaction.

Litigation

CHAPTER 9

CIVIL RIGHTS & DISCRIMINATION
(Civil Code §§ 51-53, 712-714.1, Government Code §§ 434.5, 12955-12956.2, Welfare & Institutions Code §§ 5115-5116, Health & Safety Code §§ 1597.40, 1597.531 and 4 United States Code Annotated § 5 Note)

Civ. Code § 51. Unruh Civil Rights Act.

(a) This section shall be known, and may be cited, as the Unruh Civil Rights Act.

(b) All persons within the jurisdiction of this state are free and equal, and no matter what their sex, race, color, religion, ancestry, national origin, disability, medical condition marital status, or sexual orientation are entitled to the full and equal accommodations, advantages, facilities, privileges, or services in all business establishments of every kind whatsoever.

(c) This section shall not be construed to confer any right or privilege on a person that is conditioned or limited by law or that is applicable alike to persons of every sex, color, race, religion, ancestry, national origin, disability, medical condition marital status, or sexual orientation.

(d) Nothing in this section shall be construed to require any construction, alteration, repair, structural or otherwise, or modification of any sort whatsoever, beyond that construction, alteration, repair, or modification that is otherwise required by other provisions of law, to any new or existing establishment, facility, building, improvement, or any other structure, nor shall anything in this section be construed to augment, restrict, or alter in any way the authority of the State Architect to require construction, alteration, repair, or modifications that the State Architect otherwise possesses pursuant to other laws.

(e) For purposes of this section:

(1) "Disability" means any mental or physical disability as defined in Section 12926 of the Government Code.

(2) "Medical condition" has the same meaning as defined in subdivision (h) of Section 12926 of the Government Code.

(3) "Religion" includes all aspects of religious belief, observance, and practice.

(4) "Sex" has the same meaning as defined in subdivision (p) of Section 12926 of the Government Code.

(5) "Sex, race, color, religion, ancestry, national origin, disability, medical condition, marital status, or sexual orientation" includes a perception that the person has any particular characteristic or characteristics within the listed categories or that the person is associated with a person who has, or is perceived to have, any particular characteristic or characteristics within the listed categories.

(6) "Sexual orientation" has the same meaning as defined in subdivision (q) of Section 12926 of the Government Code.

(f) A violation of the right of any individual under the Americans with Disabilities Act of 1990 (Public Law 101-336) shall also constitute a violation of this section.

Civ. Code § 51.1. Actions Requiring Copy Of Petition And Brief To Be Served On State Solicitor General.

If a violation of Section 51, 51.5, 51.7, 51.9, or 52.1 is alleged or the application or construction of any of these sections is in issue in any proceeding in the Supreme Court of California, a state court of appeal, or the appellate division of a superior court, each party shall serve a copy of the party's brief or petition and brief, on the State Solicitor General at the Office of the Attorney General. No brief may be accepted for filing unless the proof of service shows service on the State Solicitor General. Any party failing to comply with this requirement shall be given a reasonable opportunity to cure the failure before the court imposes any sanction and, in that instance, the court shall allow the Attorney General reasonable additional time to file a brief in the matter.

Civ. Code § 51.2. Housing Discrimination Based On Age Prohibited.

(a) Section 51 shall be construed to prohibit a business establishment from discriminating in the sale or rental of housing based upon age. Where accommodations are designed to meet the physical and social needs of senior citizens, a business establishment may establish and preserve that housing for senior citizens, pursuant to Section 51.3, except housing as to which Section 51.3 is preempted by the prohibition in the federal Fair Housing Amendments Act of 1988 (Public Law 100-430) and implementing regulations against discrimination on the basis of familial status. For accommodations constructed before February 8, 1982, that meet all the criteria for senior citizen housing specified in Section 51.3, a business establishment may establish and preserve that housing development for senior citizens without the housing development being designed to meet physical and social needs of senior citizens.

(b) This section is intended to clarify the holdings in *Marina Point, Ltd. v. Wolfson (1982) 30 Cal. 3d 72 and O'Connor v. Village Green Owners Association (1983) 33 Cal. 3d 790.*

(c) This section shall not apply to the County of Riverside.

(d) A housing development for senior citizens constructed on or after January 1, 2001, shall be presumed to be designed to meet the physical and social needs of senior citizens if it includes all of the following elements:

(1) Entryways, walkways, and hallways in the common areas of the development, and doorways and paths of access to and within the housing units, shall be as wide as required by current laws applicable to new multifamily housing construction for provision of access to persons using a standard-width wheelchair.

(2) Walkways and hallways in the common areas of the development shall be equipped with standard height railings or grab bars to assist persons who have difficulty with walking.

(3) Walkways and hallways in the common areas shall have lighting conditions which are of sufficient brightness to assist persons who have difficulty seeing.

(4) Access to all common areas and housing units within the development shall be provided without use of stairs, either by means of an elevator or sloped walking ramps.

(5) The development shall be designed to encourage social contact by providing at least one common room and at least some common open space.

(6) Refuse collection shall be provided in a manner that requires a minimum of physical exertion by residents.

(7) The development shall comply with all other applicable requirements for access and design imposed by law, including, but not limited to, the Fair Housing Act (42 U.S.C. Sec. 3601 et seq.), the Americans with Disabilities Act (42 U.S.C. Sec. 12101 et seq.), and the regulations promulgated at Title 24 of the California Code of Regulations that relate to access for persons with disabilities or handicaps. Nothing in this section shall be construed to limit or reduce any right or obligation applicable under those laws.

(e) Selection preferences based on age, imposed in connection with a federally approved housing progam, do not constitute age discrimination in housing.

Civ. Code § 51.3. Establishing And Preserving Accessible Housing For Senior Citizens.

(a) The Legislature finds and declares that this section is essential to establish and preserve specially designed accessible housing for senior citizens. There are senior citizens who need special living environments and services, and find that there is an inadequate supply of this type of housing in the state.

(b) For the purposes of this section, the following definitions apply:

(1) "Qualifying resident" or "senior citizen" means a person 62 years of age or older, or 55 years of age or older in a senior citizen housing development.

(2) "Qualified permanent resident" means a person who meets both of the following requirements:

(A) Was residing with the qualifying resident or senior citizen prior to the death, hospitalization, or other prolonged absence of, or the dissolution of marriage with, the qualifying resident or senior citizen.

(B) Was 45 years of age or older, or was a spouse, cohabitant, or person providing primary physical or economic support to the qualifying resident or senior citizen.

(3) "Qualified permanent resident" also means a disabled person or person with a disabling illness or injury who is a child or grandchild of the senior citizen or a qualified permanent resident as defined in paragraph (2) who needs to live with the senior citizen or qualified permanent resident because of the disabling condition, illness, or injury. For purposes of this section, "disabled" means a person who has a disability as defined in subdivision (b) of Section 54. A "disabling injury or illness" means an illness or injury which results in a condition meeting the definition of disability set forth in subdivision (b) of Section 54.

(A) For any person who is a qualified permanent resident under this paragraph whose disabling condition ends, the owner, board of directors, or other governing body may require the formerly disabled resident to cease residing in the development upon receipt of six months' written notice; provided, however, that the owner, board of directors, or other governing body may allow the person to remain a resident for up to one year after the disabling condition ends.

(B) The owner, board of directors, or other governing body of the senior citizen housing development may take action to prohibit or terminate occupancy by a person who is a qualified permanent resident under this paragraph if the owner, board of directors, or other governing body finds, based on credible and objective evidence, that the person is likely to pose a significant threat to the health or safety of others that cannot be ameliorated by means of a reasonable accommodation; provided, however, that the action to prohibit or terminate the occupancy may be taken only after doing both of the following:

(i) Providing reasonable notice to and an opportunity to be heard for the disabled person whose occupancy is being challenged, and reasonable notice to the coresident parent or grandparent of that person.

(ii) Giving due consideration to the relevant, credible, and objective information provided in the hearing. The evidence shall be taken and held in a confidential manner, pursuant to a closed session, by the owner, board of directors, or other governing body in order to preserve the privacy of the affected persons. The affected persons shall be entitled to have present at the hearing an attorney or any other person authorized by them to speak on their behalf or to assist them in the matter.

(4) "Senior citizen housing development" means a residential development developed, substantially rehabilitated, or substantially renovated for, senior citizens that has at least 35 dwelling units. Any senior citizen housing development which is required to obtain a public report under Section 11010 of the Business and Professions Code and which submits its application for a public report after July 1, 2001, shall be required to have been issued a public report as a senior citizen housing development under Section 11010.05 of the Business and Professions Code. No housing development constructed prior to January 1, 1985, shall fail to qualify as a senior citizen housing development because it was not originally developed or put to use for occupancy by senior citizens.

(5) "Dwelling unit" or "housing" means any residential accommodation other than a mobilehome.

(6) "Cohabitant" refers to persons who live together as husband and wife, or persons who are domestic partners within the meaning of Section 297 of the Family Code.

(7) "Permitted health care resident" means a person hired to provide live-in, long-term, or terminal health care to a qualifying resident, or a family member of the qualifying resident providing that care. For the purposes of this section, the care provided by a permitted health care resident must be substantial in nature and must provide either assistance with necessary daily activities or medical treatment, or both. A permitted

health care resident shall be entitled to continue his or her occupancy, residency, or use of the dwelling unit as a permitted resident in the absence of the senior citizen from the dwelling unit only if both of the following are applicable:

(A) The senior citizen became absent from the dwelling due to hospitalization or other necessary medical treatment and expects to return to his or her residence within 90 days from the date the absence began.

(B) The absent senior citizen or an authorized person acting for the senior citizen submits a written request to the owner, board of directors, or governing board stating that the senior citizen desires that the permitted health care resident be allowed to remain in order to be present when the senior citizen returns to reside in the development. Upon written request by the senior citizen or an authorized person acting for the senior citizen, the owner, board of directors, or governing board shall have the discretion to allow a permitted health care resident to remain for a time period longer than 90 days from the date that the senior citizen's absence began, if it appears that the senior citizen will return within a period of time not to exceed an additional 90 days.

(c) The covenants, conditions, and restrictions and other documents or written policy shall set forth the limitations on occupancy, residency, or use on the basis of age. Any such limitation shall not be more exclusive than to require that one person in residence in each dwelling unit may be required to be a senior citizen and that each other resident in the same dwelling unit may be required to be a qualified permanent resident, a permitted health care resident, or a person under 55 years of age whose occupancy is permitted under subdivision (h) of this section or under subdivision (b) of Section 51.4. That limitation may be less exclusive, but shall at least require that the persons commencing any occupancy of a dwelling unit include a senior citizen who intends to reside in the unit as his or her primary residence on a permanent basis. The application of the rules set forth in this subdivision regarding limitations on occupancy may result in less than all of the dwellings being actually occupied by a senior citizen.

(d) The covenants, conditions, and restrictions or other documents or written policy shall permit temporary residency, as a guest of a senior citizen or qualified permanent resident, by a person of less than 55 years of age for periods of time, not less than 60 days in any year, that are specified in the covenants, conditions, and restrictions or other documents or written policy.

(e) Upon the death or dissolution of marriage, or upon hospitalization, or other prolonged absence of the qualifying resident, any qualified permanent resident shall be entitled to continue his or her occupancy, residency, or use of the dwelling unit as a permitted resident. This subdivision shall not apply to a permitted health care resident.

(f) The condominium, stock cooperative, limited-equity housing cooperative, planned development, or multiple-family residential rental property shall have been developed for, and initially been put to use as, housing for senior citizens, or shall have been substantially rehabilitated or renovated for, and immediately afterward put to use as, housing for senior citizens, as provided in this section; provided, however, that no housing development constructed prior to January 1, 1985, shall fail to qualify as a senior citizen housing development because it was not originally developed for or originally put to use for occupancy by senior citizens.

(g) The covenants, conditions, and restrictions or other documents or written policies applicable to any condominium, stock cooperative, limited-equity housing cooperative, planned development, or multiple-family residential property that contained age restrictions on January 1, 1984, shall be enforceable only to the extent permitted by this section, notwithstanding lower age restrictions contained in those documents or policies.

(h) Any person who has the right to reside in, occupy, or use the housing or an unimproved lot subject to this section on January 1, 1985, shall not be deprived of the right to continue that residency, occupancy, or use as the result of the enactment of this section.

(i) The covenants, conditions, and restrictions or other documents or written policy of the senior citizen housing development shall permit the occupancy of a dwelling unit by a permitted health care resident during any period that the person is actually providing live-in, long-term, or hospice health care to a qualifying resident for compensation. For purposes of this subdivision, the term "for compensation" shall include provisions of lodging and food in exchange for care.

(j) Notwithstanding any other provision of this section, this section shall not apply to the County of Riverside.

Civ. Code § 51.4. Senior Housing Constructed Prior To 1982 - Exemption From Design Requirements.

(a) The Legislature finds and declares that the requirements for senior housing under Sections 51.2 and 51.3 are more stringent than the requirements for that housing under the federal Fair Housing Amendments

Act of 1988 (Public Law 100-430) in recognition of the acute shortage of housing for families with children in California. The Legislature further finds and declares that the special design requirements for senior housing under Sections 51.2 and 51.3 may pose a hardship to some housing developments which were constructed before the decision in *Marina Point Ltd. v. Wolfson (1982), 30 Cal. 3d 721.* The Legislature further finds and declares that the requirement for specially designed accommodations in senior housing under Sections 51.2 and 51.3 provides important benefits to senior citizens and also ensures that housing exempt from the prohibition of age discrimination is carefully tailored to meet the compelling societal interest in providing senior housing.

(b) Any person who resided in, occupied, or used, prior to January 1, 1990, a dwelling in a senior citizen housing development which relied on the exemption to the special design requirement provided by this section prior to January 1, 2001, shall not be deprived of the right to continue that residency, occupancy, or use as the result of the changes made to this section by the enactment of Chapter 1004 of the Statutes of 2000.

(c) This section shall not apply to the County of Riverside.

Civ. Code § 51.5. Discrimination By Business Establishment Prohibited.

(a) No business establishment of any kind whatsoever shall discriminate against, boycott or blacklist, or refuse to buy from, contract with, sell to, or trade with any person in this state on account of any characteristic listed or defined in subdivision (b) or (e) of Section 51, or of the person's partners, members, stockholders, directors, officers, managers, superintendents, agents, employees, business associates, suppliers, or customers, because the person is perceived to have one or more of those characteristics, or because the person is associated with a person who has, or is perceived to have, any of those characteristics.

(b) As used in this section, "person" includes any person, firm, association, organization, partnership, business trust, corporation, limited liability company, or company.

(c) This section shall not be construed to require any construction, alteration, repair, structural or otherwise, or modification of any sort whatsoever, beyond that construction, alteration, repair, or modification that is otherwise required by other provisions of law, to any new or existing establishment, facility, building, improvement, or any other structure, nor shall this section be construed to augment, restrict, or alter in any way the authority of the State Architect to require construction, alteration, repair, or modifications that the State Architect otherwise possesses pursuant to other laws.

Civ. Code § 51.6. Gender Tax Repeal Act of 1995.

(a) This section shall be known, and may be cited, as the Gender Tax Repeal Act of 1995.

(b) No business establishment of any kind whatsoever may discriminate, with respect to the price charged for services of similar or like kind, against a person because of the person's gender.

(c) Nothing in subdivision (b) prohibits price differences based specifically upon the amount of time, difficulty, or cost of providing the services.

(d) Except as provided in subdivision (f), the remedies for a violation of this section are the remedies provided in subdivision (a) of Section 52. However, an action under this section is independent of any other remedy or procedure that may be available to an aggrieved party.

(e) This act does not alter or affect the provisions of the Health and Safety Code, the Insurance Code, or other laws that govern health care service plan or insurer underwriting or rating practices.

(f) (1) The following business establishments shall clearly and conspicuously disclose to the customer in writing the pricing for each standard service provided:

(A) Tailors or businesses providing aftermarket clothing alterations.

(B) Barbers or hair salons.

(C) Dry cleaners and laundries providing services to individuals.

(2) The price list shall be posted in an area conspicuous to customers. Posted price lists shall be in no less than 14-point boldface type and clearly and completely display pricing for every standard service offered by the business under paragraph (1).

(3) The business establishment shall provide the customer with a complete written price list upon request.

(4) The business establishment shall display in a conspicuous place at least one clearly visible sign, printed in no less than 24-point boldface type, which reads: "CALIFORNIA LAW PROHIBITS ANY BUSINESS ESTABLISHMENT FROM DISCRIMINATING, WITH RESPECT TO THE PRICE CHARGED FOR SERVICES OF SIMILAR OR LIKE KIND, AGAINST A PERSON BECAUSE OF THE PERSON'S GENDER. A COMPLETE PRICE LIST IS AVAILABLE UPON

Civil Rights

REQUEST."

(5) A business establishment that fails to correct a violation of this subdivision within 30 days of receiving written notice of the violation is liable for a civil penalty of one thousand dollars ($1,000).

(6) For the purposes of this subdivision, "standard service" means the 15 most frequently requested services provided by the business.

Civ. Code § 51.7. Freedom From Violence; "Sexual Orientation" Defined.

(a) All persons within the jurisdiction of this state have the right to be free from any violence, or intimidation by threat of violence, committed against their persons or property because of political affiliation, or on account of any characteristic listed or defined in subdivision (b) or (e) of Section 51, or position in a labor dispute, or because another person perceives them to have one or more of those characteristics. The identification in this subdivision of particular bases of discrimination is illustrative rather than restrictive.

(b) This section does not apply to statements concerning positions in a labor dispute which are made during otherwise lawful labor picketing.

Civ. Code § 51.8. Discrimination In Granting Franchises Prohibited.

(a) No franchisor shall discriminate in the granting of franchises solely on account of any characteristic listed or defined in subdivision (b) or (e) of Section 51 of the franchisee and the composition of a neighborhood or geographic area reflecting any characteristic listed or defined in subdivision (b) or (e) of Section 51 in which the franchise is located. Nothing in this section shall be interpreted to prohibit a franchisor from granting a franchise to prospective franchisees as part of a program or programs to make franchises available to persons lacking the capital, training, business experience, or other qualifications ordinarily required of franchisees, or any other affirmative action program adopted by the franchisor.

(b) Nothing in this section shall be construed to require any construction, alteration, repair, structural or otherwise, or modification of any sort whatsoever, beyond that construction, alteration, repair, or modification that is otherwise required by other provisions of law, to any new or existing establishment, facility, building, improvement, or any other structure, nor shall anything in this section be construed to augment, restrict, or alter in any way the authority of the State Architect to require construction, alteration, repair, or modifications that the State Architect otherwise possesses pursuant to other laws.

Civ. Code § 51.9. Elements Required For Cause Of Action For Sexual Harrassment.

(a) A person is liable in a cause of action for sexual harassment under this section when the plaintiff proves all of the following elements:

(1) There is a business, service, or professional relationship between the plaintiff and defendant. Such a relationship may exist between a plaintiff and a person, including, but not limited to, any of the following persons:

(A) Physician, psychotherapist, or dentist. For purposes of this section, "psychotherapist" has the same meaning as set forth in paragraph (1) of subdivision (c) of Section 728 of the Business and Professions Code.

(B) Attorney, holder of a master's degree in social work, real estate agent, real estate appraiser, accountant, banker, trust officer, financial planner loan officer, collection service, building contractor, or escrow loan officer.

(C) Executor, trustee, or administrator.

(D) Landlord or property manager.

(E) Teacher.

(F) A relationship that is substantially similar to any of the above.

(2) The defendant has made sexual advances, solicitations, sexual requests, demands for sexual compliance by the plaintiff, or engaged in other verbal, visual, or physical conduct of a sexual nature or of a hostile nature based on gender, that were unwelcome and persistent or severe.

(3) There is an inability by the plaintiff to easily terminate the relationship.

(4) The plaintiff has suffered or will suffer economic loss or disadvantage or personal injury, including, but not limited to, emotional distress or the violation of a statutory or constitutional right, as a result of the conduct described in paragraph (2).

(b) In an action pursuant to this section, damages shall be awarded as provided by Section 52.

(c) Nothing in this section shall be construed to limit application of any other remedies or rights provided under the law.

(d) The definition of sexual harrassment and the standards for determining liability set forth in this section shall be limited to determining liability only with regard to a cause of action brought under this section.

Civ. Code § 51.10. Riverside County - Housing Discrimination Based Upon Age Prohibited.

(a) Section 51 shall be construed to prohibit a business establishment from discriminating in the sale or rental of housing based upon age. A business establishment may establish and preserve housing for senior citizens, pursuant to Section 51.11, except housing as to which Section 51.11 is preempted by the prohibition in the federal Fair Housing Amendments Act of 1988 (Public Law 100-430) and implementing regulations against discrimination on the basis of familial status.

(b) This section is intended to clarify the holdings in *Marina Point, Ltd., v. Wolfson (1982) 30 Cal.3d 721*, and *O'Connor v. Village Green Owners Association (1983) 33 Cal.3d 790*.

(c) *Selection preferences based on age, imposed in connection with a federally approved housing progam, do not constitute age discrimination in housing.*

(d) This section shall only apply to the County of Riverside.

Civ. Code § 51.11. Riverside County - Establishing And Preserving Accessible Housing For Senior Citizens.

(a) The Legislature finds and declares that this section is essential to establish and preserve housing for senior citizens. There are senior citizens who need special living environments, and find that there is an inadequate supply of this type of housing in the state.

(b) For the purposes of this section, the following definitions apply:

(1) "Qualifying resident" or "senior citizen" means a person 62 years of age or older, or 55 years of age or older in a senior citizen housing development.

(2) "Qualified permanent resident" means a person who meets both of the following requirements:

(A) Was residing with the qualifying resident or senior citizen prior to the death, hospitalization, or other prolonged absence of, or the dissolution of marriage with, the qualifying resident or senior citizen.

(B) Was 45 years of age or older, or was a spouse, cohabitant, or person providing primary physical or economic support to the qualifying resident or senior citizen.

(3) "Qualified permanent resident" also means a disabled person or person with a disabling illness or injury who is a child or grandchild of the senior citizen or a qualified permanent resident as defined in paragraph (2) who needs to live with the senior citizen or qualified permanent resident

because of the disabling condition, illness, or injury. For purposes of this section, "disabled" means a person who has a disability as defined in subdivision (b) of Section 54. A "disabling injury or illness" means an illness or injury which results in a condition meeting the definition of disability set forth in subdivision (b) of Section 54.

(A) For any person who is a qualified permanent resident under paragraph (3) whose disabling condition ends, the owner, board of directors, or other governing body may require the formerly disabled resident to cease residing in the development upon receipt of six months' written notice; provided, however, that the owner, board of directors, or other governing body may allow the person to remain a resident for up to one year, after the disabling condition ends.

(B) The owner, board of directors, or other governing body of the senior citizen housing development may take action to prohibit or terminate occupancy by a person who is a qualified permanent resident under paragraph (3) if the owner, board of directors, or other governing body finds, based on credible and objective evidence, that the person is likely to pose a significant threat to the health or safety of others that cannot be ameliorated by means of a reasonable accommodation; provided, however, that action to prohibit or terminate the occupancy may be taken only after doing both of the following:

(i) Providing reasonable notice to and an opportunity to be heard for the disabled person whose occupancy is being challenged, and reasonable notice to the coresident parent or grandparent of that person.

(ii) Giving due consideration to the relevant, credible, and objective information provided in that hearing. The evidence shall be taken and held in a confidential manner, pursuant to a closed session, by the owner, board of directors, or other governing body in order to preserve the privacy of the affected persons. The affected persons shall be entitled to have present at the hearing an attorney or any other person authorized by them to speak on their behalf or to assist them in the matter.

(4) "Senior citizen housing development" means a residential development developed with more than 20 units as a senior community by its developer and zoned as a senior community by a local governmental entity, or characterized as a senior community in its governing documents, as these are defined in Section 1351, or qualified as a senior community under the federal Fair Housing Amendments Act of 1988, as amended. Any senior citizen housing development which is required to obtain a public

report under Section 11010 of the Business and Professions Code and which submits its application for a public report after July 1, 2001, shall be required to have been issued a public report as a senior citizen housing development under Section 11010.05 of the Business and Professions Code.

(5) "Dwelling unit" or "housing" means any residential accommodation other than a mobilehome.

(6) "Cohabitant" refers to persons who live together as husband and wife, or persons who are domestic partners within the meaning of Section 297 of the Family Code.

(7) "Permitted health care resident" means a person hired to provide live-in, long-term, or terminal health care to a qualifying resident, or a family member of the qualifying resident providing that care. For the purposes of this section, the care provided by a permitted health care resident must be substantial in nature and must provide either assistance with necessary daily activities or medical treatment, or both. A permitted health care resident shall be entitled to continue his or her occupancy, residency, or use of the dwelling unit as a permitted resident in the absence of the senior citizen from the dwelling unit only if both of the following are applicable:

(A) The senior citizen became absent from the dwelling due to hospitalization or other necessary medical treatment and expects to return to his or her residence within 90 days from the date the absence began.

(B) The absent senior citizen or an authorized person acting for the senior citizen submits a written request to the owner, board of directors, or governing board stating that the senior citizen desires that the permitted health care resident be allowed to remain in order to be present when the senior citizen returns to reside in the development. Upon written request by the senior citizen or an authorized person acting for the senior citizen, the owner, board of directors, or governing board shall have the discretion to allow a permitted health care resident to remain for a time period longer than 90 days from the date that the senior citizen's absence began, if it appears that the senior citizen will return within a period of time not to exceed an additional 90 days.

(c) The covenants, conditions, and restrictions and other documents or written policy shall set forth the limitations on occupancy, residency, or use on the basis of age. Any such limitation shall not be more exclusive than to require that one person in residence in each dwelling unit may be required to be a senior citizen and that each other resident in the same dwelling unit may be required to be a qualified permanent resident, a permitted health care resident, or a person under 55 years of age whose occupancy is permitted under subdivision (g) of this section or subdivision (b) of Section 51.12. That limitation may be less exclusive, but shall at least require that the persons commencing any occupancy of a dwelling unit include a senior citizen who intends to reside in the unit as his or her primary residence on a permanent basis. The application of the rules set forth in this subdivision regarding limitations on occupancy may result in less than all of the dwellings being actually occupied by a senior citizen.

(d) The covenants, conditions, and restrictions or other documents or written policy shall permit temporary residency, as a guest of a senior citizen or qualified permanent resident, by a person of less than 55 years of age for periods of time, not more than 60 days in any year, that are specified in the covenants, conditions, and restrictions or other documents or written policy.

(e) Upon the death or dissolution of marriage, or upon hospitalization, or other prolonged absence of the qualifying resident, any qualified permanent resident shall be entitled to continue his or her occupancy, residency, or use of the dwelling unit as a permitted resident. This subdivision shall not apply to a permitted health care resident.

(f) The covenants, conditions, and restrictions or other documents or written policies applicable to any condominium, stock cooperative, limited-equity housing cooperative, planned development, or multiple-family residential property that contained age restrictions on January 1, 1984, shall be enforceable only to the extent permitted by this section, notwithstanding lower age restrictions contained in those documents or policies.

(g) Any person who has the right to reside in, occupy, or use the housing or an unimproved lot subject to this section on or after January 1, 1985, shall not be deprived of the right to continue that residency, occupancy, or use as the result of the enactment of this section by Chapter 1147 of the Statutes of 1996.

(h) A housing development may qualify as a senior citizen housing development under this section even though, as of January 1, 1997, it does not meet the definition of a senior citizen housing development specified in subdivision (b), if the development complies with that de-finition for every unit that becomes occupied after January 1, 1997, and if the development was once within that definition, and then became noncompliant with the definition as the result of any one of the following:

(1) The development was ordered by a court or a local, state, or federal enforcement agency to allow persons other than qualifying residents, qualified permanent residents, or permitted health care residents to reside in the development.

(2) The development received a notice of a pending or proposed action in, or by, a court, or a local, state, or federal enforcement agency, which action could have resulted in the development being ordered by a court or a state or federal enforcement agency to allow persons other than qualifying residents, qualified permanent residents, or permitted health care residents to reside in the development.

(3) The development agreed to allow persons other than qualifying residents, qualified permanent residents, or permitted health care residents to reside in the development by entering into a stipulation, conciliation agreement, or settlement agreement with a local, state, or federal enforcement agency or with a private party who had filed, or indicated an intent to file, a complaint against the development with a local, state, or federal enforcement agency, or file an action in a court.

(4) The development allowed persons other than qualifying residents, qualified permanent residents, or permitted health care residents to reside in the development on the advice of counsel in order to prevent the possibility of an action being filed by a private party or by a local, state, or federal enforcement agency.

(i) The covenants, conditions, and restrictions or other documents or written policy of the senior citizen housing development shall permit the occupancy of a dwelling unit by a permitted health care resident during any period that the person is actually providing live-in, long-term, or hospice health care to a qualifying resident for compensation.

(j) This section shall only apply to the County of Riverside.

Civ. Code § 51.12. Riverside County - Continuing Occupancy Of Certain Exempt Housing.

(a) The Legislature finds and declares that the requirements for senior housing under Sections 51.10 and 51.11 are more stringent than the requirements for that housing under the federal Fair Housing Amendments Act of 1988 (Public Law 100-430).

(b) Any person who resided in, occupied, or used, prior to January 1, 1990, a dwelling in a senior citizen housing development which relied on the exemption to the special design requirement provided by Section 51.4 as that section read prior to January 1, 2001, shall not be deprived of the right to continue that residency, or occupancy, or use as the result of the changes made to this section by the enactment of Senate Bill 1382 or Senate Bill 2011 at the 1999-2000 Regular Session of the Legislature.

(c) This section shall only apply to the County of Riverside.

Civ. Code § 52. Penalty For Discrimination.

(a) Whoever denies, aids or incites a denial, or makes any discrimination or distinction contrary to Section 51 or 51.5, or 51.6,is liable for each and every offense for the actual damages, and any amount that may be determined by a jury, or a court sitting without a jury, up to a maximum of three times the amount of actual damage but in no case less than four thousand dollars ($4,000), and any attorney's fees that may be determined by the court in addition thereto, suffered by any person denied the rights provided in Section 51 or 51.5, or 51.6.

(b) Whoever denies the right provided by Section 51.7 or 51.9, or aids, incites, or conspires in that denial, is liable for each and every offense for the actual damages suffered by any person denied that right and, in addition, the following:

(1) An amount to be determined by a jury, or a court sitting without a jury, for exemplary damages.

(2) A civil penalty of twenty-five thousand dollars ($25,000) to be awarded to the person denied the right provided by Section 51.7 in any action brought by the person denied the right, or by the Attorney General, a district attorney, or a city attorney. An action for that penalty brought pursuant to Section 51.7 shall be commenced within three years of the alleged practice.

(3) Attorney's fees as may be determined by the court.

(c) Whenever there is reasonable cause to believe that any person or group of persons is engaged in conduct of resistance to the full enjoyment of any of the rights described in this section, and that conduct is of that nature and is intended to deny the full exercise of those rights , the Attorney General, any district attorney or city attorney, or any person aggrieved by the conduct may bring a civil action in the appropriate court by filing with it a complaint. The complaint shall contain the following:

(1) The signature of the officer, or, in his or her absence, the individual acting on behalf of the officer, or the signature of the person aggrieved.

(2) The facts pertaining to the conduct.

(3) A request for preventive relief, including an application for a permanent or temporary injunction, restraining order, or other order against the person or persons responsible for the conduct, as the complainant

deems necessary to ensure the full enjoyment of the rights described in this section.

(d) Whenever an action has been commenced in any court seeking relief from the denial of equal protection of the laws under the Fourteenth Amendment to the Constitution of the United States on account of race, color, religion, sex, national origin, or disability, the Attorney General or any district attorney or city attorney for or in the name of the people of the State of California may intervene in the action upon timely application if the Attorney General of any district attorney or city attorney certifies that the case is of general public importance. In that action the people of the State of California shall be entitled to the same relief as if it had instituted the action.

(e) Actions brought pursuant to this section are independent of any other actions, remedies or procedures that may be available to an aggrieved party pursuant to any other law.

(f) Any person claiming to be aggrieved by an alleged unlawful practice in violation of Section 51 or 51.7 may also file a verified complaint with the Department of Fair Employment and Housing pursuant to Section 12948 of the Government Code.

(g) This section does not require any construction, alteration, repair, structural or otherwise, or modification of any sort whatsoever beyond that construction, alteration, repair, or modification that is otherwise required by other provisions of law, to any new or existing establishment, facility, building, improvement, or any other structure, nor does this section augment, restrict, or alter in any way the authority of the State Architect to require construction, alteration, repair, or modifications that the State Architect otherwise possesses pursuant to other laws.

(h) For the purposes of this section, "actual damages" means special and general damages. This subdivision is declaratory of existing law.

Civ. Code § 52.1. Interference With Exercise Of Civil Rights; Remedies.

(a) If a person or persons, whether or not acting under color of law, interferes by threats, intimidation, or coercion, or attempts to interfere by threats, intimidation, or coercion, with the exercise or enjoyment by any individual or individuals of rights secured by the Constitution or laws of the United States, or of the rights secured by the Constitution or laws of this state, the Attorney General, or any district attorney or city attorney may bring a civil action for injunctive and other appropriate equitable relief in the name of the people of the State of California, in order to protect the peaceable exercise or enjoyment of the right or rights secured. An action brought by the Attorney General, any district attorney, or any city attorney may also seek a civil penalty of twenty-five thousand dollars ($25,000). If this civil penalty is requested, it shall be assessed individually against each person who is determined to have violated this section and the penalty shall be awarded to each individual whose rights under this section are determined to have been violated.

(b) Any individual whose exercise or enjoyment of rights secured by the Constitution or laws of the United States, or of rights secured by the Constitution or laws of this state, has been interfered with, or attempted to be interfered with, as described in subdivision (a), may institute and prosecute in his or her own name and on his or her own behalf a civil action for damages, including, but not limited to, damages under Section 52, injunctive relief, and other appropriate equitable relief to protect the peaceable exercise or enjoyment of the right or rights secured.

(c) An action brought pursuant to subdivision (a) or (b) may be filed either in the superior court for the county in which the conduct complained of occurred or in the superior court for the county in which a person whose conduct complained of resides or has his or her place of business. An action brought by the Attorney General pursuant to subdivision (a) also may be filed in the superior court for any county wherein the Attorney General has an office, and in that case, the jurisdiction of the court shall extend throughout the state.

(d) If a court issues a temporary restraining order or a preliminary or permanent injunction in an action brought pursuant to subdivision (a) or (b), ordering a defendant to refrain from conduct or activities, the order issued shall include the following statement: VIOLATION OF THIS ORDER IS A CRIME PUNISHABLE UNDER SECTION 422.77 OF THE PENAL CODE.

(e) The court shall order the plaintiff or the attorney for the plaintiff to deliver, or the county clerk to mail, two copies of any order, extension, modification, or termination thereof granted pursuant to this section, by the close of the business day on which the order, extension, modification, or termination was granted, to each local law enforcement agency having jurisdiction over the residence of the plaintiff and any other locations where the court determines that acts of violence against the plaintiff are likely to occur. Those local law enforcement agencies shall be designated by the plaintiff or the attorney for the plaintiff. Each appropriate law enforcement agency receiving any order, extension, or modification of any order issued pursuant to this section shall serve forthwith one copy

Civil Rights

thereof upon the defendant. Each appropriate law enforcement agency shall provide to any law enforcement officer responding to the scene of reported violence, information as to the existence of, terms, and current status of, any order issued pursuant to this section.

(f) A court shall not have jurisdiction to issue an order or injunction under this section, if that order or injunction would be prohibited under Section 527.3 of the Code of Civil Procedure.

(g) An action brought pursuant to this section is independent of any other action, remedy, or procedure that may be available to an aggrieved individual under any other provision of law, including, but not limited to, an action, remedy, or procedure brought pursuant to Section 51.7.

(h) In addition to any damages, injunction, or other equitable relief awarded in an action brought pursuant to subdivision (b), the court may award the petitioner or plaintiff reasonable attorney's fees.

(i) A violation of an order described in subdivision (d) may be punished either by prosecution under Section 422.77 of the Penal Code, or by a proceeding for contempt brought pursuant to Title 5 (commencing with Section 1209) of Part 3 of the Code of Civil Procedure. However, in any proceeding pursuant to the Code of Civil Procedure, if it is determined that the person proceeded against is guilty of the contempt charged, in addition to any other relief, a fine may be imposed not exceeding one thousand dollars ($1,000), or the person may be ordered imprisoned in a county jail not exceeding six months, or the court may order both the imprisonment and fine.

(j) Speech alone is not sufficient to support an action brought pursuant to subdivision (a) or (b), except upon a showing that the speech itself threatens violence against a specific person or group of persons; and the person or group of persons against whom the threat is directed reasonably fears that, because of the speech, violence will be committed against them or their property and that the person threatening violence had the apparent ability to carry out the threat.

(k) No order issued in any proceeding brought pursuant to subdivision (a) or (b) shall restrict the content of any person's speech. An order restricting the time, place, or manner of any person's speech shall do so only to the extent reasonably necessary to protect the peaceable exercise or enjoyment of constitutional or statutory rights, consistent with the constitutional rights of the person sought to be enjoined.

Civ. Code § 53. Discriminatory Provisions On Ownership Or Use Of Real Property Void.

(a) Every provision in a written instrument relating to real property that purports to forbid or restrict the conveyance, encumbrance, leasing or mortgaging of that real property to any person because of any characteristic listed or defined in subdivision (b) or (e) of Section 51 is void, and every restriction or prohibition as to the use or occupation of real property because of any characteristic listed or defined in subdivision (b) or (e) of Section 51 is void.

(b) Every restriction or prohibition, whether by way of covenant, condition upon use or occupation, or upon transfer of title to real property, which restriction or prohibition directly or indirectly limits the acquisition, use or occupation of that property because of any characteristic listed or defined in subdivision (b) or (e) of Section 51 is void.

(c) In any action to declare that a restriction or prohibition specified in subdivision (a) or (b) is void, the court shall take judicial notice of the recorded instrument or instruments containing the prohibitions or restrictions in the same manner that is takes judicial notice of the matters listed in Section 452 of the Evidence Code.

Gov't Code § 12955. Discrimination In Housing Prohibited.

It shall be unlawful:

(a) For the owner of any housing accommodation to discriminate against or harass any person because of the race, color, religion, sex, sexual orientation, marital status, national origin, ancestry, familial status, source of income, or disability of that person.

(b) For the owner of any housing accommodation to make or to cause to be made any written or oral inquiry concerning the race, color, religion, sex, sexual orientation, marital status, national origin, ancestry, familial status, or disability of any person seeking to purchase, rent or lease any housing accommodation.

(c) For any person to make, print, or publish, or cause to be made, printed, or published any notice, statement, or advertisement, with respect to the sale or rental of a housing accommodation that indicates any preference, limitation, or discrimination based on race, color, religion, sex, sexual orientation, marital status, national origin, ancestry, familial status, source of income, or disability or an intention to make any such preference, limitation, or discrimination.

(d) For any person subject to the provisions of Section 51 of the Civil Code, as that section applies to housing accommodations, to discriminate against any person on the basis of sex, sexual orientation, color, race, religion, ancestry, national origin, familial status, marital status, disability, source of income, or on any other basis prohibited by that section.

(e) For any person, bank, mortgage company or other financial institution that provides financial assistance for the purchase, organization, or construction of any housing accommodation to discriminate against any person or group of persons because of the race, color, religion, sex, sexual orientation, marital status, national origin, ancestry, familial status, source of income, or disability in the terms, conditions, or privileges relating to the obtaining or use of that financial assistance.

(f) For any owner of housing accommodations to harass, evict, or otherwise discriminate against any person in the sale or rental of housing accommodations when the owner's dominant purpose is retaliation against a person who has opposed practices unlawful under this section, informed law enforcement agencies of practices believed unlawful under this section, has testified or assisted in any proceeding under this part, or has aided or encouraged a person to exercise or enjoy the rights secured by this part. Nothing herein is intended to cause or permit the delay of an unlawful detainer action.

(g) For any person to aid, abet, incite, compel, or coerce the doing of any of the acts or practices declared unlawful in this section, or to attempt to do so.

(h) For any person, for profit, to induce any person to sell or rent any dwelling by representations regarding the entry or prospective entry into the neighborhood of a person or persons of a particular race, color, religion, sex, sexual orientation, marital status, ancestry, disability, source of income, familial status, or national origin.

(i) For any person or other organization or entity whose business involves real estate-related transactions to discriminate against any person in making available a transaction, or in the terms and conditions of a transaction, because of race, color, religion, sex, sexual orientation, marital status, national origin, ancestry, source of income, familial status, or disability.

(j) To deny a person access to, or membership or participation in, a multiple listing service, real estate brokerage organization, or other service because of race, color, religion, sex, sexual orientation, marital status, ancestry, disability, familial status, source of income, or national origin.

(k) To otherwise make unavailable or deny a dwelling based on discrimination because of race, color, religion, sex, sexual orientation, familial status, source of income, disability, or national origin.

(l) To discriminate through public or private land use practices, decisions, and authorizations because of race, color, religion, sex, sexual orientation, familial status, marital status, disability, national origin, source of income, or ancestry. Discrimination includes, but is not limited to, restrictive covenants, zoning laws, denials of use permits, and other actions authorized under the Planning and Zoning Law (Title 7 (commencing with Section 65000)), that make housing opportunities unavailable. Discrimination under this subdivision also includes the existence of a restrictive covenant, regardless of whether accompanied by a statement that the restrictive covenant is repealed or void. This paragraph shall become operative on January 1, 2001.

(m) As used in this section, "race, color, religion, sex, sexual orientation, marital status, national origin, ancestry, familial status, source of income, or disability" includes a perception that the person has any of those characteristics or that the person is associated with a person who has, or is perceived to have, any of those characteristics.

(n) To use a financial or income standard in the rental of housing that fails to account for the aggregate income of persons residing together or proposing to reside together on the same basis as the aggregate income of married persons residing together or proposing to reside together.

(o) In instances where there is a government rent subsidy, to use a financial or income standard in assessing eligibility for the rental of housing that is not based on the portion of the rent to be paid by the tenant.

(p) (1) For the purposes of this section, "source of income" means lawful, verifiable income paid directly to a tenant or paid to a representative
of a tenant.

(2) For the purposes of this section, it shall not constitute discrimination based on source of income to make a written or oral inquiry concerning the level or source of income.

Gov't Code § 12955.1. "Discrimination" Defined.

(a) For purposes of Section 12955, "discrimination" includes, but is not limited to, a failure to design and construct a covered multifamily dwelling in a manner that allows access to, and use by, disabled persons by providing, at a minimum, the following features:

(1) All covered multifamily dwellings shall have at least one building entrance on an accessible route, unless it is impracticable to do so because of the terrain or unusual characteristics of the site. The burden of establishing impracticability because of terrain or unusual site characteristics is on the person or persons who designed or constructed

the housing facility.

(2) All covered multifamily dwellings with a building entrance on an accessible route shall be designed and constructed in a manner that complies with all of the following:

(A) The public and common areas are readily accessible to and useable by persons with disabilities.

(B) All the doors designed to allow passage into and within all premises are sufficiently wide to allow passage by persons in wheelchairs.

(C) All premises within covered multifamily dwelling units contain the following features of adaptable design:

(i) An accessible route into and through the covered dwelling unit.

(ii) Light switches, electrical outlets, thermostats, and other environmental controls in accessible locations.

(iii) Reinforcements in bathroom walls to allow later installation of grab bars around the toilet, tub, shower stall, and shower seat, where those facilities are provided.

(iv) Useable kitchens and bathrooms so that an individual in a wheelchair can maneuver about the space.

(b)(1) For purposes of Section 12955, "discrimination" includes, but is not limited to, a failure to design and construct 10 percent of the multistory dwelling units in buildings without an elevator that consist of at least four condominium dwelling units or at least three rental apartment dwelling units in a manner that incorporates an accessible route to the primary entry level entrance and that meets the requirements of paragraph (2) of subdivision (a) with respect to the ground floor, at least one bathroom on the primary entry level and the public and common areas. Any fraction thereof shall be rounded up to the next whole number. For purposes of this subdivision, "elevator" does not include an elevator that serves only the first ground floor or any nonresidential area. In multistory dwelling units in these buildings without elevators, the "primary entry level entrance" means the principal entrance through which most people enter the dwelling unit, as designated by the California Building Standards Code or, if not designated by California Building Standards Code, by the building official. To determine the total number of multistory dwelling units subject to this subdivision, all multistory dwelling units in the buildings subject to this subdivision on a site shall be considered collectively. This subdivision shall not be construed to require an elevator within an individual multistory dwelling unit or within a building subject to this subdivision. This subdivision shall apply only to multistory dwelling units in a building subject to this subdivision for which an application for a construction permit is submitted on or after July 1, 2005.

(2) Notwithstanding subdivision (c), the Division of the State Architect and the Department of Housing and Community Development may adopt regulations to clarify, interpret, or implement this subdivision, if either of them deem it necessary and appropriate.

(c) Notwithstanding Section 12935, regulations adopting building standards necessary to implement, interpret, or make specific the provisions of this section shall be developed by the Division of the State Architect for public housing and by the Department of Housing and Community Development for all other residential occupancies, and shall be adopted pursuant to Chapter 4 (commencing with Section 18935) of Part 2.5 of the Health and Safety Code. Prior to the effective date of regulations adopted pursuant to this subdivision, existing federal accessibility standards that provide, to persons with disabilities, greater protections than existing state accessibility regulations shall apply. After regulations pursuant to this subdivision become effective, particular state regulations shall apply if they provide, to persons with disabilities, the same protections as, or greater protections than, the federal standards. If particular federal regulations provide greater protections than state regulations, then those federal standards shall apply. If the United States Department of Housing and Urban Development determines that any portion of the state regulations are not equivalent to the federal standards, the federal standards shall, as to those portions, apply to the design and construction of covered multifamily dwellings until the state regulations are brought into compliance with the federal standards. The appropriate state agency shall provide notice pursuant to the Administrative Procedures Act (Chapter 5 (commencing with Section 11500) of Part 5 of Division 3 of Title 2) of that determination.

(d) In investigating discrimination complaints, the department shall apply the building standards contained in the California Building Standards Code to determine whether a covered multifamily dwelling is designed and constructed for access to and use by disabled persons in accordance with this section.

(e) The building standard requirements for persons with disabilities imposed by this section shall meet or exceed the requirements under the federal Fair Housing Amendments Act of 1988 (Public Law 100-430) and its implementing regulations (24 C.F.R. 100.1 et seq.) and the existing state law building standards contained in the California Building Standards

Code.

Gov't Code § 12955.1.1. "Covered Multifamily Dwellings" And "Multistory Dwelling Unit" Defined.

For purposes of Section 12955.1, the following definitions shall apply:

(a) "Covered multifamily dwellings" means both of the following:

(1) Buildings that consist of at least four condominium dwelling units or at least three rental apartment dwelling units if the buildings have at least one elevator. For purposes of this definition, dwelling units within a single structure separated by firewalls do not constitute separate buildings.

(2) The ground floor dwelling units in buildings that consist of at least four condominium dwelling units or at least three rental apartment dwelling units if the buildings do not have an elevator. For purposes of this definition, dwelling units within a single structure separated by firewalls do not constitute separate buildings.

(b) "Multistory dwelling unit" means a condominium dwelling unit or rental apartment with finished living space on one floor and the floor immediately above or below it or, if applicable, the floors immediately above and below it.

Gov't Code § 12955.2. "Familial Status" Defined.

For purposes of this part, "familial status" means one or more individuals under 18 years of age who reside with a parent, another person with care and legal custody of that individual, a person who has been given care and custody of that individual by a state or local governmental agency that is responsible for the welfare of children, or the designee of that parent or other person with legal custody of any individual under 18 years of age by written consent of the parent or designated custodian. The protections afforded by this part against discrimination on the basis of familial status also apply to any individual who is pregnant, who is in the process of securing legal custody of any individual under 18 years of age, or who is in the process of being given care and custody of any individual under 18 years of age by a state or local governmental agency responsible for the welfare of children.

Gov't Code § 12955.3. "Disability" Defined.

For purposes of this part, "disability" includes, but is not limited to, any physical or mental disability as defined in Section 12926.

Gov't Code § 12955.4. Religious Preference Allowed.

Nothing in this part shall prohibit a religious organization, association or society, or any nonprofit institution or organization operated, supervised, or controlled by or in conjunction with a religious organization, association, or society, from limiting the sale, rental, or occupancy of dwellings that it owns or operates for other than a commercial purpose to persons of the same religion or from giving preference to those persons, unless membership in that religion is restricted on account of race, color, or national origin.

Gov't Code § 12955.5. Data Collection By Government Allowed.

Nothing in this part shall preclude the government from establishing programs to collect information relating to discriminatory housing practices.

Gov't Code § 12955.6. Fair Housing Amendments Acts of 1988 Is Minimum Standard.

Nothing in this part shall be construed to afford to the classes protected under this part, fewer rights or remedies than the federal Fair Housing Amendments Act of 1988 (P.L. 100-430) and its implementing regulations (24 C.F.R. 100.1 et seq.), or state law relating to fair employment and housing as it existed prior to the effective date of this section. Any state law that purports to require or permit any action that would be an unlawful practice under this part shall to that extent be invalid. This part may be construed to afford greater rights and remedies to an aggrieved person than those afforded by federal law and other state laws.

Gov't Code § 12955.7. Retaliation For Compliance Prohibited.

It shall be unlawful to coerce, intimidate, threaten, or interfere with any person in the exercise or enjoyment of, or on account of that person having exercised or enjoyed, or on account of that person having aided or encouraged any other person in the exercise or enjoyment of, any right granted or protected by Section 12955 or 12955.1.

Gov't Code § 12955.8. Elements Of Violation Of Article.

For purposes of this article, in connection with unlawful practices:

(a) Proof of an intentional violation of this article includes, but is not limited to, an act or failure to act that is otherwise covered by this part, that demonstrates an intent to discriminate in any manner in violation of this part. A person intends to discriminate if race, color, religion, sex, sexual

Civil Rights

orientation, familial status, marital status, disability, national origin, or ancestry is a motivating factor in committing a discriminatory housing practice even though other factors may have also motivated the practice. An intent to discriminate may be established by direct or circumstantial evidence.

(b) Proof of a violation causing a discriminatory effect is shown if an act or failure to act that is otherwise covered by this part, and that has the effect, regardless of intent, of unlawfully discriminating on the basis of race, color, religion, sex, sexual orientation, familial status, marital status, disability, national origin, or ancestry. A business establishment whose action or inaction has an unintended discriminatory effect shall not be considered to have committed an unlawful housing practice in violation of this part if the business establishment can establish that the action or inaction is necessary to the operation of the business and effectively carries out the significant business need it is alleged to serve. In cases that do not involve a business establishment, the person whose action or inaction has an unintended discriminatory effect shall not be considered to have committed an unlawful housing practice in violation of this part if the person can establish that the action or inaction is necessary to achieve an important purpose sufficiently compelling to override the discriminatory effect and effectively carries out the purpose it is alleged to serve.

(1) Any determination of a violation pursuant to this subdivision shall consider whether or not there are feasible alternatives that would equally well or better accomplish the purpose advanced with a less discriminatory effect.

(2) For purposes of this subdivision, the term "business establishment" shall have the same meaning as in Section 51 of the Civil Code.

Gov't Code § 12955.9. Qualifying Senior Housing Allowed To Discriminate Based On Familial Status.

(a) The provisions of this part relating to discrimination on the basis of familial status shall not apply to housing for older persons.

(b) As used in this section, "housing for older persons" means any of the following:

(1) Housing provided under any state or federal program that the Secretary of Housing and Urban Development determines is specifically designed and operated to assist elderly persons, as defined in the state or federal program.

(2) Housing that meets the standards for senior housing in

Sections 51.2, 51.3, and 51.4 of the Civil Code, except to the extent that those standards violate the prohibition of familial status discrimination in the federal Fair Housing Amendments Act of 1988 (Public Law 100-430) and implementing regulations.

(3) Mobilehome parks that meet the standards for "housing for older persons" as defined in the federal Fair Housing Amendments Act of 1988 and implementing regulations.

(c) For purposes of this section, the burden of proof shall be on the owner to prove that the housing qualifies as housing for older persons.

Gov't Code § 12956. Relevant Records Maintained During Legal Action.

Upon notice that a verified complaint against it has been filed under this part, any owner of housing accommodations shall maintain and preserve any and all rental records or any other written materials relevant to the complaint, until the complaint is fully and finally disposed of and all appeals or related proceedings terminated.

Gov't Code § 12956.1. Amending Documents To Remove Discriminatory Language.

(a) As used in this section, "association," "governing documents," and "declaration" have the same meanings as set forth in Section 1351 of the Civil Code.

(b)(1) A county recorder, title insurance company, escrow company, real estate broker, real estate agent, or association that provides a copy of a declaration, governing document, or deed to any person shall place a cover page or stamp on the first page of the previously recorded document or documents stating, in at least 14-point boldface type, the following:

"If this document contains any restriction based on race, color, religion, sex, familial status, marital status, disability, national origin, source of income as defined in subdivision (p) of Section 12955, or ancestry, that restriction violates state and federal fair housing laws and is void, and may be removed pursuant to Section 12956.2 of the Government Code. Lawful restrictions under state and federal law on the age of occupants in senior housing or housing for older persons shall not be construed as restrictions based on familial status."

(2) The requirements set forth in paragraph (1) shall not apply to documents being submitted for recordation to a county recorder.

(c) Any person who records a document for the express purpose of adding a racially restrictive covenant is guilty of a misdemeanor. The county recorder shall not incur any liability for recording the document. Notwithstanding any other provision of law, a prosecution for a violation of this subdivision shall commence within three years after the discovery of the recording of the document.

Gov't Code § 12956.2. Recording A Restrictive Covenant Modification.

(a)　A person who holds an ownership interest of record in property that he or she believes is the subject of an unlawfully restrictive covenant in violation of subdivision (l) of Section 12955 may record a document titled Restrictive Covenant Modification. The county recorder may choose to waive the fee prescribed for recording and indexing instruments pursuant to Section 27361 in the case of the modification document provided for in this section. The modification document shall include a complete copy of the original document containing the unlawfully restrictive language with the unlawfully restrictive language stricken.

(b)　Before recording the modification document, the county recorder shall submit the modification document and the original document to the county counsel who shall determine whether the original document contains an unlawful restriction based on race, color, religion, sex, sexual orientation, familial status, marital status, disability, national origin, source of income as defined in subdivision (p) of Section 12955, or ancestry. The county counsel shall return the documents and inform the county recorder of its determination. The county recorder shall refuse to record the modification document if the county counsel finds that the original document does not contain an unlawful restriction as specified in this paragraph.

(c)　The modification document shall be indexed in the same manner as the original document being modified. It shall contain a recording reference to the original document in the form of a book and page or instrument number, and date of the recording.

(d)　Subject to covenants, conditions, and restrictions that were recorded after the recording of the original document that contains the unlawfully restrictive language and subject to covenants, conditions, and restrictions that will be recorded after the Restrictive Covenant Modification, the restrictions in the Restrictive Covenant Modification, once recorded, are the only restrictions having effect on the property. The effective date of the terms and conditions of the modification document shall be the same as the effective date of the original document.

(e)　The county recorder shall make available to the public Restrictive Covenant Modification forms.

(f)   If the holder of an ownership interest of record in property causes to be recorded a modified document pursuant to this section that contains modifications not authorized by this section, the county recorder shall not incur liability for recording the document. The liability that may result from the unauthorized recordation is the sole responsibility of the holder of the ownership interest of record who caused the modified recordation.

(g)   This section does not apply to persons holding an ownership interest in property that is part of a common interest development as defined in subdivision (c) of Section 1351 of the Civil Code if the board of directors of that common interest development is subject to the requirements of subdivision (b) of Section 1352.5 of the Civil Code.

Welf. & Inst. Code § 5115. Lanterman Developmental Disabilities Services Act.

(a)   It is the policy of this state, as declared and established in this section and in the Lanterman Developmental Disabilities Services Act, Division 4.5 (commencing with Section 4500), that mentally and physically handicapped persons are entitled to live in normal residential surroundings and should not be excluded therefrom because of their disability.

(b)   In order to achieve uniform statewide implementation of the policies of this section and those of the Lanterman Developmental Disabilities Act, it is necessary to establish the statewide policy that the use of property for the care of six or fewer mentally disordered or otherwise handicapped persons is a residential use of such property for the purposes of zoning.

Welf. & Inst. Code § 5116. Residential Use Zoning Of Group Homes.

Pursuant to the policy stated in Section 5115, a state-authorized, certified, or licensed family care home, foster home, or group home serving six or fewer mentally disordered or otherwise handicapped persons or dependent and neglected children, shall be considered a residential use of property for the purposes of zoning if such homes provide care on a 24-hour-a-day basis.

Such homes shall be a permitted use in all residential zones, including, but not limited to, residential zones for single-family dwellings.

Health & Safety Code § 1597.40. Restrictions Against Group Homes Void; Increased Security Deposit Allowed.

(a) It is the intent of the Legislature that family day care homes for children should be situated in normal residential surroundings so as to give children the home environment which is conducive to healthy and safe development. It is the public policy of this state to provide children in a family day care home the same home environment as provided in a traditional home setting. The Legislature declares this policy to be of statewide concern with the purpose of occupying the field to the exclusion of municipal zoning, building and fire codes and regulations governing the use or occupancy of family day care homes for children, except as specifically provided for in this chapter, and to prohibit any restrictions relating to the use of single-family residences for family day care homes for children except as provided by this chapter.

(b) Every provision in a written instrument entered into relating to real property which purports to forbid or restrict the conveyance, encumbrance, leasing, or mortgaging of the real property for use or occupancy as a family day care home for children, is void and every restriction or prohibition in any such written instrument as to the use or occupancy of the property as a family day care home for children is void.

(c) Except as provided in subdivision (d), every restriction or prohibition entered into, whether by way of covenant, condition upon use or occupancy, or upon transfer of title to real property, which restricts or prohibits directly, or indirectly limits, the acquisition, use, or occupancy of such property for a family day care home for children is void.

(d) (1) A prospective family day care home provider, who resides in a rental property, shall provide 30 days' written notice to the landlord or owner of the rental property prior to the commencement of operation of the family day care home.

(2) For family day care home providers who have relocated an existing licensed family day care home program to a rental property on or after January 1, 1997, less than 30 days' written notice may be provided in cases where the department approves the operation of the new location of the family day care home in less than 30 days, or the home is licensed in less than 30 days, in order that service to the children served in the former location not be interrupted.

(3) A family day care home provider in operation on rental or leased property as of January 1, 1997, shall notify the landlord or property owner in writing at the time of the annual license fee renewal, or by March 31, 1997, whichever occurs later.

(4) Notwithstanding any other provision of law, upon commencement of, or knowledge of, the operation of a family day care

home on his or her property, the landlord or property owner may require the family day care home provider to pay an increased security deposit for operation of the family day care home. The increase in deposit may be required notwithstanding that a lesser amount is required of tenants who do not operate family day care homes. In no event, however, shall the total security deposit charged exceed the maximum allowable under existing law.

(5) Section 1596.890 shall not apply to this subdivision.

Health & Safety Code § 1597.531. Liability Insurance Or Signed Affidavits Required; Naming Association As Additional Insured.

(a) All family day care homes for children shall maintain in force either liability insurance covering injury to clients and guests in the amount of at least one hundred thousand dollars ($100,000) per occurrence and three hundred thousand dollars ($300,000) in the total annual aggregate, sustained on account of the negligence of the licensee or its employees, or a bond in the aggregate amount of three hundred thousand dollars ($300,000). In lieu of the liability insurance or the bond, the family day care home may maintain a file of affidavits signed by each parent with a child enrolled in the home which meets the requirements of this subdivision. The affidavit shall state that the parent has been informed that the family day care home does not carry liability insurance or a bond according to standards established by the state. If the provider does not own the premises used as the family day care home, the affidavit shall also state that the parent has been informed that the liability insurance, if any, of the owner of the property or the homeowners' association, as appropriate, may not provide coverage for losses arising out of, or in connection with, the operation of the family day care home, except to the extent that the losses are caused by, or result from, an action or omission by the owner of the property or the homeowners' association, for which the owner of the property or the homeowners' association would otherwise be liable under the law. These affidavits shall be on a form provided by the department and shall be reviewed at each licensing inspection.

(b) A family day care home that maintains liability insurance or a bond pursuant to this section, and that provides care in premises that are rented or leased or uses premises which share common space governed by a homeowners' association, shall name the owner of the property or the homeowners' association, as appropriate, as an additional insured party on the liability insurance policy or bond if all of the following conditions are met:

(1) The owner of the property or governing body of the homeowners' association makes a written request to be added as an additional insured party.

(2) The addition of the owner of the property or the homeowners' association does not result in cancellation or nonrenewal of the insurance policy or bond carried by the family day care home.

(3) Any additional premium assessed for this coverage is paid by the owner of the property or the homeowners' association.

(c) As used in this section, "homeowners' association" means an association of a common interest development, as defined in Section 1351 of the Civil Code.

Health & Safety Code § 13132.7. Mandatory Fire Retardant Roof Covering Materials In Designated Fire Hazard Zones.

(a) Within a very high fire hazard severity zone designated by the Director of Forestry and Fire Protection pursuant to Article 9 (commencing with Section 4201) of Chapter 1 of Part 2 of Division 4 of the Public Resources Code and within a very high hazard severity zone designated by a local agency pursuant to Chapter 6.8 (commencing with Section 51175) of Part 1 of Division 1 of Title 5 of the Government Code, the entire roof covering of every existing structure where more than 50 percent of the total roof area is replaced within any one-year period, every new structure, and any roof covering applied in the alteration, repair, or replacement of the roof of every existing structure, shall be a fire retardant roof covering that is at least class B as defined in the Uniform Building Code, as adopted and amended by the State Building Standards Commission.

(b) In all other areas, the entire roof covering of every existing structure where more than 50 percent of the total roof area is replaced within any one-year period, every new structure, and any roof covering applied in the alteration, repair, or replacement of the roof of every existing structure, shall be a fire retardant roof covering that is at least class C as defined in the Uniform Building Code, as adopted and amended by the State Building Standards Commission.

(c) Notwithstanding subdivision (b), within state responsibility areas classified by the State Board of Forestry and Fire Protection pursuant to Article 3 (commencing with Section 4125) of Chapter 1 of Part 2 of Division 4 of the Public Resources Code, except for those state responsibility areas designated as moderate fire hazard responsibility zones, the entire roof covering of every existing structure where more than 50 percent of the total roof area is replaced within any one-year period, every new structure, and any roof covering applied in the alteration, repair, or replacement of the roof of every existing structure, shall be a fire retardant roof covering that is at least class B as defined in the Uniform Building Code, as adopted and amended by the State Building Standards Commission.

(d) (1) Notwithstanding subdivision (a), (b), or (c), within very high fire hazard severity zones designated by the Director of Forestry and Fire Protection pursuant to Article 9 (commencing with Section 4201) of Chapter 1 of Part 2 of Division 4 of the Public Resources Code or by a local agency pursuant to Chapter 6.8 (commencing with Section 51175) of Part 1 of Division 1 of Title 5 of the Government Code, the entire roof covering of every existing structure where more than 50 percent of the total roof area is replaced within any one-year period, every new structure, and any roof covering applied in the alteration, repair, or replacement of the roof of every existing structure, shall be a fire retardant roof covering that is at least class A as defined in the Uniform Building Code, as adopted and amended by the State Building Standards Commission.

(2) Paragraph (1) does not apply to any jurisdiction containing a very high fire hazard severity zone if the jurisdiction fulfills both of the following requirements:

(A) Adopts the model ordinance approved by the State Fire Marshal pursuant to Section 51189 of the Government Code or an ordinance that substantially conforms to the model ordinance of the State Fire Marshal.

(B) Transmits, upon adoption, a copy of the ordinance to the State Fire Marshal.

(e) The State Building Standards Commission shall incorporate the requirements set forth in subdivisions (a), (b), and (c) by publishing them as an amendment to the California Building Standards Code in accordance with Chapter 4 (commencing with Section 18935) of Part 2.5 of Division 13.

(f) Nothing in this section shall limit the authority of a city, county, city and county, or fire protection district in establishing more restrictive requirements, in accordance with current law, than those specified in this section.

(g) This section shall not affect the validity of an ordinance, adopted prior to the effective date for the relevant roofing standard specified in subdivisions (a) and (b), by a city, county, city and county, or fire protection district, unless the ordinance mandates a standard that is less stringent than the standards set forth in subdivision (a), in which case the

Civil Rights

ordinance shall not be valid on or after the effective date for the relevant roofing standard specified in subdivisions (a) and (b).

(h) Any qualified historical building or structure as defined in Section 18955 may, on a case-by-case basis, utilize alternative roof constructions as provided by the State Historical Building Code.

(i) The installer of the roof covering shall provide certification of the roof covering classification, as provided by the manufacturer or supplier, to the building owner and, when requested, to the agency responsible for enforcement of this part. The installer shall also install the roof covering in accordance with the manufacturer's listing.

(j) No wood roof covering materials shall be sold or applied in this state unless both of the following conditions are met:

(1) The materials have been approved and listed by the State Fire Marshal as complying with the requirements of this section.

(2) The materials have passed at least five years of the 10-year natural weathering test. The 10-year natural weathering test required by this subdivision shall be conducted in accordance with standard 15-2 of the 1994 edition of the Uniform Building Code at a testing facility recognized by the State Fire Marshal.

(k) The Insurance Commissioner shall accept the use of fire retardant wood roof covering material that complies with the requirements of this section, used in the partial repair or replacement of nonfire retardant wood roof covering material, as complying with the requirement in Section 2695.9 of Title 10 of the California Code of Regulations relative to matching replacement items in quality, color, and size.

(l) No common interest development, as defined in Section 1351 of the Civil Code, may require a homeowner to install or repair a roof in a manner that is in violation of this section. The governing documents, as defined in Section 1351 of the Civil Code, of a common interest development within a very high fire severity zone shall allow for at least one type of fire retardant roof covering material that meets the requirements of this section.

Civ. Code § 712. Real Estate Sales; Prohibitions Of Signs Void; Permissible Displays.

(a) Every provision contained in or otherwise affecting a grant of a fee interest in, or purchase money security instrument upon, real property in this state heretofore or hereafter made, which purports to prohibit or restrict the right of the property owner or his or her agent to display or have displayed on the real property, or on real property owned by others with their consent, or both, signs which are reasonably located, in plain view of the public, are of reasonable dimensions and design, and do not adversely affect public safety, including traffic safety, and which advertise the property for sale, lease, or exchange, or advertise directions to the property, by the property owner or his or her agent is void as an unreasonable restraint upon the power of alienation.

(b) This section shall operate retrospectively, as well as prospectively, to the full extent that it may constitutionally operate retrospectively.

(c) A sign which conforms to the ordinance adopted in conformity with Section 713 shall be deemed to be of reasonable dimension and design pursuant to this section.

Civ. Code § 713. Display Of "For Sale" Signs.

(a) Notwithstanding any provision of any ordinance, an owner of real property or his or her agent may display or have displayed on the owner's real property, and on real property owned by others with their consent, signs which are reasonably located, in plain view of the public, are of reasonable dimensions and design, and do not adversely affect public safety, including traffic safety, as determined by the city, county or city and county, advertising the following:

(1) That the property is for sale, lease or exchange by the owner or his or her agent.

(2) Directions to the property.

(3) The owner's or agent's name.

(4) The owner's or agent's address and telephone number.

(b) Nothing in this section limits any authority which a person or local governmental entity may have to limit or regulate the display or placement of a sign on a private or public right-of-way.

Civ. Code § 714. Voidability Of Covenants Restricting Solar Energy Systems; Application For Approval; Penalties.

(a) Any covenant, restriction, or condition contained in any deed, contract, security instrument, or other instrument affecting the transfer or sale of, or any interest in, real property, and any provision of a governing document, as defined in subdivision (j) of Section 1351, that effectively prohibits or restricts the installation or use of a solar energy system is void and unenforceable.

(b) This section does not apply to provisions that impose reasonable restrictions on solar energy systems. However, it is the policy of the state to promote and encourage the use of solar energy systems and to remove

Civil Rights

obstacles thereto. Accordingly, reasonable restrictions on a solar energy system are those restrictions that do not significantly increase the cost of the system or significantly decrease its efficiency or specified performance, or that allow for an alternative system of comparable cost, efficiency, and energy conservation benefits.

(c)(1) A solar energy system shall meet applicable health and safety standards and requirements imposed by state and local permitting authorities.

(2) A solar energy system for heating water shall be certified by the Solar Rating Certification Corporation (SRCC) or other nationally recognized certification agencies. SRCC is a nonprofit third party supported by the United States Department of Energy. The certification shall be for the entire solar energy system and installation.

(3) A solar energy system for producing electricity shall also meet all applicable safety and performance standards established by the National Electrical Code, the Institute of Electrical and Electronics Engineers, and accredited testing laboratories such as Underwriters Laboratories and, where applicable, rules of the Public Utilities Commission regarding safety and reliability.

(d) For the purposes of this section:

(1) (A) For solar domestic water heating systems or solar swimming pool heating systems that comply with state and federal law, "significantly" means an amount exceeding 20 percent of the cost of the system or decreasing the efficiency of the solar energy system by an amount exceeding 20 percent, as originally specified and proposed.

(B) For photovoltaic systems that comply with state and federal law, "significantly" means an amount not to exceed two thousand dollars ($2,000) over the system cost as originally specified and proposed, or a decrease in system efficiency of an amount exceeding 20 percent as originally specified and proposed.

(2) "Solar energy system" has the same meaning as defined in paragraphs (1) and (2) of subdivision (a) of Section 801.5.

(e) (1) Whenever approval is required for the installation or use of a solar energy system, the application for approval shall be processed and approved by the appropriate approving entity in the same manner as an application for approval of an architectural modification to the property, and shall not be willfully avoided or delayed.

(2) For an approving entity that is a homeowners' association, as defined in subdivision (a) of Section 1351, and that is not a pubic entity,

both of the following shall apply:

(A) The approval or denial of an application shall be in writing.

(B) If an application is not denied in writing within 60 days from the date of receipt of the application, the application shall be deemed approved, unless that delay is the result of a reasonable request for additional information.

(f) Any entity, other than a public entity, that willfully violates this section shall be liable to the applicant or other party for actual damages occasioned thereby, and shall pay a civil penalty to the applicant or other party in an amount not to exceed one thousand dollars ($1,000).

(g) In any action to enforce compliance with this section, the prevailing party shall be awarded reasonable attorney's fees.

(h) (1) A public entity that fails to comply with this section may not receive funds from a state-sponsored grant or loan program for solar energy. A public entity shall certify its compliance with the requirements of this section when applying for funds from a state-sponsored grant or loan program.

(2) A local public entity may not exempt residents in its jurisdiction from the requirements of this section.

Civ. Code § 714.1. Restrictions By Common Interest Development On Installation Of Solar Energy Systems In Common Areas.

Notwithstanding Section 714, any association, as defined in Section 1351, may impose reasonable provisions which:

(a) Restrict the installation of solar energy systems installed in common areas, as defined in Section 1351, to those systems approved by the association.

(b) Require the owner of a separate interest, as defined in Section 1351, to obtain the approval of the association for the installation of a solar energy system in a separate interest owned by another.

(c) Provide for the maintenance, repair, or replacement of roofs or other building components.

(d) Require installers of solar energy systems to indemnify or reimburse the association or its members for loss or damage caused by the installation, maintenance, or use of the solar energy system.

Gov't Code § 434.5. Restrictions On Right To Display U.S. Flag Void.

(a) As used in this section, the following terms have the following meaning:

(1) "Legal right" means the freedom of use and enjoyment

generally exercised by owners and occupiers of land.

(2) "Local government agency" means a county, city, whether general law or chartered, city and county, town, municipal corporation, school district or other district, political subdivision, or any board, commission, or agency thereof, or other local agency.

(b)(1) No person, private entity, or governmental agency shall adopt any rule, regulation, or ordinance, or enter into any agreement or covenant, that prevents any person or private entity that would otherwise have the legal right to display a Flag of the United States on private property from exercising that right, unless it is used as, or in conjunction with, an advertising display.

(2) Nothing in this subdivision shall be construed to prevent a city, county, or city and county from imposing reasonable restrictions as to the time, place, and manner of placement or display of a Flag of the United States when necessary for the preservation of the public's health, safety, or order.

(c) (1) A local government agency may not adopt any policy or regulation that prohibits or restricts an employee of that agency from displaying a Flag of the United States, or a pin of that flag, on his or her person, in his or her workplace, or on a local government agency vehicle operated by that employee.

(2) Nothing in this subdivision shall be construed to prevent a local government agency from imposing reasonable restrictions as to the time, place, and manner of placement or display of a Flag of the United States when necessary for the preservation of the order or discipline of the workplace.

(d) No restrictions solely to promote aesthetic considerations shall be imposed pursuant to paragraph (2) of subdivision (b) or paragraph (2) of subdivision (c).

FEDERAL

4 USCA § 5 Note. (Public Law No. 109-243) "Freedom To Display the American Flag Act of 2005."

(a) This Act may be cited as the "Freedom to Display the American Flag Act of 2005".

(b) For purposes of this Act--

(1) the term "flag of the United States" has the meaning given the term "flag, standard, colors, or ensign" under section 3 of title 4, United States Code;

Civil Rights

(2) the terms "condominium association" and "cooperative association" have the meanings given such terms under section 604 of Public Law 96399 (15 U.S.C. 3603);

(3) the term "residential real estate management association" has the meaning given such term under section 528 of the Internal Revenue Code of 1986 (26 U.S.C. 528); and

(4) the term "member"--

(A) as used with respect to a condominium association, means an owner of a condominium unit (as defined under section 604 of Public Law 96399 (15 U.S.C. 3603)) within such association;

(B) as used with respect to a cooperative association, means a cooperative unit owner (as defined under section 604 of Public Law 96399 (15 U.S.C. 3603)) within such association; and

(C) as used with respect to a residential real estate management association, means an owner of a residential property within a subdivision, development, or similar area subject to any policy or restriction adopted by such association.

(c) A condominium association, cooperative association, or residential real estate management association may not adopt or enforce any policy, or enter into any agreement, that would restrict or prevent a member of the association from displaying the flag of the United States on residential property within the association with respect to which such member has a separate ownership interest or a right to exclusive possession or use.

(d) Nothing in this Act shall be considered to permit any display or use that is inconsistent with--

(1) any provision of chapter 1 of title 4, United States Code, or any rule or custom pertaining to the proper display or use of the flag of the United States (as established pursuant to such chapter or any otherwise applicable provision of law); or

(2) any reasonable restriction pertaining to the time, place, or manner of displaying the flag of the United States necessary to protect a substantial interest of the condominium association, cooperative association, or residential real estate management association.

CHAPTER 10

VEHICLE CODE REGULATIONS
(Vehicle Code §§ 22658,22658.1 & 22853)

Veh. Code § 22658. Vehicle Removal From Private Property.

(a) The owner or person in lawful possession of private property, including an association of a common interest development as defined in Section 1351 of the Civil Code, may cause the removal of a vehicle parked on the property to a storage facility that meets the requirements of subdivision (n) under any of the following circumstances:

(1) There is displayed, in plain view at all entrances to the property, a sign not less than 17 by 22 inches in size, with lettering not less than one inch in height, prohibiting public parking and indicating that vehicles will be removed at the owner's expense, and containing the telephone number of the local traffic law enforcement agency and the name and telephone number of each towing company that is a party to a written general towing authorization agreement with the owner or person in lawful possession of the property. The sign may also indicate that a citation may also be issued for the violation.

(2) The vehicle has been issued a notice of parking violation, and 96 hours have elapsed since the issuance of that notice.

(3) The vehicle is on private property and lacks an engine, transmission, wheels, tires, doors, windshield, or any other major part or equipment necessary to operate safely on the highways, the owner or person in lawful possession of the private property has notified the local traffic law enforcement agency, and 24 hours have elapsed since that notification.

(4) The lot or parcel upon which the vehicle is parked is improved with a single-family dwelling.

(b) The tow truck operator removing the vehicle, if the operator knows or is able to ascertain from the property owner, person in lawful possession of the property, or the registration records of the Department of Motor Vehicles the name and address of the registered and legal owner of the vehicle, shall immediately give, or cause to be given, notice in writing to the registered and legal owner of the fact of the removal, the grounds for the removal, and indicate the place to which the vehicle has been removed. If the vehicle is stored in a storage facility, a copy of the notice shall be given to the proprietor of the storage facility. The notice provided for in this section shall include the amount of mileage on the vehicle at the time of removal and the time of the removal from the property. If the tow truck operator does not know and is not able to ascertain the name of the owner or for any other reason is unable to give the notice to the owner as provided in this section, the tow truck operator shall comply with the requirements of subdivision (c) of Section 22853 relating to notice in the same manner as applicable to an officer removing a vehicle from private property.

(c) This section does not limit or affect any right or remedy that the owner or person in lawful possession of private property may have by virtue of other provisions of law authorizing the removal of a vehicle parked upon private property.

(d) The owner of a vehicle removed from private property pursuant to subdivision (a) may recover for any damage to the vehicle resulting from any intentional or negligent act of a person causing the removal of, or removing, the vehicle.

(e) (1)   Any owner or person in lawful possession of private property, or an association of a common interest development, causing the removal of a vehicle parked on that property is liable for double the storage or towing charges whenever there has been a failure to comply with paragraph (1), (2), or (3) of subdivision (a) or to state the grounds for the removal of the vehicle if requested by the legal or registered owner of the vehicle as required by subdivision (f).

(2) A property owner or owner's agent or lessee who causes the removal of a vehicle parked on that property pursuant to the exemption set forth in subparagraph (A) of paragraph (1) of subdivision (1) and fails to comply with that subdivision is guilty of an infraction, punishable by a fine of one thousand dollars ($1,000).

(f) An owner or person in lawful possession of any private property, or an association of a common interest development, causing the removal of a vehicle parked on that property shall notify by telephone or, if impractical, by the most expeditious means available, the local traffic law enforcement agency within one hour after authorizing the tow. An owner or person in lawful possession of private property, an association of a common interest development, causing the removal of a vehicle parked on that property, or the tow truck operator who removes the vehicle, shall state the grounds for the removal of the vehicle if requested by the legal or registered owner of that vehicle. A towing company that removes a vehicle from private property in compliance with subdivision (1) is not responsible in a situation relating to the validity of the removal. A towing company that removes the vehicle under this section shall be responsible for the following:

(1) Damage to the vehicle in the transit and subsequent storage of the vehicle.

(2) The removal of a vehicle other than the vehicle specified by the owner or other person in lawful possession of the private property.

(g) (1) (A) Possession of a vehicle under this section shall be deemed to arise when a vehicle is removed from private property and is in transit.

(B) Upon the request of the owner of the vehicle or that owner's agent, the towing company or its driver shall immediately and unconditionally release a vehicle that is not yet removed from the private property and in transit.

(C) A person failing to comply with subparagraph (B) is guilty of a misdemeanor.

(2) If a vehicle is released to a person in compliance with subparagraph (B) of paragraph (1), the vehicle owner or authorized agent shall immediately move that vehicle to a lawful location.

(h) A towing company may impose a charge of not more than one-half of the regular towing charge for the towing of a vehicle at the request of the owner, the owner's agent, or the person in lawful possession of the private property pursuant to this section if the owner of the vehicle or the vehicle owner's agent returns to the vehicle after the vehicle is coupled to the tow truck by means of a regular hitch, coupling device, drawbar, portable dolly, or is lifted off the ground by means of a conventional trailer, and before it is removed from the private property. The regular towing charge may only be imposed after the vehicle has been removed from the property and is in transit.

(i) (1) (A) A charge for towing or storage, or both, of a vehicle under this section is excessive if the charge exceeds the greater of the following:

(i) That which would have been charged for that towing or storage, or both, made at the request of a law enforcement agency under an agreement between a towing company and the law enforcement agency that exercises primary jurisdiction in the city in which is located the private property from which the vehicle was, or was attempted to be, removed, or if the private property is not located within a city, then the law enforcement agency that exercises primary jurisdiction in the county in which the private property is located.

(ii) That which would have been charged for that towing or

storage, or both, under the rate approved for that towing operator by the California Highway Patrol for the jurisdiction in which the private property is located and from which the vehicle was, or was attempted to be, removed.

(B) A towing operator shall make available for inspection and copying his or her rate approved by the California Highway Patrol, if any, with in 24 hours of a request without a warrant to law enforcement, the Attorney General, district attorney, or city attorney.

(2) If a vehicle is released within 24 hours from the time the vehicle is brought into the storage facility, regardless of the calendar date, the storage charge shall be for only one day. Not more than one day's storage charge may be required for any vehicle released the same day that it is stored.

(3) If a request to release a vehicle is made and the appropriate fees are tendered and documentation establishing that the person requesting release is entitled to possession of the vehicle, or is the owner's insurance representative, is presented within the initial 24 hours of storage, and the storage facility fails to comply with the request to release the vehicle or is not open for business during normal business hours, then only one day's storage charge may be required to be paid until after the first business day. A business day is any day in which the lienholder is open for business to the public for at least eight hours. If a request is made more than 24 hours after the vehicle is placed in storage, charges may be imposed on a full calendar day basis for each day, or part thereof, that the vehicle is in storage.

(j) (1) Any person who charges a vehicle owner a towing, service, or storage charge at an excessive rate, as described in subdivision (h) or (i), is civilly liable to the vehicle owner for four times the amount charged.

(2) A person who knowingly charges a vehicle owner a towing, service, or storage charge at an excessive rate, as described in subdivision (h) or (i), or who fails to make available his or her rate as required in subparagraph (B) of paragraph (1) of subdivision (i), is guilty of a misdemeanor, punishable by a fine of not more than two thousand five hundred dollars ($2,500), or by imprisonment in the county jail for not more than three months, or by both that fine and imprisonment.

(k) (1) A person operating or in charge of a storage facility where vehicles are stored pursuant to this section shall accept a valid credit card or cash for payment of towing and storage by a registered owner, the legal owner, or the owner's agent claiming the vehicle. A credit card shall be in the name of the person presenting the card. "Credit card" means "credit card" as defined in subdivision (a) of Section 1747.02 of the Civil Code, except for the purposes of this section, credit card does not include a credit card issued by a retail seller.

(2) A person described in paragraph (1) shall conspicuously display, in that portion of the storage facility office where business is conducted with the public, a notice advising that all valid credit cards and cash are acceptable means of payment.

(3) A person operating or in charge of a storage facility who refuses to accept a valid credit card or who fails to post the required notice under paragraph (2) is guilty of a misdemeanor, punishable by a fine of not more than two thousand five hundred dollars ($2,500), or by imprisonment in the county jail for not more than three months, or by both that fine and imprisonment.

(4) A person described in paragraph (1) who violates paragraph (1) or (2) is civilly liable to the registered owner of the vehicle or the person who tendered the fees for four times the amount of the towing and storage charges.

(5) A person operating or in charge of the storage facility shall have sufficient moneys on the premises of the primary storage facility during normal business hours to accommodate, and make change in, a reasonable monetary transaction.

(6) Credit charges for towing and storage services shall comply with Section 1748.1 of the Civil Code. Law enforcement agencies may include the costs of providing for payment by credit when making agreements with towing companies as described in subdivision (i).

(1) (1) (A) A towing company shall not remove or commence the removal of a vehicle from private property without first obtaining written authorization from the property owner or lessee, including an association of a common interest development, or an employee or agent thereof, who shall be present at the time of removal and verify the alleged violation, except that presence and verification is not required if the person authorizing the tow is the property owner, or the owner's agent who is not a tow operator, of a residential rental property of 15 or fewer units that does not have an onsite owner, owner's agent or employee, and the tenant has verified the violation, requested the tow from that tenant's assigned parking space, and provided a signed request or electronic mail, or has called and provides a signed request or electronic mail within 24 hours, to the property owner or owner's agent, which the owner or agent shall provide to the towing company within 48 hours of authorizing the tow. The signed request or electronic mail shall contain the name and address of the tenant, and the date and time the tenant requested the tow. A towing company shall obtain within 48 hours of receiving the written authorization to tow a copy of a tenant request required pursuant to this subparagraph. For the purpose of this subparagraph, a person providing the written authorization who is required to be present on the private property at the time of the tow does not have to be physically present at the specified location of where the vehicle to be removed is located on the private property.

(B) The written authorization under subparagraph (A) shall include all of the following:

(i) The make, model, vehicle identification number, and license plate number of the removed vehicle.

(ii) The name, signature, job title, residential or business address and working telephone number of the person, described in subparagraph (A), authorizing the removal of the vehicle.

(iii) The grounds for the removal of the vehicle.

(iv) The time when the vehicle was first observed parked at the private property.

(v) The time that authorization to tow the vehicle was given.

(C) (i) When the vehicle owner or his or her agent claims the vehicle, the towing company prior to payment of a towing or storage charge shall provide a photocopy of the written authorization to the vehicle owner or the agent.

(ii) If the vehicle was towed from a residential property, the towing company shall redact the information specified in clause (ii) of subparagraph (B) in the photocopy of the written authorization provided to the vehicle owner or the agent pursuant to clause (i).

(iii) The towing company shall also provide to the vehicle owner or the agent a separate notice that provides the telephone number of the appropriate local law enforcement or prosecuting agency by stating "If you believe that you have been wrongfully towed, please contact the local law enforcement or prosecuting agency at (insert appropriate telephone number)." The notice shall be in English and in the most populous language, other than English, that is spoken in the jurisdiction.

(D) A towing company shall not remove or commence the removal of a vehicle from private property described in subdivision (a) of Section 22953 unless the towing company has made a good faith inquiry to determine that the owner or the property owner's agent complied with Section 22953.

(E) (i)   General authorization to remove or commence removal of a vehicle at the towing company's discretion shall not be delegated to a towing company or its affiliates except in the case of a vehicle unlawfully parked within 15 feet of a fire hydrant or in a fire lane, or in a manner which interferes with an entrance to, or exit from, the private property.

(ii)   In those cases in which general authorization is granted to a towing company or its affiliate to undertake the removal or commence the removal of a vehicle that is unlawfully parked within 15 feet of a fire hydrant or in a fire lane, or that interferes with an entrance to, or exit from, private property, the towing company and the property owner, or owner's agent, or person in lawful possession of the private property shall have a written agreement granting that general authorization.

(2)   If a towing company removes a vehicle under a general authorization described in subparagraph (E) of paragraph (1) and that vehicle is unlawfully parked within 15 feet of a fire hydrant or in a fire lane, or in a manner that interferes with an entrance to, or exit from, the private property, the towing company shall take, prior to the removal of that vehicle, a photograph of the vehicle that clearly indicates that parking violation. Prior to accepting payment, the towing company shall keep one copy of the photograph taken pursuant to this paragraph, and shall present that photograph and provide, without charge, a photocopy to the owner or an agent of the owner, when that person claims the vehicle.

(3)   A towing company shall maintain the original written authorization, or the general authorization described in subparagraph (E) of paragraph (1) and the photograph of the violation, required pursuant to this section, and any written requests from a tenant to the property owner or owner's agent required by subparagraph (A) of paragraph (1), for a period of three years and shall make them available for inspection and copying within 24 hours of a request without a warrant to law enforcement, the Attorney General, district attorney, or city attorney.

(4)   A person who violates this subdivision is guilty of a misdemeanor, punishable by a fine of not more than two thousand five hundred dollars ($2,500), or by imprisonment in the county jail for not more than three months, or by both that fine and imprisonment.

(5)   A person who violates this subdivision is civilly liable to the owner of the vehicle or his or her agent for four times the amount of the towing and storage charges.

(m) (1)   A towing company that removes a vehicle from private property under this section shall notify the local law enforcement agency of that tow after the vehicle is removed from the private property and is in transit.

(2) A towing company is guilty of a misdemeanor if the towing company fails to provide the notification required under paragraph (1) within 60 minutes after the vehicle is removed from the private property and is in transit or 15 minutes after arriving at the storage facility, whichever time is less.

(3) A towing company that does not provide the notification under paragraph (1) within 30 minutes after the vehicle is removed from the private property and is in transit is civilly liable to the registered owner of the vehicle, or the person who tenders the fees, for three times the amount of the towing and storage charges.

(4) If notification is impracticable, the times for notification, as required pursuant to paragraphs (2) and (3), shall be tolled for the time period that notification is impracticable. This paragraph is an affirmative defense.

(n) A vehicle removed from private property pursuant to this section shall be stored in a facility that meets all of the following requirements:

(1) (A) Is located within a 10-mile radius of the property from where the vehicle was removed.

(B) The 10-mile radius requirement of subparagraph (A) does not apply if a towing company has prior general written approval from the law enforcement agency that exercises primary jurisdiction in the city in which is located the private property from which the vehicle was removed, or if the private property is not located within a city, then the law enforcement agency that exercises primary jurisdiction in the county in which is located the private property.

(2) (A) Remains open during normal business hours and releases vehicles after normal business hours.

(B) A gate fee may be charged for releasing a vehicle after normal business hours, weekends, and state holidays. However, the maximum hourly charge for releasing a vehicle after normal business hours shall be one-half of the hourly tow rate charged for initially towing the vehicle, or less.

(C) Notwithstanding any other provision of law and for purposes of this paragraph, "normal business hours" are Monday to Friday, inclusive, from 8 a.m. to 5 p.m., inclusive, except state holidays.

(3) Has a public pay telephone in the office area that is open and accessible to the public.

(o) (1) It is the intent of the Legislature in the adoption of subdivision (k) to assist vehicle owners or their agents by, among other things, allowing payment by credit cards for towing and storage services, thereby expediting the recovery of towed vehicles and concurrently promoting the safety and welfare of the public.

(2) It is the intent of the Legislature in the adoption of subdivision (l) to further the safety of the general public by ensuring that a private property owner or lessee has provided his or her authorization for the removal of a vehicle from his or her property, thereby promoting the safety of those persons involved in ordering the removal of the vehicle as well as those persons removing, towing, and storing the vehicle.

(3) It is the intent of the Legislature in the adoption of subdivision (g) to promote the safety of the general public by requiring towing companies to unconditionally release a vehicle that is not lawfully in their possession, thereby avoiding the likelihood of dangerous and violent confrontation and physical injury to vehicle owners and towing operators, the stranding of vehicle owners and their passengers at a dangerous time and location, and impeding expedited vehicle recovery, without wasting law enforcement's limited resources.

(p) The remedies, sanctions, restrictions, and procedures provided in this section are not exclusive and are in addition to other remedies, sanctions, restrictions, or procedures that may be provided in other provisions of law, including, but not limited to, those that are provided in Sections 12110 and 34660.

(q) A vehicle removed and stored pursuant to this section shall be released by the law enforcement agency, impounding agency, or person in possession of the vehicle, or any person acting on behalf of them, to the legal owner or the legal owner's agent upon presentation of the assignment, as defined in subdivision (b) of Section 7500.1 of the Business and Professions Code; a release from the one responsible governmental agency, only if required by the agency; a government-issued photographic identification card; and any one of the following as determined by the legal owner or the legal owner's agent: a certificate of repossession for the vehicle, a security agreement for the vehicle, or title, whether paper or electronic, showing proof of legal ownership for the vehicle. Any documents presented may be originals, photocopies, or facsimile copies, or may be transmitted electronically. The storage facility shall not require any documents to be notarized. The storage facility may require the agent of the legal owner to produce a photocopy or facsimile copy of its repossession agency license or registration issued pursuant to Chapter

11 (commencing with Section 7500) of Division 3 of the Business and Professions Code, or to demonstrate, to the satisfaction of the storage facility, that the agent is exempt from licensure pursuant to Section 7500.2 or 7500.3 of the Business and Professions Code.

Veh. Code § 22658.1. Damage To Fence While Removing Vehicle; Location And Notification Of Property Owner By Towing Company.

(a) Any towing company that, in removing a vehicle, cuts, removes, otherwise damages, or leaves open a fence without the prior approval of the property owner or the person in charge of the property shall then and there do either of the following:

(1) Locate and notify the owner or person in charge of the property of the damage or open condition of the fence, the name and address of the towing company, and the license, registration, or identification number of the vehicle being removed.

(2) Leave in a conspicuous place on the property the name and address of the towing company, and the license, registration, or identification number of the vehicle being removed, and shall without unnecessary delay, notify the police department of the city in which the property is located, or if the property is located in unincorporated territory, either the sheriff or the local headquarters of the Department of the California Highway Patrol, of that information and the location of the damaged or opened fence.

(b) Any person failing to comply with all the requirements of this section is guilty of an infraction.

Veh. Code § 22853. Notice To Department Of Justice And Proprietor Of Storage Garage; Reports; Notice To Owner.

(a) Whenever an officer or an employee removing a California registered vehicle from a highway or from public property for storage under this chapter does not know and is not able to ascertain the name of the owner or for any other reason is unable to give notice to the owner as required by Section 22852, the officer or employee shall immediately notify, or cause to be notified the Department of Justice, Stolen Vehicle System, of its removal. The officer or employee shall file a notice with the proprietor of any public garage in which the vehicle may be stored. The notice shall include a complete description of the vehicle, the date, time, and place from which removed, the amount of mileage on the vehicle at the time of removal, and the name of the garage or place where the vehicle is stored.

Vehicle

(b) Whenever an officer or an employee removing a vehicle not registered in California from a highway or from public property for storage under this chapter does not know and is not able to ascertain the owner or for any other reason is unable to give the notice to the owner as required by Section 22852, the officer or employee shall immediately notify, or cause to be notified, the Department of Justice, Stolen Vehicle System. If the vehicle is not returned to the owner within 120 hours, the officer or employee shall immediately send, or cause to be sent, a written report of the removal by mail to the Department of Justice at Sacramento and shall file a copy of the notice with the proprietor of any public garage in which the vehicle may be stored. The report shall be made on a form furnished by that department and shall include a complete description of the vehicle, the date, time, and place from which the vehicle was removed, the amount of mileage on the vehicle at the time of removal, the grounds for removal, and the name of the garage or place where the vehicle is stored.

(c) Whenever an officer or employee or private party removing a vehicle from private property for storage under this chapter does not know and is not able to ascertain the owner or for any other reason is unable to give the notice to the owner as required by Section 22852 and if the vehicle is not returned to the owner within a period of 120 hours, the officer or employee or private party shall immediately send, or cause to be sent, a written report of the removal by mail to the Department of Justice at Sacramento and shall file a copy of the notice with the proprietor of any public garage in which the vehicle may be stored. The report shall be made on a form furnished by that department and shall include a complete description of the vehicle, the date, time, and place from which the vehicle was removed, the amount of mileage on the vehicle at the time of removal, the grounds for removal, and the name of the garage or place where the vehicle is stored.

Vehicle

CHAPTER 11

MANAGER CERTIFICATION
(Business & Professions Code §§ 11500-11506)

Bus. & Prof. Code § 11500. Definitions.

For purposes of this chapter, the following definitions apply:

(a) "Common interest development" means a residential development identified in subdivision (c) of Section 1351 of the Civil Code.

(b) "Association" has the same meaning as defined in subdivision (a) of Section 1351 of the Civil Code.

(c) "Financial services" means acts performed or offered to be performed, for compensation, for an association, including, but not limited to, the preparation of internal unaudited financial statements, internal accounting and bookkeeping functions, billing of assessments, and related services.

(d) "Management services" means acts performed or offered to be performed in an advisory capacity for an association including, but not limited to, the following:

(1) Administering or supervising the collection, reporting, and archiving of the financial or common area assets of an association or common interest development, at the direction of the association's board of directors.

(2) Implementing resolutions and directives of the board of directors of the association elected to oversee the operation of a common interest development.

(3) Implementing provisions of governing documents, as defined in Section 1351 of the Civil Code, that govern the operation of the common interest development.

(4) Administering association contracts, including insurance contracts, within the scope of the association's duties or with other common interest development managers, vendors, contractors, and other third-party providers of goods and services to an association or common interest development.

(e) "Professional association for common interest development managers" means an organization that meets all of the following:

(1) Has at least 200 members or certificants who are common interest development managers in California.

(2) Has been in existence for at least five years.

(3) Operates pursuant to Section 501(c) of the Internal Revenue Code.

(4) Certifies that a common interest development manager has met the criteria set forth in Section 11502 without requiring membership in the association.

(5) Requires adherence to a code of professional ethics and standards of practice for certified common interest development managers.

Bus. & Prof. Code § 11501. "Common Interest Development Manager."

(a) "Common interest development manager" means an individual who for compensation, or in expectation of compensation, provides or contracts to provide management or financial services, or represents himself or herself to act in the capacity of providing management or financial services to an association. Notwithstanding any other provision of law, an individual may not be required to obtain a real estate or broker's license in order to perform the services of a common interest development manager to an association.

(b) "Common interest development manager" also means any of the following:

(1) An individual who is a partner in a partnership, a shareholder or officer in a corporation, or who, in any other business entity acts in a capacity to advise, supervise, and direct the activity of a registrant or provisional registrant, or who acts as a principal on behalf of a company that provides the services of a common interest development manager.

(2) An individual operating under a fictitious business name who provides the services of a common interest development manager.

This section may not be construed to require an association to hire for compensation a common interest development manager, unless required to do so by its governing documents. Nothing in this part shall be construed to supersede any law that requires a license, permit, or any other form of registration, to provide management or financial services. Nothing in this section shall preclude a licensee of the California Board of Accountancy from providing financial services to an association within the scope of his or her license in addition to the preparation of reviewed and audited financial statements and the preparation of the association's tax returns.

Bus. & Prof. Code § 11502. "Certified Common Interest Development Manager."

In order to be called a "certified common interest development manager," a person shall meet one of the following requirements:

(a) Prior to July 1, 2003, has passed a knowledge, skills, and aptitude examination as specified in Section 11502.5 or has been granted a certification or a designation by a professional association for common interest development managers, and who has, within five years prior to July 1, 2004, received instruction in California law pursuant to paragraph (1) of subdivision (b).

(b) On or after July 1, 2003, has successfully completed an educational curriculum that shall be no less than a combined 30 hours in coursework described in this subdivision and passed an examination or examinations that test competence in common interest development management in the following areas:

(1) The law that relates to the management of common interest developments, including, but not limited to, the following courses of study:

(A) Topics covered by the Davis-Stirling Common Interest Development Act, contained in Title 6 (commencing with Section 1350) or Part 4 of Division 2 of the Civil Code, including, but not limited to, the types of California common interest developments, disclosure requirements pertaining to common interest developments, meeting requirements, financial reporting requirements, and member access to association records.

(B) Personnel issues, including, but not limited to, general matters related to independent contractor or employee status, the laws on harassment, the Unruh Civil Rights Act, the California Fair Employment and Housing Act, and the Americans with Disabilities Act.

(C) Risk management, including, but not limited to, insurance coverage, maintenance, operations and emergency preparedness.

(D) Property protection for associations, including, but not limited to, pertinent matters relating to environmental hazardous such as asbestos, radon gas, and lead-based paint, the Vehicle Code, local and municipal regulations, family day care facilities, energy conservation, Federal Communications Commission rules and regulations, and solar energy systems.

(E) The business affairs of associations, including, but not limited to, necessary compliance with federal, state, and local law.

(F) Basic understanding of governing documents, codes, and regulations relating to the activities and affairs of associations and common interest developments.

(2) Instruction in general management that is related to the managerial and business skills needed for management of a common interest development, including, but not limited to, the following:

(A) Finance issues, including, but not limited to, budget preparation; management; administration or supervision of collection, reporting, and archiving of the financial or common area assets of an association or common interest development; bankruptcy laws; and assessment collection.

(B) Contract negotiation and administration.

(C) Supervision of employees and staff.

(D) Management of maintenance programs.

(E) Management and administration of rules, regulations, parliamentary procedures.

(F) Management and administration of architectural standards.

(G) Management and administration of the association's recreational programs and facilities.

(H) Management and administration of owner and resident communications.

(I) Training and strategic planning for the association's board of directors and its committees.

(J) Implementation of association policies and procedures.

(K) Ethics, professional conduct, and standards of practice for common interest development managers.

(L) Current issues relating to common interest developments.

(M) Conflict avoidance and resolution mechanisms.

Bus. & Prof. Code § 11502.5. Competency Examinations.

The course related competency examination or examinations and education provided to a certified common interest development manager pursuant to Section 11502 by any professional association for common interest development managers, or any postsecondary educational institution, shall be developed and administered in a manner consistent with standards and requirements set forth by the American Educational Research Association's "Standards for Educational and Psychological Testing," and the Equal Employment Opportunity Commission's "Uniform

Guidelines for Employee Selection Procedures," the Civil Rights Act, the California Fair Employment and Housing Act, and the Americans with Disabilities Act of 1990, or the course or courses that have been approved as a continuing education course or an equivalent course of study pursuant to the regulations of the Real Estate Commissioner.

Bus. & Prof. Code § 11503. Exception.

A "certified common interest development manager" does not include a common interest development management firm.

Bus. & Prof. Code § 11504. Disclosures.

On or before September 1, 2003, and annually thereafter, a person who either provides or contemplates providing the services of a common interest development manager to an association shall disclose to the board of directors of the association the following information:

(a) Whether or not the common interest development manager has met the requirements of Section 11502 so he or she may be called a certified common interest development manager.

(b) The name, address, and telephone number of the professional association that certified the common interest development manager, the date the manager was certified, and the status of the certification.

(c) The location of his or her primary office.

(d) Prior to entering into or renewing a contract with a community association, the common interest development manager shall disclose to the governing board of the community association whether the fidelity insurance of the community manager or his or her employer covers the current year's operating and reserve funds of the association. This requirement may not be construed to compel an association to require a common interest development manager to obtain or maintain fidelity insurance.

(e) Whether the common interest development manager possesses an active real estate license.

This section may not preclude a common interest development manager from disclosing information as required in Section 1363.1 of the Civil Code.

Bus. & Prof. Code § 11505. Unfair Business Practice.

It is an unfair business practice for a common interest development manager, a company that employs the common interest development manager, or a company that is controlled by a company that also has a financial interest in a company employing that manager, to do any of the following:

(a) On or after July 1, 2003, to hold oneself out or use the title of "certified common interest development manager" or any other term that implies or suggests that the person is certified as a common interest development manager without meeting the requirements of Section 11502.

(b) To state or advertise that he or she is certified, registered, or licensed by a governmental agency to perform the functions of a certified common interest development manager.

(c) To state or advertise a registration or license number, unless the license or registration is specified by a statute, regulation, or ordinance.

(d) To fail to comply with any item to be disclosed in Section 11504 of this code, or Section 1363.1 of the Civil Code.

Bus. & Prof. Code § 11506. Expiration.

This part shall be subject to the review required by Division 1.2 (commencing with Section 473). *This part shall remain in effect only until January 1, 2015, and as of that date is repealed, unless a later enacted statute, that is enacted before January 1, 2015, deletes or extends that date.*

CHAPTER 12

SIGNIFICANT JUDICIAL DECISIONS AFFECTING COMMON INTEREST DEVELOPMENTS
(Cases decided within the past year are shown in bold print.)

Published court decisions play an important role in the American legal system by providing precedent upon which courts in the future may rely in deciding similar disputes. They also provide guidance to the public on how citizens should conduct themselves in order to comply with the law. Virtually all published decisions come from appellate courts. In California the appellate courts are the Courts of Appeal at the intermediate appellate level and the Supreme Court at the top level. Below the appellate courts are the trial courts. They rarely publish decisions.

To appreciate the significance of a particular judicial decision it is helpful to understand the basic structure of the judicial system. There are two independent judicial systems in the United States that operate concurrently- the state court system and the federal court system. State courts generally handle matters of local concern, such as individual rights and property rights of state citizens. State court decisions comprise the vast majority of those involving common interest developments. Federal courts are generally concerned with enforcement of federal laws, such as federal constitutional rights, federal housing laws, bankruptcy, federal income taxation and disputes between citizens of different states. Federal courts sometimes touch upon matters involving common interest developments. Appellate courts in both systems review trial court decisions based upon evidence that is preserved in a judicial record. The trial court decision may be appealed if the trial court's decision is in dispute. Ultimately, the final decision making authority is a supreme court in both state and federal systems. The higher the court the higher the precedential value of a decision.

In alphabetical order by court, this chapter contains overviews of the most significant judicial decisions of the last 30 years concerning the operation and administration of common interest developments in California.

CALIFORNIA SUPREME COURT

Aas v. Superior Court (2001) 24 Cal.4th 627; 101 Cal.Rptr.2d 718 (subject: construction defect litigation). A homeowners' association may not recover in tort (e.g., negligence, strict liability, etc.) for construction defects that have not yet resulted in property damage. The remedy for non-damage related defects lies in theories of breach of contract and breach of express and implied warranty.

Citizens For Covenant Compliance v. Anderson (1995) 12 Cal.4th 345, 47 Cal.Rptr.2d 898 (subject: CC&R enforcement). A CC&R restriction may be enforced even though neither the restriction nor the CC&Rs are referenced in a deed if the CC&R restriction appears as a matter of record in the public record at the time of purchase. Prior to this decision CC&R restrictions could not be enforced if they were not referenced in a deed or other document conveying title. This rule was made retroactive so that it applies to all past and future transfers.

Erlich v. Menezes (1999) 21 Cal.4th 543, 87 Cal.Rptr.2d 886 (subject: construction defect). A homeowner cannot recover emotional distress damages for defective construction of a home, regardless of whether the theory of recovery is breach of contract or negligence. California does not allow recovery for emotional distress arising solely out of property damage.

Foxgate Homeowners Assn. v. Bramalea California , Inc. (2001) 26 Cal.4th 1, 92 Cal.Rptr.2d 916 (subject: admissibility of evidence developed during mediation). No evidence of communications made during a mediation may be admitted or considered in a subsequent judicial proceeding absent an express statutory exception.

Golden Gateway Center v. Golden Gateway Tenants Asn. (2001) 26 Cal.4th 1013, 111 Cal.Rptr.2d 336 (subject: right to distribute literature in privately owned apartment complex). The free speech clause of the California Constitution does not prevent the owner of an apartment complex from prohibiting the distribution of literature by a tenant's group on those portions of the premises not open to the general public. California's free speech clause applies only if the property is freely and openly accessible to the public. This case is applicable in the closely analogous situation of a private common interest development.

Haggis v. City of Los Angeles (2000) 22 Cal.4th 490, 93 Cal.Rptr.2d 327 (subject: construction defect litigation). A municipality is immune from liability for failure to perform discretionary acts in the investigation and evaluation of conditions at a proposed building project which later cause damage to a residential structure.

Jiminez v. Superior Court (2002) 29 Cal.4th 473, 127 Cal.Rptr.2d 614 (subject: construction defect litigation). Manufacturers of component parts that are installed in mass-produced homes can be subject to strict liability in tort when their products cause harm. The plaintiffs were allowed to recover in tort for damage that defective windows caused to other parts of the homes.

Lamden v. La Jolla Shores Clubdominium Association (1999) 21 Cal.4th 249, 87 Cal.Rptr.2d 237 (subject: CC&R enforcement). A court will defer to a board's authority and presumed expertise in discretionary decisions regarding the maintenance and repair of a common interest development, provided that the decisions are based upon reasonable investigation, made in good faith and with regard to the best interest of the association, and are within the scope of authority given to the board under the relevant statutes and CC&Rs.

Lantzy v. Centrex Homes (2003) 31 Cal.4th 363, 2 Cal.Rptr.3d 655 (subject: construction defect litigation). In an action brought by homeowners against a developer alleging latent defects, equitable tolling did not apply to the 10-year statute of limitations set forth in Code Civ. Proc. § 337.15 while the developer's promises or attempts to repair the defect were pending. However, equitable estoppel may suspend the 10-year statute of limitations.

Montrose Chemical Corp. v. Admiral Insurance Co. (1995) 10 Cal.4th 645, 42 Cal.Rptr.2d 324 (subject: liability insurance coverage for property damage). All general liability insurance policies in force during a continuous or progressive loss to property over a period of time spanning several policy periods are available to provide coverage for the loss. The fact that the loss is known during an earlier policy period does not eliminate coverage. All such policies are available to provide coverage to the insured. This rule applies only to third party liability coverage. It does not apply to first party property damage coverage. See *Larkspur Isle Condominium Owners Assn. v. Farmers Insurance Group (1994) 31 Cal.*

App.4th 106, 37 Cal.Rptr.2d 3.

Nahrstedt v. Lakeside Village Condominium Assn. (1994) 8 Cal.4th 361, 33 Cal.Rptr.2d 63 (subject: CC&R enforcement). CC&R restrictions, including pet restrictions, are presumed reasonable and will be enforced uniformly against all association members unless the restrictions are arbitrary, impose burdens on the property that substantially outweigh the restriction's benefits to the development's residents or violate a fundamental public policy.

Pollard v. Saxe & Yolles Dev. Co. (1974) 12 Cal.3d 374, 115 Cal. Rptr. 648 (subject: construction defect litigation). An association can sue a builder/developer for construction defects under the theory of breach of implied warranty when residential buildings are not reasonably fit for their intended purpose.

Regents of the Univ. of Cal. v. Hartford Acc. & Indem. Co. (1978) 21 Cal.3d 624, 147 Cal.Rptr. 486 (subject: construction defect litigation). An action for latent construction defects is subject to a two-step statute of limitations analysis. The action must be filed within three or four years of discovery of the defective condition(s), depending on whether the action rests on negligent injury to the property (Civ. Proc. § 338) or on breach of warranty (Civ. Proc. § 337). But in either case, the action must be filed within ten years of the date of substantial completion of the development or it will be time barred (Civ. Proc. § 337.15).

Riley v. Bear Creek Planning Commission (1976) 17 Cal.3d 500, 131 Cal.Rptr. 381 (subject: CC&R enforcement). A deed restriction contained in every deed in a restricted subdivision as a part of a general plan of common restrictions may be enforced against all owners even without a recorded set of CC&Rs.

Villa De Las Palmas Homeowners Association v. Terifaj (2004) 33 Cal.4th 73, 14 Cal.Rptr.3d 67, (subject: CC&R enforcement). A use restriction duly adopted by an amendment to the CC&Rs after an owner acquires his unit is enforceable against that owner through an injunctive relief action, even though the owner disagrees with the amendment. Subsequently adopted use restrictions, like the original CC&R provisions, are presumptively valid and the burden of proving otherwise rests on the challenging owner. The association is entitled to recover its attorney fees and court costs as the prevailing party in a successful action to enforce a subsequent amendment.

Walnut Creek Manor v. Fair Employment and Housing Commission (1991) 54 Cal.3d 245, 284 Cal.Rptr. 718 (subject: housing discrimination). The California Fair Employment and Housing Act (FEHA) (Government Code §§ 12900 et seq.) authorizes the Fair Employment Commission to award compensatory damages for out-of-pocket expenses but not for emotional distress. It may award a maximum of $1,000 for a single "course of discriminatory conduct against the same individual on the same unlawful basis." The commission is not authorized to impose multiple, cumulative penalties based upon a single course of conduct.

Warfield v. Peninsula Golf & Country Club (1995) 10 Cal.4th 594, 42 Cal.Rptr.2d 50 (subject: discrimination). A private social club engaged in incidental income producing activities is a "business establishment" under the Unruh Civil Rights Act (California Civil Code §§ 51-53) which prohibits discrimination on the basis of "sex, race, color, religion, ancestry, national origin, or disability" in all business establishments. The act extends to private nonprofit organizations that engage in minimal business activity. The penalties include treble actual damages and attorney fees. This case probably applies to community associations.

Woodland Hills Residents Assn. v. City Council (1979) 23 Cal.3d 917, 154 Cal.Rptr. 503 (subject: association litigation). Code of Civil Procedure §1021.5, authorizing an award of attorney fees under the private attorney general doctrine, applies to an action by a residential association that successfully challenges a city's improper approval of a subdivision map for an adjoining parcel.

CALIFORNIA COURT OF APPEAL

1231 Euclid Homeowners Association v. State Farm Fire & Casualty Co. (2006) 135 Cal.App.4th 1008; 37 Cal.Rptr.3d 795 (subject: association insurance coverage). A homeowners' association's voluntary withdrawal of an insurance claim for property damage after the damage was inspected by both the association and the insurance carrier and believe to be below the policy deductible operates as final resolution of the claim even if further damage is later discovered after the claim period has expired. Notably the claim was not reasserted for nearly 8 years.

A & B Painting & Drywall, Inc. v. Superior Court (1994) 25 Cal. App.4th 349, 30 Cal.Rptr.2d 418 (subject: construction defect litigation). The 10-year statute of limitation of Code of Civil Procedure § 337.15 is the outside limit for an action against a developer or contractor for latent defects.

Adelman v. Associated Internat. Ins. Co. (2001) 90 Cal.App.4th 352, 108 Cal.Rptr.2d 788 (subject: association insurance coverage). Individual homeowners have no right to sue an insurance company under an insurance policy issued only to the association and not naming the individual homeowners as insured parties in the policy. The insurance company's duty to perform under the policy runs only to the association, and the association is the proper party to bring an enforcement action if the policy provisions are breached.

Alfaro v. Community Housing Improvement System & Planning Association, Inc. (2009) 171 Cal.App.4th 263, 89 Cal.Rptr.3d 659 (subject: CC&R enforcement). Plaintiffs were owners of 22 single-family residences in a community housing development aimed at creating affordable housing for households of low and moderate income families. The homes in the development were subject to deed restrictions that required the properties to remain affordable to subsequent buyers with low and moderate incomes as established by governmental regulation. Plaintiffs claimed they were surprised to learn of this deed restriction after they had invested in the properties and when no mention was made in the purchase documents. They sought to rescind the sales or recover damage for failure to disclose the restriction. The CC&Rs and some deeds contained the restriction while other deeds did not. The Court of Appeal held that those deeds that did disclose the restriction created actual knowledge on the part of the purchasers as a matter of law defeating their claims of non-disclosure. But as to those owners whose deeds did not contain the restriction, the court allowed the action to proceed against the seller for damages on the basis of nondisclosure. But see Citizens For Covenant Compliance v. Anderson (1995) 12 Cal.4th 345.

Alpert v. Villa Romano Homeowners Assn. (2000) 81 Cal.App.4th 1320, 96 Cal.Rptr.2d 364 (subject: association liability). A homeowners' association has a duty to warn or protect nonresident, as well as resident, pedestrians from known hazardous defects of sidewalks on association property.

Arias v. Katella Townhouse Homeowners Assn., Inc. (2005) 127 Cal. App.4th 836, 26 Cal.Rptr.3d 131 (subject: attorney fee awards). An owner brought an action against the association for failure to maintain and repair the common area, causing toxic mold to develop around her unit. The association made a statutory settlement offer (Code of Civil Procedure § 998) and the owner declined. After the settlement offer expired, the association made voluntarily payments to the owner for various items of loss but did not pay the full amount of the claim. By statute the prevailing party in such an action is entitled to recover attorney fees. However, if the amount of the judgment is less than the association's settlement offer, the association - not the owner - is the prevailing party and entitled to its attorney fees. The issue faced by the court was whether the amount of post-offer voluntary payments by the association should be added to the amount of the judgment obtained by the owner at trial to determine the owner's total recovery. The court found that the voluntary payments should be added to the judgment, the total of both then exceeded the statutory settlement offer, and therefore the owner was entitled to her attorney fees.

Auburn Woods I Homeowners Association v. Fair Employment & Housing Commission (Elebiari) (2004) 121 C.A.4th 1578, 18 Cal. Rptr.3d 669 (subject: discrimination). The California Fair Employment & Housing Act (FEHA)(Gov. Code § 12900 et seq.) requires an association, among others controlling residential housing, "to make reasonable accommodations in rules, policies, practices, or services when these accommodations may be necessary to afford a disabled person equal opportunity to use and enjoy a dwelling." Two condominium owners filed a complaint with the Fair Employment & Housing Commission (FEHC) alleging that an association violated the FEHA by attempting to enforce a no-pet restriction in the CC&Rs (pre-enactment of Civil Code § 1360.5) prohibiting them from keeping a small dog to alleviate severe depression and enable them to function more productively. The therapeutic effect of the pet was supported by a physician's statement, although the dog was not a "service dog" as defined in Civil Code § 54.1. The FEHC found against the association, and the association sought to have the administrative ruling overturned in court. The Court of Appeal upheld the FEHC's findings and further held that the commission's findings were entitled to judicial deference when supported by substantial evidence. Substantial evidence means evidence supporting the FECH's findings when evaluated in the light most favorable to the commission's findings and indulging in all reasonable inferences in supporting those findings. The Court of Appeals noted: "We reiterate that the FEHC did not rule that companion pets are always a reasonable accommodation for individuals with mental disabilities. Each inquiry is fact-specific and requires a case-by-case determination." However, the court provided little guidance for future cases.

Avner v. Longridge Estates (1969) 272 Cal.App.2d 607, 77 Cal.Rptr. 633 (subject: construction defect litigation). A builder/developer may be held strictly liable (i.e., without fault) for defective soil conditions in subdivision lots that later result in property damage.

Assilzadeh v. California Federal Bank (2000) 82 Cal.App.4th 399, 98 Cal.Rptr.2d 176 (subject: seller liability for nondisclosure). An institutional lender which acquires a condominium unit through foreclosure cannot be held liable to a subsequent purchaser of the unit for nondisclosure of the specifics of construction defect litigation.

B.C.E. Dev., Inc. v. Smith (1989) 215 Cal.App.3d 1142, 264 Cal.Rptr. 55 (subject: CC&R enforcement). A developer who no longer has any ownership interest in a subdivision may still sue to enforce architectural restrictions if the CC&Rs so provide.

Bear Creek Master Assn. v. Edwards (2005) 130 Cal.App.4th 1470, 31 Cal.Rptr.3d 337 (subject: association operating problems). A trust acquired a parcel in master planned community which had been subdivided into 8 condominium units, but no structures had yet been built on the property. The trust refused to pay association assessments on the theory that assessments were chargeable only to a "condominium," which had to be part of an actual, existing structure. The court found that the definition of a "condominium" includes subdivided air space and the fact that the trust had not sold any individual condominium units was irrelevant to the existence and ownership of the condominium by the trust. The trust thus owed a duty to pay assessments and refusal to do so could result in foreclosure. See also *Park Place Estates Homeowners Assn. v. Naber (1994) 29 Cal.App.4th 427, 35 Cal.Rptr.2d 51.*

Beehan v. Lido Isle Community Assn. (1977) 70 Cal.App.3d 858, 137 Cal.Rptr. 528 (subject: CC&R enforcement). An association may exercise prudent business discretion in deciding whether or not to sue for a violation of the governing documents.

Bein v. Brechtel-Jochim Group, Inc. (1992) 6 Cal.App.4th 1387, 8 Cal.Rptr.2d 351 (subject: access to private property). A process server may serve a subpoena or other legal process on an individual living in a gated community by delivering it to the gate guard if the process server is refused entry to the subdivision. Code of Civil Procedure § 415.21 provides that an authorized process server, upon presentation of identification confirming that the person is either a registered process server or a representative of a county sheriff or marshal, must be granted access to a gated community for a reasonable period of time to serve process.

Berryman v. Merit Property Management, Inc. (2007) 152 Cal. App.4th 1544; 62 Cal.Rptr.3d 177 (subject: association operating problems). An owner of a home located in two associations was required by the property management company to pay $100 in document fees and $225 in transfer fees to each association on the sale of the home, for a total of $550. The owner brought suit claiming that the charges violated Civil Code § 1368, the Unfair Competition Law (Business & Professions Code § 17200 et seq.), the Consumers Legal Remedies Act (Civil Code § 1750 et seq.), and various tort theories. The court dismissed the case on all grounds. Relying on *Brown v. Professional Community Management, Inc. (2005) 127 Cal.App.4th 532, 25 Cal.Rptr.3d 617*, the court found that Civil Code § 1368 applies only to charges by an association and not by a third party vendor (i.e., the management company). It found that the practice of charging documentation and transfer fees by a management company is a product of market forces and not subject to statutory control. Accordingly, the allegations of other violations of law were not sustainable as well.

Biagini v. Hyde (1970) 3 Cal.App.3d 877, 83 Cal.Rptr. 875 (subject: CC&R enforcement). No physical injury or financial harm need be shown in an action to enforce the CC&Rs.

Bliler v. Covenant Control Comm. (1988) 205 Cal.App.3d 18, 252 Cal. Rptr. 50 (subject: age restrictions and discrimination). Age restrictions that meet the requirements of Civil Code § 51.3 may be imposed on a subdivision converted to senior citizen housing, even though the subdivision was not originally developed for that purpose.

Bodily v. Parkmont Village Green Homeowners Assn., Inc. (1980) 104 Cal.App.3d 348, 163 Cal.Rptr. 658 (subject: CC&R enforcement). An agreement between a developer and an owners' association suspending the developer's obligation to pay assessments on unsold lots is a material change in the public offering that requires the prior approval of the Department of Real Estate. Without such approval the association may disregard the agreement and recover all unpaid assessments.

Broadmoor San Clemente Homeowners Assn. v. Nelson (1994) 25 Cal.App.4th 1, 30 Cal.Rptr.2d 316 (subject: CC&R enforcement). California Fair Employment & Housing Act (Government Code § 12955 et seq.) and the Federal Fair Housing Act of 1968 (42 United States Code § 3604(f)(1)) authorize the operation of residential care facilities for the elderly even where a CC&R provision prohibits business or commercial activity within a subdivision.

Brown v. Professional Community Management Co. (2005) 127 Cal.App.4th 532, 25 Cal.Rptr.3d 617 (subject: association operating problems). A owner brought suit against the association and its property management company challenging the legality of certain fees charged by the property manager for providing collection services to the association, which fees were then passed along to the delinquent owner. The owner claimed that the fees charged by the property manager were limited by Civil Code §1366.1 to actual out-of-pocket costs. The statute prohibits an association from charging fees or assessments in excess of the costs for which the fee or assessment is charged. The court held that the limitations of Civil Code § 1366.1 do not to a property manager or other association vendors. The amounts charged by third party vendors are controlled by market forces, not by the Davis-Stirling Common Interest Development Act (Civil Code §§ 1350 et seq.), and their charges can be passed along to the owner in appropriate circumstances.

Cabrini Villas Homeowners Assn. v. Haghverdian (2003) 111 Cal.App.4th 683, 4 Cal.Rptr.3d 192 (subject: mail service/CC&R enforcement). A request for ADR made pursuant to Cal. Civ. Code § 1354 may be served by any form of mail providing return receipt. A homeowner who never signed the return receipt waived any defect in service by failing to raise the issue in the trial court. Architectural control provisions in the CC&Rs are enforceable unless it can be reasonably inferred that a decision was discriminatory (the owner was required to remove a room air-conditioning unit installed in an exterior wall).

Calemine v. Samuelson (2009) 171 Cal.App.4th 153, 89 Cal.Rptr.3d 495 (subject: association/owner liability). A buyer of a condominium sued the seller for failure to disclosure a history of litigation over water intrusion in the common garage even though the problem had been disclosed. The seller was a party to a lawsuit against the developer for water intrusion, knowledgeable of the ineffectiveness of the initial repairs, and additional repairs when the initial repairs proved only partially effective. The initial repairs resulted in a second lawsuit against the repair contractor. The seller indicated in his real estate disclosure statement (Civil Code § 1102.6) that he was aware of flooding, drainage and grading problems during heavy rains. The listing agent disclosed occasional water damage in the garage. Neither prior litigation was disclosed. After the sale the garage flooded three times and the buyer sued the seller. The Court of Appeal held that the seller's disclosures concerning the existence of water intrusion were adequate, but remanded the case for trial to determine whether the seller's nondisclosure of the prior two lawsuits had a material affect on the buyer's decision to purchase the property. The law of California is that a seller may be subject to liability if he fails to disclose a material fact that affects the value or desirability of the property. Generally, whether the undisclosed matter was sufficient materiality to affect the value or desirability of the property is a question of fact for the judge or jury.

California Riviera Homeowners Assn. v. Superior Court (1996) 37 Cal.App.4th 1599, 56 Cal.Rptr.2d 564 (subject: CC&R enforcement). An owner may not bring an action against an association for recording a "notice of violation" against the owner's property even if the notice is inaccurate or unjustified. However, a "notice of violation" is not a recordable document. See also *Wilton v. Mountain Wood Homeowners Assn. (1993) 18 Cal.App.4th 565, 22 Cal.Rptr.2d 471*.

Cancun Homeowners Assn. v. City of San Juan Capistrano (1989) 215 Cal.App.3d 1352, 265 Cal. Rptr. 288 (subject: construction defect litigation). A municipal building inspector is immune from liability for failure to disapprove landfill with less than 90% compaction where city ordinance called for compaction to that standard but left some discretion with the building official on compliance.

Castaneda v. Olsher (2005) 132 Cal.App.4th 624 , 33 Cal.Rptr.3d 827 (subject: association liability). A mobile home park owner may have a duty to protect park residents from potential gang-related violence where the park has a history of violent gang activity.

Cebular v. Cooper Arms Homeowners Association (2006) 142 Cal. App.4th 106; 47 Cal.Rptr.3d 666 (subject: CC&R enforcement). A stock cooperative was converted into condominiums. Under the terms of the CC&Rs of the newly formed condominium project, assessments were allocated among the members according to their voting rights which was carried over from the stock cooperative method of allocation. The allocation was challenged by a member as "wholly arbitrary" because the division did not reflect the value, location, square footage, elevation or ocean views of units. The Court of Appeal held that the unusual method of allocation was justified for historical reasons, and when judged against the deferential standard of presumptive reasonableness given to CC&R provisions, it was not "wholly arbitrary" nor did it violate public policy. In the words of one judge, "[m]y sympathy with plaintiff's plight is tempered by the fact that when he purchased his unit, he should have considered the governing documents to determine his rights and liabilities."

Chantiles v. Lake Forest II Master Homeowners Assn. (1995) 37 Cal.App.4th 914, 45 Cal.Rptr.2d 1 (subject: voting rights and inspection of secret ballots). There is no absolute right to inspect secret ballots after an annual election - even by an incumbent candidate-director - where less intrusive ways of verifying the vote count are available which preserve the privacy of member votes. Article I, Section 1 of the California Constitution guarantees association members the right to privacy in their voting decisions, even though some votes are cast by proxy, and that right must be balanced against the need to verify election results. Less intrusive inspection methods include a confidentiality agreement, obscuring voter names, or independent review by a neutral person or by the court.

Chapala Management Corp. v. Stanton (2010) 186 Cal.App.4th 1532, ___Cal.Rptr.3d ___, (subject: CC&R enforcement). The Court of Appeal upheld a trial court decision that an association, through its architectural committee, acted properly in requiring an owner to remove two new casement windows that did not comply with the association's approved color scheme for windows and awarded the association its attorney fees and costs.

Chee v. Amanda Goldt Property Management (2006) 143 Cal.App.4th 1360; 50 Cal.Rptr.3d 40 (subject: association/owner liability). The owner of a condominium leased his unit to an tenant through a property management company. The tenant obtained by the property manager owned a terrier that attacked another elderly resident. The injured resident sued the association, the owner of the condominium, his property manager and the dog owner. The dog owner filed for bankruptcy. The action was dismissed as to the other parties because the plaintiff could not establish that any of the defendants had actual knowledge of the dog's dangerous propensities and the ability to control or prevent the harm.

Citizens Against Gated Enclaves v. Whitley Heights Civic Association (1994) 23 Cal.App.4th 812, 28 Cal.Rptr.2d 451 (subject: access to private property). A city may not permit a gated community to close a public street into a subdivision as a crime prevention measure. Vehicle Code § 21101.6 prohibits public officials from authorizing any type of entry device that restricts public access to public streets. (Note: Vehicle Code § 21101(a) does permit closure of a public street when it is no longer needed for vehicle access.)

City of Oceanside v. McKenna (1989) 215 Cal.App.3d 1420, 264 Cal. Rptr. 275 (subject: CC&R enforcement). A CC&R leasing restriction is valid and enforceable in a condominium project subsidized by a local redevelopment agency to provide low-cost permanent housing to local residents. Such a restriction, if enforced in a uniform manner, does not violate Civ. Code § 711 (which prohibits unreasonable restraints on alienation of property) because the restriction is intended to further the goals of redevelopment.

Clarendon America Ins. Co. v. Starnet Ins. Co. (2010) 186 Cal. App.4th 1397, ___Cal.Rptr.3d ___(subject: construction defect litigation). The Calderon Act (Civil Code §§ 1375 et seq.), passed by the Legislature in 1995, requires common interest associations to give notice to a builder, developer, or general contractor of construction defects before suing. The Calderon Act's purpose is to encourage settlement of construction defect disputes and to discourage unnecessary litigation. To commence the Calderon process, an association serves a "Notice of Commencement of Legal Proceeding" on the builder, developer or general contractor containing certain specified information. Service of the notice triggers a period of

not to exceed 180 days, during which the parties are required to attempt to resolve the dispute. The issue presented in this case was whether the service of a Calderon notice was sufficient to trigger insurance coverage under a commercial general liability policy issued to the builder, even though "suit" had not yet been filed as required by the policy. The Court of Appeal, in a case of first impression, held that service of a Calderon notice is commencement of a "civil proceeding" sufficient to satisfy the policy requirements.

Clark v. Rancho Santa Fe Association (1989) 216 Cal.App.3d 606, 265 Cal.Rptr. 41 (subject: CC&R enforcement). A board may exercise its discretion and aesthetic judgment in deciding whether to approve or disapprove an application for an architectural modification, provided its decision is reasonable and made in good faith. In making such determinations, associations have wide latitude in their decision-making. See also *Dolan-King v. Rancho Santa Fe Assn. (2000) 81 Cal.App.4th 948, 97 Cal.Rptr.2d 269.*

Clear Lake Riviera Community Association v. Cramer (2010) 182 Cal.App.4th 459, ___ Cal.Rptr.3d ___ (subject: CC&R enforcement). An owner disregarded warnings that the home he planned to construct would violate the height restrictions in the association's governing documents and went ahead with construction anyway. The resulting home exceeded the height restriction by 9 feet and severely impinged on the views of at least two neighbors. The association brought an action to require the owner to modify the home to bring it into compliance with the restriction. The Court of Appeal affirmed a trial court decision in the association's favor finding the height restriction enforceable even though adopted as a rule rather than a CC&R provision. The court also affirmed a ruling that the owners would be required to modify his home to conform to the restrictions rather than pay damages, even though the modifications would cost some $200,000.

Cohen v. Kite Hill Community Assn. (1983) 142 Cal.App.3d 642, 191 Cal.Rptr. 209 (subject: CC&R enforcement). An owners' association must exercise its authority to approve or disapprove architectural modifications in a manner consistent with the CC&Rs. The association cannot grant approvals prohibited by the CC&Rs nor immunize itself from liability by standing behind an exculpatory clause in the CC&Rs purporting to insulate the board from any liability for improper action.

Cohen v. S & S Construction Co. (1983) 151 Cal.App.3d 941, 201 Cal.Rptr. 173 (subject: developer liability). A developer who controls an association board is liable to the homeowners for failure to enforce the CC&Rs and cannot be immunized by an exculpatory clause contained in the declaration.

Costa Serena Owners Coalition v. Costa Serena Architectural Committee (2009) 175 Cal.App.4th 1175, 97 Cal.Rptr.3d 170 **(subject: CC&R enforcement). Costa Serena is an adult planned dev**elopment built in the 1970s in seven phases that comprise 724 homes. Each of the seven phases had its own CC&Rs providing for their expiration on December 31, 2006, unless extended by a vote of 75% of the owners. In 1987 the seven phases were unified into a single community governed by a single set of unified CC&Rs. In 1999 the unified CC&Rs were amended to provide that the termination date of the unified CC&Rs could be extended beyond December 31, 2006 by a vote of a majority of the owners. In 2006 the unified CC&Rs were amended by a majority vote to extended to the term of the CC&Rs from the end of year 2006 to the end of year 2039. A coalition of owners sought to invalidate the extension in an effort to eliminate an age restriction limiting occupancy to residents over 55 on the ground of irregularities in the adoption of the unified CC&Rs in 1987. The Court of Appeal held that any such irregularities were barred by the 4-year statute of limitation of Code of Civil Procedure § 343 and the CC&R extension to year 2039 was valid. (The Court of Appeal may have been influenced by the public policy in favor of extending CC&Rs. Civil Code § 1357(a) states: "The Legislature further finds and declares that it is in the public interest to provide a vehicle for extending the term of the declaration if owners having more than 50 percent of the votes in the association choose to do so.")

Creekridge Townhome Owners Association, Inc. v. C. Scott Whitten, Inc. (2009) 177 Cal.App.4th 251, 99 Cal.Rptr.3d 258 (subject: construction defect litigation). The Court of Appeal held that the discovery of a moisture problem in only one of 61 units in a townhome complex was insufficient to give the homeowners' association notice of latent construction defects. The Court of Appeal distinguished the prior case of Landale-Cameron Court, Inc. V. Ahonen (2007) 155 C.A.4th 1401, where the statute of limitation was found to bar claims when leaks were discovered in at least 3 of a project's total of eight condominium units, on the grounds that moisture in only one of 61 units was not analogous to the almost 40% failure evidenced in Landale.

Crestmar Owners Association v. Stapakis (2007) 157 Cal.App.3d 1223, 69 Cal.Rptr.3d 231 (subject: association operating problems). An owners association brought an action to quiet title to two parking spaces. The CC&Rs provided that all parking spaces not transferred by the developer/converter to condominium buyers after a period of 3 years would be conveyed to the owners association. More than 20 years later two parking spaces had still not been conveyed. The developer/converter then conveyed the two parking spaces to himself. The owners association challenged the conveyance. The developer/converter defended on the grounds that the statute of limitation had run on the association's claim. The Court of Appeal affirmed a ruling that the statute of limitation for a quiet title action does not begin to run until an adverse claim is made on the property. Here the adverse claim was the developer/converter' conveyance to himself.

Cutujian v. Benedict Hills Estates Assn. (1996) 41 Cal.App.4th 1379, 49 Cal.Rptr.2d 166 (subject: CC&R enforcement). The statute of limitation for a claim against an association for failure to perform its duties under the CC&Rs begins to run when a demand is made on the association, not when property damage occurs. (Note: Normally, the statute of limitation for property damage begins to run when appreciable property damage occurs. This case is unique because the owner who brought suit acquired the property long after the damage began. The precedential value of this case may be limited to similar cases where the owner's acquisition postdates injury and the owner takes action promptly after purchase.)

Damon v. Ocean Hills Journalism Club (2000) 85 Cal.App.4th 468, 102 Cal.Rptr.2d 205 (subject: association liability). An action for defamation brought by a former association manager against several association members, two board members and a private association journalism club was dismissed pursuant to California's anti-SLAPP statute (Code of Civil Proc. § 425.16), which is directed against litigation filed without merit to dissuade the exercise of free speech rights. The anti-SLAPP statute applied here because the evidence showed the alleged defamatory statements were made "in a place open to the public or in a public forum" and concerned an issue of public interest within the meaning of the statute, and the manager failed to show at a preliminary hearing that he would probably prevail at trial. Notably, the public forum requirement was satisfied by an "open board meeting" pursuant to Civil Code § 1363.05 and a newsletter distributed only to association members.

Davert v. Larson (1985) 163 Cal.App.3d 407, 209 Cal.Rptr. 445 (subject: association/owner liability). Individual owners of an unincorporated association may be personally liable for association liabilities. (This case is partially superseded by Civil Code § 1365.9 which provides limited immunity to owners if specified insurance is maintained.)

Deane Gardenhome Assn. v. Denktas (1993) 13 Cal.App.4th 1394, 16 Cal.Rptr.2d 816 (subject: CC&R enforcement). An association may be prevented from enforcing architectural restrictions where, through informal action of its officers or directors, the association leads an owner to believe that architectural approval has been granted and the owner carries out modifications in reliance on that advice. In order to avoid this problem, officers and directors should follow established procedures for review of architectural submissions by the full board or architectural committee.

Devonwood Condominium Owners Association v. Farmers Ins. Exchange (2008) 162 Cal.App.4th 1498, 77 Cal.Rptr.3d 88 (subject: insurance coverage). In a fire damage case, a condominium association and its property insurer disputed the insurer's duty to pay for interior painting. Pursuant to the policy provisions the matter was submitted for appraisal conducted by an independent panel. The panel returned an appraisal divided in two parts: one for the structural damage and the other for painting. The trial court entered judgment on the appraisal in favor of the association. The Court of Appeal reversed stating that the trial court had exceeded its authority in simply awarding the damage found for both structural and painting by the appraisal panel without analyzing whether coverage existed for painting damage under the policy provisions.

Dey v. Continental Central Credit (2009) 170 Cal.App.4th 721, 88 Cal.Rptr.3d 241 (subject: association operating problems). An owner brought an action against the association for unfair competition (Business & Professions Code §§ 17200 et seq.) based on a fee the association imposed upon him to collect a debt he owed the association. The owner contended that the fee was not reasonably related to the actual cost of collection as provided in Civil Code § 1366.1. The fee imposed was that charged by the association's management company. The Court of Appeal, relying on Brown v. Professional Community Management, Inc. (2005) 127 Cal.App.4th 532, ruled the fees imposed by a management company are not illegal unless they exceed the association's costs, and the association's costs necessarily include fees charged by the management for its services. In a broader sense, the amounts charged by third party vendors are controlled by market forces, not Civil Code § 1366.1, and such charges can be passed along to owners in appropriate circumstances.

Doheny Park Terrace Homeowners Assn. v. Truck Ins. Exchange (2005) 132 Cal.App.4th 1076, 34 Cal.Rptr.3d 157 (subject: association operating problems). A homeowners' association sued its insurance company in 2003 for coverage due to earthquake damage in the 1994 earthquake. The initial claim was rejected by the carrier in 1994. The policy required the association to bring suit within one year from denial of a claim, although by statute (Code of Civil Procedure § 340.9) any such claim were revived provided suit was filed by December 31, 2000. Nonetheless, the court held that an association could pursue a belated claim after December 31, 2000 if it can establish that the insurance company deliberately misled the association by misrepresenting the extent of coverage or the amount of damage was within the deductible. Neither the contractual limitation nor the statutory limitation on the time within which to bring an action preclude a later action based on misrepresentation or fraud.

Dolan-King v. Rancho Santa Fe Assn. (2000) 81 Cal.App.4th 965, 97 Cal.Rptr.2d 280 (subject: CC&R enforcement). A homeowner challenging the architectural decision of an association in court has the burden of proving that the association's decision was unreasonable and arbitrary under the circumstances. A decision is unreasonable and arbitrary "when it bears no rational relationship to the protection, preservation, operation or purpose of the affected land." Unrecorded use restrictions (e.g., rules, guidelines, etc.) may not be given a presumption of reasonableness, but evaluated under a straight "reasonableness" test. Nevertheless, the burden of proof is on the challenging homeowner to prove the "unreasonableness" of an unrecorded restriction.

Duffey v. Superior Court (1992) 3 Cal.App.4th 425, 4 Cal.Rptr.2d 334 (subject: CC&R enforcement). An association may sue to enforce a

CC&R provision without joining individual owners other than the owner directly in violation. Other owners may or may not choose to become involved in the enforcement action, but whether the other owners join or not, the decision of the court will be binding on all owners.

East Hilton Drive Homeowners Assn. v. Western Real Estate Exch., Inc. (1982) 136 Cal.App.3d 630, 186 Cal.Rptr. 267 (subject: construction defect litigation). Legal claims based upon strict liability and breach of implied warranty apply only to the original builder/developer. They do not extend to a successor owner/investor who acquires a residential subdivision after construction is complete, even though the units have never been occupied before sale by the successor owner/investor.

ECC Construction, Inc. v. Ganson (2000) 82 Cal.App.4th 572, 98 Cal.Rptr.2d 292 (subject: association operating problems). Individual condominium owners are not personally liable for the debts of an incorporated homeowners' association, except to the extent that the alter ego doctrine applies to them individually or they owe money to the association. Also, Civil Code § 1369 requires a contractor to apportion a mechanics' lien and notify each condominium owner of the fraction of the total debt secured by that owner's unit before pursuing enforcement proceedings.

Eichler Homes, Inc. v. Anderson (1970) 9 Cal.App.3d 224, 87 Cal.Rptr. 893 (subject: construction defect litigation). The sellers of component parts used in the construction of residential housing expressly and impliedly warrant that the component parts are reasonably fit for their intended purpose. Failure of those component parts will give rise to an action for damages.

Ekstrom v. Marquesa at Monarch Beach Homeowners Association (2009) 168 Cal.App.4th 1111, 86 Cal.Rptr.3d 145 (subject: CC&R enforcement). In a planned development, individual owners brought an action to enforce an express CC&R provision requiring all trees on a lot to be trimmed so as to not exceed the roof line, unless the tree did not obstruct the view from other lots. The association took the position that, because trimming a palm tree would effectively require its removal, the restriction did not apply to palm trees. The Court of Appeal affirmed a trial court decision compelling the association to enforce the tree trimming restriction regardless of the type of tree. The court held that the "judicial deference rule" of Lamden v. La Jolla Shores Clubdominium Homeowners Association cannot be used to justify a direct violation of the CC&Rs. Rather it applies to the discretionary decision-making in areas such as maintenance and repair. The court also found that the 4 year statute of limitations applicable to action to enforce CC&Rs (Code of Civil Procedure § 337) did not commence until the owners demanded enforcement rather than from the date of violation.

El Escorial Owners Association v. DLC Plastering, Inc. (2007) 154 Cal.App.4th 1337, 65 Cal.Rptr.3d 524 (subject: construction defect litigation). In a complicated case, the Court of Appeal held, among other things: (1) a suspended corporation may not prosecute or defend a construction defect lawsuit, but its insurance carrier may intervene in the lawsuit to protect its interest so long as it does so in its own name and not the name of the suspended corporation, (2) a trial court has considerable discretion to calculate and allocate damages in making a determination of a good faith settlement, (3) all parties responsible for construction defects, regardless of whether their acts are successive or contemporaneous, are jointly and severally liable as joint tortfeasors, (4) an association successful in a construction defect action is entitled to recover not only expert fees in formulating a repair plan but also for the expense of investigating and evaluating a construction defect claim, and (5) the trial court has discretion to allocate attorney fees to be awarded a party between those claims where attorneys fees are recoverable and those where they are not.

Elnekave v. Via Dolce Homeowners Association (2006) 142Cal. App.4th 1193; 48 Cal.Rptr.3d 663 (subject: association litigation). Code of Civil Procedure § 664.6 provides that "[i]f parties to pending litigation stipulate, in writing signed by the parties outside the presence of the court or orally before the court, for settlement of the case, or part thereof, the court, upon motion, may enter judgment pursuant to the terms of the settlement." In this case an owner sued the association and others over the presence of mold and mold related expenses. A settlement was reached in open court. The association was represented in court by its property manager and its insurance carrier, both of whom agreed to the settlement and represented to the court that they possessed authority to settle on behalf of the association. One party sought to enforce the settlement; the other resisted. The Court of Appeal held that the words "the parties" in the statute mean the actual parties named in the lawsuit and that the presence of the property manager and insurance representative were insufficient to meet the requirement. For an in-court oral settlement agreement to be enforceable, an officer or director of the association must be present in court and approve it.

Expressions at Rancho Niguel Assn. v. Ahmanson Developments, Inc. (2001) 86 Cal.App.4th 1135, 103 Cal.Rptr.2d 895 (subject: construction defect litigation). Equitable indemnity principles, rather than joint and several liability principles apply in apportioning losses among subcontractors. Thus, the financial liability is allocated based on comparative fault and culpability.

Farber v. Bay View Terrace Homeowners Association (2006) 141 Cal. App.4th 1007; 46 Cal.Rptr.3d 425 (subject: association/owner litigation). A condominium owner sued the former owner for an undisclosed roof leak. The former owner cross-complained against the current owner and the association for a judicial declaration of her rights and duties vis-a-vis the unit buyer and the association relating to responsibility for roof repairs. Her action against the association was dismissed. The Court of Appeal held that once an owner divests himself or herself of any ownership interest in a common interest development, the former owner loses standing to enforce the CC&Rs, unless the CC&Rs specifically confer such standing. Here, they did not.

Fidelity Mortgage Trustee Service, Inc. v. Ridgegate East Homeowners Assn. (1994) 27 Cal.App.4th 503, 32 Cal.Rptr.2d 521 (subject: association operating problems). In the absence of an agreement to the contrary, a trustee service may recover its legal expense from the association and/or the property manager in successfully defending an action for wrongful foreclosure of an assessment lien, even where the association, property manager and the trustee service all acted properly. An agent (i.e., the foreclosure service) forced to defend a suit based upon actions taken at the direction of a principal (i.e., the association or property manager) is entitled to indemnification for such expenses under principles of agency law regardless of wrongdoing.

Foothill Village Homeowners Association v. Bishop (1999) 68 Cal. App.4th 1364, 81 Cal.Rptr.2d 195 (subject: earthquake insurance). A lender holding a security interest in a condominium has no right to the proceeds of an earthquake insurance policy without a specific provision to that effect in the loan agreement.

Franklin v. Marie Antoinette Condominium Assn. (1993) 19 Cal. App.4th 824, 23 Cal.Rptr.2d 744 (subject: CC&R enforcement). An association may assert an exculpatory clause in the CC&Rs as a defense to an action for breach of contract based upon allegations of failure to maintain the common area as required by the CC&Rs. The association here was found free of fault in the discharge of its duties. The exculpatory clause merely shifted the risk of a no-fault loss to the owner. But see *Cohen v. Kite Hill Community Assn. (1983) 142 Cal.App.3d 642, 191 Cal. Rptr. 209*, holding that an exculpatory clause may not be used to protect an association from at-fault liability.

Geertz v. Ausonio (1992) 4 Cal.App.4th 1363, 6 Cal.Rptr.2d 318. (subject: construction defect litigation). Different statutes of limitation apply to latent and patent defects. Whether a defect is latent or patent for statute of limitation purposes is a question of fact that must be decided at trial on the basis of factual evidence.

Greenbriar Homes Communities, Inc. v. Superior Court (2004) 117 Cal.App.4th 337, 11 Cal.Rptr.3d 371 (subject: construction defect litigation). A clause in a purchase agreement for a new home requiring all claims for construction defects not resolved by mediation to be resolved by reference to an extra-judicial private referee/arbitrator is enforceable against original purchasers who signed the purchase agreement, but not enforceable against subsequent owners who bought after the original sale and did not sign the original purchase agreement.

Golden Rain Foundation v. Franz (2008) 163 Cal.App.4th 1141, 78 Cal.Rptr.3d 226 (subject: cooperative apartment projects). A trustee's operations in providing management and administrative services for corporations that were formed primarily to provide cooperative apartment housing fall within the definition of a common interest development under Civil Code § 1351(c). The trustee was not a management "agent" because it held title to common facilities and was not compensated for its services. The apartments were a common interest development because the residents owned separate interests and were members of the association. The recorded declaration for the apartments was adequate to meet the requirements of CC&Rs.

Haley v. Casa Del Rey Homeowners Association (2007) 153 Cal. App.4th 863; 63 Cal.Rptr.3d 514 (subject: CC&R enforcement).

Homeowners brought an action against an association and other owners for, among other things, encroachments into the common area off some back patios. The association passed a CC&R amendment giving it discretion to allow patio extensions into the common area by the percentage required in the CC&Rs. The owners also alleged discriminatory enforcement of the CC&Rs. The Court of Appeal found the amendment valid and that the association did not engage in selective enforcement because it chose not to enforce every violation. Relying on *Lamden v. La Jolla Shores Clubdominium Homeowners Association (1999) 21 Cal.4th 249, 87 Cal. Rptr.2d 237*, the court stated that the association "had discretion to select among means for remedying violations of the CC&Rs without resorting to expensive and time-consuming litigation, and the courts should defer to that discretion." The association recovered over $185,000 in attorney fees and costs against the plaintiff homeowners. See also, *Beehan v. Lido Isle Community Association (1977) 70 Cal.App.3d 858, 137 Cal.Rptr. 528.*

Harbor View Hills Community Assn. v. Torley (1992) 5 Cal.App.4th 343, 7 Cal.Rptr.2d 96 (subject: CC&R enforcement). A CC&R provision allowing the prevailing party to recover attorney fees in an action for collection of assessment may provide a basis for recovering attorney fees in other related types of CC&R disputes. (See also, Civil Code § 1354(f) which provides an alternate basis for an award of attorney fees to the prevailing party in a CC&R enforcement action.)

Harvey v. The Landing Homeowners Association (2008) 162 Cal. App.4th 809, 76 Cal.Rptr.3d 41 (subject: CC&R enforcement). Plaintiff sued his owners association and certain members of its board of directors for trespass, breach of fiduciary duty, and injunctive relief when the board of directors determined that fourth floor homeowners could exclusively use up to 120 square feet of inaccessible common area attic space adjacent to their units for rough storage. The Court of Appeal affirmed a trial court ruling that the board acted within its authority under the CC&Rs which gave the board authority to grant an owner exclusive use of common area provided the area was nominal in size and did not unreasonably interfere with any other owner's use or enjoyment of the project. The court also affirmed the decision to grant sitting directors the right to receive the benefit of the board's decision because a disinterested majority of the directors approved the grant. (See also Civil Code §1363.07(a)(3)(E) authorizing the board to grant exclusive use to an owner to transfer the burden of management and maintenance of any common area that is generally inaccessible and is not of general use to the membership at large.)

Heather Farms Homeowners Assn. v. Robinson (1994) 21 Cal. App.4th 1568, 26 Cal.Rptr.2d 758 (subject: CC&R enforcement). A court has discretion to determine whether there is a prevailing party for the purposes of awarding attorney fees in an action resolved by settlement and mutual dismissals. Civil Code § 1354(f) and many governing documents authorize an award of attorney fees to the prevailing party in a CC&R enforcement action, but a party must obtain a net benefit in order to be a prevailing party in a lawsuit and mutual dismissals do not equate to a net benefit for either party.

Heiman v. Workers' Compensation Appeals Board (2007) 149 Cal. App.4th 724, 57 Cal.Rptr.3d 56 (subject: association liability). A property manager unwittingly hired an unlicensed and uninsured contractor to perform gutter work at a community association. On the first day of work one of the contractor's employees fell and was seriously injured. The unlicensed contractor, the property manager and the association were held to be co-employers of the injured worker under Labor Code § 2750.5 and responsible for payment of all workers' compensation benefits and any tort liability arising from the accident.

Hellman v. La Cumbre Golf & Country Club (1992) 6 Cal.App.4th 1224, 8 Cal.Rptr.2d 293 (subject: association operating problems). An owner living adjacent to a golf course cannot compel the golf course operator to change the line of play so that golf balls do not land on his property, especially where the owner purchased the property with knowledge of the golf hazard and is unable to prove a continuing nuisance through incidents of actual damage.

Huntington Landmark Adult Community Assn. v. Ross (1989) 213 Cal.App.3d 1012, 261 Cal.Rptr. 875 (subject: age discrimination). Age restrictions may be enforced against condominium owners provided the project falls within the definition of senior citizen housing under Civil Code § 51.3.

Inco Development Corp. v. Superior Court (2005) 131 Cal.App.4th 1014, 31 Cal.Rptr.3d 872 (subject: construction defect litigation). The 10-year statute of limitation under Code of Civil Procedure § 337.15 for latent construction defects is not tolled or suspended from running while the developer is in bankruptcy. Normally, the filing of a bankruptcy petition operates as an automatic stay of the commencement or continuation of a judicial proceeding against the debtor under 11 U.S.C § 362; however, since Code of Civil Procedure § 337.15 is a "statute of repose" it is treated differently from statutes of limitation. 11 U.S.C. § 108 does allow any claim that cannot be brought during the pendency of bankruptcy to be brought within 30 days after the termination of the bankruptcy proceeding. That was not done in this case.

Ironwood Owners Assn. IX v. Solomon (1986) 178 Cal.App.3d 766, 224 Cal.Rptr. 18 (subject: CC&R enforcement). An association must follow its own internal disciplinary procedures before seeking relief in court.

Jaffee v. Huxley Architecture (1988) 200 Cal.App.3d 1188, 246 Cal.Rptr. 432 (subject: construction defect litigation). In an action by the association for construction defects, the builder/developer may not seek indemnity from individual board members for contributory fault in failing to maintain the property. Such claims may be asserted only as an affirmative defense to the association's action for damages.

James F. O'Toole Co., Inv. v. Los Angeles Kingsbury Court Owners Assn. (2005) 126 C.A.4th 549, 23 Cal.Rptr.3d 894 (subject: association operating problems). An owner obtained a $140,196.59 judgment against a 46-unit homeowners association. The association did not pay the judgment. The owner pursued post-judgment enforcement proceedings and the association claimed its assets were exempt from execution under Civil Code § 1366(c) because all assessments went to "essential services". The Court of Appeals rejected this argument finding that the exemption applies only to "regular assessments" and not to "special assessments" or "emergency assessments". The court ordered the association to impose a special emergency assessment to pay the judgment and, when the association failed to do so, ordered the appointment of a receiver to carry out the trial court's order.

Kaplan v. Fairway Oaks Homeowners Assn. (2002) 98 Cal.App.4th 715, 120 Cal.Rptr.2d 158 (subject: attorney fee awards). In actions brought to challenge the validity of an election of the board of directors, the prevailing party is entitled to attorney fees under Civ. Code § 1354, which was amended in 1993 to refer to "governing documents" rather than the "declaration." Thus, actions brought to enforce voting rights under the bylaws are treated the same as actions brought to enforce the CC&Rs.

Kaye v. Mount La Jolla Homeowners Assn. (1988) 204 Cal.App.3d 1476, 252 Cal.Rptr. 67 (subject: association/owner liability). In an action against the association for failure to maintain common area, owners cannot recover damages measured by both cost of repair *and* diminution in value, but are limited to one of the two.

King v. Magnolia Homeowners Assn. (1988) 205 Cal.App.3d 1312, 253 Cal.Rptr.140 (subject: association/owner liability). A service provider assumes the risk of obvious hazardous conditions when working on association property and cannot hold an association responsible for injury or damage resulting therefrom.

Kovich v. Paseo Del Mar Homeowners' Assn. (1996) 41 Cal.App.4th 863, 48 Cal. Rptr.2d 758 (subject: association operating problems). An association has no legal duty to disclose the existence of construction defects or related litigation to a prospective purchaser, at least where it does not voluntarily undertake to provide such information. The duty to disclose such information is on the seller. The only information an association is legally obligated to provide is set forth in Civil Code § 1368.

Kriegler v. Eichler Homes, Inc. (1969) 269 Cal.App.3d 224, 74 Cal. Rptr. 749 (subject: construction defect litigation). Builder/developers may be held strictly liable for construction defects in mass produced residential housing. Such housing also carries an implied warranty that it is reasonably fit for its intended purpose.

La Jolla Mesa Vista Improvement Assn. v. La Jolla Mesa Vista Homeowners Assn. (1990) 220 Cal.App.3d 1187, 269 Cal.Rptr. 825 (subject: association operating problems). An owner's written consent to extending the term of the CC&Rs is irrevocable for a reasonable period of time while other owners' consents are being obtained, unless the governing documents specifically permit previously cast ballots to be revoked. The rule promotes stability and certainty in continuous existence of common interest developments.

Laguna Publishing Co. v. Golden Rain Foundation (1982) 131 Cal.

App.3d 816, 182 Cal.Rptr. 813 (subject: association operating problems). A private, gated residential community can exclude unsolicited newspapers from distributing within the community, provided it does not discriminate between similar newspapers engaged in similar activity.

Laguna Royale Owners Assn. v. Darger (1981) 119 Cal.App.3d 670, 134 Cal.Rptr.136 (subject: association operating problems). Architectural review must be exercised in a reasonable, fair and nondiscriminatory manner.

Landale-Cameron Court, Inc. v. Ahonen (2007) 155 Cal.App.4th 1401, 66 Cal.Rptr.3d 776 (subject: construction defect litigation). The Court of Appeal held that a construction defect lawsuit was barred by the 3-year statute of limitation for property damage (Code of Civil Procedure § 338) where the president of the association had knowledge of water intrusion in at least 3 of the project's total of eight condominium units and observed a handy man trying to repair roof leaks more than three years before suit was filed. See also, *Creekridge Townhome Owners Association, Inc. v. C. Scott Whitten, Inc. (2009)177 Cal.App.4th 251* (different result).

Larkspur Isle Condominium Owners' Assn. v. Farmers Ins. Group (1994) 31 Cal.App.4th 106, 37 Cal.Rptr.2d 3 (subject: association operating problems). First party insurance is coverage that insures the policyholder's own property. Third party insurance is coverage that insures the policyholder against his own liability for negligent injury to property of another. In a first party case, only the first policy on the risk during a progressive loss spanning several policy periods is available to provide coverage. Coverage is "triggered" when the loss "manifests" or becomes apparent upon reasonable inspection. This is called the "manifestation rule." A different rule applies in third party coverage cases. See *Montrose v. Chemical Corp. v. Admiral Insurance Co. (1995) 10 Cal.4th 645, 42 Cal.Rptr.2d 324.*

Lauriedale Associates, Ltd. v. Wilson (1992) 7 Cal.App.4th 1439, 9 Cal.Rptr.2d 774 (subject: construction defect litigation). A developer who is sued for construction defects and inadequate assessments cannot cross-complain for indemnity against the individual unit owners. The developer may obtain equivalent protection by asserting an affirmative defense which will allow an offset against the association's damage claim to the extent that the damage is caused or aggravated by the individual unit owners. Civil Code § 1365.9 provides limited immunity from civil liability to individual owners if the association carries a certain level of prescribed liability insurance; however, the limited immunity extends only to tort claims and not other types of liability. See also *Jaffee v. Huxley Architecture (1988) 200 Cal.App.3d 1188, 246 Cal.Rptr. 432*, and Civil Code § 1365.7 for similar protection for association officers and directors.

Liebler v. Point Loma Tennis Club (1995) 40 Cal.App.4th 1600, 47 Cal.Rptr.2d 783 (subject: CC&R enforcement). An association has the authority to create rules prohibiting nonresident owners from using the common recreational facilities where the intent of the CC&Rs is to have one set of users per unit. The association has the authority to impose fines based upon a rule authorizing such fines. The case may be in conflict with *MaJor v. Miraverde Homeowners Assn. (1992) 7 Cal.App.4th 618, 9 Cal. Rptr.2d 237.*

MaJor v. Miraverde Homeowners Assn. (1992) 7 Cal.App.4th 618, 9 Cal.Rptr.2d 237 (subject: CC&R enforcement). A rule prohibiting a nonresident owner from using the common area recreation facilities when the unit is occupied by another family member is unenforceable. The family member in this case was an 82-year old woman who did not utilize the recreational facilities and there was no issue of double usage. The case did not rule on whether an owner who leases a unit and delegates all rights of use to the common area may be prohibited from using the facilities but indicated that a different rule might apply in such a case. This case may be in conflict with *Liebler v. Point Loma Tennis Club (1995) 40 Cal. App.4th 1600, 47 Cal.Rptr.2d 782.*

Marina Green Homeowners Assn. v. State Farm Fire & Casualty Co. (1994) 25 Cal.App.4th 200, 30 Cal.Rptr.2d 364 (subject: association operating problems). California Insurance Code § 10087 requires an insurance company providing homeowner insurance to also offer earthquake coverage; however, the requirements of Section 10087 do not apply to an association master policy in a development of more than four units. Section 10087 applies only to individually owned condominium units and residential structures of not more than four units.

Marquez Knolls Property Owners Association, Inc. v. Executive Risk Indemnity, Inc. (2007) 153 Cal.App.4th 228; 62 Cal.Rptr.3d 510 (subject: association insurance). A dispute arose between adjacent owners and the association over the construction of a patio enclosure. One set of owners sued the association for disapproving the structure and requiring its removal. The association tendered the defense and indemnity of the lawsuit to its insurance carrier, which denied coverage on the basis of an exclusion for any claim arising out of the "design, construction, renovation or rehabilitation or any building, structure or other improvement on the property." The Court of Appeal held the exclusion did not apply because the activities of the association involved only the review and disapproval of the alteration carried out by an owner. The association was not involved in any way in the design, construction, renovation or rehabilitation of the patio enclosure. The policy language excluded only involvement in the design, construction, renovation or rehabilitation by the association itself. Therefore, the claim was covered by the policy and the insurance carrier had a duty to defend and indemnify the association.

Martin v. Bridgeport Community Association, Inc. (2009) 173 Cal.App.4th 1024, 93 Cal.Rptr.3d 405 (subject: association operating problems). The owners of a home in a planned development purchased the property for occupancy by their daughter and son-in-law and gave the occupants a power of attorney to deal on their behalf with the association. It was later determined that the size of the lot was smaller than represented in the purchase documents. In negotiations with the developer and the association, the occupants (i.e., not the owners) reached an agreement on a lot line adjustment that would increase the lot size by approximately 5,600 square feet. The association reneged on the agreement and the occupants sued for specific performance of the agreement. Although the occupants held an assignment of all rights from the owners to prosecute the litigation, the Court of Appeal ruled that the "occupants", as distinct from the "owners", had no standing to pursue claims of the owners to recover an interest in real property, which is not assignable, and they were not proper parties to the agreement to the lot line adjustment. The court went on to hold that although the occupants were bound by the association's governing documents, that fact did not give them an independent right to sue the association for enforcement of the governing documents. Under Civil Code § 1354 enforcement rights lie with the association and owners alone. Occupants without an ownership interest do not have standing to enforce the governing documents.

Mission Shores Association v. Pheil (2008) 166 Cal.App.4th 789, 83 Cal.Rptr.3d 108 (subject: CC&R enforcement). An owners association filed a petition in Superior Court to reduce the percentage of votes necessary to amend its CC&Rs pursuant to Civil Code § 1356. The association sought to limit residential leases to a minimum of 30 days. The amendment garnered 59% of the vote but not the 67% required by the CC&Rs to change leasing rights. An owner objected that he had purchased in reliance on the developer's representations that he was free to rent for any term without restriction. The Court of Appeal held that the rental restriction was reasonable, and was not arbitrary or capricious, in restricting rentals to 30 days or more to ensure that the property would not become "akin to a hotel" and to preserve the character of the community. The court noted that similar restrictions are found in many city and county ordinances, and are not contrary to public policy. Notably, the court also stated that the enforcement remedies in the CC&Rs apply to tenants as well as owners and may be enforced against both by the association, so long as the enforcement does not violate public policy.

Moran v. Oso Valley Greenbelt Assn. (2004) 117 Cal.App.4th 1029, 12 Cal.Rptr.3d 343 (subject: association operating problems). In an action brought by an owner to recover costs and attorney fees in inspecting association records, the trial court has discretion whether or not to award such expenses depending on the facts of a particular case. The court will take into consideration such factors as delay in production, prevaricating tactics, and charging more than the reproduction cost.

Morgan v. Veach (1943) 59 Cal.App.2d 682, 139 P.2d 976 (subject: CC&R enforcement). An association or an owner may require removal of a structure built in violation of building restrictions.

Nelson v. Avondale Homeowners Association (2009) 172 Cal.App.4th 857, 91 Cal.Rptr.3d 726 (subject: association operating problems). An owner, who was both a religious and medical counselor, gave up his business office and conducted business from his condominium where he received clientele. The association's governing documents prohibited a "home business". The owner made no attempt to obtain the approval of the association or the local municipality before conducting a home business. The association imposed a $200 fine for the violation, revoked all guest passes until the owner provided a non-commercial guest list and offered to make "reasonable accommodation" for the owner to service his clientele by mail until he could re-establish an outside office. The owner filed suit claiming discrimination based on disability and religion in violation of the California Fair Employment and Housing Act (Gov't Code §§ 12900 et seq.) and for various other causes of action, including injunctive relief. The Court of Appeal affirmed a trial court ruling denying relief stating that the owner was unlikely to prevail on the merits and therefore injunctive relief was inappropriate.

Oak Park Calabasas Condominium Association v. State Farm Fire & Casualty Co. (2006) 137 Cal.App.4th 557; 40 Cal.Rptr.3d 263 (subject: association insurance). An association may not simply refuse to pay a contractor and when the contractor sues, transfer its contractual liability to its insurance carrier under the provisions of its directors and officers liability which provide coverage for a negligent act or omission. Moreover, the association's deliberate act in not paying its contractor lacked the fortuity of unanticipated consequences normally required to trigger insurance coverage.

Ocean Harbor House Homeowners Association v. California Coastal Com. (2008) 163 Cal.App.4th 215, 77 Cal.Rptr.3d 432 (subject: governmental permits). An owners association sought a coastal development permit from the California Coastal Commission to build a seawall to protect the condominium complex from erosion that threatened its structural integrity. The commission granted the permit, but as a condition required the association to pay a mitigation fee to the state that over five years would total $5.3 million in present value. The association appealed the amount of the mitigation fee. The Court of Appeal affirmed the amount of the fee finding that it was roughly proportional to the value of one acre of beach front property the seawall would eliminate over time.

Oceanside Community Assn. v. Oceanside Land Co. (1983) 147 Cal. App.3d 166, 195 Cal.Rptr. 14 (subject: developer liability). A covenant recorded by a developer which restricts property to use as a golf course for 99 years for the benefit of the adjacent residential development is enforceable against a subsequent purchaser of the restricted property.

Orndorff v. Christiana Community Builders (1990) 217 Cal.App.3d 683, 266 Cal.Rptr. 193 (subject: construction defect litigation). The standard measure of damage for injury to property is the cost of repair or diminution in value, whichever is less; however, when the injured property has special or unique value to the owner, the owner may elect between either measure of damage but may not recover both.

Ostayan v. Nordhoff Townhomes Homeowners Assn. (2003) 110 Cal. App.4th 120, 1 Cal.Rptr.3d 528 (subject: disclosure). An association is not required to notify its members when filing suit against its insurance company for damages, unless a contrary provision is present in the association's governing documents.

Pacific Hills Homeowners Association v. Prun (2008) 160 Cal. App.4th 1557; 73 Cal.Rptr.3d 653 (subject: CC&R enforcement). In a planned development, owners installed a gate and a fence in violation of the height and setback requirements of the CC&Rs and architectural guidelines adopted as rules. More than four years transpired before the association commenced an enforcement action. The owners defended on the grounds that the 4-year statute of limitation (Code of Civil Procedure § 337) that applies to written documents controlled rather than the 5-year statute of limitation (Code of Civil Procedure § 336(b)) that applies to a restriction of the use of land. The Court of Appeal affirmed the trial court's ruling that the 5-year statute of limitation controls both the enforcement of CC&R provisions and the rules, and therefore the association's enforcement action was timely.

Pacifica Homeowners' Assn. v. Wesley Palms Retirement Community (1986) 178 Cal.App.3d 1147, 224 Cal.Rptr. 380 (subject: association operating problems). A landowner has no natural right to air, light, or an unobstructed view unless created by the legislature, local government or by private parties through an easement or CC&R provision.

Palacin v. Allstate Insurance Co. (2004) 119 Cal.App.4th 855, 14 Cal.Rptr.3d 731 (subject: insurance coverage). Owner sued her insurance carrier for wrongful denial of coverage for water damage to the walls and floors of her condominium unit. The policy covered all items "which are your insurance responsibility as expressed or implied under the governing rules of the condominium." The carrier claimed that damage to the walls and floors were the association's insurance responsibility under the governing documents and therefore there was no coverage under the owner's policy. The Court of Appeal held that the owner's insurance obligations may be determined not only from the language of the policies involved but also from the language of the governing documents and the actual practices of the owners and the association in obtaining insurance coverage.

Palacio Del Mar Homeowners Association v. McMahon (2009) 174 Cal.App.4th 1386, 95 Cal.Rptr.3d 445 (subject: CC&R enforcement). The association obtained a $40,000 judgment against an owner who operated the association website. As part of the post-judgment enforcement proceeding, the association sought an order requiring the owner to turn over his rights of the domain name to the association. The Court of Appeal held that the association was not entitled to a "turn over" order under the post-judgment enforcement statutes because they did not authorize the turn over of "intangible" property such as a domain name. The association also failed to show that the domain name was in his "possession" because it was registered in his wife's name and serviced by Network Solutions. Neither the wife nor Network Solutions was a party to the litigation.

Pamela W. v. Millson (1994) 225 Cal. App.4th 950, 30 Cal.Rptr.2d 690 (subject: association operating problems). An association does not have a duty to take steps to protect against criminal activity absent prior knowledge of similar criminal activity in the neighborhood, even though a condominium project may be located in a high crime area. But a duty may arise when the association becomes aware that criminal acts are likely to occur in the absence of crime prevention measures.

Palm Valley Homeowners Assn. v. Design MTC (2001) 85 Cal.App.4th 553, 102 Cal.Rptr.2d 350 (subject: association operating problems.). A corporation suspended for failure to file a required information statement with the California Secretary of State, as well as for non-payment of taxes, may not prosecute or defend a lawsuit. Counsel who knowingly violates this rule may be subject to sanctions by the trial court.

Paradise Hills Assn. v. Procel (1991) 235 Cal.App.3d 1528, 1 Cal. Rptr.2d 514 (subject: construction defect litigation). A developer may not stop distribution of truthful information about construction defects by owners who already live in the development. Such action is an unconstitutional prior restraint on the exercise of free speech guaranteed by the First Amendment of the United States Constitution. However, distribution of false information may be actionable trade defamation.

Park Place Estates Homeowners Assn. v. Naber (1994) 29 Cal. App.4th 427, 35 Cal.Rptr.2d 51 (subject: association operating problems). An owner may not withhold assessments owed to the association on the grounds that the owner is entitled to recover money or damages from the association for some other obligation. The Davis-Stirling Common Interest Development Act establishes a strong public policy against allowing an owner to offset assessments against any other obligation allegedly owed by the association to the owner.

Park Redlands Covenant Control Comm. v. Simon (1986) 181 Cal. App.3d 87, 226 Cal.Rptr. 199 (subject: age restrictions and discrimination). An age restriction requiring all residents to be over age 45 does not meet the requirements of Civ. Code § 51.3.

Parkwoods Community Association v. California Insurance Guarantee Association (2006) 141 Cal.App.4th 1362; 46 Cal.Rptr.3d 921 (subject: association insurance). California Insurance Guarantee Association (CIGA) is a quasi-governmental agency created to pay covered claims against insolvent property and casualty insurance carriers authorized to do business in California. However, financial assistance is available from CIGA only when no other insurance is available to cover the claim. The court held that a partially exhausted policy of excess insurance constitutes "other insurance available to cover the claim" to the extent that its limits have not been completely exhausted and therefore CIGA had no obligation to contribute to settlement of a construction defect lawsuit.

Peak Investments v. South Peak Homeowners Association (2006) 140 Cal.App.4th 1363; 44 Cal.Rptr.3d 892 (subject: association operating problems). Civil Code § 1356 allows the association or an owner to petition the court for an order reducing the percentage required to amend the CC&Rs when the CC&Rs require a super-majority (e.g., 67%, 75%, etc.) to approve the amendment, but before petitioning the court the amendment first must be put to a vote and approved by majority of the owners. The question addressed in this case is whether the pre-petition vote must result in approval by a majority of the total voting power of the association or by a majority of the votes actually cast. The Court of Appeal held that the statute requires pre-petition approval by a majority of all owners; not a majority of those casting votes.

Pinnacle Museum Tower Association v. Pinnacle Market Development (2010) 187 Cal.App.4th 24, 113 Cal.Rptr.3d 399 (subject: construction defect litigation). The Court of Appeal affirmed the denial of a developer's petition to compel arbitration in an action for construction defects. The court held that (1) an arbitration provision

in the CC&Rs prepared and recorded by the developer did not constitute an "agreement" sufficient to waive the constitutional right to a jury trial (Article I, Section 16, of the California Constitution) in an action for construction defects brought by a homeowners association, and (2) the jury waiver provision in the purchase and sale agreements signed by the individual homeowners were not enforceable against the association. See also Villa Vincenza Homeowners Association v. Nobel Court Development, LLC, (2010) 185 Cal.App.4th 23, ___Cal. Rptr.3d ___.

Posey v. Leavitt (1991) 229 Cal.App.3d 1236, 280 Cal.Rptr. 568 (subject: CC&R enforcement). Construction of a deck encroaching on common area in violation of the CC&Rs is actionable by the association or any owner. If the association fails or refuses to act, any owner may sue to have the encroachment removed even if the association granted erroneous approval. Civil Code § 1354(a) provides that unless the CC&Rs state otherwise, CC&R restrictions may be enforced by either the association or an owner. (Note: In a CC&R enforcement action involving less that $5,000 in monetary damages, Civil Code § 1354 requires the parties to attempt to resolve the matter through alternative dispute resolution, such as mediation or arbitration, before proceeding to litigation or certain penalties attach.)

Queen Villas Homeowners Association v. TCB Property Management (2007) 149 Cal.App.4th 1; 56 Cal.Rptr.3d 528 (subject: association operating problems). A homeowners' association brought suit against its property management company for failure to disclose and thwart a single board member from self-dealing in providing liaison services in connection with a separate construction defect lawsuit. Apparently, the director was paid for her "services" by the property manager without the requisite board approval. The property manager defended the suit based upon a standard indemnification clause under which the association agreed to defend, indemnify and hold harmless the manager from all claims arising out of the manager's performance of its duties under the management agreement, excluding only claims involving the manager's sole negligence or willful misconduct. The Court of Appeal held this type of classic indemnity clause relates only to third party claims and not to claims between the association and the manager themselves. Such protection can only be achieved by a very clearly drafted exculpatory clause not present in the agreement under review. The court pointed out that to rule otherwise would allow the manager to disregard its duties under the management agreement with impunity. (Note: exculpatory clauses may be subject to challenge as contrary to public policy under Civil Code § 1668.)

Rancho Santa Fe Association v. Dolan-King (2004) 115 Cal.App.4th 28, 8 Cal.Rptr.3d 614 (subject: CC&R enforcement). Unrecorded rules designed to act as guidelines in helping homeowners evaluate architectural modifications are subject to the test of reasonableness, and, provided they meet that test, are enforceable against an owners. In a lawsuit over the proper interpretation of the rules, the prevailing party is entitled to attorney fees and court costs. In this case, the Court of Appeal upheld an attorney fee award in favor of the association in the amount of $318,293.50.

Raven's Cove Townhouse, Inc. v. Knuppe Dev. Co. (1981) 114 Cal. App.3d 783, 171 Cal.Rptr. 334 (subject: developer liability). Developer appointed directors can be held personally liable for decisions that benefit the developer's interests at the expense of the association and its members. Also, the cost of repair is the proper measure of damage in a construction defect lawsuit.

Ritter & Ritter, Inc. Pension & Profit Plan v. The Churchill Condominium Association (2008) 166 Cal.App.4th, 82 Cal.Rptr.3d 389 (subject: association operating problems). Condominium owners sued their association and the individual directors for breach of the CC&Rs, breach of fiduciary duty and injunctive relief for failure to plug utility openings or penetrations in concrete slab floors that separated upper from lower units in a 13-story building. Odors from lower floors were able to pass through the openings and affect the units above. The original construction plans called for the openings to be closed. Building codes in effect at the time of original construction did not require they be closed; current building codes did require closure of new buildings but not a retrofit of existing, nonconforming conditions. The retrofit work adjacent to plaintiffs' units could have been accomplished for $2,700 per unit. A jury found the association had breached its duty to maintain the common areas as required by the CC&Rs and also found the individual directors were not individually liable. The Court of Appeal affirmed the jury verdict and the trial court's award against the association of $531,159 in attorney fees and related legal expense.

Ruiz v. Harbor View Community Association (2005) 134 Cal.App.4th

1456; 37 Cal.Rptr.3d 133 (subject: association/owner litigation). Owners filed a defamation lawsuit against an association stemming from the denial of the owners' conceptual plans to rebuild their house. The defamation claims were based on two letters written by association counsel. The association challenged the suit on the grounds that the letters were in furtherance of free speech and protected by Code of Civil § 425.16 (anti-SLAPP). That statute provides a special motion to strike a complaint against a person arising from any act of that person in furtherance of the person's right of petition or free speech under federal or state law. The statute protects all defendants, including corporate associations, from interference with the valid exercise of their constitutional rights, particularly the right of freedom of speech or petition the government for redress of grievances. These protections extend to private conduct that impacts a private community as well as public community.

Ruoff v. Harbor Creek Community Assn. (1992) 10 Cal.App.4th 1624, 13 Cal.Rptr.2d 755 (subject: association/owner liability). Individual condominium owners, as well as the association, may be held individually liable for injuries sustained as a result of hazardous conditions in the common area. Civil Code § 1365.9, enacted after the *Ruoff* case and in response to it, now gives limited immunity to individual owners if the association carries a certain level of liability insurance; however, the limited immunity extends only to tort claims.

Salawy v. Ocean Towers Housing Corporation (2004) 121 Cal.App.4th 644, 17 Cal.Rptr.3d 427 (subject: CC&R enforcement). Owners brought an action against their apartment cooperative for oral promises made to reimburse them for out-of-pocket expenses incurred in vacating the apartment building during large-scale renovation following the Northridge earthquake in 1994. The trial court dismissed the complaint based on what it determined to be superseding provisions of the governing documents and certain defenses available to directors under the same documents. The trial court then awarded the association $15,000 in attorney fees. The Court of Appeal reversed the attorney fee award holding that Civil Code § 1354 only authorizes an award of attorney fees in an action to "enforce" the governing documents; not in an action by an owner to enforce an oral promise where provisions of the governing documents are used merely as a defense. But see *Kaplan v. Fairway Oaks Homeowners Association (2002) 98 Cal.App.4th 715, 120 Cal.Rptr.2d 158.*

Salton Sea Area Property Owners Assn. v. M. Penn Phillips Co. *(1977) 75 Cal.App.3d 184, 141 Cal.Rptr. 895* (subject: construction defect litigation). An association has standing to represent its members in a lawsuit upon a determination that the association can fairly and adequately represent the members' interests, notwithstanding the fact that the association itself has not been damaged and has no contractual relationship with the defendant. (See also Code of Civil Procedure §§ 382 and 383.)

Seligman v. Tucker (1970) 6 Cal.App.3d 691, 86 Cal.Rptr. 187 (subject: CC&R enforcement). A view restriction forbidding the erection of a structure on any lot to a height which unreasonably obstructs the view from any other lot is not too vague or uncertain to be enforceable, but a specific height limitation would also be valid.

Share v. Casiano Bel-Air Homeowners Assn. (1989) 215 Cal.App.3d 515, 263 Cal.Rptr. 753 (subject: association operating problems). An owner who prevails in a CC&Rs dispute with an association is entitled to recover attorney fees. (See also Civil Code § 1354(c).)

Siegel v. Anderson Homes (2004) 118 Cal.App.4th 994, 13 Cal. Rptr.3d 462 (subject: construction defects litigation). Subsequent owners of homes brought an action for construction defects and an issue arose over whether the original owners or the subsequent owners had the right to bring the action for construction defects. The Court of Appeal held that subsequent owners could bring an action for construction defect provided that appreciable damage first became apparent to a reasonable person during their period of ownership. If the damage first became apparent prior to their purchase, the claim for construction defects belonged to the prior owners. When the damage became apparent is a question of fact for the judge or jury at trial. The sale of property does not automatically transfer the right to bring an action for damages possessed by a prior owner, but such a right can be transferred from the seller to the purchaser in the purchase contract.

Siena Court Homeowners Association v. Green Valley (2008) 164 Cal.App.4th 1416, 79 Cal.Rptr.3d 915 (subject: construction defect litigation). A condominium owners association brought an action against its developer for construction defects. The association that sued shared certain recreation facilities with a second owners association. The second association sought to intervene or become part of the first association's construction defect lawsuit some two years after it was commenced because the statute of limitation had run on its own action against the developer. The court denied the application on the grounds that the addition of a new party as a plaintiff would increase the complexity and introduce new issues not already before the court. Since the second association could not show that it was an indispensable party in the first association's lawsuit, the trial court properly exercised its discretion to deny the request.

Smith v. Laguna Sur Villas Community Assn. (2000) 79 Cal.App.4th 639, 94 Cal.Rptr.2d 321 (subject: association attorney client privilege). An incorporated association is a separate legal entity distinct from its members, and it may assert the attorney-client privilege to protect all communications (including billings) between the attorney and the association against disclosure to the members of the association. Directors who have an absolute right to request privileged information in their capacity as directors lose that right when they cease to be directors.

Smith v. Superior Court (1990) 217 Cal.App.3d 950, 266 Cal.Rptr. 253 (subject: association/owner liability). The statute of limitation for an action by an owner against an association for breach of fiduciary duty and negligence is 3 years. California Code of Civil Procedure § 359 provides that an action against directors of a corporation must be brought within 3 years after the discovery of the wrongful acts by the aggrieved party. But see, *Briano v. Rubio (1996) 46 Cal.App4th 1167, 54 Cal.Rptr.2d 408,* criticizing *Smith.*

Standard Fire Insurance Co. v. The Spectrum Community Association (2006) 141 Cal.App.4th 1117; 46 Cal.Rptr.3d 804 (subject: construction defect litigation). A general liability insurance policy issued to real estate developer before any of the units were sold must provide coverage for property damage claims that occur during the policy period, even though the damage took place before a homeowners' association came into existence and the claims are not asserted until after the developer have sold all of the units and divested itself of any interest in the property.

Starlight Ridge South Homeowners Association v. Hunter-Bloor (2009) 177 Cal.App.4th 440, 99 Cal.Rptr.3d 20 (subject: CC&R enforcement). Starlight Ridge is a planned development. Under its

CC&Rs the association is responsible for the maintenance, repair and replacement of the "landscape maintenance areas" and all improvements and facilities thereon. A separate CC&R provision requires each owner to "maintain, repair, replace and keep free from debris or obstructions the drainage system and devices, if any, located on his Lot." A drainage channel or V-ditch that crossed over a portion of an owner's property was is poor condition and partially collapsed. The association requested the owner to perform repairs. The owner declined on the ground that the V-ditch was in the "landscape maintenance areas" and an association responsibility. The association sought judicial relief. The Court of Appeal ruled in favor of the association largely on the ground that in interpreting a legal document (i.e., the CC&Rs) a court will resolve an ambiguity by reference to the rule that a specific provision will take precedence over a more general provision. Here, the CC&Rs specifically stated that the owner was responsible for maintaining the V-ditch, and that specificity overrode the more general provision that the association was responsible for the landscape maintenance areas.

Stearman v. Centex Homes (2000) 78 Cal.App.4th 611, 92 Cal.Rptr.2d 761 (subject: construction defect litigation). A homeowners' association can recover under strict liability for defective components in a building that cause injury or damage to other components of the building, regardless of whether injury or damage has occurred to persons or property apart from the structure itself. Also, expert fees incurred by the association in having professionals investigate construction defects and formulate an appropriate repair plan are recoverable as damages in a lawsuit.

Stonegate Homeowners Association v. Staben (2006) 144 Cal. App.4th 740; 50 Cal.Rptr.3d 709 (subject: construction defect litigation). An association has a valid claim against a subcontractor arising from the subcontractor's defective work, even if there is no privity of contract between the association and the subcontractor. Regardless of the contractual arrangement between the general contractor and the subcontractor, the subcontractor has a duty to perform the work in a good and workmanlike manner according to standards in the industry. See also, *La Jolla Village Homeowners Association v. Superior Court (1989) 212 Cal.App.3d 1131, 261 Cal.Rptr. 146.*

Thaler v. Household Finance Corp. (2000) 80 Cal.App.4th 1093, 95 Cal.Rptr.2d 779 (subject: lien priority of assessment lien). An assessment does not have priority over a prior recorded mortgage or deed of trust regardless of language in the CC&Rs purporting to give an assessment lien priority over a prior recorded encumbrance.

Ticor Title Ins. Co. v. Rancho Santa Fe Assn. (1986) 177 Cal.App.3d 726, 223 Cal.Rptr. 175 (subject: CC&R enforcement). In interpreting governing documents, a specific provision will control over a general provision. A provision requiring written approval of 2/3 of the owners for modification of setback requirements will control over a general provision giving the board the power to make regulations for the general welfare of the owners.

Tilly v. CZ Master Association (2005) 131 Cal.App.4th 464, 32 Cal. Rptr.3d 151 (subject: association operating problems). A security guard sued a homeowners' association for negligence, negligent supervision and premises liability for injuries he suffered when responding to complaints about a youth party. He attempted to arrest two party-goers and was assaulted. The court dismissed the action finding that the association had no duty to restrict youth parties, no control over the party, and did not require the security guard to confront potentially violent persons. The basic scope of the guards duties was to observe and report misconduct. See also *Pamela W. v. Millson (1994) 225 Cal.App.4th 950, 30 Cal.Rptr.2d 690.*

Titus v. Canyon Lake Property Owners Association (2004) 118 Cal. App.4th 906, 13 Cal.Rptr.3d 807 (subject: association liability). An association had no duty to protect a passenger in a private vehicle driven by an intoxicated driver on association property where neither the association nor its security company acted in any way to increase the risk of such an accident and neither had reason to foresee that such an accident would occur. The mere authority to make and enforce traffic rules within the community was insufficient to create a heighten standard of care on the part of the association.

Tomko Woll Group Architects, Inc. v. Superior Court (1996) 46 Cal. App.4th 1326, 54 Cal.Rptr.2d 300 (subject: construction defect litigation). The 4-year statute of limitation of Code of Civil Procedure § 337.1 for commencement of an action based upon personal injury or property damage arising out of a patent (or obvious) construction defect begins to run upon substantial completion of the project; not when the deficiency is discovered or when the injury or damage is sustained.

Trend Homes, Inc. v. Superior Court (2005) 131 Cal.App.4th 950, 32 Cal.Rptr.3d 411 (subject: construction defect litigation). A clause in a purchase agreement for a new home requiring all claims for construction defects not resolved by mediation to be resolved by reference to an extra-judicial private referee/arbitrator is enforceable against original purchasers who signed the purchase agreement, but not enforceable against subsequent owners who bought after the original sale and did not sign the original purchase agreement. See also *Greenbriar Homes Communities, Inc. v. Superior Court (2004) 117 Cal.App.4th 337, 11 Cal.Rptr.3d 371;* but see *Pardee Construction Co. v. Superior Court (2002) 100 Cal.App.4th 1081, 1086, 123 Cal.Rptr.2d 288,* for a contrary ruling.

Treo @ Kettner Homeowners Assn. v. Superior Court (2008) 166 Cal.App.4th 1055, 83 Cal.Rptr.3d 318 (subject: construction defect litigation). A condominium owners association sued the developer and others for construction defects. The developer written CC&Rs required all disputes between the association and the developer be decided by a referral to a non-judicial third party (e.g., a retired judge, etc.) pursuant to Code of Civil Procedure § 638. On appeal the CC&R provision requiring non-judicial disposition violated Article I, Section 16, of the California Constitution and Code of Civil Procedure § 631 which ensures the right to trial by jury unless the parties waive the protection after a dispute has arisen. See also *Grafton Partners v. Superior Court (2005) 36 Cal.4th 944, 32 Cal.Rptr.3d 5.*

Turner v. Vista Pointe Homeowners Association (2010) 180 Cal. App.4th 676, ___ Cal.Rptr.3d ___ (subject: CC&R enforcement). Homeowners filed suit against the association alleging various claims for failure of the association to grant a variance for unapproved modifications to an outdoor patio, including a casita, that was built more than a foot higher than the approved height. The association denied a variance, in part, because of a protesting neighbor. The association responded to the suit by a motion to dismiss the complaint on the grounds that its actions in enforcing architectural restrictions were protected free speech activities and subject to dismissal pursuant to California's anti-SLAPP statute (Code of Civil Procedure § 425.16). The Court of Appeal held that not every communication about the enforcement of architectural restrictions is protected freedon of

speech. **The court further found that the association's actions in this case were not taken in furtherance of its right of free speech and therefore not protected by the anti-SLAPP statute. See also, Ruiz v. Harbor View Community Association (2005) 134 Cal.App.4th 1456, 37 Cal.Rptr.3d 133; and Damon v. Ocean Hills Journalism Club (2000) 85 Cal.App.4th 468, 102 Cal.Rptr.2d 205.**

Vaughn v. Dame Construction Co. (1990) 223 Cal.App.3d 144, 272 Cal.Rptr. 261 (subject: construction defect litigation). An owner who sues for construction defects may continue to prosecute the action even after that owner sells the property. Given the duty of disclosure in California, presumably the sale price will be reduced to reflect the existence of disclosed defects. If repairs have been carried out, the seller who actually paid for the repairs has suffered the damage.

Villa Milano Homeowners Association v. Il Davorge (2000) 84 Cal. App.4th 819, 102 Cal.Rptr.2d 1 (subject: construction defect litigation). A binding arbitration clause in CC&Rs inserted by the developer and designed to preclude homeowners and homeowners' associations from pursuing an action for construction defects in court is unenforceable as it circumvents other statutory protections, is unconscionable and violates public policy, but the rule is expressly limited to claims for construction defects and does not extend to other types of disputes that may arise in the homeowners association context.

Villa Vincenza Homeowners Association v. Nobel Court Development, LLC (2010) 185 Cal.App.4th 23, ___ Cal.Rptr.3d ___ (subject: construction defect litigation). An arbitration provision in the CC&Rs for a common interest development recorded by the developer, did not constitute an "agreement" sufficient to waive the constitutional right to a jury trial (Article I, Section 16, of the California Constitution) for construction defect claims brought by a homeowners association. See also Pinnacle Museum Tower Association v. Pinnacle Market Development (2010) 187 Cal.App.4th 24, 113 Cal.Rptr.3d 399; Treo @ Kettner Homeowners Association v. Superior Court (2008) 166 Cal.App.4th 1055, 83 Cal.Rptr.3d 318.

Ward v. Superior Court (1997) 55 Cal.App.4th 60, 63 Cal.Rptr.2d 731 (subject: CC&R enforcement). An association may not record a "notice of noncompliance" or "notice of violation" against a property for a violation of the governing documents. Recordable documents are governed by statute. No statute authorizes the recordation of a "notice of noncompliance" or "notice of violation." Individuals cannot create a recordable document by private agreement or by a CC&R provision.

Windham At Carmel Mountain Ranch Assn. v. Superior Court (2003) 109 Cal.App.4th 1162, 135 Cal.Rptr.2d 824 (subject: construction defect litigation). An association may have a cause of action against a developer for breach of implied warranty with respect to the common areas of condominium. The association has the requisite privity of contract as implied by Cal. Code Civ. Proc. § 383. Further, Civ. Code § 945 makes this privity explicit for condominiums sold on or after January 1, 2003.

Wilton v. Mountain Wood Homeowners Assn. (1993) 18 Cal.App.4th 565, 22 Cal.Rptr.2d 471 (subject: association operating problems). Recording an assessment lien by an association is absolutely privileged under California Civil Code § 47(b) and not actionable even if the lien is without merit.

Winston Square Homeowners Assn. v. Centex West, Inc. (1989) 213 Cal.App.3d 282, 261 Cal.Rptr. 605 (subject: construction defect litigation). The trial court may award special master fees as a recoverable cost to the prevailing party in a construction defect action. Additionally, attempted repairs by a developer will only toll the applicable limitation period as to the specific defect repaired.

Woodridge Escondido Property Owners Association v. Nielsen (2005) 130 Cal.App.4th 559, 30 Cal.Rptr.3d 15 (subject: CC&R enforcement). An owner in a planned development constructed a wood deck that encroached on an easement area between two adjacent homes with the permission of the association's architectural committee. The CC&Rs prohibited the installation of "any permanent structure other than irrigation systems" in the easement area. The board of directors later found that the architectural committee has erroneously approved the deck, ordered the owner to remove the deck, and offered to pay the cost of removal. The owner refused and the association brought suit to require the removal of the deck from the easement area. The court found that because the CC&Rs expressly prohibit the construction of a permanent structure in the easement area, the association did not act arbitrarily in demanding the removal of the structure even after approving it. The court further found that the association did not have the authority to approve the construction of any structure in the easement area in violation of the CC&Rs. The association was allowed to recover its attorney fees.

UNITED STATES FEDERAL COURT OF APPEAL

Southern California Housing Rights Center v. Los Feliz Towers Homeowners Association, 426 F.Supp.2d 1061 (C.D. Cal. 2005) (subject: discrimination). A disabled condominium owner and an advocacy group filed an action in U.S. Federal District Court against a condominium association for housing discrimination under the Fair Housing Amendments Act (FHAA), the American With Disabilities Act (ADA), and state law. The association refused to grant the disabled owner's request to use the more convenient general manager's parking space rather than her deeded parking space, although the association offered to provide her with valet service as an alternative, which she rejected. The court dismissed the ADA claim because the association is a private entity and does not provide a place of "public accommodation." However, the court held she was entitled to proceed with her claim under the FHAA and state law as to whether the association failed to make a "reasonable accommodation" for her disability.

Opera Plaza Residential Parcel Owners Assn. v. Hoang, 376 F.3d 831 (9th Cir. 2004) (subject: CC&R enforcement). An action to obtain a declaratory ruling on the validity or invalidity of a satellite dish restriction must be brought in state court or by petition of the Federal Communications Commission. It may not be brought in federal court despite a Federal Communications Commission regulation indicating federal or state courts may hear such petitions. No action may be taken by an association to enforce a satellite dish restriction other than to file suit in state court or petition the Federal Communications Commission. See also, 47 Code of Federal Regulations §§ 1.4000(a) and 1.4000(e).

CHAPTER 13

California Association of Community Managers Standardized Management Agreement, Code of Ethics, Board Member Code of Ethics and Board Member Commitment Pledge

---

CACM Standardized Management Agreement*

Preliminary Recitals

A. REAL PROPERTY COVERED BY THIS AGREEMENT:

Common Interest Development:
Location:
Declaration Recordation No.:
Tract No.:
# of Residential Living Units:
Development Type:
Developer:
Address:

*This CACM Standardized Management Agreement is intended to be viewed only as a "sample" contract with guidelines. It is not intended to be utilized as a legal document or provide legal advice. Management firms and/or associations should consult legal counsel to best protect their own respective interests.

B. "ASSOCIATION" AS PARTY TO THIS AGREEMENT

Association: _____ , a California Mutual Benefit
Non-Profit Corporation
Address:

C. MANAGING AGENT ("AGENT") AS PARTY TO THIS AGREEMENT:

Name:
Address:
Principal:

D. DEFINITIONS

1. **"Association"** shall mean a corporation formed under the California state Corporation Code, or an unincorporated California Association, its successors and assigns. As used in this agreement, "Association" shall specifically represent _____ .

2. **"Base Fee"** shall mean the monthly fee as identified in Section 8, (A, B, and C) and covers agent's basic contractual services and usual and customary office expenses, exclusive of all extraordinary services which may occur by Board direction as identified in Section 9 and Exhibit A of this agreement.

3. **"Board"** of **"Board of Directors"** shall mean the Board of Directors of the Association, elected pursuant to the Bylaws of the Association.

4. **"Budget"** shall mean a written, itemized estimate of the expenses to be incurred by the Association in performing its functions under its Declaration and Bylaws.

5. **"Common Area"** shall mean all the real property and improvements, including without limitation, streets, open parking areas, landscape areas and recreational facilities, which are owned or controlled by the Association for the common use and enjoyment of all the owners.

6. **"Common Interest Development"** means any of the following: (1) a condominium project, (2) a planned development, or (3) a stock cooperative.

7. **"Definitions"**. The terms **"Association"**, **"Owner"**, or **"Managing Agent"**, herein or any pronoun used in the place thereof, shall mean and include the masculine and the feminine, the singular or the plural number and jointly and severally, individuals, firms or corporations, and each of their respective successors, executors, administrators, and assignees as the context so indicates.

8. **"Governing Documents"** shall mean the Declaration of Covenants, Conditions and Restrictions and other documents, such as By-Laws, operating rules of the association, which govern the operation of the common interest development or association.

9. **"Maintenance Assessments"**. As used in this Agreement, the term "Assessments" shall mean those rates established and approved by the Board of Directors, which the Association members are bound to pay as their share of the common expenses. The term "Association" as used herein shall mean an association consisting of all the Owners of units in the Common Interest Development (CID) organized under the laws of the State of California for the purpose of administering the Common Interest Development (CID) established by the Declaration of Covenants, Conditions and Restrictions ("Declarations") for the real property.

E. MISCELLANEOUS

In consideration of the covenants herein, the Association as described in B above enters into this Agreement with the Agent to manage the property described in A above for the compensation provided in Section 8 and for the term as set forth in Section 11 and subject to the Agency Agreement, "Scope of Services", Terms and Conditions set forth hereafter which are Pages 3 through 18 incorporated and made a part of this Agreement. These documents are to be construed as one integrated written Agreement between the parties, and include the recitals.

This written Agreement supersedes any and all prior representations, understandings and communications, and may be modified only by written agreement of the parties. Any oral agreements or modifications are expressly invalid.

This Agreement will be construed in accordance with, and governed by, the laws of the State of California. If any term, provision, covenant or condition of this Agreement, including the Scope of Services, should be found by a Court of competent jurisdiction to be invalid, all other provisions shall continue in full force and effect, and shall in no way be affected, impaired or invalidated.

If any legal proceeding is necessary to enforce or interpret the provisions of this Agreement, the prevailing party shall be entitled to its reasonable attorney's fees and legal costs, in addition to any other relief to which such party may be entitled. The parties agree that this Agreement shall be effective as of the date set forth in the TERM OF CONTRACT. (Section 11)

If the Association is incorporated, it is understood and so assured by the signer that the person signing on behalf of Association is a duly elected officer thereof and has corporate authority to execute contracts. If Association is unincorporated, and this Agreement is signed by both parties prior to the first (organizational) homeowners meeting, it is understood and assured by the person signing on behalf of Association that the Association automatically assumes or will assume the full legal obligations of this Agreement for the full term stated in this Agreement, and that no provisions to the contrary are or will be included in the Association's Covenants, Conditions and Restrictions or Bylaws.

ARTICLE II. APPOINTMENT AND ACCEPTANCE
Scope of Services

The Association hereby exclusively engages the Agent and appoints the Agent to manage the Association under the sole direction of the Board of Directors upon the terms and conditions hereinafter set forth. The relationship between the Association and Agent is one of Principal and Agent.

The Managing Agent (hereinafter called "Agent"), will deliver services reasonably necessary to provide Association with management services on behalf of the Association's Board of Directors, and strictly within the scope of this agreement.

1. MANAGING AGENT'S SERVICES AND RESPONSIBILITIES

1.1   The Association hereby appoints the Agent and the Agent hereby accepts appointment, on the terms and conditions hereinafter provided, as the Agent for the Association.

1.2 The Association retains the primary responsibility for enforcement of provisions of the Association's governing documents and contractual agreements and assumes liability for any and all acts and occurrences which relate to the actions of the association and its actions concerning the real property covered by this contract.

1.3 Agent will undertake reasonable efforts to implement the lawful decisions of the Board of Directors and in accordance with the Terms and Conditions of this Agreement, subject to the compensation schedule set forth herein. Agent will not be obligated to implement any decision which: a) is contrary to the terms of this Agreement, applicable laws or governing documents, b) would involve transactions or services outside the Agent's expertise, knowledge or licenses, or c) would involve transactions or services which are not set forth in this Agreement.

1.4 It will be the responsibility of Agent, during the term of this Agreement, to perform the duties as set forth in this Agreement, consistent with the plans and directives of the Association's Board of Directors, and to perform such other acts as are reasonably necessary to discharge Agent's responsibilities.

2. FINANCIAL MANAGEMENT

2.1 Maintenance Assessments. The Agent will provide for the collection and deposit of all maintenance assessments, and establish, at its sole discretion, a separate checking account or accounts, with any federally insured institution(s), as is customary with other Associations managed by Agent for the deposit and protection of Association's operating funds.

2.2 Association Operating Funds. Agent will establish and maintain Association funds, in a bank of Agent's choice whose deposits are federally insured, and in a manner to indicate the custodial nature thereof, a separate bank account as Agent of Association for the deposit of monies of Association, with authority to draw thereon for any payments to be made by the Agent to discharge any liabilities or obligations incurred pursuant to this Agreement and for the payment of the Agent's fee, all of which payments are subject to the limitations of this Agreement. From funds collected, Agent will cause to be paid the expenses for the operation of Association in accordance with the approved budget or as otherwise authorized by Association's Board of Directors. Any service fees charged for banking services or account maintenance by the bank shall be the responsibility of the association and shall be a charge against Association's operating and/or money market accounts.

2.3   Delinquent Accounts. Agent is authorized to take reasonable steps for collection of delinquent accounts. In the event such efforts fail, Agent will have authority to record a lien against the delinquent owner's unit in accordance with the Declarations and the approved collection policy. The Agent is authorized to assess the delinquent account a late charge and a delinquent processing charge, along with other charges for collection & lien fees, reflective of the costs of collection, accounting, payment plan monitoring and legal proceedings. All such assessments are to be deposited into the account of the Association. Agent shall be paid 50% of any late charges paid by homeowners. Statutory interest may be charged commencing 30 days after any due date. Reasonable costs of collection, including attorney's fees, are authorized to be charged and collected per Exhibit A.

2.4   Disbursement Authorization. Agent is authorized and shall make all disbursements from Association funds for liabilities incurred on behalf of Association. Association acknowledges Agent's role as Paymaster, accordingly, such disbursements may be made via paper drafts or electronically at the discretion of Agent. Agent is authorized to utilize all fraud control systems and methods available to Agent for the protection of Association's funds. Agent is hereby granted authority to make any non-budget expenditures as provided in this section at its own discretion up to $1,000.00 In addition, Agent shall have the authority to make normal and usual expenditures as prescribed by the Board of Directors and/or by the Association's approved operating budget. Agent will obtain approval for any extraordinary expenses of the Association as needed.

Emergency repairs involving imminent danger to life or property, or immediately necessary for the preservation and safety of the property, or for the safety of the Members, or required to avoid the suspension of any necessary service to the complex, may be made by the Agent irrespective of the cost limitation imposed by this section.

Agent will establish Association's reserve accounts at Association's direction. Agent makes no warranty or representations regarding the security or yield of any reserve investment. Except for the disbursements provided for above, all reserve account disbursements will be signed by two members of the Board of Directors.

2.5   Accounting and Financial Statements. Agent will maintain a set of accounting records in accordance with generally accepted industry standards.

a.   Agent will distribute monthly to all members of the Board of Directors a financial statement for the previous month, including copies of the Balance Sheet, Statement of Income and Expenses, Schedules of Cash Investments, reserve allocations, and a check register of disbursements.

b.   Agent shall reconcile all bank statements received by Agent and shall provide to the Board copies of both statements and reconciliations.

c.   Agent will cooperate with auditors in their performance of audits and reviews of Association's records and their preparation of applicable tax returns in accordance with Exhibit A.

d.   Agent will, upon direction from the Board of Directors, distribute to all members, at Association expense, copies of annual financial reports, budgets, collection policies, and all other publications and reports deemed necessary by the Board of Directors and applicable laws.

2.6   Budget Preparation. Agent will prepare and submit to the Board of Directors a proposed budget. Any budget draft will be subject to final approval by the Board of Directors and the Board shall retain full responsibility for the appropriateness of data contained in the budget. Any decision to adopt Agent's proposed budget, or to amend it for adoption will be reserved to and exercised solely by the Association's Board of Directors.

2.7   In the event Association elects to have an outside firm perform a reserve study, Agent agrees to cooperate with said outside firm and to furnish any and all necessary forms and documents in Agent's possession, upon request.

3. PHYSICAL MANAGEMENT

3.1   Maintenance. Agent will assist the Board of Directors in its responsibilities for the upkeep, maintenance and management of Common Area and the equipment, pursuant to the Association's documents and within the scope of this Agreement.

3.2   Agent will receive maintenance requests and/or complaints concerning the Association's Common Areas, and communicate them to appropriate Association contractors and vendors for correction, repairs and maintenance.

3.3   Agent will provide a 24-hours per day, 7 days per week call center to assist or refer emergencies in the Common Areas of the Association. Serious matters will be reported to the Association's Board of Directors with appropriate recommendations for the purpose of receiving further instructions from the Board on how to proceed.

3.4   Agent will perform monthly general reviews of the Association Common Areas and facilities from ground level, and will submit findings, action taken and recommendations to the Board of Directors, to assist in preserving the aesthetics of the common areas. Agent shall also make additional periodic reviews of the common area as it deems necessary to satisfy its duties under the terms of this Agreement. The Agent shall not be required to review the Common Areas during its reviews from any other perspective than from ground level. Agent is authorized to initiate routine repairs to the Common Areas and facilities, so long as such repairs and maintenance are in compliance with the Board's adopted management plan for the Association, or Section 2.4 herein.

3.5   Bids for Hiring, Supervising and Discharging Third Party Contractors.
        a. Agent will, upon receipt of instructions or upon resolution of the Board of Directors, request bids from insured vendors of Agent's and Board's selection, with a minimum of two (2) and a maximum of three (3) bids for the types of third party goods or services that Agent believes, in his sole discretion, are likely to cost $<<amount>> or more. Those items for which the Board requests bids that are in the Agent's sole discretion likely to less than $<<amount>> will not be let out for bid, and Agent shall be under no duty to solicit bids for those items. Should the Board wish for Agent to solicit bids for an item costing less than $<<amount>>, Agent shall be entitled to an hourly fee in accordance with Section 9.1 of this agreement. Specifications for all items shall be included with the Board's request, and the Board shall be solely responsible for establishing the standards, specifications or criteria for work to be let out for bid. Agent will endeavor to make helpful suggestions; however, the final decision in establishing standards, specifications and criteria shall be the Association

Board's.

b. Agent will, upon receipt of the Board's instructions or resolution, discharge Association contractors that the Board decides are not performing up to the standards, specifications or criteria established by the Board of Directors. Agent, on the basis of an operation schedule, job standards and compensation rates approved by the Association shall investigate, secure and pay third parties in order to maintain and operate the Association. Any contract for such third party contractors will be a direct contract between the Association and the third party contractor, and Agent will act solely as the Agent of the Association in negotiations and maintenance of said contract, and not as a contracting party. Compensation for the services of all third party contractors shall be paid by the Association. Under no circumstance does Agent make any representations or warranties for the work performed by any third party contractor.

4. ADMINISTRATIVE MANAGEMENT AND CONSULTING

4.1   Agent will organize the records and documents it receives from the Association or their prior manager or management company in accordance with its normal procedures. Within sixty (60) days from receipt of complete records, Agent shall render financial statements in their usual form showing the financial status of Association, or, if the records are inadequate to prepare such financial statements, Agent shall submit a written recommendation to Association. If such recommendation suggests a review or audit by a third party, or additional investigation and organization of information that will permit the publication of financial statements, Agent will provide estimated cost of performing such services.

4.2   Agent will write or delegate letters and communicate as necessary to assist the Board in carrying out its responsibilities.

4.3   Agent will counsel and advise Board of Directors and its committees in their day-to-day operations.

4.4   Agent will assist in interpretation of the rules of the Association and suggest possible steps of enforcement.

4.5   Agent will provide, at Association's sole cost and expense, material and expertise in the development of methods of communication to the homeowners (rules and regulations, etc.), as necessary.

4.6   Meeting Notices. At the request of the Board, and at the Association's sole cost and expense, Agent will send notices of Association meetings, prepare the Agenda for said meeting, circulate minutes of any such meetings as prepared by the Recording Secretary, and effect instructions as approved by the Board of Directors.

4.7   Agent will attend up to twelve (12) monthly meetings of the Board of Directors in any calendar year. Time in excess of two (2) hours per meeting or fraction thereof that lasts after 9:00 p.m. shall be charged at the rate schedule in accordance with Section 9.1 of this agreement.

4.8   Agent will attend meetings scheduled Monday through Thursday, except holidays. Meetings held on days other than those identified herein, and which the Agent agrees to attend, will be charged at the rate on Section 9.1 of this agreement.

4.9   Agent will not be obligated to attend special meetings of the membership or of the Board of Directors or the Association's committees. However, if Agent is requested to attend and accepts, Association will pay Agent at the rate schedule in accordance with Section 9.1 of this agreement, per hour for each hour or fraction thereof that such meeting last, plus mileage at IRS rate per mile as applicable.

4.10   At the Association's sole cost and expense, Agent will assist in preparation for Association Annual Membership Meeting, including notices, proxies and agenda, and will attend and participate in conducting the meeting if so requested by the Board of Directors.

4.11   Agent will not be responsible to record and/or type minutes of regular meetings of the Board of Directors or the Annual Meeting of the Association. Upon request by the Board of Directors, Agent shall coordinate a third party to serve as recording secretary, the costs for which shall be borne by the Association.

4.12   Association Records. Agent will maintain possession of all records of the affairs of the Association throughout the term of this

Agreement. While Agent will put forth every effort to maintain association records in good order, Agent makes no representation or warranty as to the accuracy and/or completeness of such records. Accuracy and/or completeness of the Association records remains the responsibility of the Association.

4.13 Owner Review of Records. Agent will make allowable Association records available for review to Association members. Association agrees that Agent shall charge a fee to the homeowner in accordance with Section 9.1 for records research and for the scheduling and monitoring of such a review.

4.14 Special Mailings and newsletters requested by the Board as prepared by the Association, shall be duplicated and mailed at the expense of the Association. All requests for duplication of additional copies of project documents, correspondence, reports, etc., will be at the expense of the Association.

5. TERMINATION OF AGREEMENT

5.1 Termination. Either party may terminate this agreement by providing sixty (60) days written notice to the other. This termination provision may be invoked with or without cause. Upon such notice of termination, both parties agree that this agreement shall remain in full force and effect for the entire sixty (60) days.

5.2. Arbitration Provision. In the event of a dispute over the performance and/or non-performance by either party in this agreement, the alleging party shall offer arbitration to the offending party prior to initiating legal action to gain compliance with the terms and conditions set forth by this agreement.

Prior to requesting arbitration, the alleging party must provide the offending party written notice of the dispute. Such notice shall allow for a reasonable time, not to exceed thirty (30) days, for the offending party to comply with this agreement. After the expiration of said thirty days the alleging party can proceed to binding arbitration or can elect to file suit. Upon acceptance of a written demand for arbitration the dispute shall be submitted to arbitration with a single arbitrator mutually selected by the parties from a list of five arbitrators submitted by the American Arbitration Association. The determination of the arbitrator shall be binding upon both parties. The arbitration shall be conducted pursuant to the rules of the American Arbitration Association and shall be submitted within 120 days of submission. Upon making a written demand for arbitration, the dispute shall be submitted promptly to an arbitrator mutually selected by the parties and the determination of the arbitrator shall be binding upon both parties. If the arbitrator shall determine that offending party has committed a material breach of this agreement, then such finding shall furnish the aggrieved party with the right to terminate the contract 30 days after the final decision of the arbitrator and the offending party shall bear all costs of the arbitration proceeding. In the event that the parties cannot mutually select a single arbitrator, the arbitrator will be selected by the American Arbitration Association from the remaining names. The arbitrator shall award the prevailing party its costs including reasonable attorney fees.

5.3   Termination Fee. The Association acknowledges that Agent will incur extraordinary costs in the transition period after termination such as the generation of special reports identifying the inventory of records, the inventory of current activities, processing the transitional documents, mechanically and physically transporting books, records and documents, and meeting with the Association and/or Agent's successor to describe, define and explain the Association's documents, instruments and records, and the functioning of the community. Consequently, Association agrees that all such transitional services shall be deemed to be extraordinary services for which Agent shall be compensated as hereafter set forth. In any event, however, the compensation for these transitional services shall not exceed the sum of the most recent monthly fee, including extras, payable under the Contract.

5.4   Attorney Fees and Costs. Should any party hereto retain counsel for the purpose of enforcing or preventing the breach of any provision hereof, including, but not limited to, instituting any action of proceeding or arbitration to enforce any provision hereof, for damages by reason of such party's rights or obligations hereunder or for any other judicial remedy, then the prevailing party shall be entitled to be reimbursed by the losing party for all such costs and expenses incurred thereby, including, but not limited to, reasonable attorney's fees and costs for services rendered to such prevailing party.

5.5   Condemnation. Upon taking of the entire or a substantial portion of the Project through lawful condemnation proceedings by any governmental party, either party may terminate this agreement by serving 30 days written notice by certified mail to the other party.

6. RECORDS RETENTION

6.1   The Association's current records shall be kept at the Agent's office. Such records shall be available for inspection and copying during Agent's normal business hours in accordance with California state laws and Association document provisions, Monday through Friday. Agent shall be entitled to charge and receive copying and document research costs, as set forth in Exhibit A, from anyone requesting copies of records or documents, before making such copies. Agent shall be entitled to reasonable notice prior to such inspection or copying of records.

6.2   Homeowner Lists. Agent shall maintain a current list of homeowners in the Association in accordance with the information supplied to Agent. Reasonable efforts will be made to keep this list accurate, but it shall be the responsibility of the Association to advise Agent of address or ownership changes. Agent shall not be obligated to search official records for such transfers of ownership unless specifically requested to do so by the Board at hourly rates set forth in this agreement. Agent will record changes of address of ownership upon advice from owners or escrow, with supporting documentation.

6.3   Correspondence. Agent will maintain documents and complete files for all current correspondence relating to Association, such as incoming unit owner correspondence, violation and architectural control letters, contracts, purchase orders, filing with public agencies, insurance policies and information and other related documents.

6.4   All records and correspondence regarding Association are and will remain the sole property of Association. Agent agrees to return any and all such records and correspondence to the Association, or to an entity or person designated by the Board of Directors upon termination of this Agreement. Such records will be available for pick up at Agent's office or such other designated location as may be agreed upon. Electronic media, such as computer tape, discs, and general electronically stored data bases are the sole property of the Agent and any duplication or transference of information shall be at the sole discretion of the Agent with all costs and charges to be paid by the requesting party.

6.5   Agent agrees to maintain storage of Association records and correspondence at Association sole cost and expense per Exhibit A.

7.   INSURANCE AND INDEMNIFICATION

AGENT'S INSURANCE

7.1   Agent will, throughout the term of this Agreement, and at Agent's expense, maintain the following insurance coverage:

a.   Fidelity Bond with coverage for all Agent's employees, when applicable, to protect Association funds, if any.

b.   Agent's liability insurance and comprehensive general liability coverage, including automobile liability, completed operations, blanket contractual and personal injury coverage, with combined single limits of $1,000,000 property damage and liability.

c.   Workers Compensation Insurance in the statutory amount, covering any of Agent's employees.

d.   Errors and Omissions coverage with limits of $1,000,000.

ASSOCIATION INSURANCE

7.2   Association will maintain at its sole expense a policy of comprehensive general liability, Directors and Officers, worker's compensation and property insurance (as necessary) in accordance with the Association's Declaration and applicable California law.

7.3   Association shall name Agent as an additional named insured on the Association's policies of comprehensive general liability and directors and officers insurance and said insurance policies will cover Agent for any and all claims and losses indemnified by Association pursuant to Section 7.5. Agent will be provided with insurance certificates identifying Agent as   additional named insured showing the amount of coverage to be furnished to the Agent.

7.4   In the mutual interest of Association and Agent, both parties agree that fidelity insurance coverage protecting Association funds shall be placed with The Hartford Insurance's Master Fidelity, so long as such coverage is available. The limits of the Master Fidelity policy shall be no less than the total amount of the Association's reserve funds plus three (3) months total assessment income.

7.5   Agent will maintain reasonable communication with Association's insurance agent and will assist the Board in reviewing and renewing insurance coverage, including solicitation of bids for such coverage. The Board of Directors is solely responsible for maintaining insurance coverage for the Association, and for ensuring the adequacy of coverage.

INDEMNIFICATION

7.6   Association shall indemnify, defend at its sole cost, and hold harmless Agent and its employees, agents, officers and directors from and against any and all claims, demands, losses, costs, expenses, obligations, liabilities, judgments, orders and damages, including interest, penalties and attorney's fees, that Agent shall incur or suffer which arise, result from, or relate to the performance by Agent of its duties under this agreement, except for the willful misconduct or gross negligence of Agent. This provision shall survive any termination of this Agreement.

7.7   Agent will be responsible only for any willful misconduct and gross negligence where such liability is due to the sole conduct of Agent and/or its employees in the performance of its duties under this Agreement.

8. COMPENSATION

In consideration of Agent's acceptance of its appointment hereunder and the performance of services as set forth herein, the compensation to which the Agent will be entitled will consist of fees for basic services (Base Fee) which are considered due upon execution of this agreement, but are paid monthly, along with those fees and costs for special or extraordinary services as set forth in Exhibit A.

a.   Agent shall be paid in advance on the first day of each month without prior Association approval Agent's base monthly fee of _____ .

b.   The base fee, as defined, shall be net to Agent and is exclusive of the Association's operating expenses and costs. The base fee shall be superseded by the adoption of a new annual association budget indicating an adjusted base fee for management services. Adoption of the annual budget by the Association's Board of Directors shall constitute an approval of a base fee change under this agreement, but in no event shall the base fee be less than the amount stated in A of this section.

c.   Agent and Association agree that the base fee for services identified in paragraph A above, is based upon the estimated time necessary to fulfill Agent's duties defined by this Agreement. Association and Agent agree that time in excess of _____ hours in the aggregate, shall be billed to Association in accordance with Section 9.1 herein. In the event Agent performs its duties under this Agreement in fewer hours than identified herein in any given month, the remaining hours will be carried forward to the following month. **Agent understands the time investment necessary to assist Association at the inception of this Agreement. Accordingly, Agent will not charge for excessive time for a period of four months from the date of commencement.**

8.1   Agent's Fees and Costs. Any base fees and costs due the Agent will be paid promptly each month on the first of each month. Any monies due and billed and not paid to Agent by the fifteenth (15th) of each month will carry a 1.5% per month late fee which will be added to the balance due and will be subject to further late charges until paid. Interest at the maximum legal rate to be charged thirty (30) days after any amounts are delinquent.

8.2   Reimbursable Administrative Operating Expenses. The Association shall be responsible to reimburse Agent for all postage, Xerox, fax and other usual office expenses incurred by Agent on Association's behalf. Association will also reimburse Agent for all reasonable expenses incurred on behalf of the Association including, but not limited to, those expenses listed in Exhibit A attached hereto as utilized in special projects (special mailings, newsletters, etc.), as may be amended from time to time, and included herein. Said costs will be reimbursed on a monthly basis as incurred and billed.

8.3   Deduction of Agent's Compensation. Association will be obligated to pay, and Agent shall receive as compensation for its services under this Agreement the sum provided for in this section herein and above at the times therein set forth. Agent is entitled to deduct such compensation when due from the funds then in its possession. Agent's compensation covers normal and usual administration expenses of Agent related to actions of the Board of Directors including costs of travel, as authorized by the Board of Directors.

9. SPECIAL OR EXTRAORDINARY SERVICES

9.1   Association shall pay Agent compensation as follows: Principals $_____ per hour, Community Administrator $_____ per hour, Accounting and Clerical Personnel $_____ per hour, or a specific rate as given below, for services performed on behalf of Association outside the normal course of operation or outside the parameters of this agreement.

9.2   Agent may be required to perform additional services beyond the scope of these services, for which the above fees, or the current rates that are then applicable, will be charged by the work performed. Examples of such services are, but not limited to:

a.   Assistance in adhering to requirements of laws and regulations which may be passed during the term of the Agreement, that require Agent participation.

b.   Agent will be paid per hour, portal to portal, for work performed by Agent on behalf of Association, including but not limited to, appearance at court, at hearings, depositions, claims negotiations and processing of insurance losses or reconstruction, performing committee functions, such as monitoring, reporting and updating of any architectural progress and violations within the common areas, development status reports, bank loans, investments, maintenance, construction defect matters, financial reconstruction, discovery on Association's acts prior to the original commencement date of this agreement.

c.   Agent will only be paid for the services identified above if performing said services cannot be accomplished, along with Agent's other duties defined herein, within the hours prescribed by Section 8, paragraph C of this Agreement.

10. ASSOCIATION SET-UP FEE

10.1   Agent shall be paid a one-time, non-refundable fee of $_____ at the commencement of this agreement to off-set the costs of setting up the Association's records. Not included in such set-up fee are bank charges or independent accountant's fee which may also be incurred.

11. TERM OF CONTRACT

11.1   Commencement Date. After execution of this contract by the Association's Board of Directors, Agent's compensation shall commence upon the day indicated in the following paragraph.

11.2   This Agreement shall commence _____ and shall continue in full force and effect for twelve months, and hereinafter from year to year. This agreement shall automatically renew for a like term at each anniversary of the commencement date, subject to the termination provisions contained in this agreement.

12. AGENT AND ASSOCIATION PROTECTION

AGENT EMPLOYEES

12.1   Agent spends significant amounts of time and money to hire and train employees for the operation of this and other Associations. Association derives and benefits from Agent's experience in managing, and their hiring and training procedures. Association agrees it will not hire, retain, or contract with any past or present employee, partner, officer, or co-owner of agent or its parent company or divisions in any capacity whatsoever for a period of six (6) months following the termination of this agreement or any extension thereof. Association agrees to pay Agent the sum of Ten Thousand Dollars ($10,000.00) as liquidated damages if it breaches this provision of the contract. Both parties agree that this is a reasonable sum due to the extensive training and trade secrets that Agent provides, as well as expectation of continued income and allotment of resources, and further with respect to the difficulty in establishing the amount of actual damages.

COMPANY TRADE SECRETS

12.2   Association will have access to and be dealing with trade secrets of Agent, such as: confidential information pertaining to client lists; procedures, processes and documentation relating to management of Agent's client Associations; and programs, software, procedures and techniques relating to data processing and financial reporting. Association agrees to hold any such trade secrets or confidential information, attained during the course of this Agreement, in the strictest confidence, and shall retain a total confidentiality, giving value to protecting them from Agent's competitors. This provision shall survive the termination of this Agreement.

12.3   All materials of a confidential nature, prepared and utilized in Agent's performance of their duties under this Agreement, shall remain the exclusive property of Agent, and shall be retained in Agent's possession.

13. MISCELLANEOUS

13.1   Advances and Charges. Agent will not be required to perform any act or duty hereunder involving the expenditure of money unless Agent shall have in its possession sufficient funds of the Association available. Therefore, if at any time the funds in the possession of Agent are not sufficient to pay the charges incident to this Agreement, Agent shall not be responsible to advance its own funds for any reason, and the Association agrees, in such cases, that upon notice thereof by Agent, the Association shall make immediate arrangements to make funds available to cover the insufficiency. Agent shall promptly notify Association of any deficiency in the account necessary to pay the charges incident to this Agreement.

13.2   Agent shall receive communications and directions from any Association director, and shall act with the assumption that said director is acting on behalf of the entire Board. Should a conflict arise between directors, Agent shall consider the President as the representative of the Association with authority to act on behalf of Association. Should the President be unavailable to resolve such a conflict, then the Vice President shall serve in this capacity. Agent may, but is not required to, submit any matter, direction, instruction or the like to the Board of Directors and shall then follow the direction of the Board of Directors.

The Association Board of Directors understands its fiduciary duties, and agrees to govern the Association in a business like manner, acting in good faith and in the best interest of the association and in accordance with the adopted community management plan, the Association's governing documents and applicable state and federal laws.

13.3   Successors and Assigns. This Agency Agreement will be binding upon and inure to the benefit of the successors and assigns of the Association. This Agency Agreement shall be binding on the parties hereto, their heirs, executors, administrators, successors and assignees, and constitutes the full agreement except that subsequent changes or additional provisions must be in writing and executed by both parties.

Notwithstanding the preceding sentence, the Agent shall not assign its interest under this Agreement except in connection with the sale of all or substantially all of the assets of its management business. In the event of such a sale, Agent shall be released from all liability by the Association.

13.4   Association and Agent acknowledge that they have carefully read and reviewed this Agreement and each term and provision contained herein and by execution of this Agreement show their informed and voluntary consent thereto. The parties hereby agree that, at the time this Agreement is executed, the terms of this Agreement are commercially reasonable and effectuate the intent and purposes of the Association and Agent with respect to the service agreement.

14. DISCLAIMER

No representation or recommendation is made by the Agent, its employees, or the California Association of Community Managers as to the legal sufficiency, legal effect, or other consequences of this Agreement. The parties shall rely solely upon the advice of their own legal counsel as to the legal and other consequences of this Agreement.

By affixing signatures below, both Association and Management agree to the terms, conditions and provisions specified by this Management Service Agreement, dated _____.

_____ ASSOCIATION   AGENT: _____
(Name of Association)   (Management Firm Name)

BY: _____   BY: _____

TITLE: _____   TITLE: _____

DATE: _____   DATE: _____

EXHIBIT "A"

INDIVIDUAL PROPERTY OWNER CHARGES: (Billed Directly to Individual Property Owners)

A. Escrow Transactions
1. Transfer & Set-up Fee *$ _____ ; $ _____ (for new developments)
2. Refinance Fee *$ _____
3. Association Documents - Complete sets only **$ _____
4. Homeowner Certifications: $ _____
* Includes statement of account, budget, fidelity bond and financial statement.
** Includes CC&R's, Bylaws, Articles of Incorporation, Rules & Regulations

B. Collection Charges (Billed to Association for Homeowner Reimbursement)

1. Intent to Lien Letter & Tracking Fee: $ _____
2. Preparation & Recording of Lien: $ _____
3. Late Charges: 50% of amount collected from homeowner
4. Payment Plan Administration: $ _____ per unit per month
5. Processing Returned Checks: $ _____ per check + bank charges

C. Architectural Review Fees (Billed Directly to Homeowner upon Submittal)

1. Plan Review and Packaging for ARC Submittal per submittal: $ _____ *(For custom home development only)*
2. Modification and Addition Plan Review per submittal: $ _____ *(After initial construction of home)*
3. Progress Reviews and Compliance Reports: No Charge

D. Reimbursable Association Administrative Operating Costs/ Expenses
The following charges are reimbursable Administrative Operating Expenses incurred on behalf of the Association. An invoice to substantiate each charge at the time of payment will be provided.

Telephone Toll Calls: Actual Cost
Postage: Actual Cost
Certified/UPS/Fed Ex: $ _____ plus charges

Homeowners' Listings: $ _____ per page

Fax Charges (incoming & outgoing): $_____ per page

Distribution Stickers/Keys/Openers: $_____ each plus costs

Labels/Address Sheets: $ _____ each (special mailings only)

Mailing Charges: $ _____ (special mailings only)

Fold/Staple: $ _____ (special mailings only)

Envelopes - Small: $ _____ (special mailings only)

           Large: $ _____ each

Special Check Processing: $ _____ per check

Photocopies: $ _____ per page

Folders/Postcards: $ _____ each

Year-end 1099's; Payroll Tax Returns: $_____ each + costs

Special Assessments - First Month: $ N/A

                   Each Add'l Month: $ N/A

Check Stock/Micr Ink: $ _____ per check

Document Storage: $ _____ per box per month

Payroll Processing Fee: 10% of gross payroll or $ _____ per check

           (whichever is greater)

Vendor Filing Fee: $_____ per vendor

Off-Site Document Retrieval: Actual Cost

Agent is authorized to purchase supplies for Association including, but not limited to, check stock, data disks, copier use, and telephone toll calls made for Association business.

Note: The foregoing list is intended to identify the major areas of service which are extraordinary expenses. There may be additional charges for which the Association will be charged. In such cases, the Agent will provide cost estimates prior to engaging any additional service. The above fees may be subject to change without notice or subject to change due to implementation of new law(s).

CACM CODE OF PROFESSIONAL ETHICS
AND STANDARDS OF PRACTICE

CERTIFICATION

CACM[sm] certifies that this Code of Professional Ethics and Standards of Practice was adopted by the Board of Directors of CACM[sm] at a duly constituted meeting of the Board on February 17, 1994, amended at a duly constituted meeting of the Board of Directors on July 7, 1997, May 19, 2000, August 15, 2001, March 31, 2004, July 25, 2007, and September 9, 2009.

RECITALS

A. In order to promote and enhance a high level of professional conduct among its membership, the California Association of Community Mangers, Inc.[sm] ("CACM") hereby adopts the following Code of Professional Ethics and Standards of Practice.

B. The Code of Professional Ethics and Standards of Practice have been adopted by the Board of Directors of CACM as the official rules of conduct which apply to all individual Managers ("MEMBERS") whether or not they are also a Certified Community Association Manager ("CCAM") and non-member Certified Managers of CACM, and to any affiliated management firm recognized by CACM, while performing services related to the practice of management of community associations (a Common Interest Development ["CID"] as defined in Title 6 of Part 4 of Division 2 of the California Civil Code commencing at Section 1350), including complete association management, financial services, administrative services and/or independent consulting for a Member, client or employer ("client").

Note: "Member" also includes "Non-member Certified Manager"

C. A Member engaged in the practice of community association management must observe all rules of conduct incorporated in the Code of Professional Ethics and Standards of Practice.

D. A Member shall not permit anyone under the Member's supervision, to carry out on the Member's behalf, either with or without compensation, anything which, if carried out by the Member, would place the Member in violation of the rules of conduct under the Code of Professional Ethics and Standards of Practice. Where the subordinate of a Member violates the Code of Professional Ethics or Standards of Practice while performing functions for a Member's client and under the general supervision of a Member, the Member shall be accountable for the violation as if the violation was committed by the Member.

E.   All Rules of Ethics and Standards of Practice contained herein shall be subordinate to all governmental regulations.

F.   Any word of general usage contained herein shall be interpreted in light of the prevailing definition as contained in the then current edition of Webster's Unabridged Dictionary.

CODE

1.00   General Standards

Loyalty, Fidelity and Integrity - The Member shall act with loyalty, fidelity and integrity in all aspects of the Member's relationship with the client and in all aspects of representing the client to third parties.

The Member shall be honest and forthright in all of the Member's professional dealings. The Member shall not misrepresent, either by affirmative statement or material omission, the Member's qualifications, experience or capabilities in the field of community association management.

The Member shall honor all client confidences and shall treat the business affairs and records of the client as confidential unless directed or authorized otherwise by competent authority. The Member shall refuse to make available to business vendors the names, addresses and telephone numbers of the members of a community association without the prior consent of a majority of the Board of Directors of the community association.

Professional Competence - The Member shall accept only those engagements which the Member, or the Member's firm, can reasonably expect to perform with professional competence.

Due professional care - The Member shall exercise due professional care in the performance of duties.

• *Standard of Practice 1-01: Education*

a. The Member shall strive to keep informed of new developments in community association management, including but not limited to, legal and accounting principles applicable to community associations.

b. The Member shall seek continuing education in community association management through attendance at professional courses of CACM^{sm}, CAI, IREM, BOMA and other similar professional associations related to the practice of management of community associations.

c. The Member shall encourage officers, Board members, and committee chairs of clients to participate in courses and seminars which will improve their abilities to serve community association members.

• *Standard of Practice 1-02: Use of CCAM Designation.*

Only an individual is a Member, not a firm; and only a Member, not a firm, may be a Certified Community Association Manager (CCAM). Neither a Member nor others of an organization engaged in community association management shall hold themselves out to anyone as being a Certified Community Association Manager (CCAM) at any time before accreditation or after the expiration, suspension or termination of membership or membership status.

• *Standard of Practice 1-03: Member Staff Support.*

The Member shall have sufficient qualified staff and administrative personnel, or a formal arrangement with necessary consultants, to ensure the capable handling of the client's interests.

• *Standard of Practice 1-04: Compliance.*

a. The Member shall comply with the provisions of

1) California Civil Code, Division 2, Part 4, Title 6 - Common Interest Developments, commencing at Section 1350,

2) California Corporations Code, Title 1, Division 1- General Corporation Law, commencing at Section 100, and Division 2, Part 3- Non-profit Mutual Benefit Corporations, commencing at Section 7310, and

3) Business and Professions Code, commencing at Section 11500, et seq.

4) other applicable codes, statutes, laws and regulations.

b. The Member shall comply with the Code of Professional Ethics and Standards of Practice of CACM.

c. The Member shall comply with all lawful provisions of the client's governing documents.

d. The Member shall comply with all lawful provisions of written contracts in which the Member is a party.

2.00   Integrity and Objectivity

The Member shall not knowingly misrepresent facts in order to benefit the Member, or the Member's company, or any affiliate, including family relations, of the Member or the Member's company. All representations made to a community association which has engaged the Member must be made with the best interest of the community association in mind.

3.00   Technical Standards

The Member shall comply with all standards that are currently in force or may from time to time be adopted and promulgated by the California Association of Community Managers.

• *Standard of Practice 3-01: Inspection:*

In accordance with the management agreement, a Member shall make, or cause to be made, regular physical inspections of the common property and assets of its clients. Such inspections shall be defined as "reasonable inspections" such as those made by a reasonably prudent person exercising ordinary care, not an "expert inspection" such as one made by a licensed architect, engineer or construction specialist.

• *Standard of Practice 3-02: Maintenance.*

a. The Member shall recommend that a reserve study be prepared in a professional manner and reviewed and updated in accordance with California State law.

b. The Member shall recommend that the client shall establish and implement a preventive maintenance program.

• *Standard of Practice 3-03: Legal.*

a. The Member shall not engage in the unlicensed practice of law. This provision, however, does not prevent a Member from rendering a business judgment nor does this provision prevent a Member from appearing on behalf of a client where authorized to do so by law.

b. The Member shall advise clients when the Member believes legal counsel should be retained and assist the client in retaining qualified counsel.

c. The Member shall recommend that a legal review, where appropriate, by an attorney knowledgeable in community association law be considered for all legal issues, including but not limited to, major contracts, association rules, enforcement procedures and association documents.

d. The Member shall recommend that the community association implement an Injury Prevention Program in compliance with CAL-OSHA requirements and standards pursuant to California Labor Code Section 6401.7.

e. The Member shall become familiar with and develop a working knowledge of the community association's governing documents.

f. The Member shall recommend that written rules be established and published to the community association membership and the publication and implementation of a consistent enforcement policy based on federal, state and local laws and regulations, the property's covenants, conditions and restrictions, and the association's articles of incorporation and bylaws. The Member shall make all reasonable effort to assure that the adopted policies are in full compliance with these documents.

• *Standard of Practice 3-04: Accurate Financial Records.*

A Member shall, at all times, cause to be kept and maintained current and accurate records of all financial transactions, properly marked for identification, concerning the business entity and assets managed for a client, and cause to be prepared financial statements in sufficient detail to allow the client's Board and auditor to determine the status of the association's accounts and financial operations. Such records shall be made available for inspection by the client in accordance with the governing documents and applicable law.

• *Standard of Practice 3-05: Expenditure of Funds.*

A Member shall advise and, when authorized, shall endeavor to expend client's funds to achieve the greatest benefit for the client.

• *Standard of Practice 3-06: Commingling and Security of Funds.*

Except as provided for in California Civil Code Section 1363.2, the Member shall not commingle the Member's funds or other client's funds with any of the funds of a management client. The Member shall deposit all such funds in an FDIC insured financial institution as required by the governing documents, and California law.

• *Standard of Practice 3-07: Budgetary & Finance*

a. The Member shall act as a fiduciary on behalf of the client in handling the client's financial affairs and shall put the client's interests above the Member's own in handling the client's financial affairs.

b. The Member shall recommend that the community association comply with the fiscal requirements of California laws, in addition to the community association's legal documents.

c. The Member shall advise clients when the Member believes the services of a Certified Public Accountant should be retained and assist clients in retaining qualified accounting and tax advice.

d. The Member shall recommend that the community association file, in a timely manner, applicable quarterly and fiscal year-end tax returns and reports and make required periodic deposits with the IRS, the California Franchise Tax Board, and with other applicable federal, state, and local agencies.

e. The Member shall make financial records available for inspection and copying by an authorized representative of the community association upon reasonable notice during regular business hours.

• *Standard of Practice 3-08: Reserve Investment.*

a. The Member shall recommend that the community association invest association funds in accordance with the association's legal documents and recommend that the primary objectives in investing should be safety first, liquidity second, then yield and then other considerations. Recommended investments should be limited to deposit accounts insured by the FDIC, or U.S. Treasury Securities or other full faith and credit obligations of the Federal Government or money funds which invest exclusively in these instruments and which are FDIC or SIPC insured.

b. The Member, unless qualified to do so by education or professional experience, shall refrain from giving investment advice to community association clients and, when such advice is requested, recommend qualified investment professionals.

• *Standard of Practice 3-09: Insurance*

a. The Member shall advise the client of the need to obtain insurance.

b. The Member shall recommend that the community association obtain professional advice on insurance coverage consistent with the requirements established in the community association governing documents, and ensure annual review of those requirements and coverage.

c. The Member shall recommend that the community association maintain appropriate property casualty insurance.

d. The Member shall recommend that the community association maintain appropriate liability insurance.

e. The Member shall recommend that the community association acquire an appropriate level of Directors and Officers liability insurance.

f. The Member shall recommend that the Board of Directors provide adequate fidelity bond/insurance coverage extending to the board and community association employees.

g. The Member shall recommend that workers' compensation insurance be part of the overall insurance package whether or not the community association has regular employees.

h. If the Member is an independent agent, rather than an employee of the community association, the Member shall recommend that the management entity be named as an additional insured under the association insurance contracts.

• *Standard of Practice 3-10: Communications.*

a. The Member shall maintain a Record of Membership including the names and addresses of the community association members as provided by the membership.

b. The Member shall recommend that the community association have regular communications with the membership.

c. The Member shall assist the community association in dissemination of information as defined in the community association's governing documents, and as required by the Civil and Corporations Codes of the State of California.

• *Standard of Practice 3-11: Transfer of Property to Client.*

a. At the conclusion of any engagement for a client, upon receipt of a written request from the client, the Member shall produce Client Property and Client Records to the person designated by the client. Client Property and Client Records shall be produced as soon as reasonably practical after receipt of client's written request to do so, regardless of any dispute over termination or fees.

b. As used herein, "Client Property" means the client's physical property, such as manuals (e.g., for operation, maintenance or warranty of elevators, pool heaters, HVAC systems, etc.), security gate transponders, and pool keys.

c. As used herein, "Client Records" means hard files and electronically stored information maintained by the Members in the ordinary course of business which the client is legally required to maintain by California state law and/or which is reasonably necessary for the client's continued operation. "Client Records" includes, at a minimum, all items presented to an association Board of Directors for their consideration.

d. The Member shall produce Client Records in the form in which they have been kept by the Member or in a form which the Member reasonably believes will be useable by the client. The Member shall produce Client Records in a manner which is convenient, not burdensome, and inexpensive to the Member. The Member need not produce Client Records which are not reasonbly available because of undue burden or expense. The Member need not produce Records which might include proprietary or other trade secret information developed by the Member for use in the Member's management business. The Member need not produce records which have been lost, damaged, altered or overwritten as the result of routine good faith operation of an electronic information system. The Member need not produce working papers or electronic data developed or created by the Member. The Member need not produce records of telephone conversations or emails, unless they previously have been printed and included in a board packet or vendor/project file.

e. The Member's obligation to honor all client confidences and to treat the business affairs and records of the client as confidential continues after the conclusion of the engagement for a client.

f. In their contracts with clients, Member may provide for different definitions of "Client Property" and "Client Records" or a longer period within which they must be produced other than those stated above, as long as those definitions and time period are reasonable.

4.00   Professional Courtesy

The Member shall exhibit professional courtesy to all community association management professionals. The Member shall be fair in making representations and shall refrain from making defamatory comments about others involved in the community association management profession.

The Member shall assist other Members in achieving the Standards of Practice as set forth herein.

The Member shall not make false, fraudulent, misleading or deceptive statements in the marketing of property management services or the solicitation of business.

All Members are encouraged to promote fair and open competition and shall avoid unlawful restraints of trade.

The Member shall refrain from causing tortious interference with contractual relationships between community association management professionals and their clients. The Member shall refrain from unlawful intentional interference with prospective economic advantage.

• *Standard of Practice 4-01: Marketing*

a. Ethical marketing may include, but is not limited to, general mailings and advertising of promotional pieces or distributions which contain no false, fraudulent, misleading or deceptive statements or claims.

b. Management marketing programs are encouraged to include: (i) a description of CACM, (ii) a copy of the CACM Code of Professional Ethics and Standards of Practice, (iii) a description of the CCAM requirements, and (iv) a description of a PCAM, CPM, AMS, or other professional designations.

c. Except as prohibited for interference with contract, if invited by the Board of Directors, it is permissible to meet with that Executive body and/or a Committee of the Association and to propose services.

d. Ethical marketing does not include the use of any proprietary information of another Member or firm. Proprietary information includes, but is not limited to: (i) Client lists, (ii) Pricing schedules, (iii) Internal policy and procedures manuals, etc.

5.00   Conflict of Interest

Members shall avoid any real or apparent conflicts of interest with their clients/employer. In the event of a real or apparent conflict of interest, the Member shall promptly disclose all pertinent information regarding the conflict to the client and allow the client to make an informed decision as to whether to continue the relationship on the then existing basis or to make an appropriate change in the relationship to accommodate the conflict. The decision on how to deal with a real conflict of interest shall rest with the client and not with the Member.

Recommendations to a client of vendors, suppliers or contractors that have any financial or other than independent third party relationship to the Member, or a family relation or employee of the Member, must be disclosed to the client by the Member at the time the recommendation is made.

• *Standard of Practice 5-01: Non-management Services.*

The Member may provide goods or services to clients, other than community association management services, provided there is full written disclosure on no less than an annual basis as to all aspects that may influence the use of these services. The disclosure shall specifically include any Compensation paid directly to the Member as a result of contracting for these services, prior to the award of any contract to provide such goods or services.

a. Where the management contract provides for specific charges or a specific mark-up for goods or services, the requirement for disclosure is met.

b. Where a contract for goods or services is to be competitively bid and the member or an allied, related and/or affiliated company of the Member is a bidder such bid shall be based on precise written specifications provided to each bidder. The Member shall employ a sealed bid process wherein all bids are received sealed and are opened in the presence of the client board or its designated representative other than the Member.

6.00   Gratuities

It shall be the policy of the California Association of Community Managers to discourage the acceptance by Members of gifts, entertainment, or other favors from existing or prospective clients, vendors or suppliers who act on behalf of the Member's clients, when such acceptance can unduly influence the Member.

No Member, or employee of a member, may accept any unearned fees or other forms of remuneration that may actually be, or appear to be, a conflict of interest.

• *Standard of Practice 6-01: Referral Fees.*

The Member is prohibited from receiving undisclosed referral fees, deferred compensation, commissions or similar gratuities in cash or in kind for recommending to or purchasing material or services on behalf of a client.

a. The acceptance of any gratuity in cash is prohibited.

b. The acceptance of any gratuity by gift certificate, or in kind, including but not limited to, meals, entertainment, housing, transportation, professional services or, of any other nature, having a cumulative value in excess of three hundred dollars ($300.00) from any one person or business in any twelve (12) month period shall be fully disclosed to all clients which have procured services from the providing person or business and to all clients who contemplate the procurement of such services.

c. Under no circumstances shall a member or employee of any member solicit any gratuity, in cash or in kind, on their own behalf or on behalf of another member(s) or employee(s), regardless of value or type from any one person or business.

7.00   Use of Client Funds

The Member may not misuse any funds being held for a client under a fiduciary relationship.

8.00   Limitations of Practice

The Member, who has contracted with a client to perform community association management services, and who is also engaged in the practice of another profession, may perform other professional services provided there is full disclosure to the client.

9.00   Enforcement

Each Member, as a condition of membership in the California Association of Community Managers, agrees to be bound by and to abide by this Code of Professional Ethics and Standards of Practice and by duly adopted amendments hereto, and to voluntarily participate in compliance, disciplinary proceedings, discipline and/or, binding arbitration as required by the Professional Standards Committee or Appeals Committee.

The Member subject to disciplinary action may, after hearing, be subject to censure, suspension or termination of membership or membership status.

AMENDMENT

This Code of Professional Ethics and Standards of Practice supersedes and replaces all prior versions of this document and shall have prospective as well as retroactive effect from the inception date of CACM[sm] to the date of subsequent modification or termination. This Code of Professional Ethics and Standards of Practice may be amended from time to time by vote of a majority of the Executive Committee of CACM[sm] cast at a duly constituted meeting.

The signatory below agrees to abide by the Code of Professional Ethics and Standards of Practice of the California Association of Community Managers as stated above and as shall be duly amended from time to time; and to be subject to procedures for compliance and/or disciplinary action.

_____   _____
Signature   Date

_____
Print Name

_____
Address

_____

CACM BOARD MEMBER CODE OF ETHICS
(Sample)

As a Board member, you need to be aware that more is expected of those in leadership roles. Review the following statements. Signing this Code of Ethics solidifies your commitment to honest Board service.

<u>As a member of this Board, I will:</u>

◆ Be committed to fulfilling the mission and vision of the XYZ HOA.

◆ Keep all confidential Board information, confidential.

◆ Focus my efforts on the XYZ HOA and not my personal goals.

◆ Serve on a committee and/or task force in a leadership capacity.

◆ Refrain from using my service on this Board for my own personal advantage or for the advantage of my friends or associates.

◆ Respect and support the majority decisions of the Board.

◆ Immediately disclose to the Board any perceived or real conflict of interest as soon as I have knowledge of the potential conflict.

◆ Approach all Board issues with an open mind, prepared to make the best decisions for everyone involved.

◆ Do nothing to violate the trust of those who elected or appointed me to the Board or of those we serve.

◆ Never exercise authority as a Board member except when acting in a Board meeting or as I am delegated by the Board or its President.

◆ Continue to maintain the XYZ HOA Board member candidate qualifications.

◆ Consider myself a trustee of this organization and do my best to ensure that it is well maintained, financially secure, growing and always operating within the best interest of those we serve.

_____   _____

BOARD MEMBER SIGNATURE   DATE

BOARD MEMBER COMMITMENT PLEDGE
(Sample)

I,_____, recognizing the vital responsibility I am undertaking in serving as a member of the Board of Directors of the XYZ HOA, I hereby pledge to carry out in a trustworthy and diligent manner the duties and obligations of my role as a Board member.

MY ROLE:

I acknowledge that my primary role as a Board member is (1) to understand, support and ensure fidelity to the XYZ HOA mission and vision, and (2) to carry out the functions of the office of Board Member and/or Officer as stated in the Bylaws.

My role as a Board member will focus on the development of the broad policies (e.g., long term vision, overall financial philosophy, etc.) that govern the implementation of institutional plans and purposes.

MY COMMITMENT:

I will exercise the duties and responsibilities of this office with integrity, fidelity and care.

I PLEDGE TO:

♦ Maintain a good working relationship with other Board members.

♦ Keep up to date on the organization's major programs and services.

♦ Follow trends and important developments in the HOA and substantive field of interest. Educate myself about the needs of the constituents I serve.

♦ Act knowledgeable and prudently when making recommendations.

♦ Recommend qualified individuals with relevant skills and experience as possible nominees for the Board.

♦ Prepare for and participate at board and committee meetings.

♦ Participate in the strategic planning process.

♦ Willingly volunteer and use my special skills to further the organization's mission and vision.

♦ Complete all assignments in a timely manner.

♦ Listen respectfully to other's points of view.

♦ Take advantage of opportunities to enhance the organization's public image by periodically speaking to leaders in the community about the work of the XYZ HOA.

♦ Respect the confindentiality of the Board's Executive sessions.

♦ Speak for the Board or XYZ HOA only when authorized to do so.

♦ Suggest agenda items for future Board and committee meetings.

♦ Aid and advise the president when my help is requested.

♦ Avoid burdening the staff with requests for special favors.

♦ Ensure that any communication with the Community Manager does not undermine the relationship between the Board and the Manager.

♦ Avoid, in fact and perception, conflicts of interest that might embarrass the Board or organization, and disclose to the Board, in a timely manner, any possible conflicts.

If, for any reason, I find myself unable to carry out the above duties as best as I can, I agree to resign my position as a Board member/officer.

_____   _____
BOARD MEMBER SIGNATURE   DATE

CHAPTER 14

BASIC PARLIAMENTARY PROCEDURE

1. GENERAL

Parliamentary procedure originated in the English Parliament as a way of debating public affairs even when matters became heated. The rules were introduced to meetings in America with the first settlers from England and, as we know them today, were established in 1876 by Henry M. Robert when he published his first manual on parliamentary law entitled Robert's Rules of Order. The original procedural system has evolved into a sophisticated set of rules that has become the standard method of conducting business at organizational meetings.

The purpose of this segment of the book is to set forth the basic rules of parliamentary procedure so that they can easily be understood and adapted to fit the needs of your organization. It is important to remember that parliamentary procedure, while allowing for democratic rule, should be flexible enough to protect the rights of all members, including the opposition. A sense of fair play can be established by providing everyone with an opportunity to be heard. Like any system, parliamentary procedure works when it is used properly by those in charge and treats with respect the rights of all members.

This is a basic summary of a complex set of rules that will serve as a guide for most routine matters. However, when technical issues arise it may be necessary to consult a primary text on parliamentary procedure.

2. ORDER OF BUSINESS

Organizations using parliamentary procedure usually follow a fixed order of business. The following is a typical example:

1. CALL TO ORDER: The chairperson says, "The meeting will please come to order."
2. ROLL CALL: Members say "present" as their names are called.

3. READING AND APPROVAL OF MINUTES: The secretary reads the minutes of the last meeting and calls for approval, modification or addition by motion.

4. OFFICERS' REPORTS: Often limited to a report without discussion from officers (e.g., treasurer), but others may report at this time.

5. COMMITTEE REPORTS: First come reports from "standing" committees or permanent committees, then come reports from "ad hoc" or special committees, usually in the order of importance.

6. SPECIAL BUSINESS: Important business previously designated for consideration at the meeting.

7. UNFINISHED BUSINESS: Business left over from previous meetings.

8. NEW BUSINESS: Introduction and discussion of new topics.

9. ANNOUNCEMENTS: Informing the members of other subjects and events germane to the business of the organization.

10. ADJOURNMENT: The meeting ends by vote or general consensus recorded in the minutes; or under special circumstances by the chair's decision if time of adjournment was prearranged by vote.

3. TYPES OF MOTIONS

There are four types of motions:
1) Main motions
2) Subsidiary motions
3) Privileged motions
4) Incidental motions

Each type has a specific purpose and a relative priority. The order of precedence is: privileged motions, subsidiary motions and then main motions. Incidental motions have no order of precedence; they must be decided as soon as they arise.

1. MAIN MOTIONS introduce subjects to the assembly for its consideration. They cannot be made when another motion is before the

assembly. Only one main motion may be considered at a time, but it must yield to privileged, subsidiary and incidental motions. For example, a main motion might be introduced as follows: "I move that we purchase..."

2. SUBSIDIARY MOTIONS change or affect how the main motion is handled and they are voted on before the main motion. Subsidiary motions include a motion to amend, a motion to refer to committee, a motion to postpone, a motion to limit or extend debate, a motion to close debate and a motion to table. A subsidiary motion may be introduced by saying, "I move the question be amended by striking out . . ."

3. PRIVILEGED MOTIONS are the most urgent. They usually deal with a special or important matter not directly related to the pending business. Some examples are: a motion to recess, a motion to adjourn at a predetermined time, a question to complain about heat, noise or other conditions, a question to protest breach of rules or conduct, a question to avoid improper matter, etc.

4. INCIDENTAL MOTIONS raise questions of procedure that relate to other pending motions and must be considered before a vote on the related motion. For example, an incidental motion may involve a motion to appeal the chair's decision to the assembly, a motion to suspend the rules, a point of order, a parliamentary inquiry, a request to withdraw a motion, a request for division of the motion into parts, verification of a vote, a motion for reconsideration of hasty action, etc.

4. CONSIDERATION OF MOTIONS

Generally, a motion is in order if it relates to the business at hand and is presented at the right time. It must not be obstructive, frivolous or against the by-laws. Usually, a second is required. A second indicates that another member would like to consider the motion. A second is not required for certain types of motions, but if a second is required, the motion will die without a second. The procedure of a second prevents spending time on a question that interests only one person.

Once made, most motions can be amended by striking out, inserting, or both at once. Amendments, however, must relate to the subject presented by the main motion. Both the main motion and all amendments are debatable. Parliamentary procedure guards the right to free and full debate on most motions. Some privileged and incidental motions are not debatable.

Some motions are so important that the speaker may be interrupted to make them. After the interruption has been attended to the original speaker regains the floor.

Most motions require a majority vote. But motions concerning the rights of the assembly or its members need a 2/3 vote to be adopted. Once passed, most motions can be re-debated and re-voted to give the members a chance to change their minds. The move to reconsider, however, must come from the winning side.

5. PRESENTING A MOTION

A motion proposes that the assembly take a stand or take action on some issue. A member can present a motion by making a proposal with the introduction, "I move . . ." A member may second a motion expressing support for the decision to discuss another member's motion. Following a second, if a second is required, a member may debate the pending motion or related business by giving an opinion or raising a question about the business at hand. Finally, a member may call for a vote on the disposition of the motion.

The procedure for presenting a motion is relatively simple. First, the member should wait until the last speaker is finished and obtain the floor by addressing the chair. The member should say, "Mr. or (Ms.) Chairperson (or President)" and give his or her name. The chair will recognize the member by repeating the member's name. Next, the member should state the motion in clear and concise terms. The motion should be stated affirmatively, not negatively. For example, a motion should be phrased, "I move that we . . ." instead of, "I move that we do not . . ." All motions should avoid personalities, innuendo and irrelevancies.

Once the motion has been made, the member should wait for a second. Another member will second the motion by saying, "I second the motion." Or, if a second is not immediately forthcoming, the chair will call for a second. If there is no second and one is required for the motion, the motion will not be considered.

Following a second, the chair will say, "It is moved and seconded that we . . ." and debate will commence. The motion is now "assembly property" that cannot be changed without the consent of the members by a vote.

A pending motion may be expanded. The initial moving member, however, is allowed to speak first. The mover should direct all comments to the chair. Keep to time limits for speaking as stated in the by-laws or as predetermined by the members or the chair. The other members may speak after the mover is finished, and the mover may speak again after all other members have finished speaking. A mover may speak only twice unless a motion is passed by a 2/3 vote to suspend the rules authorizing the mover to more than two turns.

At the conclusion of debate, the chair will ask, "Are you ready for the question?" If there is no more discussion, a vote is taken. Alternatively, a motion for a previous question may be adopted.

6. VOTING ON A MOTION

The method of voting on a motion depends on the situation and the by-laws. Generally, there are five methods of voting on a motion: 1) by a voice vote, 2) by a show of hands, 3) by a roll call, 4) by a ballot and 5) by general consent.

A voice vote is taken by the chair asking those in favor to say "Aye" and those opposed to say "No." This method may be used for a majority vote only. It may not be used for a 2/3 vote. A member may move for an exact count at his or her option on any type of vote.

A vote by a show of hands is taken by members raising their hands as sight verification of or as an alternative to a voice vote. It does not require a count. However, any member may move for an exact count.

A vote by roll call is taken by the chair calling out the name of each member who then answers "Yes" or "No" as his or her name is called. The secretary will record the roll call vote as taken when a record of each person's vote is needed.

A vote taken by ballot requires the members to write their vote on a slip of paper. This method of voting is used when secrecy is desired.

A vote by general consent is used when a motion is not likely to be opposed. It is introduced by the chair saying, "If there is no objection, . . ." Members show agreement by their silence. If a member says, "I object," the matter must be put to a roll call or ballot vote.

A motion (or question) is pending so long as it has been stated by the chair but not yet voted on. The last motion stated by the chair is the first pending. The main motion is always the last voted on.

A vote can be delayed for either a predetermined period or indefinitely. Postponement involves two types of motions: a motion to table or a motion to postpone indefinitely. A motion to table is often used in an attempt to "kill" a motion. There is always the option to "take from the table" later by a motion for reconsideration by the assembly. A tabled motion will remain tabled until reconsidered. A motion to postpone indefinitely allows members to dispose of a motion without making a decision for or against the matter presented. It is useful in the case of a badly chosen main motion for which either a "Yes" or "No" vote would have undesirable consequences. Again, a motion postponed indefinitely may be reconsidered when a motion for reconsideration is passed.

7. TWENTY TIPS FOR A SUCCESSFUL MEETING

1. RESPECT TRADITION. Follow established parliamentary procedure.

2. Have a WRITTEN AGENDA and stick to it.

3. Allot a DESIGNATED AMOUNT OF TIME for each controversial matter and schedule after routine business.

4. RESTATE EACH MOTION so that it may be recorded accurately and understood fully. Repeat again if necessary.

5. CONTROL DISCUSSION and debate through the chair. Require recognition before allowing a member to speak.

6. LIMIT DISCUSSION to matters pertinent to the pending motion.

7. PERMIT FULL DEBATE even if it requires delaying a vote until the next meeting.

8. ALLOW ALL SIDES TO SUBMIT privileged, subsidiary and incidental motions.

9. RAISE A POINT OF ORDER whenever there is an error, mistake, omission or misunderstanding.

10. DO NOT USE parliamentary technicalities for tactical advantage alone.

11. CALL FOR A FINAL VOTE on all motions and in the proper order of their respective precedence.

12. DISPOSE OF ALL NON-CONTROVERSIAL MATTERS by a general consensus vote.

13. REQUIRE A VOTE BY BALLOT on all important contested

matters.

14. ALLOW THE CHAIR to resolve procedural questions unless an appeal is taken to the assembly questioning the chair's action.

15. RECORD ALL MOTIONS WHETHER THEY ARE defeated or succeed. Record non-controversial motions adopted by general consensus.

16. DO NOT RECORD individual opinion, personal criticism, comments made in debate, motives behind motions or motions that have been withdrawn.

17. PERMIT THE ENTIRE ASSEMBLY to decide when debate should end.

18. DO NOT SPEND VALUABLE MEETING TIME worrying about who is right or wrong. Nothing is as important as it seems at first.

19. BE WILLING TO LOSE A BATTLE OR TWO in order to win the war.

20. GET ACQUAINTED with a good lawyer, CPA and parliamentarian.

CHAPTER 15

USEFUL FORMS AND CHECKLISTS

Form No. 1   Board Resolution
Form No. 2   Revenue Ruling 70-604 Election Resolution
Form No. 3   Notice of Annual Membership Meeting
Form No. 4   Notice of Special Membership Meeting
Form No. 5   Notice of Regular Board Meeting
Form No. 6   Notice of Special Board Meeting
Form No. 7   Consent to Action Without Board Meeting
Form No. 8   Notice of Executive Session Board Meeting
Form No. 9   Proxy Form
Form No. 10   Proxy Revocation Form
Form No. 11   Ballot Form
Form No. 12   Sample Secret Ballot and Instructions
Form No. 13   Alternative Dispute Resolution Requirements
Form No. 14   Request for Alternative Dispute Resolution
Form No. 15   Request to Meet and Confer (IDR)
Form No. 16   Response to Request for ADR Resolution
Form No. 17   Pre-Lien Notice (Notice of Delinquent Assessment)

Checklist No. 1 Transition From Developer Control
Checklist No. 2 Board of Directors Meeting Standard Agenda
Checklist No. 3 Association Duties
Checklist No. 4 Quarterly Financial Review
Checklist No. 5 Annual Financial Review
Checklist No. 6 Rule Enforcement
Checklist No. 7 Construction Contract Review

Note: The forms and checklists in this chapter are for the reader's use. They may be duplicated without the express written permission of the author.

FORM NO. 1

MODEL HOMEOWNERS' ASSOCIATION
RESOLUTION OF THE BOARD OF DIRECTORS

RECITALS

Whereas, ___(state date, time of meeting)___

Whereas, ___(state facts upon which resolution is based)___

Whereas, ___(state additional facts, as necessary)___

RESOLUTION

It is hereby resolved by the Board of Directors for the Model Homeowners' Association that ___(state substance of resolution)___

_____

_____

_____

_____

_____

Executed this _____ day of _____, 2011

By: _____
Secretary
Model Homeowners' Association

FORM NO. 2

RESOLUTION FOR IRS REVENUE RULING 70-604 ELECTION- EXCESS INCOME APPLIED TO THE FOLLOWING YEAR'S ASSESSMENTS

RESOLUTION OF THE _____ ASSOCIATION

RE: EXCESS INCOME APPLIED TO THE FOLLOWING YEAR'S ASSESSMENTS - REVENUE RULING 70-604

WHEREAS, the _____ Association is a non profit, mutual benefit corporation duly organized and existing under the laws of the State of California; and

WHEREAS, the members desire that the corporation shall act in full accordance with the rulings and regulations of the Internal Revenue Service;

NOW, THEREFORE, the members hereby adopt the following resolution by and on behalf of the _____ Association:

RESOLVED, that any excess of membership income over membership expenses for the year ended _____ shall be applied against the subsequent tax year member assessments as provided by IRS Revenue Ruling 70-604.

This resolution is adopted and made a part of the minutes of the meeting of _____ .

BY: _____
President

ATTESTED: _____
Secretary

FORM NO. 3

MODEL HOMEOWNERS' ASSOCIATION
NOTICE TO HOMEOWNERS

ANNUAL MEMBERSHIP MEETING

Date: _____

Time: _____

Location: _____

   Notice is hereby given that the annual meeting of Model Homeowners' Association will be held on ___(date)___, at ___(time)___. The issues to be discussed will include ___(describe issues to be discussed or reference an attached meeting agenda)___. There will be a vote of the membership on the following issues: ___(list items on the ballot)___. Pursuant to Civ. Code § 1363.03(b), each ballot received by the inspector of elections shall be treated as a member present at a meeting for purposes of establishing a quorum. Members who will be unable to attend the meeting should return their ballots to _(name and address of the inspector(s) of elections_ by ___(date)___.

   The meeting will be held at the ___(name of facility)___, located at _(address of facility)___. Directions to the ___(name of facility)___ are available from ___(name and phone number of person who can give directions - or enclose a map showing directions to the facility from the development)___.

                              Board of Directors
                              Model Homeowners' Association

FORM NO. 4

MODEL HOMEOWNERS' ASSOCIATION
NOTICE TO HOMEOWNERS

SPECIAL MEMBERSHIP MEETING

Date: _____

Time: _____

Location: _____

Notice is hereby given that on __(date)__, at __(time)__, there will be a special meeting of the members of the Model Homeowners' Association to discuss __(describe issues to be discussed or reference an attached meeting agenda)__. There will be a vote of the membership on the following issues: __(list items on the ballot)__. Members who will be unable to attend the meeting should execute the enclosed proxy and return it to the (name and address of individual in charge of collecting proxies) by (date).

The meeting will be held at the __(name of facility)__, located at (address of facility). Directions to the __(name of facility)__ are available from (name and phone number of person who can give directions - or enclose a map showing directions to the facility from the development).

Board of Directors
Model Homeowners' Association

FORM NO. 5

MODEL HOMEOWNERS' ASSOCIATION
NOTICE TO HOMEOWNERS

REGULAR BOARD OF DIRECTORS MEETING

Date: _____

Time: _____

Location: _____

Notice is hereby given that the regular _(monthly/ quarterly)_ meeting of the Board of Directors for the Model Homeowners' Association will be held on ___(date)___, at ___(time)___. The issues to be discussed will include _(describe issues to be discussed or reference an attached meeting agenda)_.

The meeting will be held at the ___(name of facility)___, located at _(address of facility)___. Directions to the ___(name of facility)_ are available from _(name and phone number of person who can give directions - or enclose a map showing directions to the facility from the development)_.

Board of Directors
Model Homeowners' Association

FORM NO. 6

MODEL HOMEOWNERS' ASSOCIATION
NOTICE TO HOMEOWNERS

SPECIAL BOARD OF DIRECTORS MEETING

Date: _____

Time: _____

Location: _____

    Notice is hereby given that a special meeting of the Board of Directors for the Model Homeowners' Association will be held on ___(date)___, at ___(time)___. The issues to be discussed will include _(describe issues to be discussed or reference an attached meeting agenda)_.

    The meeting will be held at the ___(name of facility)___, located at (address of facility) . Directions to the (name of facility) are available from (name and phone number of person who can give directions - or enclose a map showing directions to the facility from the development).

                  Board of Directors
                  Model Homeowners' Association

FORM NO. 7

MODEL HOMEOWNERS' ASSOCIATION
CONSENT TO EMERGENCY
ACTION WITHOUT BOARD MEETING

We, the undersigned, being all the directors of __(Homeowner Association)__ , a California non-profit corporation, hereby consent to the following emergency action by the Board of Directors without a meeting:

_____

_____

_____

(Description of action to be taken)

Dated: _____

(Signature of Director

_____

(Signature of Director)

_____

(Signature of Director)

_____

(Signature of Director)

_____

(Signature of Director)

[Please note, this document must be filed with the minutes of the Board of Directors meeting.]

FORM NO. 8

MODEL HOMEOWNERS' ASSOCIATION
NOTICE OF EXECUTIVE SESSION

Date: _____

Time: _____

Location: _____

    Notice is hereby given that at meeting of the Board of Directors for the Model Homeowners' Association held on _____(date)_____, at ___(time),___ the Board will adjourn into executive session to consider the following issues: _____

_____

(generally describe issues to be discussed or reference an attached meeting agenda).

    [For meetings off-site: Directions to the _____(name of facility) are available from_____(name and phone number of person who can give directions - or enclose a map showing directions to the facility from the development).]

Board of Directors
Model Homeowners' Association

[Please note, this document should be filed with the records of the Board of Directors and any matter discussed in executive session should be generally noted in the minutes of the immediately following meeting that is open to the entire membership.]

FORM NO. 9

MODEL HOMEOWNERS' ASSOCIATION
PROXY FOR ANNUAL MEETING

I/we, _____ , hereby designate _____ to act on my/our behalf at the _____meeting to be held on __(date)__ at __(location of meeting)__, California. I/we authorize to exercise my/our vote on all matters which come regularly before the (annual membership)__ at the __(date)__ meeting as follows: _____

_____

_____

_____

_____

(Brief description of the item to be voted on.)

Date: _____   Signature: _____
                                        (unit owner)

Date: _____   Signature: _____
                                        (co-owner)

Please note: Any instruction given in a proxy issued for an election that directs the manner in which the proxy holder is to cast the vote shall be set forth on a separate page of the proxy that can be detached and given to the proxy holder to retain. The proxy holder shall cast the member's vote by secret ballot. (Civ. Code § 1363.03)

FORM NO. 10

MODEL HOMEOWNERS' ASSOCIATION
PROXY REVOCATION

I/we, _____ , hereby revoke our proxy executed on _____.
(Name of board president or person authorized by proxy) is not authorized
to exercise my/our vote at the ____(board/membership)____ meeting on
(date) at (location) , California.

I/we understand that if I/we do not execute a new proxy or personally
vote at the meeting my/our vote will not be counted on any matter.

Date:_____   Signature: _____
                                                (Owner)

Date: _____   Signature: _____
                                              (Co-owner)

FORM NO. 11

MODEL HOMEOWNERS' ASSOCIATION SOLICITATION MATERIALS & BALLOT*

The owner(s) of each unit are entitled to cast one vote per unit owned. Please read the following ballot measure(s) carefully and indicate whether you wish to vote for or against each ballot measure listed. Your vote will be cast in accordance with your choice as set forth on this ballot form.

The association must receive executed ballots from at least _(number of votes needed for a quorum)_ homeowners for this vote to be valid. In addition, each measure must be approved by _(percentage of homeowners needed to pass measure)_ of the homeowners in order to be enacted. All ballots must be returned to _(i.e., Association's office/property management company)_ by _(date)_ .*

_____

_____

(Set forth a description of the proposed action to be voted on.)

I/We, hereby, cast my/our vote for or against the above action as follows: _____ For _____ Against

*You must allow a reasonable time for return of the ballots.

* See Form 12, Sample Secret Ballot Form and Instructions, which meet the requirements of Civil Code § 1363.03. Secret ballots must be used when voting for assessments, election of board of directors, amendments to the governing documents, grant of exclusive use common area, and when required by the association's governing documents. See also Chapter 17 for a sample set of election rules.

FORM NO. 12

SAMPLE SECRET BALLOT
(Pursuant to Civil Code § 1363.03)

Candidate: _____

Candidate: _____

Candidate: _____

Candidate: _____

Candidate: _____

<u>Board Resolution:</u>

BE IT RESOLVED, _____

_____

_____

_____

_____ FOR _____ AGAINST

SECRET BALLOT INSTRUCTIONS
(Must be separate from the ballot itself)

Cast your ballot by indicating your choice and inserting it into the envelope marked Secret Ballot Envelope. **Do not sign or write your name or unit/lot number on the Secret Ballot or Secret Ballot Envelope.** Place the Secret Ballot Envelope into the Owner Identification Envelope and seal it. On the outside of the Owner Identification Envelope in the upper left hand corner, print your name, sign your name below your printed name and print your address.

Either mail or hand deliver the signed and sealed Owner Identification Envelope (with sealed Secret Ballot Envelope inside) to the Inspector(s) of Elections noted on the outside of the Owner Identification Envelope. To be counted, your ballot must be received by_____ P.M. on _____.

FORM NO. 13

SUMMARY OF ALTERNATIVE DISPUTE
RESOLUTION REQUIREMENTS
(Civil Code §§ 1369.510 - 1369.590)

1. An association, owner or member of an association may not file an action in Superior Court seeking either: (a) declaratory or injunctive relief to enforce the governing documents, the Davis-Stirling Common Interest Development Act, or the Corporations Code, or (b) in conjunction with a claim for $7,500 or less (other than assessments), unless the parties have endeavored to submit their dispute to alternative dispute resolution (ADR), which includes mediation, arbitration, conciliation, or other nonjudicial procedure that involves a neutral party in the decision making process. The ADR process may be binding or non-binding.

2. This requirement does not apply to disputes within the jurisdiction of the Small Claims Court or disputes over assessments.

3. The ADR process is commenced by one party serving the other party with a Request For Resolution. It must contain the following:
    a. A brief description of the dispute;
    b. A request for ADR; and
    c. A notice that the party receiving the Request For Resolution must respond within 30 days or the Request For Resolution will be deemed rejected.
    d. If the person on whom the Request For Resolution is served is an owner, a copy of the statutes governing ADR. Civil Code §§ 1369.510 - 1369.590.

4. Service of the Request For Resolution may be by personal delivery, first-class mail, express mail, facsimile or other means reasonably calculated to give the other party actual notice.

5. A party served with a Request For Resolution has 30 days to accept or reject the request. Failure to accept or reject is deemed a rejection.

6. If the Request For Resolution is accepted, ADR must be completed

within 90 days from the date of acceptance. The deadline can be extended by a written agreement among all parties.

7. The costs of ADR shall be shared by the parties.

8. The time to file a civil action is suspended while ADR is pending.

9. Refusal to participate in ADR may result in the loss of the right to recover attorney fees in a subsequent Superior Court action.

FAILURE OF A MEMBER OF THE ASSOCIATION TO COMPLY WITH THE ALTERNATIVE DISPUTE RESOLUTION REQUIREMENTS OF SECTION 1369.520 OF THE CIVIL CODE MAY RESULT IN THE LOSS OF YOUR RIGHT TO SUE THE ASSOCIATION OR ANOTHER MEMBER OF THE ASSOCIATION REGARDING ENFORCEMENT OF THE GOVERNING DOCUMENTS OR THE APPLICABLE LAW.

FORM NO. 14

REQUEST FOR
ALTERNATIVE DISPUTE RESOLUTION

Date: _____
Requesting Party: _____
Unit/Lot No.: _____
Address: _____

Responding Party: _____
Unit/Lot No.: _____
Address: _____
Nature of Dispute: _____
_____
_____

This Request for Alternative Dispute Resolution is being made in accordance with the provisions of California Civil Code § 1369.520 (a copy accompanies this Request.) Costs will be shared equally between the parties. You are required to respond within thirty days, or this Request will be deemed rejected. If accepted, ADR must be completed within ninety (90) days from the date of acceptance, unless extended by written stipulation.

TYPE OF ADR REQUESTED:
_____ Mediation
_____ Arbitration, non-binding
_____ Arbitration, binding (Not an option if association intends to initiate a judicial foreclosure)

FAILURE OF A MEMBER OF THE ASSOCIATION TO COMPLY WITH THE ALTERNATIVE DISPUTE RESOLUTION REQUIREMENTS OF SECTION 1369.520 OF THE CIVIL CODE MAY RESULT IN THE LOSS OF YOUR RIGHT TO SUE THE ASSOCIATION OR ANOTHER MEMBER OF THE ASSOCIATION REGARDING ENFORCEMENT OF THE GOVERNING DOCUMENTS OR THE APPLICABLE LAW.

FORM NO. 15

REQUEST TO MEET AND CONFER
(Internal Dispute Resolution)

TO: _____

DISPUTE: _____ Association would like to meet and confer with you concerning _____ _____ (i.e. some violation of the governing documents). If this dispute cannot be resolved at this time, the next step is to meet with a neutral third party to try to resolve this dispute. The suggested meeting time is _____ . Please contract _____ at _____ to confirm the time and place of the meeting. If you do not confirm this meeting, it will be assumed that you do not wish to participate in this informal procedure.

or

DISPUTE: I/We, owners of _____ would like to meet with the board or its designated representative to resolve the dispute concerning _____ _____. Please contact me at _____ to arrange a mutually convenient time and place to explain our positions and confer in good faith to resolve this dispute. (The board may not refuse this request to meet and confer.) (See Civil Code § 1363.840)

Dated: _____   By: _____

FORM NO. 16

MODEL HOMEOWNERS' ASSOCIATION
RESPONSE TO REQUEST FOR
ALTERNATIVE DISPUTE RESOLUTION

I agree to submit this dispute to alternative dispute resolution.

Responding Party: _____

Nature of Dispute: _____

_____

_____

_____

_____

Signature: _____   Date: _____

[The person(s) or entity(ies) named as responding party(ies) above are required to respond to a request for alternative dispute resolution within 30 days of receipt, or it will be deemed rejected. Responses should be sent to the requesting party at the address indicated on the request.

If you choose to accept a form of Alternative Dispute Resolution, alternative dispute resolution shall be completed within 90 days of receipt of your acceptance, unless all parties to the dispute agree otherwise in writing.]

FORM NO. 17

MODEL HOMEOWNERS' ASSOCIATION
PRE-LIEN NOTICE
(NOTICE OF DELINQUENT ASSESSMENT)

To: _____

Address: _____

Date: _____

"IMPORTANT NOTICE: IF YOUR SEPARATE INTEREST IS PLACED IN FORECLOSURE BECAUSE YOU ARE BEHIND IN YOUR ASSESSMENTS, IT MAY BE SOLD WITHOUT COURT ACTION"

1. Pursuant to Civil Code § 1367.1, a lien will be placed on the property at _____ unless all delinquent assessments, fees, costs, and charges are paid in full within 30 days of receipt of the postmark of this notice. The amount of the delinquent assessment is as follows:

a.   Delinquent __(regular, special or reimbursement)__ assessment(s) for the period from _____ through _____ at a rate of _____ for a total amount of _____.

b.   Costs incurred in collecting the delinquent assessment(s) are as follows:

(1)	Costs of collections	$
(2)	Late charges	$
(3)	Interest at ___% per annum	$
(4)	Attorney fees	$ 425.00
c. TOTAL CHARGES :		$

2. You have the right to examine the accounting books and records of the association between _____ and _____ at _____ , and shall not be liable to pay the costs of collection, late charges, interest or fees if it is determined that the assessment was paid on time to the association.

3. You have the right to dispute the debt noticed above by submitting a written request to "meet and confer" or participate in alternative dispute resolution with a neutral third party pursuant to Civ. Code § 1363.840 or the association's "meet and confer" program.

4. You have the right to request a meeting with the board to discuss a payment plan for the above debt if the request is sent by certified mail to the board c/o _____ within 15 days of the date of the postmark of this notice of delinquency (lien). The board, or a designated member of the board, shall meet with you in executive session within 45 days of receipt of the request to discuss a payment plan.

Payment plans may incorporate any assessments that accrue during the payment plan period. Payment plans shall not impede an association's ability to record a lien on the owner's separate interest to secure payment of delinquent assessments. Additional late fees shall not accrue during the payment plan period if the owner is in compliance with the terms of the payment plan. In the event of a default on any payment plan, the association may resume its efforts to collect the delinquent assessments from the time prior to entering into the payment plan.

5. For a full description of collection and lien enforcement procedures, please refer to the ASSOCIATION ASSESSMENT COLLECTION POLICY, attached.

Date: _____   Signed: _____

[Please note, this document must be sent to the owner by certified mail at least 30 days prior to recording a lien.]

CHECKLIST NO. 1

TRANSITION FROM DEVELOPER CONTROL

A. DOCUMENTS TO OBTAIN

√ Original recorded CC&Rs and any amendments.

√ Original corporate minute book containing articles of incorporation, bylaws, and rules and regulations.

√ Corporate seal, letterhead, books and records.

√ Original recorded condominium plan or tract map.

√ Original minutes of all board of director meetings.

√ Original minutes of all member meetings.

√ Membership roster from inception to date.

√ All bank records, including: a) checkbooks, passbooks and other access documents; b) bank statements and reconciliations; c) cancelled checks and check registers; and d) bank account and borrowing resolutions.

√ As-built plans and specifications.

√ Inventory of moveable property.

√ Tax records including: a) returns (Federal and State); b) board certifications to CPA; c) IRS and FTB correspondence; and d) audit materials.

√ Insurance policies including: a) general liability policies; b) directors and officers liability; and c) fidelity bonds.

√ Maintenance contracts and records.

√ Management contracts and records.

√ *Pro forma* operating budgets from inception to date.

√ Reserve studies and updates from inception to date.

√ Bonds - subdivision maintenance bond, etc.

√ Warranties and written contracts with product suppliers.

√ Records of accounts payable and accounts receivable from inception to date.

√ Statement of known defective conditions.

B. FINANCIAL AUDIT

√ Review financial statements.

√ Review *pro forma* operating budget.

√ Review bank statements and cancelled checks.

√ Review segregation of operation revenue from reserves.

√ Review prior reserve studies.

√ Review balances on deposit in reserve accounts.

√ Conduct an audit if discrepancies appear.

C. CONSTRUCTION AUDIT

√ Review all major systems on spot check basis including the roof system, siding system, foundation system, electrical system, plumbing system, seismic restraint system, and the landscape and drainage system.

√ Retain expert consultants as necessary.

√ Define any problems and method of repair.

√ Determine cost of repair.

√ Make demand on developer for compensation.

D. ORGANIZATION OF ASSOCIATION

√ Review governing documents for compliance with requirements for officers and directors.

√ Review committee structure for effective use.

√ Review management contracts for compliance with current needs.

√ Review service providers for adequacy.

√ Review professional consultant contracts for adequacy and conflicts of interest.

√ Establish reporting procedures for management and committees.

√ Delegate tasks to Board members and committee members.

√ Develop long range plan for overall management of project.

CHECKLIST NO. 2

STANDARD AGENDA BOARD OF
DIRECTORS MEETING

√　Call to order by President.

√　Determine whether a quorum is present.

√　If quorum is not present, adjourn and reschedule either by verbal or written notice as specified in CC&Rs or bylaws.

√　If quorum is present, proceed with meeting.

√　Adopt minutes of last meeting by: a) read minutes of the last meeting or vote to waive; b) call for corrections; and c) vote on adoption.

√　Homeowner forum.

√　Consent calendar (if appropriate).

√　Present reports including: a) treasurer; b) architectural committee; c) landscape committee; d) newsletter committee; e) maintenance committee; and f) property manager.

√　Unfinished business.

√　New business.

√　Executive session (if necessary)

√　Adjournment.

CHECKLIST NO. 3

ASSOCIATION DUTIES

√ Provide effective physical maintenance of common area and facilities for which it is responsible.

√ Establish sound financial policy and procedures, including compliance with annual reporting requirements and government filings (e.g. tax, corporate, etc.).

√ Review and adjust, as necessary, budget figures and assessment rates.

√ Establish and implement a delinquent assessment policy.

√ Establish, publicize and enforce rules and regulations, including penalties for violation.

√ Select a financial consultant and arrange for prompt preparation of necessary reports.

√ Employ a competent attorney.

√ Employ a management agent or employee and prescribe the scope of the manager's duties.

√ Establish and enforce architectural and other standards.

√ Appoint committees. Coordinate and supervise their activities to ensure effective action.

√ Develop and supervise an education and training program for board members.

√ Establish and periodically review the insurance program to ensure adequate coverage.

√ Ensure proper procedures (e.g. parliamentary, notice, etc.) are followed at all board and member meetings.

√ Periodically review bonding of personnel handling funds.

√ Communicate with members on matters that affect their property.

√ Address owner concerns before they become a real problem.

√ Avoid conflicts-of-interest and self-interest decisions.

√ Decide matters based upon the best interests of the association as a whole.

√ Understand the governing documents thoroughly.

√ Hold regular board meetings and ensure proper records are kept.

CHECKLIST NO. 4

QUARTERLY FINANCIAL REVIEW

√ Review Civil Code § 1365.5.

√ Check to determine whether the governing documents impose morestringent standards than set forth below.

√ Review a current reconciliation of the association's operating accounts.

√ Review a current reconciliation of the association's reserve accounts.

√ Review the current year's actual reserve revenues and expenses compared to the current year's budget.

√ Review the latest account statements prepared by the financial institutions where the association has its operating and reserve accounts.

√ Review an income and expense statement for the association's operating and reserve accounts.

√ Investigate any apparent discrepancies.

CHECKLIST NO. 5

ANNUAL FINANCIAL REVIEW

√   Review Civil Code § 1365.5.

√   Review CC&R financial requirements.

√   Review the most recent reserve study for compliance with Civil Code § 1365.5(d). Include the following in your review: a) review the major components with a remaining useful life of 30 years or less for which the association is responsible; b) review the probable remaining useful life of those major components as of the date of the study; c) review the estimated cost of repair, replacement, restoration and maintenance during and at the end of their remaining useful lives; d) review the total annual contribution necessary to defray the cost of repair, replacement, restoration and maintenance of those components as required; e) review the total reserve funds on deposit as of the date of the study year; and f) review the percent of reserves funded when the current amount of accumulated cash reserves is divided by the current estimate of the amount of cash reserves necessary to maintain, repair or replace the major components.

√   Review year to date expenses in all categories, including accounting, administrative, insurance, legal, maintenance, management, utilities, outside services, etc.

√   Determine whether the association anticipates any substantial increases in operating expenses for the upcoming year.

√   Determine whether there will be any capital improvements or new projects that will introduce new categories of expense into the budget and in what amount.

√   Review delinquent accounts and whether enforcement action is necessary.

√   Review the current delinquent assessment collection policy of the association for adequacy.

√   Review the draft budget for the upcoming year.

√ Review income from all sources, such as reimbursable expenses, penalties, interest, etc. (Note: interest income on reserve accounts is normally excluded from operating revenue for budget purposes.)

√ Determine whether the current monthly assessment per unit is adequate, and, if not, adjust accordingly.

√ Review prior year's income and expense figures to determine whether there are any unusual disparities and, if so, investigate.

√ Determine whether the time deadlines for financial reporting have been met in the past and ensure that they can be complied with in the future.

√ Determine whether the overall financial program is serving the best interests of the association and, if not, how it should be restructured.

√ Review prior year's income and expense figures to determine whether there are any unusual disparities and, if so, investigate.

√ Determine whether the time deadlines for financial reporting have been met in the past and ensure that they can be complied with in the future.

√ Determine whether the overall financial program is serving the best interests of the association and, if not, how it should be restructured.

CHECKLIST NO. 6

RULE ENFORCEMENT

√ Determine whether there has there been a violation or infraction of the governing documents (i.e. CC&Rs, bylaws, rules).

√ Determine whether there is sufficient evidence (i.e. witnesses and/or documents) to sustain a rule enforcement proceeding.

√ Determine whether the violator is someone subject to the restrictions in the governing documents. If not consider indirect enforcement action against the responsible owner.

√ Determine whether there is authority in the governing documents to make and enforce the rule. This should have been done at the time of enactment.

√ Determine whether the rule is reasonably related to the purposes it is intended to achieve. This should have been done at the time of enactment.

√ Determine whether the violator has received proper notice of the rule and related penalties in advance of the violation.

√ Determine whether there are any defenses to enforcement, such as lack of notice, waiver, selective enforcement, illegality, etc.

√ Give adequate notice of a hearing pursuant to an established enforcement program.

√ Conduct a hearing in accordance with established procedure. Swear in all witnesses. Give limited weight to hearsay, particularly uncorroborated or inherently untrustworthy third party statements.

√ Give the violator a full and fair opportunity to be heard and present evidence on his/her behalf.

√ Render a prompt decision based upon the evidence. The decision should be a simple, concise statement of the ultimate decision.

√ Commence and carry out enforcement without delay.

CHECKLIST NO. 7

CONSTRUCTION CONTRACT REVIEW

√ Review identity and credentials of design professional (i.e. architect/ engineer), construction manager, general contractor, specialty subcontractors, and contact person with each.

√ Review the final stamped (by the architect/engineer) and approved (by the local building department) set of drawings and specifications. If a set cannot be located, obtain a complete set immediately.

√ Review all change orders and other contract modifications.

√ Determine whether the contract has been performed to date in accordance with the written documents.

√ Determine whether the work is proceeding on schedule and, if not, why not.

√ Determine whether holdback or retention has been deducted from periodic payments to contractor(s).

√ Determine whether construction manager or other owner's representative has obtained lien releases for work covered by the periodic payments.

√ Review adequacy and effectiveness of reporting channels.

CHAPTER 16

DISCLOSURE & NOTICE DEADLINES*

1. With *Pro Forma* Operating Budget

Information	Deadline	Statutory Reference
Pro Forma Operating Budget or Summary	30 to 90 days before the beginning of fiscal year	Civ. Code § 1365(a) & (d)
Assessment & Reserve Funding Disclosure Summary	30 to 90 days before the beginning of fiscal year	Civ. Code §§ 1365(a) & (b), 1365.2
Anticipated Special Assessment for Reserves	30 to 90 days before the beginning of fiscal year	Civ. Code §§ 1365(a) (3), 1365.5(e)(5)
Assessment Collection Policy	30 to 90 days before the beginning of fiscal year	Civ. Code §§ 1365(e), 1365.1(a)
Statutory Notice of Collection Rights	30 to 90 days before the beginning of fiscal year	Civ. Code § 1365.1
Association Insurance Disclosure	30 to 90 days before the beginning of fiscal year	Civ. Code § 1365(f)
Alternative Disputes Rights Summary	30 to 90 days before the beginning of fiscal year	Civ. Code § 1369.590
Internal Dispute Resolution Procedures	30 to 90 days before the beginning of fiscal year	Civ. Code § 1363.850

* Statutory deadlines may be altered by the governing documents. Both should be reviewed to determine which controls.

Information	Deadline	Statutory Reference
Receipt & Disposition of Funds Received for Construction Defects	30 to 90 days before the beginning of fiscal year	Civ. Code § 1365(a) (2) (B)
Notice of Member Right to Minutes	30 to 90 days before the beginning of fiscal year	Civ. Code §§ 1363.05(e)
Notice of Right to Submit Secondary Address	30 to 90 days before the beginning of fiscal year	Civ. Code §§ 1367.1(k)
Architectural Review Procedures	30 to 90 days before the beginning of fiscal year	Civ. Code §§ 1378(c)

2. Assessment Increases

Information	Deadline	Statutory Reference
Notice of Assessment Increases	30 to 60 days before the assessment due date	Civ. Code § 1366(d)

3. Other Fiscal Disclosures

Information	Deadline	Statutory Reference
Review of Annual Financial Statement	120 days after end of fiscal year	Civ. Code § 1365(c)
Notice of Right to Receive Annual Financial Statement	120 days after end of fiscal year	Corp. Code § 8321
Notice of Transaction with Officer or Director	120 days after end of fiscal year	Corp. Code § 8322
Resolution of Construction Defect Claims	As soon as reasonably practicable	Civ. Code § 1375.1

4. Board Meetings

Information	Deadline	Statutory Reference
Notice of Regular Board Meetings	4 days before the meeting	Civ. Code § 1363.05(g)
Notice of Emergency Board Meeting	No prior notice required	Civ. Code § 1363.05(h)
Board Minutes Available	30 days after meeting	Civ. Code § 1363.05(d)

5. Membership Meetings

Information	Deadline	Statutory Reference
Notice of Membership Meeting	10-90 days before the meeting	Corp. Code § 7511

6. Member Disciplinary Hearings

Information	Deadline	Statutory Reference
Notification to Member	10 days prior to hearing	Civ. Code § 1363(h)
Notification of Decision	15 days after hearing	Civ. Code § 1363(h)
Schedule of Monetary Penalties	Upon adoption and when changed	Civ. Code § 1363(g)

7. Rule Adoption, Change & Reversal

Information	Deadline	Statutory Reference
Notice of Intention to Adopt or Change Rule	30 days prior to adoption or change	Civ. Code § 1357.130 (a)
Notice of Emergency Rule Adoption or Change	No prior notice required	Civ. Code § 1357.130 (a)
Notice of Rule Adoption or Rule Change	15 days after adoption or change	Civ. Code § 1357.130 (c)

Information	Deadline	Statutory Reference
Duration of Emergency Rule	120 days or shorter	Civil Code §1 357.130 (d)
Request for Meeting to Consider Rule Reversal	30 days after notice of rule adoption or change	Civil Code § 1357.140 (b)
Notice of Rule Reversal	15 days after vote on rule reversal	Civil Code § 1357.140 (g)

8. Corporate Filings

Information	Deadline	Statutory Reference
Association Information Statement	90 days of original formation and then biennially	Civ. Code § 1363.6(b)
Statement of Officers	90 days of original formation and then biennially	Corp. Code § 8210(a)
Notice of Address or Manager Change	60 days of change	Civ. Code § 1363.6(c)

9. Architectural Rules

Information	Deadline	Statutory Reference
Architectural Review Procedures	30 to 90 days before the beginning of fiscal year	Civ. Code § 1378(c)
Architectural Decision	As provided in rules	Civ. Code § 1378

10. Reserves

Information	Deadline	Statutory Reference
Reserve Study	3 years	Civ. Code § 1365.5(e)
Reserve Study Updates	Annually, if necessary	Civ. Code § 1365.5
Assessment & Reserve Funding Disclosure Summary	30 to 90 days before the beginning of fiscal year	Civ. Code § § 1365(a) & (b), 1365.2.5

Information	Deadline	Statutory Reference
Notice of Use of Reserve Funds for Operations	4 days before the meeting when resolution passed	Civ. Code § 1365.5 (c)
Notice of Use of Reserve Funds for Litigation	Next mailing to members	Civ. Code § 1365.5 (d)
Accounting of Reserve Funds for Litigation	Quarterly	Civ. Code § 1365.5 (d)
Repayment of Funds Transferred from Reserves	1 year, unless extended	Civ. Code § 1365.5 (c)
Notice to Extend Period for Repayment of Reserve Funds	4 days before the meeting when resolution passed	Civ. Code § 1365.5 (c)

11. Insurance

Information	Deadline	Statutory Reference
Association Insurance Disclosure	30 to 90 days before the beginning of fiscal year	Civ. Code § 1365(f)

12. Record Production

Information	Deadline	Statutory Reference
Production of Records for Current Fiscal Year	10 business days	Civ. Code § 1365.2(i)
Production of Records for Prior Two Fiscal Years	10 business days	Civ. Code § 1365.2(i)
Production of Records with *Pro Forma* Operating Budget or Summary	30 to 90 days before the beginning of fiscal year	Civ. Code §§ 1365.2 (i), 1365
Production of Records Required for Transfer	10 days	Civ. Code §§ 1365.2 (i), 1368(b)

Information	Deadline	Statutory Reference
Board Minutes	30 days after meeting	Civ. Code §§ 1365.2 (i), 1363.05(d)
Committee Mintues	15 days after approval of a decision	Civ. Code § 1365.2(i)
Membership Lists	5 days	Civ. Code § 1365.2(i), Corp. Code § 8330

13. Sale of Property

Information	Deadline	Statutory Reference
Governing Documents to Prospective Buyer	As soon as practicable before transfer	Civ. Code § 1368(a)
Age Restrictions to Prospective Buyer	As soon as practicable before transfer	Civ. Code § 1368(a), Gov't Code § 12956.1
Financial Records to Prospectuve Buyer	As soon as practicable before transfer	Civ. Code § 1368(a)
Assessment Statement to Prospective Buyer	As soon as practicable before transfer	Civ. Code § 1368(a)
Outstanding Violation Statement	As soon as practicable before transfer	Civ. Code § 1368(a)
Construction Defect Statement	As soon as practicable before transfer	Civ. Code § 1368(a)
Change in Assessment Statement	As soon as practicable before transfer	Civ. Code § 1368(a)

14. Elections

Information	Deadline	Statutory Reference
Delivery of Election Ballots	30 days before election	Civ. Code § 1363.03(e)
Publish Election Results	15 days after election	Civ. Code § 1363.03(g)

Information	Deadline	Statutory Reference
Retention of Ballots	1 year after election	Civ. Code § 1363.03(i)
Challenging Election Results	1 year after election	Civ. Code § 1363.09

15. Assessments, Liens & Collection

Information	Deadline	Statutory Reference
Assessment Increase	30 to 60 days before due date	Civ. Code § 1366(d)
Delinquent Assessment	15 days after due date	Civ. Code § 1366(e)
Commencement of Interest	30 days after due date	Civ. Code § 1366(e)
Pre-Lien Notice	30 days before recording a lien	Civ. Code § 1367.1(a)
Notice of Delinquent Assessment	10 days after assessment lien is recorded	Civ. Code § 1367.1(d)
Commencement of Foreclosure Proceedings	30 days or more after assessment lien is recorded	Civ. Code § 1367.1(g)
Lien Release Following Payment or Error	21 days or less after payment or discovery of error	Civ. Code §§ 1367.1(d), 1367.1(l)
Meeting to Consider Payment Plan	45 days from the date of request	Civ. Code § 1367.1(c)
Right of Redemption after Non-Judicial Foreclosure	90 days after sale	Civ. Code § 1367.4 (c)(4)
Assessment Collection Policy	30 to 90 days before the beginning of fiscal year	Civ. Code §§ 1365(e), 1367.1(a)

Information	Deadline	Statutory Reference
Notice of Right to Dispute Assessment, Inspect Records & ADR	30 days before recording a lien(with pre-lien notice)	Civ. Code § 1367.1(a)

16. Alternative Dispute Resolution (ADR)

Information	Deadline	Statutory Reference
Response to Request for Resolution	30 days of receipt	Civ. Code § 1369.530
Completion of ADR	90 days after acceptance	Civ. Code § 1369.540

17. Manager Disclosures

Information	Deadline	Statutory Reference
Prospective Manager Disclosures	90 days or less before entering into a management agreement	Civ. Code § 1363.1

18. Notice of Temporary Relocation for Pest Control

Information	Deadline	Statutory Reference
Notice of Temporary Relocation	15 to 30 days before temporary relocation	Civ. Code § 1364 (d)(2)

19. Construction Defects

Information	Deadline	Statutory Reference
Notice of Construction Defect Litigation (without statute of limitation issues)	30 days before filing suit	Civ. Code § 1368.5
Notice of Construction Defect Litigation (with statute of limitation issues)	30 days after filing suit	Civ. Code § 1368.5

Information	Deadline	Statutory Reference
Notice of Meeting of Members to Consider Rejection of Pre-Litigation Settlement Offer	15 days before meeting to consider matter	Civ. Code § 1375 (k)(D)
Meeting of Members to Consider Rejection of Pre-Litigation Settlement Offer	15 days before construction defect suit is filed	Civ. Code § 1375 (k)(D)
Notice of Resolution of Construction Defect Litigation	As soon as reasonably practicable after resolution	Civ. Code § 1375.1

CHAPTER 17

MODEL ELECTION RULES

These voting and election rules were adopted by the board on _____, 2011 and are intended to comply with the requirements of Civil Code § 1363.03(a). These rules will stay in effect until modified by the board of directors pursuant to Civil Code § 1357.100 *et seq.*

ARTICLE 1   VOTING PROCEDURES

1.1 <u>Voting by Secret Ballot.</u> Not less than 30 days prior to voting period, the association will mail to each member of the association, by first-class mail or personal delivery, a ballot, an instruction sheet, and two pre-addressed envelopes with instructions on how and where to return the ballot. In order to preserve confidentiality, a voter will not be identified by name or address on the ballot. The ballot itself is not signed by the voter, but is inserted into an envelope that is sealed. This envelope is then inserted into a second envelope addressed to the inspector(s) of election. The voter then seals the outer envelope and, in the upper left hand corner prints and signs his/her name, address, (and unit number, if applicable) which entitles him/her to vote.

1.2 <u>Voting Period.</u> Ballots may be mailed or hand delivered to the inspector(s) of election at the address designated in the instruction sheet. The ballot must be received by the inspector(s) before the end of the voting period or it will be disregarded. A voter may request a receipt upon delivery of a ballot. Once a secret ballot is received by the inspector(s), it shall be irrevocable.

1.3 <u>Tabulation of Ballots.</u> The inspector(s) of elections will count and tabulate all votes in public at a properly noticed open meeting of the owners or board of directors. Any candidate or other owners may witness the counting and tabulation of the votes. No person shall open or otherwise review any ballot prior to the time and place at which the ballots are counted and tabulated.

1.4 <u>Reporting Results.</u> The inspector(s) will promptly report the results of the election to the board. The board will record the results in the minutes of the next meeting of the board and make the results available for review by any member of the association at any time after the results are received from the inspector(s). The board will publicize the results of the election in a communication directed to all owners within 15 days of the election.

1.5 <u>Ballot Custody.</u> The sealed ballots, proxies, if any, and envelopes shall at all times remain in the custody of the Inspector(s) or at a location designated by the Inspector(s) until after the tabulation of the vote, at which time custody will be transferred to the association. They will be stored in a secure place for one year after the date of the election. In the event of a recount or other challenge to the election process, the association will, upon written request, make the ballots, proxies, if any, and envelopes available for inspection and review by owners and their authorized representatives. Any recount or other challenge to the election process will be conducted in a manner that will preserve the confidentiality of the vote.

1.6 <u>Elections by Mail-In Ballot.</u> Unless otherwise restricted by the CC&Rs or bylaws, all elections covered by these rules may be conducted by mail-in ballot alone, except for the meeting to count the votes.

1.7 <u>Modification Of Rules.</u> These rules shall be construed to conform to any legislative changes in Civil Code § 1363.03 without any further adoption procedures. Any other change in these rules shall be done only after 30 days written notice to all owners in accordance with the provisions of Civil Code § 1357.130.

ARTICLE 2   INSPECTORS OF ELECTION

2.1 <u>Inspector(s) of Elections.</u> There may be one or three inspector(s) of elections. The board of directors, in its sole discretion, shall have the power to decide on the number of inspectors and appoint persons to fill those positions. An inspector shall be any independent third party, including, but not limited to, a person under contract with the association for compensation, such as a property manager, attorney, or certified public accountant, etc. The only persons who may not serve as an inspector are sitting owners of the board of directors, candidates for the board of directors, and persons related to sitting owners of the board of directors or candidates for the board of directors.

2.2 Indemnification of Inspectors. The association will defend, indemnify and hold harmless the inspector(s) of elections from any and all claims, demands, damages, costs, liabilities and expenses arising out of his/her activities absent gross negligence or willful misconduct.

2.3 Duties of Inspectors of Elections. Inspector(s) of elections shall have the following duties: (a) perform any acts as may be proper to conduct the election with fairness to all owners in accordance with these rules; (b) determine the number of ownerships entitled to vote and the voting power of each; (c) determine the authenticity, validity, and effect of proxies, if any; (d) receive ballots; (e) hear and determine all challenges and questions in any way arising out of or in connection with the right to vote; (f) count and tabulate all votes in such a way as to preserve their secrecy; (g) determine when the polls shall close; and (h) determine the result of the election. An inspector shall perform his/her duties impartially, in good faith, to the best of his/her ability, and as expeditiously as is practical. If there are three inspectors, the decision or act of a majority shall be effective in all respects as the decision or act of all. Any report made by the inspector(s) of election is *prima facie* evidence of the facts stated in the report.

ARTICLE 3 CANDIDATES FOR THE BOARD OF DIRECTORS

3.1 Candidate Qualifications. A candidate for the board of directors shall be an owner of record of unit in the development or a resident.

3.2 Nominating Procedure. The procedures for nominating a candidate for the board of directors are as follows: (a) an owner may nominate himself or herself as a candidate; (b) an owner may nominate any other owner or resident as a candidate; or (c) the board may appoint a three person nominating committee, chaired by a board member to nominate an owner or resident as a candidate. All nominations to be included in the written ballot must be in writing and delivered to the association not less than 5 days prior to the date set for mailing the ballots to the members.

3.3 <u>Nominations from the Floor.</u> In addition, nominations may be made from the floor at the meeting at which the election is held.

ARTICLE 4   VOTING RIGHTS

4.1 <u>Voting Power.</u> The owners of each unit shall have one vote per unit, except for the election of directors, where each unit shall have one vote for each vacant director position to be elected. When two more units have been combined, the owners of the combined unit shall have all of the votes associated with all of the combined units. Where there are multiple owners of a single unit, they shall decide among themselves who among them shall cast the vote on behalf of the unit. If one vote is cast on behalf of a single unit, then it shall be conclusively presumed that the vote was cast by the authorized owner. If more than one vote is cast on behalf of a single unit, then all such votes shall be disregarded.

4.2 <u>Cumulative Voting.</u> Until such time as the association's governing documents are amended, all elections of two (2) or more directors shall be by cumulative voting.

4.3 <u>Qualifications for Voting.</u> Only members is good standing shall be allowed to vote. (See Bylaws Article 1, Section 1.2.)

4.4 <u>Proxies.</u> A "proxy" means a written authorization signed by an owner or the authorized representative of an owner that gives another owner or owners the power to vote on behalf of that owner. The owner to whom a proxy is given is called a "proxy holder". The owner who gives a proxy may restrict the proxy holder's authority to vote in accordance with his or her instructions. Any instructions that restrict the manner in which the proxy holder can vote must be set forth on a separate page and attached to the proxy, so that it can be detached and given to the proxy holder when the proxy is delivered to the inspector(s) of elections. A proxy and a ballot cannot be combined.

A proxy may not be used as a ballot. All proxies must be submitted to the inspector(s) of elections before the close of the voting period. Failure to file a proxy with the inspector(s) of elections before the close of the voting period invalidates the vote by proxy.

4.5 <u>Quorum.</u> A quorum shall be required only if so stated in the governing documents. If a quorum is required, each ballot received by the inspector(s) of elections shall be treated as an owner present at a meeting for purposes of establishing a quorum.

ARTICLE 5   ASSOCIATION ACCESS

5.1 <u>Access To Association Media.</u> If the association should ever have association media, newsletters, or internet web sites and provide access during a campaign, for purposes reasonably related to the election, to any candidate or member advocating a point of view, then the association will provide equal access to all candidates and members advocating a point of view, including those not endorsed by the board.

5.2 <u>Restrictions on Editing.</u> If the association should ever have association media, newsletters, or internet web sites and provide access during a campaign the association will not edit or redact any content from campaign communications, but may include a statement specifying that the candidate or member, and not the association, is responsible for the content of the communications. The association and its directors, officers, and agents shall be immune from liability for the content of those communications. The association may require the person submitting a potentially defamatory or obscene communication to sign an indemnity and hold harmless agreement protecting the association from liability for the publication.

5.3 <u>Access To Association Meeting Space.</u> The association will provide access to the common area meeting space by the pool during a campaign, to all candidates, including those who are not incumbents, and to all owners advocating a point of view, including those not endorsed by the board, for purposes reasonably related to the election. Access shall be provided at no cost to the owners.

5.4 <u>Campaign Fund Restrictions.</u> Association funds will not be used for campaign purposes in connection with any association board election. Funds of the association will not be used for campaign purposes in connection with any other association election except to the extent necessary to comply with duties of the association imposed by law. Campaign purposes include, but are not limited to, the following: (a) expressly advocating the election or defeat of any candidate that is on the association's election ballot; and (b) including the photograph or prominently featuring the name of any candidate on a communication from the association or its board, excepting the ballot and ballot materials, within 30 days of an election. This restriction does not prevent distribution of campaign materials as otherwise specifically allowed under the equal access provisions of these rules.

CHAPTER 18

RESOURCE LIST

**California Association of
Community Managers
(CACM)**
23461 South Pointe Dr., Ste. 200
Laguna Hills CA 92653
Tel: (949) 916-2226
Fax: (949) 916-5557
Email: info@cacm.org
www.cacm.org

**Executive Council of
Homeowners
(ECHO)**
1602 The Alameda, Suite 101
San Jose, CA 95126
Tel: (408) 297-3246
Fax: (408) 297-3517
Email: info@echo-ca.org
www.echo-ca.org

**California Legislative Action
Committee
(CAI-CLAC)**
5355 Parkford Circle
Granite Bay, CA 95746
Tel: (916) 791-4750
Fax: (916) 772-3781
Email: caiclac@aol.com
www.caicalif.org

**Community Associations
Institute (CAI)**

National Chapter:
www.caionline.org

**Bay Area/Central California
Chapter:** www.caibaycen.com

California North Chapter:
www.cai-cnc.org

Channel Islands Chapter:
www.cai-channelislands.org

Coachella Valley Chapter:
www.coachellavalleycai.org

**Greater Inland Empire
Chapter:** www.cai-grie.org

Greater Los Angeles Chapter:
www.cai-glac.org

Orange County Chapter:
www.caioc.org

San Diego Chapter:
www.cai-sd.org

Department of Real Estate
P. O. Box 1870000
2201 Broadway
Sacramento, CA 95818
Consumer help:
(916) 227-0810
Fax: (916) 227-0842
www.dre.ca.gov

Legislative Bill Room
State Capitol Room B32
Sacramento, CA 95814
Tel: (916) 445-2323

**Official California
Legislative Information**
Web site: www.leginfo.ca.gov

Secretary of State
1500 11th Street
Sacramento, CA 95814-5701
Tel: (916) 653-6814
www.ss.ca.gov

Department of Consumer Affairs
Consumer Information Division:
1625 N. Market Blvd., Suite 112
Sacramento, CA 95834
Toll Free: (800) 952-5210
www.dca.ca.gov

**California Association of
Realtors (CAR)
Executive Offices**
525 South Virgil
Los Angeles, CA 90020
Tel: (213) 739-8200
Fax: (213) 480-7724
Hot line: (213) 739-8282
www.car.org

CAR Legislative Offices
980 Ninth Street, Suite 1430
Sacramento, CA 95814
Tel: (916) 492-5200
Fax: (916) 444-2033

**Department of Insurance
Consumer Hot Line**
300 South Spring Street,
South Tower
Los Angeles, CA 90013
Toll Free: (800) 927-HELP
www.insurance.ca.gov

**California Housing Law
Project**
1107 9th Street, Suite 801
Sacramento, CA 95814
www.housingadvocates.org

**The Rewrite Program-
Document Revision**
6114 La Salle Avenue, #510
Oakland, CA 94611
Tel: (510) 595-8200
Fax: (510) 595-8600
office@condolawfirm.com
www.condobook.com

Index

Symbols

A

B

F

L

S